at all levels of government, while leaving thousands of vulnerable minds tragically scarred and families irreparably shattered in its wake.

"I would recommend this book especially to mental health professionals, child protective service workers, law enforcement personnel, and legislators, who are finding themselves repeatedly faced with difficult decisions as they encounter increasing numbers of Satanic ritual abuse stories in their work."

—George K. Ganaway, M.D.
Director, The Ridgeview Center for Dissociative Disorders, and Clinical Assistant Professor of Psychiatry, Emory University School of Psychiatry

"Like McCarthyism a generation ago, today's baseless panic about diabolical cult murderers and child molesters mask real social dilemmas . . . Jeffrey Victor discredits the facile rumor-mongering that has come to symbolize these complex troubles. He also offers tools to understand and combat the panic—tools which hopefully will redirect communities' energies away from shadowy chimeras and towards real problems. Satanic Panic is essential reading for parents, police, child welfare advocates, journalists, and policy-makers who seek sense and justice in the face of this culture's latest witch hunt."

—Debbie Nathan
Investigative Journalist

"Dr. Victor has explicated one of the most perplexing phenomena of the late twentieth century: an internationally prevalent scare that subversive cults of Satanists conspire to kidnap, torture, murder, and enslave millions of people. Satanic Panic is the first attempt by an academic sociologist to explain to a non-specialist audience the apparently diverse, unconnected trends and events that converge to produce fear and rumor. For years the American public has watched television tabloids and semi-fictional made-for-TV movies about Satanic rituals and their attendant abuses— child molesting and murder, to name a few—but now comes Dr. Victor with an intelligent, comphrensive, cross-disciplinary study that makes sense out of the fantastic, gives structure to the *hysterical, and restores meaning where confusion and tension prevail."*

—Robert Hicks
Law Enforcement Specialist

"Satanic Panic is a courageous discussion of witch hunting, a phenomenon still avoided by many academics. Victor's work places alleged information about shadowy Satanists firmly within the folklore and sociology of rural small towns, and casts much-needed light on which fears are justified by real teenage activities and which are the exaggerated anxieties of modern witch finders. His wide-ranging survey of the scholarship will allow concerned adults to link the allegedly new threat of Satanism to its ancestors: crusades against Catholics, Jews, women, and even the newly-born Christian church under Nero."

—Professor Bill Ellis
Pennsylvania State
University, Hazleton

"A chilling case study on how prone we are to scapegoat and how quick to demonize what we do not understand. Powerful, persuasive and timely."

—F. Forrester Church
Pastor of All Souls Church in
New York City and author of
God and Other Famous Liberals

"Satanic Panic is a wise and knowing book about a subject that all too often is presented in a hysterical or careless fashion. . . . I heartily recommend this book for all those who are concerned about the rise of teenage evil in our society and the social movements that accompany it. They will surely sleep better after reading Victor's balanced treatment."

—Professor Gary Alan Fine
Department of Sociology
University of Georgia

"Jeffrey Victor combines findings from psychology, sociology, history, and folklore with his own first-hand observations of rumor-panics and anti-Satanists in action. The result is a fascinating introduction to an increasingly influential social movement

and the anxieties which fuel it. This book contains information which can help halt the hysteria."

—Professor Joel Best
Department of Sociology
Southern Illinois University at
Carbondale
Author of *Threatened Children*
and *The Satanism Scare*

"Dr. Victor's insightful analysis of the social forces causing the embrace of folly is like a cold shower reducing the ardor of erroneous fantasy. It leaves you gasping but refreshed."

—Ralph Underwager, Ph.D.
Institute for Psychological
Therapies

"Jeffrey Victor provides us with what I consider to be the most comprehensive statement of the Satanic ritual phenomenon. Meticulously researched, compellingly written, and thoroughly objective, Satanic Panic *is an important contribution—coming at a time when voices of sanity are being drowned out by the cacophony of mass hysteria and mass delusion."

—Richard A. Gardner, M.D.
Clinical Professor of Child
Psychiatry
Columbia University

"Satanic Panic . . . *should be required reading for officials in the police or other government agencies who are tempted to take seriously the whole farrago of unsupported charges about human sacrifice, ritual abuse, cult survivors, and teenage Devil worship . . . This is a timely and impressive work."

—Philip Jenkins
Professor of Criminal Justice
Pennsylvania State University

"Satanic Panic *is a daring, powerful, and disturbing account of how the Satanic cult legend came to be (mis)used by ordinary people to explain many of our society's extraordinary problems."

—Elizabeth F. Loftus, Ph.D.
Department of Psychology
University of Washington

SATANIC PANIC

SATANIC PANIC

The Creation
of a
Contemporary
Legend

Jeffrey S. Victor

I.C.C. LIBRARY

Open ✱ Court
Chicago and La Salle, Illinois

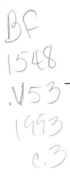

OPEN COURT and the above logo are registered in the U.S. Patent and Trademark Office.

First printing 1993
Second printing 1993

Library of Congress Cataloging-in-Publication Data

Victor, Jeffrey S.
    Satanic panic: the creation of a contemporary legend/Jeffrey S. Victor.
        p.   cm.
    Includes bibliographical references and index.
    ISBN 0-8126-9191-1.—ISBN 0-8126-9192-X (paper)
    1. Satanism—United States—Psychological aspects. 2. Satanism—United States—Public opinion. 3. Crime—United States—Public opinion. 4. Public opinion—United States. 5. Rumor—Case Studies.
I. Title.
BF1548.V53   1993
364. 1—dc20
                                     93-995
                                        CIP

This book is dedicated to the
memory of my father, Bert L. Victor,
1913–1991.

Contents

Acknowledgments

I have frequently read statements acknowledging that "this book would not have been possible, without the help of. . . ." Now, I really understand the emotional meaning underlying these words of gratitude. I have been very fortunate to have had the assistance of many people in gathering the information necessary to write this book. Many people sent me research materials, offered me suggestions, and gave my project much needed encouragement. They allayed my isolation in research and writing and enabled me to feel that I could offer something of value to other people.

Folklore specialist Bill Ellis and anthropologist Phil Stevens gave me the initial encouragement to write a book on this topic. They frequently offered me crucial insights from their knowledge of the folklore and anthropology of current and past beliefs about Satanism and societal scares. They guided me toward many unexpected paths to investigate. In many places throughout this book, their contributions are acknowledged by bibliographical references to their publications. However, it isn't possible for me to cite the full extent of the ideas they contributed to this book. I have enjoyed the personal friendship which emerged from our collaboration.

I also owe a similar great debt of gratitude to criminal justice analyst Robert Hicks, who regularly sent me huge packages of research sources, including copies of newspaper articles, research studies, governmental reports, and advertisements for training seminars on "ritualistic crime." I have cited his publications about the criminal justice aspects of the Satanic cult scare throughout this book. However, it is not possible for me to acknowledge the full benefit that I obtained from our correspondence and discussions about police Satanic cult hunters.

I want to thank anthropologist Sherrill Mulhern for her correspondence and our discussions of her research findings about Satanic cult "survivors" and their believing psychotherapists. I want to thank psychiatrist George Ganaway for our discussions about Multiple Personality Disorder and the claims of patients who say that they are "survivors" of Satanic cult torture. I want to thank journalist Debbie Nathan for our frequent discussions about her investigations of innocent women accused of the "ritual" sexual abuse of children in child-care centers. I want to thank criminologist Bill Thompson for sending me newspaper articles about the "ritual" sexual abuse scare in England and Scotland and for keeping me current with events there. I want to thank sociologist Gary Alan Fine for his critical reading of some of my work on the dissemination of Satanic cult rumors. I want to thank psychologists Ralph Underwager and his wife, Hollida Wakefield, for their constant encouragment of my research work.

Several people have made my research possible by sending me a great amount of research source information. I want to thank Paul Putnam, Human and Civil Rights Specialist of the National Education Association, for sending me several boxes of news clippings from local newspapers. I want to thank Anne Levenson of the Office for Intellectual Freedom of the American Library Association for sending me information about censorship attempts directed at libraries. I want to thank private detective Paul Ciolino for sending me legal documents about cases he investigated involving false accusations of sexual child abuse. I want to thank Gerry O'Sullivan and Vicki Copeland for sending me copies of their computer files about the activities of moral crusaders against Satanism.

Some of my former students did interview research collecting information used in this book. I would particularly like to thank Marci Abraham and Everett Seastrum for the work they did as independent study students under my direction, interviewing high school students and ministers, respectively.

Librarians at my college and city libraries gave me invaluable assistance in finding information. I owe special thanks to my good friend Pat White of the James Prendergast Library for her help in doing computer searches and for her constant encouragement. I want to thank the reference librarians of the Prendergast Library for their enthusiastic help in finding information. I would also like to thank Adena Woodard, Kathleen Barkham, and Marilyn Estok at the Jamestown Community College for their patience and initiative in pursuing my inquiries about sources of information. I want to thank Nelson Garifi for his work on the computer-generated map of rumor-panic sites.

I owe a special debt of gratitude to Gerry Wallerstein, my literary agent. Without her emotional support and confidence in my writing, and her persistence in trying to find a publisher for this book after many disappointments, this book would not have been possible.

Finally and most importantly, I want to thank my wife, Michele, and my son, Mathieu. Many ideas in this book were prompted by our conversations about teenage and family issues.

Chapter One
Rumors, Claims, and Allegations about Satanic Cult Crimes

Once men are caught up in an event they cease to be afraid. Only the unknown frightens men.

Antoine de Saint-Exupéry,
Wind, Sand and Stars[1]

Some Strange Happenings

Some really bizarre things have been happening in this country. These strange happenings may be omens of one of the biggest secret conspiracies, or one of the biggest hoaxes, in recent history.

A few examples serve to illustrate the point.

Example: A top-level leader in the Church of Jesus Christ of Latter-Day Saints (Mormons) wrote a confidential report for an internal study of the church, in which he said that he believed that the church had been infiltrated up to the highest levels, by a conspiracy of criminal Satanists who sexually torture children and ritually sacrifice babies. The confidential report was obtained by an anti-Mormon group of fundamentalist

Protestants who published it in a Salt Lake City newspaper in October, 1991. (See Chapter Thirteen.)

Example: In a small town in North Carolina, in the spring of 1989, five women and two men were arrested and charged with sexually molesting and sadistically torturing twenty-nine children in group ritualistic activities at a child-care center. Initial rumors in the community alleged that the group was a secret Satanic cult. The trial of the defendants was still in progress in 1992. (See Chapter Six.)

Example: Two adult daughters brought a suit against their seventy-six-year-old mother in San Diego in March 1991, charging her with having sexually abused and tortured them when they were children in Satanic cult rituals, conducted by groups which included their now dead father and many strangers. The women also accused their mother and the cult of having forced them to kill their own babies born out of rape and act as prostitutes to lure derelicts who were to be used in human sacrifices. (See Chapter Thirteen.)

Example: On the cold night of November 8, 1991, about five hundred people turned out in the small town of Rupert, Idaho, to attend a prayer vigil for babies ritually tortured and killed by Satanic cults. People came from as far away as Utah and Colorado to attend the event, which was organized by local ministers to commemorate the discovery of the mutilated and burned corpse of "baby X" found at a landfill two years before. Rumors had been raging wildly over the area during that time, alleging that a local Satanic cult had killed the infant in a ritual sacrifice. According to newspaper reports, almost all local people believe the allegations.[2]

Example: Just before Halloween in 1990, the *Chicago Sun-Times* newspaper carried an article headlined: "Police on Halloween Alert for Satanic Cults."[3] The article reported that signs of Satanism had been increasing since 1987 and that more than twenty-five ritual sites had been found by police in the Chicago suburbs and outlying counties. It quoted a Chicago policeman and a social worker as authorities on ritual crime and presented a list of murders and suicides in Illinois which the article associated with Satanic cult ritual crimes.

What's Going On?

This is a detective story of a different sort. It is a sociological and psychological investigation. It required the study of psychological research about people who have Multiple Personality Disorder and about emotionally disturbed teenagers. It required the study of sociological research about rumors, contemporary legends, and social movements. It required a historical study of the origins of legends from the distant past, legends reaching back to medieval Europe.

There have been a lot of allegations of bizarre and vicious crimes, but little hard evidence to follow. I didn't begin this investigation with any preconceived assumptions about these rumors, claims, and allegations. There were hundreds of clues that had to be carefully pieced together in order for me to understand what was happening in American society.

As with any allegations of crime where hard evidence is lacking, it is best to be a bit suspicious of the claims. Therefore, this investigation focusses upon the claims-makers as well as their claims. Ultimately, many clues pointed me in the direction of focussing upon the rumors, claims, and allegations about Satanic cult crimes rather than upon the object of the claims, Satanic cult crime.

This book is, therefore, not an investigation of Satanism. Readers who seek information about organized Satanic religion should look elsewhere. This is a study of rumors, claims, and allegations about Satanic cult crime and widely held beliefs about dangerous Satanic influences in society. It is a study of the underlying causes and significance of these bizarre collective phenomena.

The Claims and Claims-Makers

There is a wide range of claims about dangerous Satanism and criminal Satanic cults being circulated in American society. In brief, these claims assert that there exists a secret organization, or network, of criminals who worship Satan and who are engaged in the pornography business, forced prostitution, and drug dealing. These criminals also engage in the sexual abuse and torture of children in an effort to brainwash children into becoming life-long Devil worshippers. In their Devil worshipping rituals, these criminals kill and sacrifice infants, and sometimes adults, and commit cannibalism with the body parts. They kidnap children for ritual sacrifice and commit random murders of indigents. They actively try to recruit into their secret groups, teenagers who dabble in occult magic. Many claims-makers assert that Satanists have infiltrated all the institutions of society in order to subvert society, create chaos, and thus promote their beliefs in Satan worship. Some claims-makers even suggest that this Satanic cult conspiracy can be traced back many centuries.[4]

None of these claims are supported by reliable evidence. My research suggests that they are baseless and misleading. Moreover, these claims exploit widespread fears, particularly the anxieties parents have about their children. The claims are significant, however, because they are themselves symptoms of serious problems in American society which affect a great many people.

These claims are being made by many prominent people, not merely uneducated rubes. The claims-makers include some police officers, child protection social workers, psychotherapists, and clergymen. Almost all of them are quite sincere about the claims that they are making.

What this Book Provides

This book offers a study of many unusual social phenomena. There are widespread rumors about various kinds of Satanic cult crime. There are community and regional rumor-panics in response to stories about dangerous, local Satanic cults, often alleged to be planning to kidnap and sacrifice blond, blue-eyed children in Satanic rituals. There are people who suffer from Multiple Personality Disorder, a severe psychological disturbance, who claim that they are survivors of sexual abuse and torture by secret Satanic cults. There are arrests and trials of individuals and groups who are accused by children of sexually abusing them in bizarre Satanic cult rituals, often at child-care centers. Finally, there are organized community groups seeking to stop dangerous Satanic influences which they perceive in children's school books, in rock music, and in fantasy games.

The present investigation is guided by several basic questions. 1) What are the origins of these rumors, claims, and allegations? How did they arise and how are they being disseminated? 2) Why do so many people believe these rumors, claims, and allegations, in the absence of scientific or legal evidence to confirm them? What can explain people's receptivity to these stories? 3) What do these rumors, claims, and allegations indicate about social conditions in American society? What do they indicate about underlying anxieties and fears being experienced by Americans, and especially by those people who are particularly receptive to believing the stories?

The results of this investigation should be helpful to parents, police officers, journalists, and human service professionals who are concerned about what lies behind of the rumors, claims, and allegations about criminal Satanists. It will provide useful research findings for behavioral scientists who study crime, deviant behavior, and collective behavior. Much of the book is illustrated with direct, original research findings.[5]

All too often there is a giant gap between behavioral science research on an important social issue and practical knowledge gained from that research. I have tried to keep the twin goals of advancing behavioral science theory and offering practical applications in close discourse with each other. To that end, in the text I have deliberately avoided using unnecessary technical jargon and burdening the reader with the names of researchers and theories. Extensive notes are provided for interested readers.

On a practical level, this book offers information about the harmful consequences of the Satanic cult scare and what can be done about it. On an intellectual level, this book offers research findings which can help us to understand the social dynamics of rumor-panics, national scares, and witch hunts. These research findings enable us to better understand how societies create imaginary deviance and how societies operate to create collective fear and persecutions.

This book is a study of the social construction of imaginary deviance through the social processes of collective behavior. The first half of the book investigates the many different manifestations of the Satanism scare in the light of psychological and sociological knowledge. The second half of the book offers an analysis of the social dynamics and historical roots of the Satanism scare. The book offers a fascinating story of rather strange behavior.

Chapter Two
The Evolution of the Satanic Cult Legend

> *The flying rumours gather'd as they roll'd*
> *Scarce any tale was sooner heard than told;*
> *And all who told it added something new,*
> *And all who heard it made enlargements too.*
> Alexander Pope,
> *Temple of Flame*[1]

The Evolution of the Satanic Cult Legend

The Satanic cult legend didn't spring into existence ready-made in the 1980s. It has been evolving gradually for at least two decades. Different streams of rumors, arising from quite different sources, have gradually merged to form an elaborate story. How could the Satanic cult legend become a plausible explanation for such widely divergent social problems as pet mutilations, church desecrations, cemetery vandalism, teenage suicide, child kidnappings and missing children, child sexual abuse, and serial murder? The answer is that several social conditions transformed scattered local rumors into a contemporary legend.

The social process through which random rumors spread and become increasingly organized has been studied by sociologists. Knowledge of the preconditions of the process is still sketchy, but some specific factors are generally agreed to be important.[2] First, isolated local rumor stories need to find a channel to reach a broad, mass audience. These stories need to become "marketable" for the mass media. Second, it is necessary for some kind of "carrier" groups to take up the rumor stories as a cause and disseminate them over many years, even persisting in the face of strong skepticism. In order to disseminate the rumors widely, these carrier groups need to employ pre-existing grass-roots communication networks. Finally, it is necessary for some kinds of authority figures to legitimize the rumor stories, by publicly endorsing them as being true, or at least plausible.

The Rise of New Religions and the Anti-Cult Movement

The social changes of the 1960s gave rise to many religious groups which emerged out of the youth counterculture. Some of these groups were variations of fundamentalist and charismatic Protestantism. However, many others were even more unconventional groups, holding beliefs imported from non-Christian, Asian religions, or synthesized out of the human potential movement and ancient occult-magical traditions. Their active proselytism caused widespread resentment, as some parents "lost" children to these new religions that they labelled "cults." It was widely believed that the young people joining these cults were somehow "brainwashed" and coerced into membership.

In response, a network of local and national anti-cult organizations took form in the 1970s to fight the influence of these cults, supported mainly by the parents of "lost" children. The Cult Awareness Network and the American Family Foundation are some of the largest anti-cult organizations, with national operations. However, there are also many local groups. (The Cult Awareness Network, for example, has thirty local affiliates.)

In addition, many fundamentalist Protestant organizations developed an apparatus to engage in counter-propaganda against the proselytism of these new competitors for members.

Some examples include the Christian Research Institute and the Spiritual Counterfeits Project. There are also a host of special ministries, which have travelling evangelists who speak as "experts" on cults at churches and town meetings.

Groups such as the Unification Church (the "Moonies"), the International Society for Krishna Consciousness (the "Hare Krishnas"), and the Children of God became targets of critical and sometimes sensational mass media reports. The public image of cults became even more negative than it had been when Charles Manson's murderous groupies were labelled a "cult" in newspaper reports. The word "cult" took on the image of a potentially dangerous, fanatical group, subversive of traditional Christian and Jewish values.

The mounting worries about these new religions were turned into national outrage in November 1978 by a uniquely tragic event. In Jonestown, Guyana, 913 people were manipulated and coerced into committing mass suicide. Over 200 of them were children. They were followers of a "cult," Reverend Jim Jones's People's Temple. Thereafter, any reservoir of tolerance for new religious groups evaporated in disgust. The event was so shocking that it left a latent image in the minds of the public of any group labelled a "cult" as being prone to fanaticism and violence. Thereafter, a "cult" was seen through the lens of Jonestown. A "cult" came to mean a group led by a manipulative fanatic and having mindless followers who were brainwashed into submission to the leader's authority.

In the 1970s, small groups calling themselves followers of Satanic religion developed. However, they really didn't receive much public attention. If they were known at all, they were regarded as just another bunch of "kooks" in the exotic countercultural zoo. Even Anton LeVey, who is now touted as the Godfather of Satanism in popular accounts of the subject, was a relative unknown. His Church of Satan and several other formally organized groups calling themselves Satanists attracted no more than a few hundred active followers.[4]

At about the same time, a few newspaper reports began to appear which referred to groups labelled by police and fundamentalist clergy "informants" as "Satan cults," or Devil worshippers. These so-called "Satan cults" were small, local gangs of juvenile delinquents, often from prosperous suburbs, who mixed heavy drug abuse with make-shift black magic rituals. The few gang members who became intensely involved in magical symbols and rituals learned what they could from pop culture books on black magic, which were readily available in libraries and bookstores. When they became involved in other criminal activities beyond the use of illegal drugs, it usually consisted of killing domestic animals as part of their attempts at ritual magic. In a few cases, however, some gangs committed murders which they rationalized through their Satanic ideology.

In a celebrated case in Vineland, New Jersey, in 1971, for example, a mentally disturbed twenty-year-old youth was bound by two other teenagers and thrown into a pond to drown, supposedly at his own request for help in committing suicide. Newspapers reported the murder as being a bizarre Satanic ritual.[5] Cruelty to animals and even bizarre thrill murders are not new forms of teenage crime. What was new and unusual was the use of Satanic ideology to justify violent aggression. These gangs of juvenile criminals were harbingers of an increasing number of such sadistic miscreants in the following decades.

The generic label "Satanic cult," with its ambiguous meanings, had not yet become a familiar stereotype to most Americans. The stereotype behind that label would later bring together popular images of Satanic religion and bizarre criminal activity and result in the invention of a new category of criminality called ritual or occult crime.[6]

The Cattle Mutilation Rumors

In the mid-1970s, cattlemen in the western states began to report finding some of their cattle dead and mutilated. The soft parts of the cattle had been removed, including lips, ears, tongues, udders, and genitals. The parts appeared to have been cut off with a very sharp instrument, like a razor or scalpel. In many cases, also, the blood of the animals seemed to have been completely drained out, without any blood stains being left on the ground. No footprints or animal tracks were found around the carcasses. Cattlemen first made reports about these incidents in Kansas, Colorado, and Montana and, then, throughout the West and Midwest. There suddenly appeared to be an epidemic of these incidents.

As these reports were increasingly made public in local newspapers, rumors began to circulate, speculating about the cause of these bizarre incidents.[7] The cause was unclear. Some rumor stories claimed that strange lights had been seen in the night skies at the time of these incidents and that the cattle mutilations were probably the work of extraterrestials from UFOs. Other rumor stories claimed that Army helicopters had been seen in the isolated areas of these cattle mutilations and that they were probably the result of some kind of secret military tests.

Still other rumors linked the cattle mutilations to the finding of strange altars in areas where religious cults were believed to practice their rituals. These stories claimed that Satanic cults were killing the cattle in order to use their parts and their blood for Satanic rituals. Thus, the emerging Satanic cult legend first received widespread publicity out on the cattle ranges of the West. They offered a plausible explanation for ambiguous and disturbing events.

The cattle mutilation reports evoked widespread concern in the western states. More and more reports came to the police from angry cattlemen. They demanded that something be done to stop these senseless attacks on their property. In some areas cattlemen even organized armed vigilante patrols. Local newspapers recounted the incidents, as well as the accompanying rumor speculations, bringing them to wide public attention. Eventually, several state governments commissioned investigations and research studies to determine the causes of the cattle mutilations.

Several careful scientific studies came to the conclusion that the overwhelming majority of these incidents were due to purely natural causes. According to these studies, the cattle died from diseases, poison plants, rattlesnakes, and other ordinary hazards. Then, their soft parts were eaten by small predators.[8] Microscopic examination of the cuts revealed the uneven marks of razor-sharp teeth. Statistical studies revealed that there had been no actual increase over the normal rate of cattle deaths expected in an area. Veterinarians testified that the blood of the cattle only appeared to have been drained away because it had coagulated in the animal after the animal's death. In a very few cases, knife cuts were found, indicating that in a few cases the mutilations may have been carried out by copycat pranksters after the animals' deaths.

Even though the findings of these investigations were reported in the press, a great many people still could not believe the "official story." Rumors that Satanic cults were killing and mutilating animals for ritual sacrifices continued to circulate widely.[9] As recently as 1989, many local newspapers continued to lend credibility to claims that Satanic cults were mutilating cattle. The *Fort Worth Star-Telegram* of April 16, 1989, for example, quoted a local police "expert" in criminal Satanism as claiming to be able to identify the signs of Satanic animal mutilation.

> "Mutilated animals are found throughout the area. But, the ones that send up red flags of possible satanist activity are the ones with no blood, cattle with their organs removed and decapitated goats. Look for absence of blood. There will be absolutely none," the Seagoville officer said. "That is accomplished by first killing the animal, perhaps, by shooting coolant down its throat. Then, using a stolen blood pump, they actually suck the blood out," the officer said. "If one drop of blood falls on the ground, it's tainted and can't be used," he said.[10]

The article made no mention at all of the scientific findings which refute these claims.

Why do these cattle mutilation rumors have the power to persist, in the face of contrary scientific evidence? Some answers can be found in several sociological research studies which have investigated these rumors.[11] First, the initial rumor stories caused many people to attribute new meanings to events (the cattle deaths) which they had previously taken for granted and not questioned. The rumors distorted people's perceptions of the actual facts and caused the cattle deaths to be regarded as more peculiar than they were in reality. Second, newspaper articles, such as the one quoted above, continued to circulate the stories, because the rumor stories have dramatic "human interest" appeal for the newspapers. Scientific findings generally do not make dramatic newspaper stories compared with stories about Satanic cults. Third, local police "experts" in Satanism and "occult crime" continued to promote the rumor stories as truth, thereby helping to spread them from town to town. At the same time, the status of police as authority figures lent the rumors credibility, even though no cattle-killing Satanic cultists were ever found. These local "experts" are more easily accessible to small town newspaper reporters than are the few scientists who know about the details of the research studies. These same factors help to explain the persistence of later developments of the evolving Satanic cult legend.

Rumors about Satanism at Procter & Gamble

In 1980, the corporate headquarters of the Procter & Gamble Company began receiving letters accusing the company of having a trademark logo which contained Satanic symbolism.[12] The logo was a face on a crescent moon looking at thirteen stars which represented the original thirteen states. However, rumors circulating around the country claimed that hidden in the logo was the number "666" (found by connecting the stars) which is supposedly a Satanic symbol. Gradually, the rumor stories became more elaborate. The rumors usually claimed that the "owner" of Procter & Gamble had made a pact with the Devil and had given a share of the company's profits to the Church of Satan. According to these rumors, the "owner" had supposedly made that announcement to the public on a television talk show.

The rumors were spread in handbills given out at shopping centers and through the local newsletters of some fundamentalist churches. Boycotts were organized against the company's products. Many retailers became worried about selling Procter & Gamble products and refused to do so. In a few cases, the company's vehicles were even vandalized. By 1982, the company was receiving five hundred letters a day about its link to the

Church of Satan. It had to hire four staff members just to respond to the inquiries.

In 1982, Procter & Gamble decided to fight back. It obtained endorsements from leading fundamentalist and Catholic clergymen. The company then sent out letters from these clergymen to forty-eight thousand churches, disclaiming the rumor stories. Procter & Gamble even brought lawsuits against individuals found actively promoting these rumors in printed flyers and newsletters. Nevertheless, the rumors persisted. When they died down in one area of the country, they began anew in another area. As they died down among fundamentalist groups in the South and Midwest, they sprang up among among conservative Catholics in the North.[13]

It appears that the rumors were too strong to fight. In April 1985, Procter & Gamble announced that it would remove the offending logo from all of its products. However, even changing the logo did not stop the rumors. By the spring of 1990, similar rumor allegations were circulating again in flyers in the South and Southwest.[14] The company again was receiving about three hundred telephone calls a day about the rumor allegations.

Research sponsored by the company found that the rumors were transmitted primarily through informal communication networks beyond the reach of lawsuits: through flyers given out in churches and shopping centers and by word-of-mouth conversation.[15] The persistence of the Procter & Gamble Satanism rumor stories demonstrates the power of the fundamentalist communication network in American society and the receptiveness of fundamentalists to Satanic conspiracy rumors.

Rumors about Satanism in Child-Care Centers
The first known claim linking Satanism with the abuse of children during rituals was made in a "survivor" story, *Michelle Remembers*, which was published in 1980.[16] Some researchers suspect, but cannot prove, that early Satanic cult "survivor" stories influenced the development of later allegations of ritual child abuse. What is known with certainty, however, is that the book was used by police and prosecutors in the early 1980s in preparing cases against people accused of sexually molesting

children in day-care centers.[17] It is also known that Michelle Smith and several other "survivors" met with parents and children involved in the famous McMartin case after the case was reported in the press.[18] The initial prosecutor in the McMartin case, Glenn E. Stevens, believes that Michelle Smith and other counselors influenced the children's testimony against the accused.[19]

Rumors that Satanists were sexually molesting children in day-care centers first surfaced in the McMartin Preschool case, which began in 1983 in Manhattan Beach, California. It went on to become the longest and most expensive trial in American history, with a cost of $15 million.[20] The initial allegations linked sexual child abuse in the day-care center to rituals of a "Devil worship" cult. These allegations led to the arrest of sixty-two-year-old Peggy McMartin Buckey, her son, Raymond Buckey, and five other child-care workers. They were accused of victimizing 360 children in extremely bizarre sexual acts carried out over a period of five years.

This case was particularly important because it gave rise to the organization of volunteer groups of parents and child protection advocates, such as Believe the Children, which were committed to alerting the general public to the hidden dangers of a newly identified kind of child abuse.[21] They labelled the newly "discovered" form of child molestation, "ritual abuse." Unfortunately, the process of the trial did nothing to clarify the facts of the case. In January 1990, the only two remaining defendants, Peggy and Raymond Buckey, were found innocent of most of the charges against them. Later that year, several remaining charges against Raymond Buckey were dropped by the prosecution.[22]

Soon after the McMartin case attracted national attention, a host of other similar accusations of ritual sexual abuse swept across the country. In some cases, accusations of Satanic cult activity were made public during trials. In Kern County, California, during 1984 and 1985, a local Satanic cult rumor-panic resulted in investigations of seventy-seven people, who local police believed were involved in a criminal Satanic cult. In several panic-driven trials, dozens of people were convicted and sent to the state prison.[23] In one of those cases, for example, seven people were convicted and imprisoned for sexually molesting children as part of a Satanic cult. The only direct evidence against them came from the testimony of children, who claimed that they had been injected with drugs and forced to drink urine and engage in bizarre sexual acts with adults, as well as with other children, while the activities were being filmed. The children also accused the defendants of murdering at least twenty babies, using their blood in rituals, and engaging in cannibalism. Some of the children later recanted their stories.[24] Then, in 1990, the convictions were overturned after being appealed.

In most cases, however, the Satanic cult accusations are not brought to light in court proceedings, but they circulate in local rumors. Many prosecutors in these cases worry that some jurors might be unable to believe children's more fantastic claims about bizarre rituals, torture, orgies, and infant sacrifices. Instead, Satanic cult activity is merely implied through the use of the euphemistic term "ritual child abuse" during police investigations and legal proceedings.[25] The term "ritual abuse" has now become a vague buzz word for people who believe in the existence of secret Satanic cults.

As these cases continued, passions ran high and almost anyone who cautioned against presuming the guilt of those accused, became a "suspect" in the eyes of the outraged parents in a community. In a case in Jordan, Minnesota, for example, a policeman who vouched for the character of an accused person was soon charged with the same crimes against the children who made the accusations.[26] In another case in Chicago, two women who publicly expressed support for an accused person, shortly thereafter found their names on a list of child molesters being circulated by a concerned parents' group.[27]

These disturbing rumors are dangerous, because they arouse the outrage of decent people who too easily assume the guilt of child-care workers accused of sexually molesting children. Moreover, the accusations are supported only by the testimony of very young children, without any solid corroborating evidence. As a result, it is quite possible that many completely innocent people, mostly women, are now in prison as a consequence of these Satanic cult rumor allegations.[28] It is extremely unusual for women to sexually molest small children. Some reporters have noted the strange resemblance of this situation to the Salem witch trials, which also were brought on by the accusations of children, mainly against women.

In 1988, reporters Tom Charlier and Shirley Downing of the Memphis, Tennessee *Commercial Appeal,* published a careful study of thirty-six cases of accused ritual sexual abuse of children.[29] In these cases, only about one-fourth of those people arrested were eventually convicted and most of the convictions had little to do with any kind of ritual sexual abuse. Charlier and Downing concluded:

> Allegations of satanism—of rites involving mutilation, infant sacrifice and devil worship—have since emerged in more than 100 child sex abuse cases across the country. . . . In four years, though, investigators have found no evidence to support fears that cults are preying on the nation's children. The *Commercial Appeal* studied ritual sexual abuse allegations in 36 cases and found instead that many of the stories labeled "satanic" or "ritual" have the hallmarks of urban legends."[30]

Charlier and Downing identified some possible channels through which this urban legend was transmitted. They noted that Satanic cult sexual child abuse stories have been disseminated, since the McMartin case in 1983, by police Satan hunters across the country and through seminars, workshops, and conferences on ritual child abuse and Satanic cult crime. These conferences attract parents, social workers, therapists, police, and prosecutors. The central importance of these seminars and conferences is that they function as organizing agencies for communication networks carrying the legend.[31] What is important to note is that various "child advocates" and child-protection professionals have constructed a communication network which now disseminates the Satanic cult legend. It is propelled by the national over-reaction to concerns about child abuse, especially sexual abuse.

The reporters were able to tie one of the "carriers" of the Satanic cult legend to the McMartin Preschool case: Robert Currie, a retired television executive. Currie, whose three sons attended the McMartin Preschool, boasted to the reporters that he was the first person to expose Satanic ritualism in the case. He acted as a self-appointed detective and interviewed most of the children who made accusations of sexual abuse. Currie later worked with Kenneth Wooden as an advisor for a segment of the "20/20" television show about Satanic cult crimes.[32]

The "20/20" Show about Satanism

On May 16, 1985, the television show "20/20" carried a segment titled "The Devil Worshippers" produced by Kenneth Wooden. This was the first television show to bring claims about criminal Satanic cults to a national audience. The subject of the segment was described by the host of the "20/20" show, Hugh Downs, as: "Perverse, hideous acts that defy belief. Suicides, murders, and ritualistic slaughter of children and animals."[33] The cast of "experts" on Satanism and ritualistic crime included: policeman Dale Griffis, evangelist Mike Warnke, police detective Sandi Gallant, and psychiatrist Dr. Lawrence Pazder (author of *Michelle Remembers*). The program focussed upon murders committed by several self-proclaimed teenage Satanists. However, it also alluded to claims about animal mutilations, grave robberies, kidnapped and missing children, the ritual murder of infants, the sexual abuse of children, child pornography, and cannibalism.

An excerpt from the dialogue of the program illustrates the general tenor of the program.

Tom Jarriel (the narrator):	"Cannibalism. It's difficult to believe, but in every case we examined, children described it."
A grandmother:	"The hearts were cut out, and the children were made to chew pieces of these children's hearts, pieces of their flesh."

Jarriel:	"Is cannibalism part of the ritual?"
Ms. Gallant:	"The children have spoken about this in almost every instance. Also, human feces, or drinking the urine, or drinking human blood."[34]

The interviewer's apparently uncritical acceptance of claims about cannibalism points out how contemporary legends easily create an aura of credibility. Accusations of cannibalism have commonly accompanied the blood ritual myth in the past.[35] These stories which combine human sacrifice, the drinking of blood, and the eating of human flesh function as symbols of ultimate evil incarnate in some group. As is the case where there is much anxiety and fear, the more outrageous the storyteller's tale, the more believable it appears to be. Adults who have forgotten the rich folklore of children can easily bring themselves to believe that children couldn't possibly fabricate such seemingly bizarre stories on their own.

The historical importance of this television program is that it lent credibility to what had previously been merely local rumors. The television program seemed, to unskeptical viewers, to expose some newly discovered, sinister influence at work in our society. It is frequently cited in newspaper reports about Satanic cults, as being the first national "exposé" of the Satanic cult problem. Videotapes of the program are also sometimes used as "documentation" by "experts" on Satanic cult crime in their lecture tours.

The Toledo Dig

Shortly after the "20/20" television exposé, a strange incident once again brought claims about Satanic cults to national attention. A local sheriff of a rural county near Toledo, Ohio, named James Telb, claimed to have information obtained from "several confidential informants," that a Satanic cult had sacrificed as many as fifty to eighty victims, mostly children, whose remains were buried in a wooded lot in the village of Holland, Ohio.[36] According to Sheriff Telb, this secret Satanic cult had as many as two hundred local members who had been ritually murdering people, mostly children, since 1969.[37]

On June 21 and 22, 1985, an intensive excavation of the garbage-strewn wooded lot took place under the eyes of a national audience. Over one hundred reporters arrived to cover the Toledo dig, including television crews, all hoping to unearth a big story of mass murder by a sinister conspiracy. About fifty law enforcement officers from several states also showed up to observe the search for evidence. Dale Griffis, a police captain and supposed expert on Satanic cult crime, was hired as a consultant. (He had been one of the featured experts on the "20/20" show.)

The Toledo dig turned into an empty media show. Nothing of any substance was ever found. Nevertheless, Griffis claimed that some items found in the garbage, including a headless doll, two old curved knives, and some torn children's clothes, were "occult ritual relics" that provided evidence of Satanism at the site. Dr. Michael Pratt, an archeologist who was brought in from nearby Heidelberg University, however, did not agree with Griffis's claims. Some of the media reported Griffis's claims uncritically, not treating them with much skepticism.[38] As a result, the Toledo dig has now become a part of the evolving contemporary legend. As recently as 1989, some newspaper reporters were still referring to the events of the Toledo dig to support sensationalist claims that secret Satanic cults engage in ritual human sacrifice.[39] The folklore of the Toledo dig presaged the sensationalized and distorted news reporting of the infamous Matamoros drug gang murders.

The Matamoros Murders

Bodies of people killed in ritualized murders were found in Matamoros, Mexico in April 1989, and the discovery was easily distorted by much of the mass media to fit the Satanic cult legend. The discovery of the murders was occasioned by the disappearance of an American college student, Mark Kilroy, who had gone to Mexico on spring break a few days earlier. His body was found brutally mutilated, along with the bodies of at least twelve other victims. They had been killed by members of a drug-smuggling gang of thugs. The evidence of torture and mass murder of arbitrarily chosen victims was sensational enough for the news media. Even more sensational was evidence of the torture and murder of the victims during bizarre rituals. The leader of the drug gang, Adolfo Constanzo, employed a variety of pseudo-religious rituals to instill fear in his superstitious followers and control their loyalty to him. Constanzo created his own "black magic" belief system and rituals from the horror movie, *The Believers,* and from notions drawn from Palo Mayombe, an African religious tradition, rather than from any single existing religion.[40]

Some of the news media quickly portrayed the Matamoros murders as being the work of a Devil-worshipping cult, as if it was the first verified discovery of a Satanic cult mass murder. Even *Time* magazine initially reported the Matamoros murders in that light.[41] In rapid order, several "true crime" books appeared, the authors and publishers obviously ready to profit from the sensationalism about these supposed Satanic cult sacrifices. The contemporary legend continued to grow and accumulate a rich heritage of mythologized incidents. Now, millions of worried parents can refer to their memories of the news reporting of the Matamoros murders and find credibility for claims that secret criminal Satanists are prowling about for innocent victims.

The Power of Contemporary Legends

The Legend Has Great Mass Media Appeal

The Satanic cult legend exists because it has provided an easily available explanation for several disturbing and ambiguous phenomena—cattle believed to have been mutilated, the sexual abuse of children in day-care centers, and violent, sadistic teenage gangs. The label "Satanic cult" is so vague that it can be flexibly applied to many entirely different types of social deviants: child molesters, violent teenage gangs, psychopathic serial murderers, teenagers involved in makeshift occult ritualism, and harmless practitioners of unconventional religion.

The stereotypic image of a "Satanic cult" gradually began

to emerge in the 1970s out of the rhetoric used to attack disturbing new religious groups. The stereotype of criminal Satanism merged imagery of fanatical religious cults with that of psychopathic criminals like Reverend Jim Jones and Charles Manson.

This dramatic imagery had great mass media appeal. Satanic cult stories were first able to find a channel to a national audience when they appeared in small town newspaper reports as a possible explanation for an epidemic of spurious claims about cattle mutilations. Later, small town newspaper reports about a wide variety of crimes, from cemetery vandalism to serial murder, began to attribute the crimes to "Satanists."

The Legend Has Been Legitimized by Authority Figures

Satanic cult stories obtained credibility when certain authority figures, police "experts" in ritualistic crime, clerical "experts" on Satanism, and child protection "experts" on "ritual abuse," legitimized them as part of the discourse about social problems. They gained further credibility when television programs, such as "20/20" and television talk shows, broadcast stories about criminal Satanism to a national audience.

The Legend Promotes Certain Vested Interests

While it is true that the mass media appeal of these stories and their endorsement by some sources of authority help to account for the persistence of the Satanic cult legend, something else is crucial. The Satanic cult stories have, at the same time, served to promote a variety of vested interests in money, prestige, and social influence.

The Satanic cult stories have helped to revive national and local anti-cult organizations after a period of waning concern about new religious "cults" in the early 1980s. The stories have helped these organizations to attract increased funding, volunteer workers, and receptive audiences eager for someone to do something to fight the supposed Satanists in our society. The local police, from many areas, have organized a loose network of "experts" in Satanic cult crime, many of whom receive lucrative lecture fees as guest speakers at seminars on Satanic cult crime around the country. Police lecturers are much more likely to attract large public audiences when they speak about Satanism than when they speak about, for example, the drug problem. This is especially true in small towns, where public concern about Satanism is intense, rather than in large cities, where people are much more concerned about a broad range of very real crimes. So, the Satanism scare continues to ferment primarily in small-town and rural America, while urban Americans are largely unaware of it.

Television talk shows have mined the Satanic cult scare like a gold field. These horrific stories have proven useful in attracting large audiences of worried mothers at home with young children and it has done wonders for their ratings. In addition, many local print journalists have attracted readership with sensationalized reports about the dangers of Satanism among teenagers.

Many fundamentalists have found that the Satanic cult scare affirms their belief that Satan's evil influence is behind much of the moral corruption they see in American society. Travelling revivalists can now attract wider audiences than otherwise, including many listeners who are not fundamentalists, when they speak about the menace of Satanism for today's youth. Many of them also receive lucrative speaker's fees. The National Education Association, for example, reports that religious evangelists are now invited to speak to public school students about the psychological dangers of Satanism using the guise of being secular "experts."[42] One such "expert" is Jerry Johnston, head of Jerry Johnston Associates as well as Jerry Johnston Ministries, and author of a book on Satanism.[43]

The Procter & Gamble rumors provide evidence that the fundamentalist communication network is particularly receptive to subversion myths built upon its preconceptions about Satanism and Satan's malevolent influence in modern society. It is important to realize that the fundamentalist communication network is highly decentralized and does not simply respond to any set of religious authorities. This fact is illustrated by the denunciations of the Procter & Gamble rumors by prominent fundamentalist ministers.

Historians have documented the persistence of subversion

myths in the fundamentalist cultural tradition, which until recently have been aimed primarily at Catholicism as the main enemy.[44] Other conspiratorial enemies in fundamentalist subversion myths have included Jews, Communists, "secular humanists," and even the fictitious "Illuminati."[45] One result of the Satanic cult legend is that it enables fundamentalists and conservative Catholics to share a subversion myth in common. It also joins them in a strange alliance with secular child advocates (including some feminists) who are concerned about child abuse.

Chronology of the Satanic Cult Scare in the United States

Late 1960s, Early 1970s	Rumors about dangerous religious cults, including teenage "Devil worshippers" and Charles Manson's "Devil" cult.
1970s	Rumors about cattle mutilations and Satanic cult ritual animal sacrifices in the West and Midwest.
1980	Publication of *Michelle Remembers* by Smith and Pazder. The first Multiple Personality Disorder Satanic cult "survivor" story.
1980	Rumors accusing Procter & Gamble Company of promoting Satanism, claiming that the company logo is a Satanic symbol.
Early 1980s	Missing children kidnapping scare.
1982–84	Satanic cult rumor-panics begin.
1983	First "ritual child abuse" allegations and arrests. McMartin Preschool Case.
1984	Meeting of International Society for the Study of Multiple Personality Disorder offers presenta-

tions about Satanic cult "ritual abuse," lending credibility to the "survivor" stories of Multiple Personality Disorder patients.

1985   The "20/20" TV program episode, "The Devil Worshippers."

1988   Geraldo Rivera's TV special, "Devil Worship."

1988   Publication of Lauren Stratford's Satanic cult "survivor" story in her book *Satan's Underground.*

1988–89   Peak years in number of Satanic cult rumor-panics in communities across the United States.

1989   Matamoros murders discovered and labelled Satanic cult ritual sacrifices in tabloid press and "pop" books.

1990–91   "Ritual child abuse" scare and arrests in England.

1990   Religious magazines publish attacks on the *Impressions* series of elementary readers for promoting Satanism.

1991   Censorship attacks on school and library books alleging Satanic influences become common.

1991   News reports of allegations that Mormon Church hierarchy is infiltrated by secret Satanists who sexually abuse children in rituals.

1992   Satanic "ritual abuse" scare in San Diego.

Chapter Three
The Social Dynamics of a Rumor-Panic

> *From the dawn of civilization onwards, crowds have always undergone the influence of illusions. . . . The masses have never thirsted after truth. They turn aside from evidence that is not to their taste, preferring to deify error, if error seduce them. Whoever can supply them with illusions is easily their master; whoever attempts to destroy illusions is always their victim.*
>
> Gustave Le Bon, *The Crowd*[1]

The Community Panic of Friday the Thirteenth

In the spring of 1988, rumors about a dangerous Satanic cult spread throughout the rural areas of western New York, north-western Pennsylvania, and eastern Ohio (see Figure 1). The rumor stories made claims about secret ritual meetings, the killing of cats, dogs, and other animals, and the drinking of animal blood, and they predicted the imminent kidnapping and sacrifice of a blond, blue-eyed virgin. The stories focussed upon specific, local circumstances from town to town, yet they carried remarkably similar symbolic content. These rumors began to appear in different, distant locations at about the same time during mid-winter, and evolved to a peak of emotional extreme in a rumor-panic on Friday, the thirteenth of May.

The panic was driven by fearful and angry behavior, in

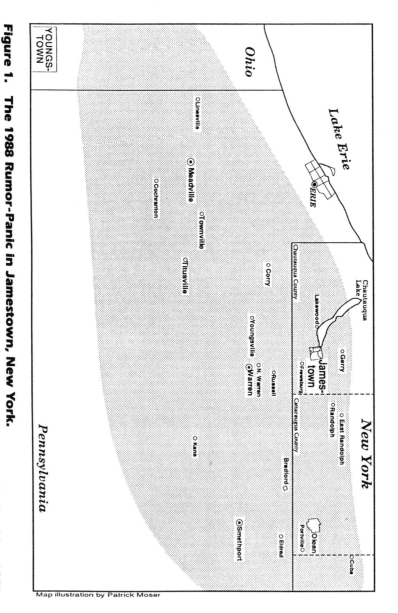

Figure 1. The 1988 Rumor-Panic in Jamestown, New York.
The shaded area of the map is the area where a Satanic rumor-panic occured during May, 1988.
Locations shown are places where rumor activity was most intense according to newspaper reports.

Map illustration by Patrick Moser

response to a threat which people perceived to exist concealed in their communities. There were abundant examples of such behavior in Jamestown, New York, where I collected most of my research information. Many parents held their children home from school out of fear that they might be kidnapped by "the cult," as they called the threat. Absences from elementary school were three to four times greater than average, according to school attendance records. Over one hundred cars showed up at a wooded park, rumored to be a Satanic cult ritual meeting site, where they were stopped by police barricades awaiting them. Some of the cars had weapons in them, such as hunting guns, knives, and clubs. At another location rumored to be a "cult" meeting site, an unused factory warehouse, about $4,000 damage was done to the musical equipment belonging to bands which practiced there and to the interior walls of the building. Several teenagers rumored to be members of the supposed "cult," perhaps because of their countercultural appearance, were victims of anonymous death threats and other types of telephone harassment. Groups of young thugs with baseball bats were seen wondering around in the downtown area during the evening hours.

The police, the youth bureau, and school officials received hundreds of telephone calls reporting bizarre incidents attributed to "the cult." People reported seeing things which did not exist, such as dead animals hanging from lamp-posts or robed figures in ritual meetings. They reported having advance knowledge of planned events which did not then occur, such as the kidnapping of particular persons. A great many people traded bits and pieces of these rumor stories on that day during passing encounters with friends and neighbors, in stores while shopping, over the telephone, at community meetings, and especially at school. The Jamestown police spent hundreds of man-hours of work investigating these allegations that day and during the preceding weeks, without finding anything to verify the great numbers of rumor stories.

The rumor-panic was a rather curious event for several reasons. A great many people were emotionally over-reacting to a perceived threat, yet there was no concrete evidence of any threat in their immediate experience. How could this happen?

On the surface of it, the behavior of many of the people might mistakenly be regarded as having been "irrational"; at least in the sense of their having no practical reason for emotionally over-reacting to the situation. There was something which seemed to rob people of their intellectual individuality, in the sense that so many people, thousands in Jamestown proper and hundreds of thousands over the entire rumor region, seemed to be bereft of their critical faculties and personal judgment.

A rumor-panic is a rather rare outburst of dramatic collective behavior. We have something more to learn from these transient social phenomena than the foibles of human behavior. An understanding of the inner social dynamics of rumor-panics teaches us about the limits of individuality and critical intellect in the face of strong social forces. Few rumor-panics have been studied in any depth, and fewer still have been studied by behavioral scientists on the scene as they emerged.

The Research Questions

I began my research immediately after the day of the rumor-panic with several fundamental questions in mind.[2] These questions were directed toward three basic aspects of the phenomena. First, I wanted to understand the rumor development process. How did the rumor stories about a dangerous Satanic cult get started? What social forces led the rumors to promote a fear with such emotional intensity? Second, I wanted to understand the rumor consensus. How did the rumor stories gain widespread credibility in the absence of any visible evidence to confirm people's fears? In other words, why was the perceived threat taken so seriously by so many people with such diverse personal conceptions of reality? In order to answer this question, I needed to understand the symbolic cultural meanings embedded in the rumor stories, meanings which could join people together in a shared explanation of what was happening to them. Third, I wanted to understand what "hidden" sources of shared social stresses could account for fears evoked by the rumor stories. This last question was prompted by my knowledge that collective behavior of such intensity usually arises from commonly shared anxieties which are reflected as metaphors in the rumor story imagery.

The Research Methods

In pursuing my research, I interviewed a wide variety of community authorities who would normally be aware of events in the community, including police investigators, school officials, youth group social workers, ministers, psychotherapists, and newspaper reporters. The Jamestown Police Department was exceptionally helpful in providing me with non-confidential information regarding their investigations of the many different rumor stories. Students from one of my courses conducted interviews with forty-nine local teenagers, parents, and informal authority figures, such as teachers and ministers. They conducted these interviews immediately after the panic erupted, while people's memories were still fresh in their minds and before they could be distorted by later circumstances. Two students did independent research studies for me. One of them interviewed a sample of thirty teenagers from the local high school to investigate whether conflicts between teenagers in different subcultures functioned to promote the rumors. The other student, who was a minister, interviewed ten fundamentalist ministers in depth concerning their beliefs about the rumor stories and about any actions they took in response.

In addition, I conducted telephone interviews with reporters from newspapers in towns distant from Jamestown, where I learned that similar rumor-panics had taken place simultaneously with the one in Jamestown. My first surprising finding was that very similar rumor stories and community panics had taken place at the same time, over a rather large section of the country.

How a Rumor-Panic Develops: The Rumor Process in One Community

In order to trace the rumor stories back to some point of origin, I decided to construct a chronology of events and rumors leading up to the Friday the thirteen panic in Jamestown. I collected these reports from the interviews. This enabled me to have a broad picture of relevant circumstances happening in Jamestown over many months. These events were circumstances which were associated with the evolution of the changing rumor stories and the eventual community panic.

This chronology makes clear one important finding of my research. Rumor-panics are the dramatic end product of a gradual evolution of symbolic meanings embedded as metaphors in rumor stories. Rumor-panics are not sudden outbursts of contagious hysteria, as much popular wisdom and some past sociological theories assert.

Chronology of Jamestown Area Events

Oct. 31, 1987

Event. A Halloween party takes place at the "warehouse," an empty factory which is used by rock bands to practice their music. About sixty people attend, some of whom wear Halloween costumes, including those of witches and wizards. This becomes the subject of gossip among teenagers who are not invited to attend. Many of the teenagers who attend have a "punk" style of hair and clothing, which is something new and is seen as strange. (Note: One of these bands, "The 10,000 Maniacs," later became internationally well known among youth.)

Gossip. Gossip circulated among many high school teenagers that the "punk" kids were using drugs and having sex orgies at the "warehouse."

Mid-Winter, 1987

Rumors. Rumors circulate in Jamestown High School about supposed teenage suicide attempts in the area.

Nov. 19, 1987

Event. The "Geraldo" TV show offers a national television program titled: "Satanic Cults and Children." The program features the plight of parents whose children have been victimized by purported Satanic cults.

In his introductory remarks, Geraldo makes the following sensational and ominous claims: "Estimates are that there are over one million Satanists in this country. The majority of them are linked in a highly organized, very secretive network. From small towns to large cities, they have attracted police and FBI attention to their Satanic ritual child abuse, child pornography, and grizzly Satanic murders. The odds are that this is happening in your town."[3]

Jan. 4, 1988   *Event.* Several worried parents call a Catholic priest about their concerns that Satanic rituals may be taking place at the "warehouse." They also express their concerns about alleged teenage suicide attempts and about the strange "dark clothing" of the "punk" kids. The parents ask the priest to "find out what is going on" at the warehouse. The priest calls the police and school officials to relate the parents' concerns. A few of them refer to the "Geraldo" show as evidence for the importance of their concern.

Jan. 1988   *Rumors.* Rumors circulate widely, asserting that the police are investigating "a list" of high school students for some unknown reason. The "list" supposedly includes all of the "punk" teenagers who go to the "warehouse." (Several parents go to the police to inquire why their teenage children are being investigated.)

Jan. 12, 1988   *Event.* 1) An article appears in the Jamestown newspaper, about the nationally reported Tommy Sullivan case. The first line of the article states: "A youth obsessed with Satanism committed suicide after stabbing his mother to death . . . officials said."[4] (See Chapter Eight for information about the Tommy Sullivan case.)

Event. 2) On the same day, the Jamestown police receive the first telephone call claiming that "punk" teenagers are involved in Satanism at the "warehouse." Over the next five months, the police receive hundreds of similar telephone calls.

Feb. 1988

Rumors. Rumors circulate widely that the "punk" kids are involved in Satanism at the "warehouse."

Early Mar. 1988

Rumors. The rumor intensity increases as more parents express a worried search for information about "what is going on" among teenagers in the community.

Late Mar. 1988

Event. A fundamentalist minister writes in his church newsletter, which circulates widely to other churches, that Satanic practices among local teenagers should be taken very seriously.

Early Apr. 1988

Rumors. Rumors circulate widely about the ritual killing of cats and about secret Satanist ritual meetings.

Event. The Jamestown Youth Bureau begins to receive telephone calls from worried parents about the rumors that local teenagers are engaged in Satanic practices. These calls increase greatly over the next weeks.

Apr. 16, 1988

Event. The Humane Society begins to receive telephone calls claiming that cats are being killed. Over the next four weeks, similar calls are received every day in increasing numbers. However, no evidence is found of any deliberately killed cats or dogs.

Apr. 16–17, 1988

Event. 1) Two out-of-town religious "experts" on Satanism speak at a local fundamentalist church, where they were invited to speak to teenagers in response to concerns of several parents about teenage Satanists in the area. One of these "experts" claims to have been a former member of a Satanic cult.

Event. 2) The two "experts" on Satanism are taken by some church youth to be shown a purported ritual meeting site, in a wooded area called "the hundred acre lot." While there, they are stopped by police, who are also there investigating the rumored "ritual site."

Event. 3) The Jamestown police investigate the rumored "ritual site." The site consists of a campfire, surrounded by trees which are spray painted with the words: "Get Stoned," "High Times," and "ZZ RATT," and symbols including a flower and a five-pointed star. (Note: *High Times* is a drug-oriented magazine and ZZ RATT is the name of a heavy metal rock band.)

Apr. 18,
1988

Event. College custodians go to the "hundred acre lot," in back of Jamestown Community College, after learning about the police investigation. There, they find twenty-five pamphlets in plastic envelopes around the alleged "ritual site." Some people who learn about the pamphlets assert that they were left there by the Satanic cult as propaganda. (These pamphlets were actually cartoon gospel tracts, published by a fundamentalist press and having an anti-Satanist message.[5])

Mid-Apr.
1988

Rumors. A rumor spreads that the police found evidence of a Satanic cult ritual meeting site in the college's "hundred acre lot."

Apr. 26,
1988

Event. The Jamestown Youth Bureau hosts a meeting between some community authorities and some of the "punk" teenagers, in order to open lines of communication. The adults are representatives from the police, schools, human service agencies, and youth clubs. The teenagers tell the adults that they feel threatened by the growing hysteria in the community, and the police tell the youth to report any potentially violent harassment to the police. (Some "punk" youth had been victims of threats and physical assaults.)

Apr. 30,
1988

Event. An article appears in the newspaper of nearby Warren, Pennsylvania, about potential violence among students at Youngsville High School (in Pennsylvania), between supposed Devil worshippers and others students. The article cites rumors about threats made with a knife and gun on a school bus. The story is retold by word of mouth in Jamestown.

Early May 1988
Rumors. Rumor stories of various threats multiply greatly. Their transmission becomes intensely active in conversations and one version or another is heard by most people in the community. These threat rumors include stories about some kind of impending violence planned by "the cult" or by some kind of vigilante group against members of "the cult." The most common rumor is that "the cult" plans to kidnap and sacrifice a blond, blue-eyed virgin on Friday the thirteenth of May.

May 10, 1988
Event. The Jamestown Police Department and Youth Bureau offer to let teenagers who fear harassment because of the rumor threats have a party in the community room of the City Hall on Friday the thirteenth, under protection of the police.

May 12, 1988
Event. An article appears in the Jamestown newspaper reporting about the rumors and citing the police as saying that no evidence has been found for any of them.[6] (This article was misinterpreted by many people to mean that the rumors actually had credibility, and that the police "were hiding something, because they didn't want to cause a panic.")

May 13, 1988
Community Panic. A rumor-panic occurs in Jamestown and much of the surrounding area. Afterwards, rumor activity rapidly declines.

May 12–15, 1988
Event. Articles appear in newspapers across western New York, northwestern Pennsylvania, and northeastern Ohio, reporting very similar rumor-panics in rural areas. All of these news reports focus upon their own local areas, with no mention that similar rumors and panics are spreading over a very large region of the country.

The Origin of the Rumors

The most common question that people have when rumors circulate, and especially when they cause a panic, is, Who or what caused the rumors to start? However, specialists in the study of rumors don't regard this question as being a central concern. The reason is that most rumors are not simply started by any person or group, nor are they a product of any single incident, no matter how distorted perceptions of that incident may be.[7] A great many rumors arise out of impersonal social dynamics.

Jean-Noel Kapferer, a French social psychologist specialized in the study of rumors, has written the most extensive compilation of research about rumors in his book, *Rumors: Uses, Interpretations and Images* (1990). Kapferer suggests that there are three kinds of rumor origins among those rumors which are not deliberately provoked by some person or group.[8] Some rumors have their origin in some kind of ambiguous event which affects many people in a stressful situation, such as a war, ethnic conflict, or a natural catastrophe like an earthquake. A second kind of rumor arises out of common, ongoing activity, when many people begin to take notice of some facts or details to which they didn't previously pay much attention. For example, people living near a nuclear power plant may take notice of the numbers of people dying from cancer in the area and speculate in conversations, that the plant has been leaking radioactivity for a long time. The combined anxieties and uncertainties about cancer and nuclear power may be enough to generate persistent rumor stories.

The third kind of rumor origin is that which gave rise to the rumor process leading to the rumor-panic about dangerous Satanic cults. Some rumors have their origin in a contemporary (or "urban") legend—one of a number of stories which continually circulate in societies and arise here or there, in one form or another, when conditions are ripe. These conditions are ones which combine ambiguous incidents with shared anxieties, which in turn become translated into the symbolism embedded in the legend. The collective behavior process is similar to what used to happened when anti-Semitic rumors about Jews kidnapping gentile children for religious sacrifice circulated in Europe and caused violent pogroms during times of social and economic stress. The anti-Semitic rumors arose from centuries long anti-Semitic legend stories.

The rumors in Jamestown about a dangerous Satanic cult and the resultant rumor-panic could not have originated in Jamestown; similar rumors arose simultaneously over a vast area. Moreover, the Satanic cult rumors could not even have had their origin anywhere in the region at the time they began to circulate. The reason is that similar Satanic cult rumors had been circulating in many rural areas of the country and giving rise to other community panics since as far back as 1983 (as we will see in the next chapter).

Nevertheless, the chronology is valuable because it points to several "catalysts" which helped to activate the Satanic cult rumor stories. One of these "catalysts" was the "Geraldo" show on November 19, 1987, and another was the widely reported news accounts of the Tommy Sullivan case. These mass media events reached an audience across the whole area simultaneously, but they did not cause the rumors. Instead, they provided symbolic imagery which shaped the direction of the rumor process. In a sense, the Satanic cult legend simply "piggybacked" onto the evolving stream of pre-existing rumor stories. Those pre-existing rumors about teenage suicide, teenagers with strange clothes, and clandestine gatherings at "the warehouse" paradoxically arose from parental anxieties (in response to the gossip of teenagers) and promoted even more anxieties about what was going on in the community.

Anxiety and Belief in Rumors

There is much research evidence gained from experiments which shows that fear-provoking rumors both satisfy the need to reduce uncertainty and provoke even more anxiety.[9] The rumors about a dangerous Satanic cult served the convenient function of focussing rising collective anxieties upon a seemingly specific threat, even though that threat was a purely imaginary one. When people suffer from anxiety due to stressful situations in their lives, they seek explanations for that anxiety.

If the reasons for people's anxiety is not quite clear to them, they are particularly likely to grasp at explanations in rumor stories which suggest that something specific in their environment is threatening their security.

The most famous rumor-panic, the "War of the Worlds" panic on October 30, 1938, illustrates these principles about anxiety and rumor in a dramatic real life situation.[10] A brief sketch of the facts of the incident goes as follows. On the eve of Halloween in 1938, Orson Wells narrated an adaptation of H. G. Wells's story, "War of the Worlds," on a radio broadcast over the CBS network. The adaptation was set in the present and was presented as if an invasion of Martians was actually taking place, this impression being created by the device of dramatized news bulletins during the hour-long program. It is estimated that as many as a million people panicked in response to their misperception of the radio show. (Many people tuned in late and didn't hear the initial disclaimer that the program was only a dramatization.) The panic was most pronounced in the mid-Atlantic states, near the fictitious first landing site of the Martians in New Jersey. In New Jersey, many families fled to their basements to avoid poison gas attacks. In Philadelphia, women and children ran screaming into the streets. Highways in the area were jammed with fleeing motorists. Hospitals were crowded with people seeking help, some of whom were in shock.

The panic was not simply an automatic response to the radio program, no matter how dramatic it might have been. The Martian invasion story, presented in the form of on-the-scene reports, certainly provoked fear, but it also built upon pre-existing anxieties. Real events in Europe, with the rising aggression of Nazi Germany, seemed to be leading to a second world war and, as a result, many people were worried that another major war was imminent. (The Munich Pact had just been reached on September 30, 1938.) In actuality, of course, events were building up to the Second World War. It started less than a year later. It is also important to recognize that the metaphorical similarity between a "War of the Worlds" and a world war made the Martian invasion story more believable.

The possibility of war with Martians was a creation of pure imagination, but possibility of war with the Nazis was no illusion.

The Cause of Panic

Most past studies of panics have explained episodes of collective panic in terms of psychiatric mental illness notions. Because the behavior appears to be so out of the ordinary, or abnormal, in the course of everyday life, these incidents are simply regarded as being "irrational." People are seen as being caught up in some kind of temporary mental disorder which is spread, like a disease, through some process of "contagion." Therefore, rumor-panics have usually been labelled incidents of "mass hysteria." However, I have deliberately avoided such mental illness terminology. In recent years, sociologists have moved toward the conclusion that the "mass hysteria" explanation of collective panics is inadequate, because it simply doesn't fit the sociological knowledge of group behavior.[11]

During the Jamestown rumor-panic, people in the community acted quite rationally to a threat that they believed to exist in the community. When parents held their children home from school, especially girls who were blond, they were acting quite reasonably in response to a threat they thought "might" possibly exist. Their perceptions of a threat arose from distortions of real events and from supposed "facts" heard from a "friend-of-a-friend," but their fears did not arise out of any kind of internal mental disorder. There are many times for all of us, when we misperceive what is happening, when what we believe is simply unfounded in the verifiable facts of the situation and we act in ways that are inappropriate to the situation. It sometimes happens in our work relationships, for example, after we learn some distressing "office rumor" through a friend-of-a-friend.

If we shift our focus of attention away from the extraordinary behavior and expression of emotion to the beliefs held by people, the cause of panic is easier to comprehend. The panic was a reaction to the rumor stories. Threat rumors became assimilated into local gossip in a process of collective story-telling. Research on threat rumors, as previously noted, indicates that they have the paradoxical effect of satisfying the need for information in matters of uncertainty and also of increasing people's collective anxiety.[12] The rumor process in Jamestown gradually increased community tensions, like a generator accelerating energy.

A central social mechanism which escalated the fear was a vicious cycle of distorted communication between parents and their children. Children brought home from school bits and pieces of schoolchildren's gossip about suicide attempts, secret rituals, and cat killings. These stories served to aggravate parental worries about dangerous influences upon their children. The parents then talked about the stories with other parents, who confirmed the worries of parents by telling them that they also heard versions of the same stories. Back home again, the parents expressed their now exaggerated fears to their children, who then took their parents' fears as evidence that the stories were indeed true and not mere gossip.

Collectively held anxiety alone cannot produce a community panic. The anxiety has to be transformed into fears of something specific.[13] That catalyst was the mass media stories about dangerous Satanism, in the "Geraldo" show, and newspaper reports about the Sullivan case. The fears of a dangerous Satanic cult became increasingly focussed in rumor story-telling, until finally another event functioned to trigger off the panic. As silly as it might seem, that precipitating event was Friday the thirteenth, encumbered with all its ominous symbolism. As if it were a poetic metaphor, the ominous thirteenth fit perfectly into the evolving collective story-telling about dark dangers of the occult. (Not surprisingly, the horror movie, *Friday, the Thirteenth,* was playing in movie theaters throughout the region. It seems that movie agents play close attention to the symbolic meanings attached to particular days.)

The community panic served a useful social function. It enabled the rising collective anxieties to be released in a kind of shared catharsis, a purge of growing community tensions. It didn't really matter that no dangerous Satanists were found and no confrontation of "the cult" and vigilantes occurred. The rumor-panic functioned much like a nightmare, which gives symbolic expression and emotional release to underlying tensions in a person's life. In the days after the rumor-panic, people could laugh at all the silliness, enjoy trading stories about what had happened that day, and go on with the normal activities of everyday life.[14]

Why So Many People Believe Bizarre Rumors: The Rumor Consensus

The simultaneously shared belief in a frightening story among thousands of people cannot be explained on the basis of personality characteristics of individuals, such as personal motives like the desire to impress others with bits of interesting gossip, or personality traits like gullibility. The thousands of people who took seriously the threat of a dangerous Satanic cult had a multitude of differing individual motives, personal beliefs about reality, and personality traits. A consensus of belief, or shared belief between thousands of people, requires some kind of unifying bond between people. The most basic bond between human beings consists of symbols (usually verbal ones) which people come to share. Communication is the link between people while the content of shared symbols is the bond, whether between husbands and wives in marital relations, or in work organizations, or in communities. Therefore, in order to understand why so many people can believe a frightening rumor story, we must first understand the process of communication and then the contents of that communication.

One young woman's experience illustrates how the communication process operated during the rumor-panic in Jamestown. Marcie was a psychology major at Jamestown Community College and seemed to me to be a very rational and reasonable person. She also happened to be a very attractive, blond, blue-eyed nineteen-year-old. On the morning of Friday the thirteenth, Marcie overheard people at the office where she worked discussing the rumor that "the cult" was planning to kidnap and sacrifice a blond, blue-eyed virgin. Her initial reaction was one of skeptical amusement. Later that day, at home, her mother repeated the same rumor story to her, angry that dangerous criminals could be on the loose in the community. The story was no longer silly and amusing gossip for Marcie. She began to seek more information and called some of her girlfriends. They too had heard the story about "the cult." Marcie then became increasingly anxious and tense. When her parents went out for the evening, Marcie asked to know the whereabouts of the family gun ("just in case something happened"). Later that evening, as her fears mounted to near panic, Marcie called me to ask if I had any facts about the rumor stories. When I answered the telephone, she was so ashamed by her unsubstantiated fears, that she immediately hung up.

Social Forces Which Influence Belief in Rumors

Marcie's reactions illustrate several principles found in research about people's belief in rumors. The communication of the rumor story from a source of authority, her mother, who took the story seriously, lent credibility to the rumor for Marcie. The consistent repetition of the same story, from clients and friends, increased its credibility. The rumor story was personally quite relevant for Marcie, because she happened to be blond and young. (I found, for example, that the rumor did not provoke much concern among Black people in the town because it was obviously not as relevant for them. On the other hand, I found evidence that it was particularly relevant for parents of young girls. In one case, for example, a mother dyed her blond daughter's hair brown.)

In addition, it is important to note that Marcie held only an ambivalent belief in the rumor story. Most people's belief in frightening rumor stories is a kind of "half-belief." I found over and over in my interviews, the aphorisms "Where there is smoke, there must be fire" and "It is better to be safe than sorry." It is an attitude of suspended skepticism that is most commonly held by people who take threat rumors seriously, rather than certainty of belief.[15]

In summary, the rumor stories about a dangerous Satanic cult were believed by so many people for several reasons. 1) The rumors were conveyed by some sources of authority, including parents, school teachers, and ministers. 2) The rumors were repeated over and over from numerous different sources. Social psychologists call this process "the consensual validation of reality," which means that people seek to validate their beliefs about reality by using what most others say is "true" as a guide to confirm their own perceptions of reality. 3) In stressful social conditions, many people readily believe that bizarre tragedies can easily happen. A key reason why bizarre threat rumors are so often taken seriously is that many people feel that it is unwise to disregard the rumors, just in case there is some truth in them. ("Where there is smoke, there must be fire.") 4) Finally, the rumors were relevant, in some ways, for a great many people. (Why the Satanic cult stories were relevant is a question we will examine in some detail shortly.)

Understanding the social process of belief formation during rumors also provides insight into the reasons so many millions of Americans are caught up in the national Satanism scare.

Communication Networks and Belief in Rumors

What accounts for the difference between people who heard the rumors and believed them and people who did not take them seriously at all?

Research on rumors has found that the rumors travel through particular communication networks and not others. People in receptive communication networks are those people most likely to believe the rumor stories, or at least, to regard them most seriously.[16]

In order to identify some of the receptive communication networks through which the rumor stories travelled, I tried to locate the school neighborhoods in Jamestown, where there was greatest reaction to the rumor stories. Parents of elementary school children in small towns commonly participate in neighborhood communication networks of similar parents, in which a common topic of shared concern is children. I reasoned that the parents who took the kidnapping rumor most seriously were also those who were most likely to keep their children home from school.

Therefore, I checked the statistics on the increased absences from schools on Friday the thirteenth at the six different elementary schools in Jamestown. Some of the elementary schools had a much higher percentage of children absent than did other schools. The highest percentage of school absences was about four times greater than the average (of previous weeks) and the lowest percentage was about two times greater than average. When I placed a map of the elementary school districts over a map of census neighborhoods, I was able to determine the socio-economic characteristics of those neighborhoods where the rumor stories resulted in greater or lesser school absences.

The parents who were most likely to hold their children home from school came from the neighborhoods disproportionately composed of families with low incomes and little education. In social class terms, these neighborhoods had high proportions of poor working class families, families which were struggling to get by financially and whose members held jobs that require little skill.

These economically stressed parents are those parents for whom it is most difficult to hold young children home from school. Most of them can't easily afford to take the day off from work to care for their children. Many of these less prosperous parents are single-parent mothers, who desperately need each day's pay. Therefore, these parents must have taken very seriously indeed, the possibility that their children might be kidnapped by "the cult."

What these findings indicate is that Satanic cult rumors are most likely to be believed and circulated by parents who are economically stressed and inadequately educated. In Jamestown, these parents are blue-collar workers, whose jobs are fast disappearing, and whose incomes have not kept up with inflation over the last twenty years.

Some past research on rumor-panics has found that poorly educated people are more likely to uncritically accept and believe in bizarre threat rumors than are well educated people.[17] The greater skepticism about threat rumors among people with greater education is partly a product of having more accurate information about a broad range of matters. However, poorly educated people are skeptical about rumors if they happen to have special knowledge about the matter of the rumor story content. In the case of the cattle mutilation rumors, for example, experienced ranchers were found to be less likely to believe the bizarre explanations of the cattle deaths than were people who knew little about raising cattle.[18]

More important to a person's skepticism about tales told by a "friend-of-a-friend" is the acquisition of critical thinking skills. Poorly educated people, for example, may have been more likely to believe Satanic cult rumors that Satanist teenagers drank cat's blood in rituals or that Satanic rituals give people some kind of special, occult power.

My research did not directly test this question, but my interviews led me to the conclusion that an inadequate education did cause many people to uncritically believe the Satanic cult stories, even though some well educated people, such as school teachers, also accepted the rumors without much skepticism.

Another communication network I investigated was that of fundamentalist Protestants. These people are disproportionately drawn from the same socio-economic level of less prosperous, working class people. As previously noted, one of my adult students, who was a Methodist minister, interviewed a sample of ten fundamentalist ministers.[19] Eight of the ministers believed that Satanic cults were "common" in the United States and these eight also believed that Satanic cults were operating in the Jamestown area. What they meant by a "Satanic cult" ranged from a group of teenagers engaged in Satanic practices to a secret organization with as many as 150 people in it in the local area.

Six of the ministers reported that they had responded to the Satanic cult rumors in some active, public way, but only in the context of their own congregations. These responses included: organizing a special prayer meeting, giving a sermon about Satanism, showing a videotape of a "Geraldo" show about Satanism to members of their congregation, writing about their concerns regarding Satanism in their church newsletter, organizing a youth group meeting concerning Satanism, and inviting special out-of-town "experts" on Satanism to speak to their congregations. Even if it was not the personal intent of the ministers to do so, these activities lent credibility to the rumor stories about a dangerous Satanic cult.

However, all the ministers indicated that they were simply responding to the concerns brought to them by members of their congregations. They were seeking ways of serving the needs of their congregations. Some of the ministers even mentioned that they felt that some members of their congregations were over-reacting to the rumors.

This information indicates that the grass roots communication networks of Protestant fundamentalists are highly receptive to belief in Satanic cult rumors and highly active in transmitting them, at least between their co-religionists.[20]

The Underlying Sources of Shared Stress

Past research suggests that rumors usually arise in groups of people who are experiencing anxiety due to some source of stress they share.[21] We also know from past studies of rumors that suddenly increased economic stress has very commonly been a source of threat rumors which blame scapegoats for life's problems. The key is to find rapid changes in many people's lives which cause misfortune and frustration.

Rapid Economic Decline
Economic stress has increased sharply in small town and rural areas of the United States since the late 1970s. According to research published by the Population Reference Bureau in 1988:

> . . . the poverty rate for the 54 million Americans who live in rural areas has climbed to 18 percent—50 percent higher than in urban areas. By 1986, one out of every five young rural

families was living below the poverty line . . . Almost one-third (32 percent) of rural families headed by someone between the ages 18 to 29 were poor in 1986, up from 19 percent in 1979.[22]

It is important to realize that this new rural poverty falls particularly hard upon young parents with children, many of whom have inadequate educations (high school or less) to find decent jobs. These parents are precisely the ones who were most likely to take the Satanic cult rumors seriously and communicate them to others.

The region where the rumor-panic took place is part of the economically declining "rust belt," where industries that used to pay good blue-collar wages are rapidly disappearing. Much of the employment in western New York and northwestern Pennsylvania was in small manufacturing companies which no longer exist. Comparatively little of it was in agriculture, so the economic problems of this region are not due to the disappearance of the family farm.

The extent of rapid economic deterioration is evident in regional economic studies. One such study of the "southern tier" counties of New York done in 1988 indicates the speed of the economic decline in the area. It found that:

1) The per capita personal income in the region dropped from 74% to 70% of the state average, between 1976 and 1984.
2) The number of people in the region receiving public assistance almost doubled between 1974 and 1985.
3) Chautauqua County [in which Jamestown is located] lost about 9% of its work force between 1979 and 1987, because of its lack of adequate job opportunities.[23]

County economic studies indicate that the area is losing well-paid manufacturing jobs very rapidly. It is true that many of these jobs are being replaced by so-called "service jobs" (like those at new fast food restaurants), but those jobs offered only about half the average salary of the skilled manufacturing jobs lost.[24] The meaning of this change, on the personal level, is that many young, poorly educated blue-collar parents can't find the kind of jobs which offered their own parents at least a comfortable living. Moreover, many older adults have lost well-paid jobs and now have to work at much lower wages. As a result, many young parents and some older adults are very frustrated and angry. This is the foundation for the widespread, free-flowing anxiety in the region.

The Breakdown of the Family

Economic stress is a common cause of family problems. Therefore, it is not surprising that an additional source of stress over the region where the rumor-panic took place is the increasing breakdown of cohesive family bonds. The family has been the central source of security, stability, and continuity in people's lives, in traditionalistic small town and rural areas of the country. It was a mutual-help and problem-solving group, which people could rely upon for emotional support and financial assistance. No longer. Over the past twenty years, small town and rural families have experienced a rapidly increasing rate of disintegration. The pressure of economic stress, on top of changing sex roles, has caused increasing marital conflict and divorce, increasing parent-child conflict, more single-mother parenting, and the increasing departure of youth seeking jobs in distant places. In addition, problems which used to be primarily ones of urban areas, such as teenage drug abuse and unwed motherhood, have battered stable family relationships.

Data from Chautauqua County's Department of Social Services, for example, provides evidence of rapidly increasing stress upon family relationships.[25] Since the early 1980s, there has been a substantial increase in the caseload of children's services, including that for child abuse, foster care, juvenile delinquency programs, and institutionalized youth. The extent of divorce is indicated by data from the Jamestown Public Schools. As of March 1986, 43 percent of the children in the city's high school were not living with both of their natural parents.[26]

It is not possible to prove that sharply increased economic and family stress formed the foundation of anxiety in people's lives which gave rise to the Satanic cult rumors. However, in the light of past research on threat rumors and scapegoating rumors, it is reasonable to conclude that it is the shared source of social stress.

Interpreting the Hidden Meanings in Rumors: Rumors as Metaphors

Now we can return to the question: Why were the seemingly bizarre threat stories about Satanism "relevant" (meaningful) to the lives of so many thousands of different individuals? In order to find answers to this question, we need to recognize that there are metaphorical meanings "hidden" in rumor stories beyond any literal meaning they hold. Rumor stories need to be translated in order for us to understand their more powerful meanings.

In his survey of research on rumors, Jean-Noel Kapferer puts the principle this way:

> Behind its apparent content, a rumor bears a second message. It is the latter that gives intense emotional satisfaction as the rumor circulates. In fact, we essentially spread hidden messages of which we are unaware.[27]

Rumors need to be interpreted for their symbolic meanings, much like myths, legends, folk tales, and poetry. However, the symbolic interpretation of persistent rumors is a tricky task. It is necessary to seek the symbolic meanings of rumors in the real-life social context of a particular culture in particular social conditions.[28] It is also necessary to recognize that there may be different frames of reference for rumors having different kinds of content. For example, rumors about contaminated foods in restaurants need to be interpreted using a different frame of reference than rumors about strange monsters in the forest. It may be quite misleading to seek *universal* symbolic meanings in rumors, that is, meanings which apply for all times and places. Finally, it is also important to recognize that complex rumors can have several levels of symbolic meaning, so that there may be several different but equally valid interpretations of rumor metaphors.[29]

The Collaborative Story-Telling Process

If we follow the analogy of comparing threat rumors and rumor-panics with nightmares, we find an appropriate framework for interpreting the Satanic cult rumors. Many psychologists believe that nightmares give symbolic expression to underlying sources of anxiety in a person's life. These anxieties are most often ones that arise from problems that a person is trying to solve but can't. In a sense, nightmares are problem-solving explorations of thought. Threat rumors, such as the Satanic cult rumors, can be interpreted as being a collaborative symbolic expression of people's shared anxieties about some threat to their well-being and their attempt to seek a solution to the problems causing those anxieties. Therefore, in interpreting the symbolic meanings hidden in the Satanic cult rumors, we need to identify shared cultural symbols (of a particular time and place) which refer to actual threats to people's well-being.

We need to see rumors as being a kind of collaborative story-telling process which constantly evolves rather than as being a fixed narrative. Therefore, when interpreting these rumors, we need to find the overall meaning in the changing flow of story-telling development.

Rumors of Teenage Suicide

The rumors about a dangerous Satanic cult built upon pre-existing rumors about teenage suicide. I found this to be true in Jamestown and in many other communities in the region.[30] Stories about teenage suicide seem to reflect the anxieties of parents about uncertain and dangerous "outside" influences upon the minds of their adolescent children. However, beyond this, the rumors can be interpreted as cultural metaphors for the loss of the family's ability to protect its children. In American society today, rumors of teenage suicide may be interpreted as omens for the failure of families to provide a protective shield against a dangerous world outside of the family, a failure to be a haven in a heartless world. These rumors arise not only from collective worries, but from collective guilt.

Rumors about Killing Cats

The rumors which followed and built upon those of teenage suicide concerned stories about the killing of cats at secret ritual meetings. These rumors added another level of symbolic meanings to the evolving metaphor.

Why did these rumors concern the killing of cats, rather than dogs, or perhaps chickens? Euro-American folklore associates cats, especially black ones, with the practice of witchcraft. In medieval Europe, cats were often burnt during times of witch hunts. Cats are symbols of black magic and symbolic omens of dangerous "evils." Even today, black cats remain symbols of "magical" events during Halloween celebrations.

However, there is a deeper meaning. Rumor stories about the killing of cats at secret rituals are metaphors for imminent danger from sources of "evil." The killing of cats is an omen.

Rumors about Kidnapping

Rumors about kidnapping are a persistent tradition in folklore. They circulate and recirculate, generation after generation, in local "urban legends" in ever new variation. There are persistent stories about the kidnapping of children at shopping malls, at entertainment parks, and in school parking lots. These rumors are symbols for parental fears for the safety of their children. Kidnapping rumors serve a useful socialization function. They communicate a message that all parents want children to learn: "Beware of strangers; don't talk to them; don't accept rides from them."

In addition, kidnapping rumors are metaphors for parental worries about their children's future in a society which is perceived to be unsafe for children. By extension, they are also symbols for worries about our children's future and the future in general.

Rumors about the Ritual Murder of a Blond Virgin

The rumor about the imminent kidnapping and ritual sacrifice of a blond, blue-eyed virgin emerged over the whole region. It has also been present in many Satanic cult rumor-panics before and after the one studied here. As such, its symbolism is a key to interpreting Satanic cult rumors.

Why do these particular kidnapping stories feature a blond, blue-eyed virgin, rather than, for example, a dark-haired, dark-eyed beauty, or perhaps a sexually promiscuous girl? The answer lies in the symbolism of the blond-haired, virgin girl. Since ancient times in European cultures, the blond virgin has been a symbol of innocence, purity, and rare beauty. It is found in folklore stories and in folk ballads.

At a deeper level, the blond virgin is a symbol for people's cherished ideals. Stories about the kidnapping and murder of a blond virgin are metaphors for attacks upon our most cherished traditional values. Such attacks arise only from the opposite of innocence and purity, from that which is most "evil." These rumors are parables about evil forces in our society. The rumor metaphor bespeaks this collective complaint: "Our most cherished values are in danger from mysterious forces of evil."

Rumors about Dangerous Satanic Cults

The Satanic cult metaphor functioned as a leitmotif throughout the evolution of the emerging rumor. It tied together the collaborative story-telling, so that the sub-themes of the story made sense as a whole. This metaphor is meaningful primarily in the cultural context of American society in recent decades and possibly would not be in many other contemporary societies. This is so because of the widespread American concern about new religious "cults" which symbolically "kidnap" children away from their parents' influence and because belief in a supernatural Satan is more common among Americans than among people in most other modern societies.[31]

The metaphor of a "Satanic cult" combines two powerful symbols: a cult and Satan. When most Americans use the word "cult," they don't do so in its technical sociological or anthropological sense, as simply a new religious group which is distinctively different from previous religious groups in a society. Instead, when people label a group a "cult," they mean to denote that it is a dangerous, manipulative, secretive, conspiratorial group. Moreover, a cult is seen as a heresy, a threat to decent, traditional cultural values.

Satan is an ancient symbol in Western tradition for powerful forces which work for evil. Satan is a symbol for forces which conspire against the legitimate authority of God and work for the destruction of God's moral order. On a deeper level, Satan is a collective symbol for evil forces working toward the destruction of the current moral order of a society. Satan is a symbol for threats to people's consensually accepted norms, values, and ideals which regulate stable relationships between people in a society. Threat rumors about Satanic cults are, therefore, metaphors for a dangerous heresy which threatens the legitimate moral order of American society, and which is causing the destruction of traditional American values.

There is another level of symbolic meaning which needs to be recognized in these rumors of Satanism. Satan is also a symbol for the loss of faith. It is Satan who conspires to tempt individuals to reject God and God's moral order. In the current cultural context of American society, rumors about Satanism are metaphors for fears about loss of faith in the traditional institutions and authorities of American society.

This interpretation fits the situation in American society today. There is abundant research evidence for the increasing "loss of faith" by Americans in their institutions and authorities since the 1960s.[32] The decline of faith and confidence in the ability of the institutions of American society to deal with people's problems is evident in the attitudes that American's hold toward the political system, toward business, toward education, and even toward organized religion.

When these rumor stories are interpreted together as a whole, they offer an emotionally powerful message in metaphorical form. Now, it can be understood why the Satanic cult rumors were meaningful and relevant to so many thousands of people. Their hidden meaning coveys the complaint: "The moral order of our society is being threatened by mysterious and powerful evil forces, and we are losing faith in the ability of our institutions and authorities to deal with the threat." When many people are experiencing economic decline and family breakdown, this message expresses precisely how they feel as their world is falling apart.

I may be quite wrong, but it seems to me that these stories about Satanism, which circulate in rumors, claims, and allegations, are no trivial matter. I believe that they are "omens" of deep-seated problems in American society. Much like nightmares, they have something important to tell us.

Symptoms of a Moral Crisis

Satanic cult rumors are symptoms of anxieties deeper than fantasy worries about secret, conspiratorial kidnappers and murderers. These rumors are collaborative messages in metaphorical form, which speak of a moral crisis. That moral crisis, as people perceive it, involves a loss of faith in the moral order of American society, a perception of the rapid decline in traditional moral values. People are saying, in essence, that "our world is falling apart, because all things good and decent are under attack by evil forces beyond our control."

This metaphor arises out of concrete sources of shared social stress in rural and small town areas of the country, areas which manifest particularly high rates of economic decline and family disintegration. The social stress is most intense for poorly educated, blue-collar workers, whose jobs are rapidly disappearing and whose families are disintegrating. Economically stressed blue-collar workers are those people who are most likely to believe the Satanic cult rumors. They are also those people who have held most uncritically to traditional American cultural values, such as the ideal of hard work, the ideal of unquestioning patriotism, the ideal of religion as a force for morality in society, and the ideal of the family as the central source of stability in life.

It has been common in the history of American culture for socio-economic tensions to become translated into moral-religious ideology, rather than to be expressed directly in terms of some purely economic ideology, as is more commonly the case in European societies. In a culture which blames financial difficulties on individual personality traits rather than impersonal social forces, the translation of problems of the "public sphere" of life (economics, politics) into problems of the "private sphere" of life (religion, morality, family relations) should not be surprising. Nor is it surprising that a major component in the informal communication network active in the dissemination of Satanic cult rumors is that of fundamentalist Protestants. The fundamentalist Protestant component is disproportionately composed of economically stressed, poorly educated blue-collar workers. They hold most tightly to traditional American cultural values which are affirmed in fundamentalist religious ideology.

Rumors, allegations, and claims about Satanism may also be a symptom of an emerging moral crisis in American society as a whole, as increasing numbers of people experience the effects of economic stress and family disintegration. If the economic decline of America accelerates as more and more well-paid blue-collar jobs disappear, it is likely that people will fantasize more conspiratorial threats and seek to find more scapegoats for their anxieties.

Chapter Four
Rumor-Panics across the Country

Perhaps no other form of crime in history has been a better index to social disruption and change, for outbreaks of witchcraft mania have generally taken place in societies which are experiencing a shift of religious focus—societies, we would say, confronting a relocation of boundaries.

Kai Erikson,
Wayward Puritans[1]

What Is a Rumor?

What makes a story a rumor? In common usage, a story is referred to as "just a rumor" when it turns out to have been false. However, this way of defining a rumor is impractical. It may take years of careful investigation to determine the truthfulness of some rumors. The accuracy of some stories may never be determined. For example, stories about a conspiracy to assassinate President Kennedy abound and it may never be possible to ascertain their truth or falsehood with a high degree of certainty.

Usually, the fabric of an elaborate rumor is false, at least in the sense that it conveys many misperceptions, distortions, and complete fabrications of actual events, even when it also recounts many events which did actually occur. However, the truth or falsehood of a story is not the central defining characteristic of a rumor.

A story can be identified as a rumor if it is a collectively shared story which is believed in the absence of any manifestly obvious evidence to substantiate it.[2] A rumor-story is widely believed to be true but cannot be confirmed by incontrovertible evidence at the time. Rumors are created and disseminated not only through word-of-mouth conversations but also through newspapers, magazines, radio, television, and privately printed materials.

Rumors usually arise when something unusual or unexpected happens and there is no easy explanation available. According to sociologist Tomatsu Shibutani, who wrote a comprehensive study of rumors, rumors originate as a substitute for "hard news."[3] Shibutani suggests that rumors are a collaborative attempt to find an explanation for a disturbing and ambiguous set of events. They usually arise when people do not trust "official" sources of news. If people lose faith in authorities, they may even regard bizarre and frightening rumor stories as being plausible because it might seem dangerous to simply disregard them. When rumors proliferate, many people feel "where there is smoke, there is fire" and begin to take rumor stories seriously.

A rumor persists when it offers a plausible explanation for people's shared anxieties.[4] Several conditions can make rumors seem plausible. Rumors gain credibility when their stories offer many dramatic details, thus giving them an aura of authenticity. They grow through a "snowball" process, as more and more people contribute supportive details to the collective story.

The most crucial support for rumors comes from eyewitness testimonials. There are always people who volunteer eyewitness accounts which seem to verify even the most bizarre rumor stories. They may do so to satisfy a variety of personal motives: to obtain attention and prestige, to express their own fantasy fears, to attack some group they hate, to amuse themselves or others, or to express some kind of mental delusion. However, the collective creation of rumors cannot be fully explained solely on the basis of these personal intentions.

Rumors need to be regarded as a social process of collaborative story-telling which expresses people's desire for a consensual explanation of ambiguous circumstances.

Community Panics in Response to Satanic Cult Rumors

Rumor-Panics

On rare occasions, fear-provoking rumor stories give rise to panics in crowds or even in whole communities. The classic case is that of the "War of the Worlds" panic, which took place in the region around New York City on October 30, 1938. The panic erupted in response to the famous radio broadcast and built upon underlying fears that another world war was about to begin in Europe. In the past, such events were termed occasions of "mass hysteria." However, that term is very misleading because it implies that some kind of contagious, temporary mental illness caused a panic.[5]

In order to avoid vague notions of what constitutes a "rumor-panic," in my research I defined a "rumor-panic" as a collective stress reaction in response to a belief in stories about immediately threatening circumstances. A rumor-panic in a community can be identified by the existence of widely occurring fear-provoked behavior. Examples of fear-provoked behavior include: 1) protective behavior, such as the widespread buying of guns or preventing children from being in public places; 2) aggressive behavior, such as group attacks on people perceived to be sources of threat, or the destruction of property; and 3) agitated information-seeking at community meetings for "news" about the threat and intensified surveillance of the community by police and vigilante groups of citizens.

Just as in the "War of the Worlds" panic, rumor-panics in response to Satanic cult stories do not arise from purely local events. The process begins when an ambiguous local event, such as a teenage suicide, vandalism of a cemetery, or the appearance of mysterious graffiti symbols on walls, becomes a concrete focus of attention for community anxiety and gossip. Thereafter, Satanic cult stories taken from newspaper articles, TV talk shows, horror movies, and folklore stories provide a plausible explanation for the ambiguous events. These stories are incorporated into local gossip and become persistent rumors. Satanic cult rumors gain credibility, as rumors usually do, because they are repeated so often that "everyone" people talk to says that they are true. This social process is called the consensual validation of reality.

The repetition of similar rumor stories from location to location across the country indicates that Satanic cult rumor-panics are a manifestation of a contemporary legend-making process in American society.

Rumor-Panics across the Country

In May 1988, when I began to search through newspapers from small towns near Jamestown, I was surprised to find that similar Satanic cult rumors appeared almost simultaneously over a vast region stretching 250 miles across parts of western New York, northwestern Pennsylvania, and eastern Ohio. This is an area consisting primarily of small towns, villages, and farmlands. The population is thinly dispersed across the area. People in any one location don't have much day-to-day contact with people from other locations. During the time of the rumor fever, people in one town didn't know that similar rumors were circulating in nearby towns. I didn't learn how widespread the rumors were, for example, until I began to telephone reporters from the newspapers of other towns.

As I searched through small town newspaper articles, I was surprised to find that similar Satanic cult rumor-panics have occurred in many communities and regions around the United States and in Canada. Eventually, I found sixty-two locations where rumor-panics have taken place. (See the map in Figure 2 and Appendix IV for detailed descriptions.) The first report of a Satanic cult rumor-panic was in 1982 and the last (as of early 1993, when this book went to press) was early in 1992. The peak years of occurrence were 1988 and 1989. After that time, the frequency of rumor-panics declined.

The data and interpretation that follows comes from an

analysis of the content of newspaper reports from thirty-one locations of rumor-panics in the United States for which I had sufficient information at the time this book was completed.

In none of these cases was any group found which resembled the stereotype of a Satanic cult, that is, a well-organized group committing crimes and justifying their actions with a "Satanic" ideology. In a few cases, authorities found groups of juvenile delinquents who had engaged in vandalism and proclaimed themselves "Satanists" but even that was unusual.

This series of rumor-panics is truly a social phenomenon without precedent. There have been many examples of community-wide rumor-panics and many examples of rumors which have swept across the nation. However, there are no other cases of a prolonged series of community rumor-panics erupting across the United States, unless one were to count race riots that took place in response to rumors. The situation is comparable to the witchcraft panics which swept across Europe in the late Middle Ages.

I believe that these rumor-panics are warning signals of deep, underlying problems in American society as a whole. The rumor-panics are like recurring collective nightmares. They are telling us about deep-seated anxieties in our society.

Behavioral Indicators of Rumor-Panics

In the western New York rumor-panic, there were many behavioral indictors of collective panic, including protective, aggressive, and information-seeking behavior. The indicators of fear-driven behavior were reported in newspapers throughout the 250-mile-wide region.

School officials from small towns and rural school districts reported hundreds of school children absent because fearful parents kept their children home. Police departments received an avalanche of telephone calls from people who reported having seen mutilated animals, Satanic graffiti symbols, lists of planned victims, and even a few human corpses. Town meetings, in which enraged parents demanded "action" from police and school authorities, were held in many locations. Prayer meetings were held in some rural fundamentalist churches, to pray for help in fighting Satan's influence. Sunday school instruction was given in some churches to warn children about the dangers of playing with occult magic rituals.

Newspaper articles about Satanic cult rumor-panics from across the country report very similar forms of collective behavior. Some of the articles, for example, reported that during rumor-panics the sale of guns increased greatly. Gun stores were sold out in a few places. Some of the articles reported the organization of local vigilante groups to patrol and search for Satanists. Emergency town meetings at churches or schools were common. Anti-Satanism "experts" from out of town were invited to give lectures about the dangers of occult practices and to provide information about how to identify Satanists. Some of these "experts" presented videotapes of television shows about Satanism as information. In many communities, absences from school increased greatly as parents held children home from school to protect them. In most locations, the local police were on alert searching for secret Satanist gangs. Sometimes innocent people were temporarily arrested on the basis of anonymous claims made by neighbors. In some locations, parents' advisory groups were set up to censor school library books which were assumed to promote occult beliefs and Satanic influences among youth. In many communities, the local newspaper published information for parents to use to identify the danger signs of Satanism among teenagers.

What Are the Underlying Causes of these Rumor-Panics?

Theories of collective behavior suggest that rumors and panics arise from shared sources of social stress, underlying conditions which cause widespread anxiety and frustration.[6] Clues to these sources of social stress may be found in the socio-economic conditions in the locations where rumor-panics have occurred. Clues may also be found in the metaphors embedded in the imagery of rumor stories. Even if rumor stories are not true in

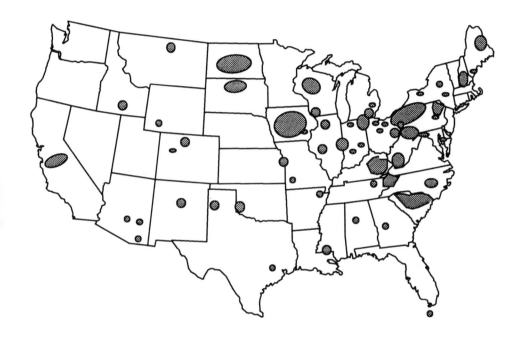

Figure 2.   Locations of Rumor-Panics in the United States.

the literal sense, they may embody symbolic messages about the shared anxieties people feel.

Economic Stress in Rural Areas and Small Towns

In every case except one (Kansas City, Missouri) these rumor-panics have occurred in rural areas and small towns rather than large cities. Rumor-panics which took place near large cities such as Pittsburgh, Pennsylvania, or Richmond, Virginia, did not penetrate into the urban areas.

The rumor-panic of Friday the thirteenth, 1988, covered a huge area of farmlands and small towns across southwestern New York and northwestern Pennsylvania. Curiously, however, it did not penetrate into Erie, Pennsylvania, the largest city in the region, having a population of about 120 thousand. People in the suburban villages near Erie became very agitated about dangerous Satanic cults, but people in Erie had not even heard the rumors about them.[7]

The location of these rumor-panics is quite curious and calls for an explanation. One possible explanation is that underlying socio-economic stresses are particularly acute in rural and small town areas. There is ample evidence for greatly increased economic stress upon unskilled, poorly educated parents due to the rapid loss of well-paid blue-collar jobs in small town America.[8] One major study published in 1988, for example, reported that "the poverty rate for the 54 million Americans who live in rural areas has climbed to 18%—50% higher than in urban areas."[9]

There is also evidence that the problems of parenting children, such as problems involving alcohol and drug abuse, juvenile crime, depression, and child abuse, have increased proportionately more in rural areas than these social problems have in urban and suburban areas.[10] In addition, the fundamentalist Protestant communication networks, which disseminate Satanic cult stories most actively, are stronger in rural and small town areas.

Parental Anxieties about the Safety of Children

Newspaper reports about Satanic cult rumor-panics reveal that the rumor stories feature surprisingly similar content across the country. About 75 percent of the stories mention animal mutilations. About 65 percent of them describe the kidnapping and ritual sacrifice of children. Many of the kidnapping stories take the form of predictions, but others claim that such crimes have already taken place secretly and have been concealed from public knowledge by the police and newspapers. Interestingly, about 40 percent of these kidnapping stories specifically mention blond, blue-eyed children or virgins.

Other rumor motifs were less common. Murder or mass murder by Satanists (without specific mention of children) was claimed to have taken place in about 20 percent of the rumors. Ritual sexual abuse of children by a Satanic cult was mentioned in only about 5 percent of the rumors. Other crimes that were referred to in only one case each included the sacrifice of human fetuses, ritual torture, sexual orgies, and teenage suicide due to Satanism.

In my research on the western New York rumor-panic, I found that the most fear-provoking rumor was that "the Satanic cult was planning to kidnap and sacrifice a blond, blue-eyed virgin." This rumor surfaced only about two weeks before the panic reached a peak of intensity on Friday the thirteenth of May, 1988. It served to focus tensions which had been growing since mid-winter, as one fear-provoking rumor built upon another.

Stories about the kidnapping and ritual sacrifice of children are the core of these Satanic cult rumors. Historical research suggests that this story motif derives from the ancient blood ritual myth. Variations of this myth commonly arise during periods of cultural crisis, when people are frustrated and fearful about rapidly changing cultural values, like they are today. (See Chapter Fourteen.)

Many parents today worry about threats to the safety and well-being of children, such as those from drug abuse, teenage pregnancy, teenage suicide, sexual molestation, and kidnapping. A great many traditionalist people are morally appalled by the existence in our society of widely available pornography, the acceptance of premarital sex, the tolerance of homosexuals, and the easy availability of abortion. Traditionalist parents regard all these conditions as being indications of moral decadence and threats to secure family life. These concerns are powerful ones for a great many Americans, as evidenced by their emergence as popular campaign issues in elections.

How Do the Rumor-Panics Get Started?

Before a rumor-panic begins, some antecedent event, or events, acts as a symbolic link with the content of the Satanic cult legend. These antecedent events also trigger increased tension in a community or region. Eventually, some antecedent event acts as a catalyst to release the built-up tensions in a climax of panic behavior. A triggering event, however, is not the cause of the panic behavior. If there was no underlying source of deep anxiety in a community, and if people did not take the stories about dangerous Satanic cults seriously, there would be no panic.

In Jamestown, New York, the rumor process started with the appearance of the new "punk" counterculture of high school students and private rock music parties attended by those youths at a warehouse rented for the purpose of band practice. Local gossip about the countercultural teenagers was gradually transformed, over months, into the symbolism of Satanic cult rumor stories. One triggering event for this transformation was a "Geraldo" talk show episode about Satanic cult influences on teenagers.[11] Another triggering event was a national news item about a teenager who killed his mother and himself, supposedly as a result of the influence of Satanism, this according to officials quoted in the news report.[12] (This was the nationally publicized Tommy Sullivan case.) Finally, months later, the date of Friday the thirteenth acted as a symbolic trigger that released the pent-up community tension in a panic.

The newspaper reports indicate that some common antecedent events occur before Satanic cult rumors give rise to community panics. These include: the sighting of so-called "Satanic" graffiti mentioned in 39 percent of the cases, cemetery vandalism mentioned in 23 percent of the cases, and some type of violent, local crime, such as a murder or suicide, mentioned in 45 percent of the cases. Other antecedent events mentioned less frequently include: a local church meeting or a police conference concerning the dangers of Satanism (16 percent), a mass media presentation about the dangers of Satanism (13 percent), conflict between local youth groups involving accusations of Satanism (13 percent), and the discovery of mutilated animals (6 percent).

It appears that antecedent to a Satanic cult rumor-panic, there is usually at least one ambiguous local event which evokes the symbolic themes of the Satanic cult legend in the people's collective imagination. The legend is used to provide a shared explanation for some disturbing local event for which there exists no easy explanation. There need not be any real danger in a community. When a group of people *believe* that something is real, it *is* real for them, at least in its consequences.

How Do the Rumors Spread?

Communication Networks and Propagandists
Rumors are spread through those communication networks which are receptive to them rather than through others in which people remain skeptical or disinterested.[13] The key factor relevant to the acceptance of the rumor stories seems to be participation in a communication network which constantly repeats the stories. In receptive communication networks, a few people actively promote the rumor stories, much like propagandists working for a cause, with little regard for verifiable facts.

Analysis of the newspaper articles indicates that in many cases, so-called "experts" on Satanism acted like propagandists for Satanic cult rumors and may have contributed to the growing fears. Sensational claims about the supposed dangers of Satanic cults made by these "experts" were reported in local news articles, often as "objective" news, without any critical evaluation of the claims. In some news reports, these claims were simply handled as being indisputable, taken-for-granted truths. As a result, these claims are likely to have lent credibility to bizarre rumor stories.

In about one-third of the rumor cases, police "experts" in Satanic cult crime were reported to have been active in promoting dramatic claims about Satanic cults. In about one-fourth of the cases, religious "experts" in detecting Satanism were similarly active in claims-making.

Here are a few of the sensational claims made by these "experts" which may have served to spread Satanic cult rumors and intensify people's fear.

> In April 1985, a local deputy sheriff in rural Union county, Ohio, claimed to have knowledge of five secret "cells" of Satanists, having at least fifteen hundred members, who came to deserted locations in the county to conduct secret ritual sacrifices of animals.[14] These claims led two months later to the famous "Toledo dig," during which teams of investigators dug up a wooded area near Toledo in search of remains of an alleged forty to fifty human sacrifices. (See Chapter Two.)

> In April 1988, a sheriff in McComb, Mississippi, claimed to the press that he had a confidential list of twenty-two members of a local Satanic cult, which he alleged were engaging in many ritual sacrifices of animals. Shortly afterwards, a rumor-panic erupted.[15]

> In May 1989, police "experts" in Satanic cult crime held a state-wide conference in New Hampshire and were quoted in newspapers as claiming that there are over two million members of Satanic cults in the United States, organized into "criminal cartels." According to these crime "experts," many of the unsolved kidnappings and serial murders in our country are committed by highly secret Satanic cults. Shortly thereafter, a state-wide rumor-panic broke out during which there was a hurried search for Satanists. Some police, for example, arrested a group of youths dressed in strange clothing while they were meeting deep in the woods. They had with them equally strange paraphernalia, including an animal skull, candles, daggers, and

swords. The police then announced to the press that they had arrested a Satanic cult caught in the act of practicing their Satanic rituals. (Although, that itself would not be illegal.) The youths' explanation of their behavior was disregarded by the police until someone checked the college at which they said they were students. It turned out that they were a group of art students practicing a Medieval play for videotaping in a secluded woods.[16]

In July 1989, a rumor-panic swept across rural areas in the Texas Panhandle near the small town of Hereford after a minister claimed to have knowledge of forty to fifty sacrificial killings by a secret Satanic cult. The minister said that he obtained his information from two women parishioners who witnessed the murders at an abandoned house in a deserted area. Local police could find no evidence to substantiate the claims.[17]

In my research on the Jamestown rumor-panic, I found that fundamentalist churches were an important part of a communication network for the dissemination of the Satanic cult rumor stories. The ministers of several of these churches gave sermons condemning occult practice and Satanism. Some churches held meetings about the Satanic cult rumors and some held special prayer sessions. A few churches invited out-of-town religious "experts" on Satanism to speak to their congregations. Members of a few of these churches even organized adult study groups which used videotapes of "Geraldo" talk shows as documentation for their studies. The rumors were discussed in some church newsletters and, thereby, circulated more widely. However, none of this should be taken as evidence that fundamentalist ministers provoked the rumor stories.

Certain groups in American society are more ideologically receptive to the symbolism of Satanic cult rumors and are more likely to actively disseminate them. These groups include small town police and fundamentalist churches. When such stories are spread on the local level, in face-to-face relations and through personal communication networks, these bizarre claims attain greater credibility than they ever could through the mass media alone. There is no more powerful way of being exposed to an outrageous or frightening story than learning about it from "a-friend-of-a-friend" who "really knows."

The Contemporary Legend-Making Process

The scholarly study of contemporary legends began attracting notice in the 1970s. Jan Harold Brunvand's first collection of "urban legends," *The Vanishing Hitchhiker*, brought this concept to the attention of scholars, as well as the general public. The concept of a contemporary legend (or urban legend) provides a new intellectual tool for understanding forms of collective behavior which were previously discussed only as being persistent rumors.

Brunvand defines urban legends as a "subclass of folk narratives . . . that—unlike fairy tales—are believed, or at least believable, and that—unlike myths—are set in the recent past and involve normal human beings rather than ancient gods or demigods."[18] Bill Ellis, who is the editor of an international newsletter about research on contemporary legends, notes that contemporary legends deal with events which are alleged to have "just happened," or with threats that have recently emerged. These stories: 1) are presented as being "news" freshly arisen from the storyteller's social setting, 2) deal with some kind of perceived emergency or social problem which urgently needs attention, and 3) express attempts to gain social control over an ambiguous situation.[19]

It is more useful to think of a contemporary legend as a process of collective behavior rather than as a fixed and unchanging narrative. The collective behavior consists primarily of the collaborative creation and communication of persistent rumor stories in ever-changing variations. A contemporary legend is, therefore, always emergent out of interaction and never finished. The story arises out of social encounters and is constantly being reshaped as people add parts, forget parts, and distort parts as the legend is told again and again.

There are thousands of contemporary legends, most of which have only local appeal and never get written down.

However, many can be recognized as belonging to generic families of legends. One such example consists of a family of stories about encounters with strange human-like creatures.[20] These stories have an ancient heritage which includes medieval tales about encounters with "wild men," vampires, dragons, and werewolves. In more recent times, there have been stories of encounters with bigfoot creatures, sasquatch, and yeti. Even more recently, extraterrestrial aliens ("ETs") from UFOs have come to play the role of the humanoid creatures in these tales. A related family of legends are ones about encounters with ghosts. There exist innumerable local folktales about the sighting of ghosts in haunted houses and at village cemeteries. Contemporary variations of this type of legend include the story about an alleged haunted house in Amityville, New York, which was celebrated in a popular book and a movie. Another contemporary version can be found in the many rumors about sightings of Elvis Presley or his ghost.

Contemporary legends such as these are likely to be amusing rather than disturbing. They don't touch our everyday lives. However, other types of contemporary legends play upon our everyday fears. Examples include persistent rumors about Halloween sadists who supposedly give children poisoned candy and rumors about gangs which kidnap children.[21] These crimes certainly do occur occasionally. That is what makes these rumors all the more frightening. However, even though the rumors most often are baseless, they continue to circulate year after year.

The Link between Legends and Rumors

There is no clear-cut distinction between persistent rumors and contemporary legends. Both are products of people's collaborative story-telling. Both commonly attempt to explain anxiety-provoking or ambiguous situations. However, most rumors are usually brief assertions, lacking a long, detailed narrative about people and events. Rumors are usually transitory and have only local significance.

In contrast, contemporary legends are usually short stories about incidents alleged to have recently occurred. These stories are set in a context of symbolic meanings which have wide significance beyond any particular location. The themes and symbolism of legends are sometimes used by people to create the content of rumor stories.[22] Legends transmit ready-made scripts which provide plausible explanations for unfamiliar and threatening circumstances. Contemporary legends, therefore, circulate in the form of persistent rumors which arise in widely distant locations.

In summary, contemporary legends, like ordinary rumors, are transmitted primarily through oral communication, and only secondarily through the mass media. These stories are also told as if they are true and widely believed "as if" they are likely to be true, just like ordinary rumors. However, the story themes are much more widespread and persistent than ordinary rumors. They are also more symbolic in their content and less tied to specific people and events. The stories communicate shared anxieties about newly-emergent, collectively perceived threats, and they are conveyed in age-old recurring motifs, or themes, which usually embody a moral-political message.

The scripts of contemporary legends can structure our preconceptions. Legends are not only "out there" in our shared culture. They are also "in us" psychologically. They are the models by which we live. They provide ready-made exemplars of goodness and evil, scenarios for working toward ideals, and explanations of tragedies. A person does not need to know all the details of a contemporary legend in order to fill in details. A good imagination will suffice. Once a set of events is viewed through the lens of a contemporary legend, there is a tendency to distort what is understood about the events in the direction of the preconceptions built into the script and symbols of the legend.

One of the most perplexing aspects of the Satanic cult legend consists of testimonial claims. There are claims made by people who say that they are former Satanists. There are claims made by psychotherapy patients who describe in detail their personal experiences as Satanic cult "survivors" of childhood ritual torture. There are teenage delinquents who claim that they are Satanists. There are violent criminals who claim that they are Satanists. There are children who give accounts of having been ritually abused in Satanic ceremonies. These testimonials are commonly offered as conclusive "evidence" of the existence of dangerous Satanic cults, even though there is no external corroborating evidence to verify any of the accounts. This is where research on contemporary legends is particularly useful.

Contemporary legends create self-fulfilling processes whereby the rumor stories are sometimes acted out or used to provide "accounts" of behavior. Folklore scholars term this process ostension.[23] The process is similar to the "copycat" modelling of criminal behavior from movies or newspaper articles. Satanic cult legend stories, for example, are used in hoaxes carried out by phoney, self-proclaimed "former satanists," who turn their stories into money making enterprises involving books and lectures. The stories are also used by some psychologically disturbed people to provide themselves and their therapists with convincing accounts of their confused mental states, as is the case with some women who have dissociative disorders who claim to be Satanic cult survivors. The stories are used to provide self-justifying accounts for criminal behavior, as is the case with some juvenile delinquents and a few violent criminals. In some cases, the stories become part of a cooperatively negotiated interpretive account for a very ambiguous situation, as is the case when children have given accounts of Satanic cult ritual sex abuse. Ostensive processes explain why similar testimonial stories are heard from people independent of each other and locations distant from each other.

Case Study of a Contemporary Legend: Anti-Semitic Rumors, France, 1968

In order to better understand how the contemporary legend-making process works, it will be useful to examine one thoroughly investigated case. A very old legend is the "white slavery legend." The script of the legend tells the story of innocent young girls who are kidnapped and forced into prostitution by well organized and powerful secret criminal networks with international connections. Thematically, it is very similar to the

Satanic cult rumors and is part of the same family of legends. The principles revealed in the following research can be applied equally to understanding the Satanic cult rumors, claims, and allegations.

In France in May 1969, rumors that Jewish clothing store merchants were kidnapping teenage girls in their stores and selling them into forced prostitution provoked a series of community-wide panics in several small provincial cities.[24] Stores owned by Jews and even ones presumed to be owned by Jews were boycotted and a few had their windows smashed. Some members of the local Jewish population received anonymous death threats.

Researchers traced the rumors back to stories about white slavery gangs, which were published in a national sensationalist tabloid magazine. The original story didn't mention Jews at all. Instead, the rumors built upon the folklore myths of European anti-Semitism which linked white slavery to Jews. As a result, the rumor stories were quite similar in different and distant provincial cities across France. Specific claims in different cities gave the stories local relevance, thereby providing the stories with apparent credibility. People across France didn't have to have contact with each other to fabricate similar stories. People in distant locations could create very similar stories because they shared the same basic cultural heritage. Many people who claimed to know about girls who disappeared in local stores, supposedly after going into changing rooms with trap doors, came forth to the police. Yet, the police could find no evidence of any girl being kidnapped. Belief in the rumor stories persisted, even though no evidence could be found to support them and even though official sources continued to deny them.

Similar rumors of white slavery popped up again in a few provincial cities in France in 1974 and in 1985 and again they were aimed at Jewish clothing store owners.[25] Researchers found that in these cases, people's vague memories of newspaper reports of the past 1968 rumors had been distorted so that they recalled only the white slavery stories rather than the fact that the stories were false.

The underlying source of social stress was not obvious. Yet, it was embedded in the symbolism of the rumor stories. The researchers identified the social stress as being social change which had caused serious generational conflict.[26] The year 1968 saw the student riots in Paris which almost overthrew the national government. Generational hostility had become intense. Parents were very worried about what was happening with their children and young people in general. In small towns, where traditionalism prevailed, parental anxieties were most intense. The new youth subculture had been developing since the early 1960s, and with it came new styles of clothing (such as miniskirts) for teenagers, unfamiliar and strange to most adults. Many new clothing stores, some owned by Jews, catered particularly to teenage girls and seemed to adults to be strange places. (One in Orleans, for example, was called "The Dungeon" and was decorated accordingly.) The underlying fear of parents was that they were "losing" their children.[27]

The white slavery legend about Jews, just like the Satanic cult legend, offers an elaborate scenario which distorts people's perceptions of unconnected incidents. The idea of a broad conspiracy provides the emotional power for the persistence of belief in the absence of any concrete evidence.

Origin of the Satanic Cult Legend

Satanic cult stories are part of a recurring cultural pattern in Western history involving the spread of subversion myths and a search for scapegoats to blame for social problems.[28] These stories arise again and again during periods of widespread cultural crisis. The social process through which this pattern arises links the motifs of ancient legends to currently popular explanations for social problems.

Satanic cult rumor stories derive from an ancient legend, usually referred to as the "blood ritual myth." It tells the story of children being kidnapped and murdered by a secret conspiracy of evil strangers who use the children's blood and body parts in religious rituals.[29] This myth is enduring because it offers universal appeal to the latent fears of parents everywhere. Variations of the myth are commonly elaborated upon with symbols of mysterious evil: graveyard robberies and the mutilation of corpses, secret meetings of people engaged in secret rituals, strange incantations, strange symbols, and people clothed in black robes with black cats, making ritual animal sacrifices and sometimes eating human body parts in cannibalistic rites. These are all interpreted as omens indicating that purity and innocence is being endangered by powerful agents of absolute evil.

The evil internal enemy in blood ritual subversion stories is usually some widely despised group in a society. Such groups function as scapegoats for anxieties caused by widespread social stresses. In ancient Rome, subversion stories claimed that Christians were kidnapping Roman children for use in secret ritual sacrifices.[30] The murder of innocent children was a symbol of the Christians' absolute evil, for only total evil preys upon total innocence. Later, during the Middle Ages, similar stories claimed that Christian children were being kidnapped by Jews for use in secret, religious ritual sacrifices. When this myth is used in anti-Semitic attacks, it is known as the "blood libel myth." (See Chapter Fourteen.) In France, just before the French Revolution, similar stories accused aristocrats of kidnapping the children of the poor to use their blood in medical baths.

Today, the blood ritual myth is constantly being reworked by the mass media to serve as popular culture entertainment. Many horror stories in pop culture novels and movies are based on a theme of kidnapping and murder carried out for a variety of unsavory purposes, such as ritual sacrifice (*The Believers*), or the use of body parts (*Coma*). Similarly, some fairy tales depict children being kidnapped, usually by witches or monsters who may cook or eat them. In this way, popular culture keeps alive and makes familiar an ancient story's themes and symbols. Satanic cult stories are fabricated out of these cultural materials.

The Satanic cult legend combines the blood ritual myth with another ancient subversion story. This second story tells us about Satan's rebellion against God and his struggle to subvert the souls of men and women and, thereby, destroy God's moral order. This particular combination of myths has a long history. It was frequently used in scapegoating attacks upon Jews, lepers, and people accused of being heretics or witches.[31] The power of this combination is that it offers both secular and sacred symbols and appeals to both secular professionals and religious traditionalists. The presumed Satanists can be regarded as either dangerous social deviants or as agents of supernatural evil, or both.

The danger of such powerful subversion mythology lies in its demand to find scapegoats. Inevitably, real living scapegoats will be found.

The Symbolism of the Satanic Cult Legend

The Satanic cult legend is an expression of what anthropologists call a revitalization movement—a social movement aimed at restoring an idealized society of past greatness and moral purity.[32] These social movements typically blame the subversion of dominant cultural values upon some kind of evil internal enemy.

The blood ritual myth and similar subversion myths usually arise at times when a society is undergoing a deep cultural crisis of values, after a period of rapid social change which causes disorganization and widespread social stress.[33] Indeed, subversion myths and their resulting witch hunts can be regarded as symptoms of a cultural crisis.[34] These stories are collective metaphors which express a society's anxieties about its future. It says, in symbolic form, that our future is threatened by mysterious forces which we cannot fully comprehend or control. Since a society's future is, to a considerable extent, embodied in its children, people's anxieties and the symbolism in the rumors focus upon dangers to children.

This metaphor is a projection of people's loss of faith in the ability of their society's institutions and authorities to solve social problems which threaten their well-being. Satan symbolizes the loss of faith in legitimate authority. The people who are most likely to take the metaphor of the Satanic cult stories seriously are those who feel the greatest threat to their faith in traditional values. In American society, these people are most likely to be religious traditionalists and socio-political conservatives.

The overall metaphor says that very powerful, secretive, evil forces threaten the moral order of society. The threat derives from a "heresy" against sacred, traditional values, which were once the solid foundation of our stable way of life. The evil enemy's values are the opposite of everything we cherish. Their power may derive from mysterious occult sources or "hidden" connections within the power elite in our society. The evil enemy image functions, just as in times of war, to confirm our society's essential goodness.

Chapter Five
Satanic Cult "Survivor" Stories

The lunatic, the lover, and the poet
Are of imagination all compact:
Such tricks hath strong imagination,
That, if it would but apprehend some joy,
It comprehends some bringer of that joy;
Or in the night, imagining some fear,
How easy is a bush supposed a bear!

William Shakespeare, *A Midsummer-Night's Dream*[1]

"Survivor" Stories

The personal testimony of people who claim to be survivors of Satanic cult torture is commonly offered as conclusive evidence for the existence of secret criminal organizations guided by Satanic religious ideology. These stories have gained credibility because some leading psychiatric authorities have come to take them quite seriously, as plausible explanations for the severe emotional problems of some of their patients. The dramatic personal testimony of some Satanic cult "survivors" has been broadcast on television talk shows to national audiences. Their stories can't easily be brushed off as the fabrications of people desperately seeking public attention. They remain a genuine scientific curiosity.

"Survivors" of Catholic Convents

The testimony of self-proclaimed "survivors" has been used throughout the centuries to lend credibility to subversion myths. In American society, for example, during the height of the anti-Catholic subversion hysteria in the 1830s and 1840s, a number of books were written by women claiming to be former nuns who escaped from forced confinement in convents where they had witnessed sexual orgies, sadistic torture, the slaughter of newborn infants, and even the practice of witchcraft.

The best-selling Catholic convent "survivor" story was published in 1836 in the sensational book *The Awful Disclosures of Maria Monk*.[2] Maria Monk claimed to be a Protestant girl who converted to Catholicism and entered a convent in Montreal in order to be educated, only to be sexually abused and tortured by priests.[3] She claimed to have seen young novices tortured and raped by priests, with the assistance of nuns. She described in detail the torture of innocent women, who were bound by leather straps, whipped, and branded with hot irons. She claimed that some women were even executed for refusing to submit themselves to lustful priests, some of whom were garroted and others who were stomped to death, while the priests and nuns laughed. Babies born in the convent were baptized immediately after birth and then strangled and thrown into a deep hole behind secret passageways. When she herself became pregnant, Maria determined to escape from the convent and to expose its hidden horrors to the public. Her *Awful Disclosures* sold so well over time, that the book surpassed the sales of any other book published before the Civil War, except for *Uncle Tom's Cabin*. The book was imitated by many other "survivors," one of whom even lent seeming support to Maria's story by claiming to have escaped from the very same convent as Maria.

Maria Monk's exposé of secret Catholic brutality was neither original nor creative. It followed from a long heritage of very similar anti-Catholic survivor stories published in Europe. Timing can account for the unusual popularity of Maria's story. *The Awful Disclosures* was published at a time of great anti-Catholic ferment in the United States and Maria's story was used as a vehicle by Protestant anti-Catholic associations to attack Catholicism in general and the mounting Irish Catholic immigration in particular. Catholic convent survivor stories were political. They provided ammunition for extremist believers in nativist Protestant ideology, who sought to gain control of American government in the name of tradition and moral purity.

The First Satanic Cult "Survivor"

The oldest known Satanic cult "survivor" testimonial was published in 1980 in the form of the book, *Michelle Remembers*.[4] The book was written by a Canadian psychiatrist, Dr. Lawrence Pazder, from a case study of one of his patients, Michelle Smith, whom he diagnosed as suffering from Multiple Personality Disorder.

According to Michelle's story, she was sexually abused and tortured during 1954 and 1955 as a child in Victoria, British Columbia, by a secret group of Satanists to which her parents belonged. She claims that she witnessed babies and adults being ritually killed and butchered and that she was even fed ashes from the burned remains of a victim. On another occasion, Michelle claims that a fetus was sliced in half in front of her and then rubbed on her body. She claims that she was frequently kept naked in a special cage that was sometimes filled with snakes. On one occasion, she says she was tied up and a mass of little red spiders was made to crawl over her and bite her. On still another occasion, she says she had horns and a tail surgically sewn into her flesh that she later ripped out. The culmination of Michelle's torture came when Satan himself visited the rituals, but she was saved by the intercession of the Virgin Mary and Jesus.

In treating Michelle, Pazder used some rather unconventional therapy. In one session, for example, Pazder arranged to have Michelle baptized a Catholic by a priest. (Curiously, Pazder who is a Catholic, later divorced his wife and married Michelle, who had divorced her spouse.)

There is no external evidence to corroborate Michelle's bizarre tale. Michelle's claims of encountering supernatural beings should provoke at least some cautious skepticism. A reporter who investigated Michelle's story found that Michelle's two sisters, who curiously were not mentioned in her book, deny her story, as does her father.[5]

Dr. Pazder had been a physician in West Africa, where he became very much interested in the study of black magic rituals in ceremonies he observed.[6] He gathered an extensive collection of photographs of these ceremonies, according to his own admission. His interest in African black magic could have influenced his preconceptions about Michelle's story and his photographs could have become cues for ideas incorporated into her imaginings.

Michelle's survivor story attracted a large audience. Even before her book was published, her story was featured in *People Weekly* magazine, which reported that the authors had received an unusually high $100,000 advance for the hardback edition and an additional $242,000 for the paperback version.[7] A version of the story quickly appeared in *The National Enquirer*, spreading the story to an even wider audience.[8] Michelle and Dr. Pazder have since appeared frequently on television, radio, and at conferences, speaking as experts on Satanic cult ritual abuse.

Michelle's story was widely disseminated. Quite likely, it became a model imitated by other self-proclaimed survivors.

Satanic Cult "Survivors" on Television

In the 1980s, the stories of Satanic cult "survivors" proliferated. They were widely disseminated in books, magazine articles, newspaper articles, on television talk shows, and on Christian radio programs.[9] Around the country, "survivors" spoke as guest "experts" at conferences for therapists, police, and religious groups on such issues as ritual child abuse, occult crime, and Satanism. Their evident emotional pain and apparent sincerity conveyed a truth to audiences in their presence, a truth that empathic ears could not easily deny. Yet, the meaning of that truth was not clear.

The largest audience by far to hear the personal testimony

and see the anguished faces of Satanic cult "survivors" were those who watched them on national television talk shows. "Survivor" stories have been featured on "Geraldo" shows titled: "Satanic Breeders: Babies for Sacrifice" in October 1988; "Satan's Black Market: Sex Slaves, Porno and Drugs" in March 1989; and "Investigating Multiple Personalities: Did the Devil Make Them Do It."[10] The "Sally Jesse Raphael" show presented two episodes titled: "Baby Breeders" in February 1989 and "Devil Babies" in July 1991.[11] In addition, three programs of "The Oprah Winfrey Show" from 1986 to 1989 presented "survivors" as guests on broadcasts about Satanism.[12]

The words of "survivor" Cheryl Horton, offered on the "Sally Jesse Raphael" show of February 28, 1989 provides an excellent example of the kind of horrifying testimony heard by TV audiences.[13] Her anguished emotional expression and the empathic involvement of Sally Jesse Raphael can be seen in the dialogue between them. The testimony is very similar to that heard by psychotherapists, even more powerfully expressed in the privacy of their offices.

Cheryl Horton: "Well, I was impregnated at 11 years old for the first time"

Sally: "By whom?"

Ms. Horton: "By a friend—I'm not sure by who the first time, the second I know it was by a friend that worked for my parents. The first time I don't know by who, but I know the baby was taken as an abortion, but it was still the shape of a fetus, it had hands. So I don't know what happened to that baby. I remember being in my bedroom and the lights were out, but yet I could see the fetus laying on the tray and it was dead. The second time I was"—

Sally: "You mean, they brought you the—the dead fetus?"

Ms. Horton: "Yes. And they left me in a room and kept the fetus on a tray, I think to brainwash me and frighten me."

Sally: "These are your parents?"

Ms. Horton:	"Yes, these are my parents."
Sally:	"Were they a member of a—some kind of cult or something?"
Ms. Horton:	"Yes, they were a member of a ritual abuse cult, and it was nationwide."
Sally:	"Okay."
Ms. Horton:	"The second time I was impregnated by a man that worked for them, and what they did was, they would always shoot me up with drugs, but when they wanted me pregnant, they would quit giving me their drugs and they started giving me fertility pills. And what the outcome of that was, I gave birth to two twins—to twins."
Sally:	"You were how old when you were—"
Ms. Horton:	"I was 12 years old at the time."
Sally:	"Fertility drugs for a 12-year-old."
Ms. Horton:	"Yes."
Sally:	"How did they get those drugs?"
Ms. Horton:	"Well, it was in a mansion in the Los Angeles area, and there was a doctor that owned the mansion, and he was a full-fledged Satanist."
Sally:	"Okay."
Ms. Horton:	"And they prescribed the fertility drugs to me, and they would set me up in a room with this man, and—well, actually, he was about 19. He was young, too, but I hold him responsible also. I gave birth to—I called them, I gave them names myself, because I don't know what they named them—Kevin and Wendy. And Kevin was let to live, he was in a bassinet, and Wendy they put on a chair—on a table—and I am very nervous and very hurt right now. And they drove a cross in her chest upside down, wooden cross."
Sally:	"In the newborn baby's chest."
Ms. Horton:	"Yes."
Sally:	"And what happened?"
Ms. Horton:	"She—they held my head and made me watch. And I was on a delivery table, and they held my head like this, to hold it down, and made me

watch them do that. And afterwards, they put me on a stretcher and took the baby, Wendy, and buried her out in the yard—after consuming some of her flesh for their communion."

Sally: "And that—I'm sorry, and that's very, very difficult for—you know, for you, I'm sure."

Ms. Horton: "It hurts a lot."

Sally: "Of course. And the boy? The twin?"

Ms. Horton: "My son Kevin was let to live for two years, and I knew to stay away from him when—when they were around, but when they weren't around, I would play with him. And he was sacrificed at—on a Halloween when he was a little over two. And what they did was, they had—and this sounds really bizarre—they had a spa, and they would use piranhas in a lot of their rituals, and they took and—his father didn't want him sacrificed, and they took and—and put his father in a trance and put drugs on him, and they can do that with people. And his father went with him to sacrifice him—my father and the doctor and his father—took and sacrificed my son over the spa with the piranhas. They cut his arm off first and then started dismembering him."

Sally: "Wow."

. . .

Ms. Horton: "I had it blocked. And I got into therapy, and my therapist said, 'There's something you have mighty blocked.' And all of a sudden I started remembering. And I had blocked it through a process called multiple personalities, and when I got into therapy, the personalities that held the memories started coming up. And today I remember it as one person, as Cheryl, because I'm integrated."[14]

Two basic questions arise from the eyewitness testimony of Satanic cult "survivors," one which is obvious and one which is not so obvious. First, can the testimony be believed, in whole or in part? Is there any corroborating evidence for any of these incredible stories? Secondly, and even more importantly, why are these stories believed by so many people, including many respected psychiatric authorities?

The Search for Evidence and Understanding

Therapists who believe the "survivor" stories point to the following forms of "evidence" for ritual abuse of children by organized Satanic cults. (1) Their patients' stories are internally consistent. (2) Their patients tell their stories with evident emotional pain. (3) Their patients reveal the same stories while under hypnosis. (4) Patients from various parts of the country report very similar stories.[15]

The same forms of "evidence" have been used by psychiatrists in the past, who claimed to have discovered Multiple Personality Disorder patients around the world who were able to report stories of past lives in which they died painful deaths centuries ago. This kind of evidence is also similar to that used to support people's reports of being abducted by aliens from UFOs. It is possible that some people have been reincarnated, that some people have been abducted by aliens, and that some people have been ritually tortured and killed by organized Satanic cults. However, claims like these must be supported by the kind of evidence that is capable of verification by careful examination and that can be used to rule out alternative interpretations of the testimonials. These same forms of "evidence," for example, are what may be expected to be found in the transmission of a contemporary legend. The burden of proof should always be upon conspiracy theorists to provide corroborating evidence. Otherwise, fear and suspicion becomes a substitute for rational evidence.

What kind of corroborating evidence would support the testimony of Satanic cult survivors? Obviously, the discovery of remains of body parts of the many infants and adults supposedly murdered would be useful, as would the identification of missing people in the communities where the murders were supposed to have occurred. No such remains have been found nor have missing persons reports been filed in the communities in question. Tracing some of the secret Satanists and their links with each other would also be useful in establishing the veracity of the stories. The history of past secret organizations indicates that they rarely remain secret for very long, especially if there are a great many people involved. This has been true of secret criminal organizations such as the Mafia, and organizations of spies and terrorists, and even secret religious groups like the murderous Thuggee of India.[16] Arrests and convictions of some of the alleged murderers and accomplices to murder in these supposedly extensive and well organized groups would be useful. Most of these murders would have occurred during the 1950s and early 1960s, when most of the self-proclaimed survivors were children and before the growth of exotic religions.[17] The claims of survivors would have us believe that organized ritual murderers could operate with impunity at a time when murder rates were low, without leaving any trace of evidence of their existence.

The Clemsford Witch Reincarnation

The study of people who reveal "memories" of a previous life in extraordinary detail while under hypnosis demonstrates the existence of little-understood mental processes and the need for a careful search for corroborating evidence. It is too easy to simply pass off bizarre claims of Satanic cult torture as being the mere lies of people seeking public attention.

In 1977, a twenty-three-year-old English woman, having no particular mental disorder, was hypnotized and regressed to memories of her "previous life" in a famous experiment.[18] Under hypnosis, the woman reported an anguished description of her trial for witchcraft in the year 1556. She did so, while speaking fluently in what seemed to be archaic English, using a vocabulary of that time. While questioned under hypnosis, she provided elaborate details of her experience—her name and those of her family members, names of people at the trial and even their physical appearance, locations, trial procedures, and details of everyday life in the sixteenth century. While recounting her story, the woman expressed great fear and intense physical pain in a manner beyond the ability of any ordinary actress. She held out her hands with fingers curled up, which she explained had been severely burned in a trial procedure in which she had been forced to grasp a hot metal bar. Later, the researcher found an obscure book about the Clemsford witch trial which confirmed all of the factual details the woman had provided under hypnosis: the names, physical descriptions of the people, and even the procedure of testing the accused by making her grasp a hot metal bar. Everything seemed to support the woman's story. Her emotional anguish appeared much too real to be faked.

In her conscious state, the woman had no memories whatsoever of the Clemsford witch trial, nor any recollection of having ever read anything about it. She seemed to have no motive to fabricate the story. She was not seeking public attention and even requested that her name not be made public, because she was confused and disturbed by what she had revealed under hypnosis.

A later, more careful investigation found crucial discrepancies in the woman's story.[13] An expert in the study of archaic English was given an audio-tape of the woman's hypnotically induced story to examine. He very quickly concluded that the language was not genuine sixteenth-century speech, but the kind of English used by contemporary writers and movie makers to suggest the flavor of speech of that time. An even more important clue was found by some careful historical research. The researcher found it in the only surviving original records of the Clemsford trial. The original records of the trial gave its date as being in 1566, rather than in 1556. The latter date and the date given by the woman under hypnosis was a printing error reproduced in reprints of the original records of the trial, and by many scholars and story writers since the nineteenth century. In other words, the woman did not relate any experience of a previous life, but rather her experience of some history story containing the telltale error in date. The story, which she perhaps read or heard on the radio, was beyond her conscious ability to recall. It might have been a radio program she had heard during her childhood that frightfully absorbed her attention and imagination at that time.

How can we understand this kind of testimony? Is it a bold lie, or is it the honest recounting of personal experience? Perhaps it would be most useful to avoid conventional notions of deliberate lying and honesty. In a sense, some people's testimony of their experiences in various unusual states of consciousness, like those under hypnosis, are "honest lies." In the case of the Clemsford witch reincarnation, the woman's testimony was an honestly recounted experience, but one that was also untrue to the actual social context of her experience.

One thing is clear. Memories recounted by people during hypnotic trance states are not photographic recordings of their past experience. People's memories during trance states are constructed from their current interpretation of their past experience, their memories of childhood fantasies, and vivid imaginings designed to please others. Martin Segall, the Director of the Society for Ethical Hypnosis, noted in a letter to me, in response to my questions about the hypnotically regressed memories of Satanic cult survivors:

> In my personal opinion, based upon what I have gleaned to date, unless there can be corroborating evidence, such as cross-referenced dates, events, etc., such testimony is worthless. Regressed memories are definitely not infallible. There always remains the possibility of hallucinations, fantasy, and, above all, the possibility of contaminating the testimony by improper questioning.[20]

Demon Possession and Multiple Personality Disorder

Most of the women who claim to be survivors of Satanic cults have been diagnosed by psychotherapists as suffering from Multiple Personality Disorder (MPD). The problem is that it is not clear whether these women are reporting the actual underlying trauma (childhood torture) which caused their mental disorder, or whether their claims are simply another manifestation of their disorder.

The behavior and emotional reactions of people who suffer

from MPD are remarkably similar to those found among people who claim to be possessed by demons in societies where witchcraft and exorcism are part of culturally accepted reality.[21] The possessed are people who easily go into self-induced trance, or hypnotic states of consciousness.[22] They express themselves during these trance states, as if their minds are controlled by entities or forces which are beyond their will, much like another inner self. Commonly, they have no conscious memories of what they say or do during their altered states of consciousness (although this is not always the case). They often exhibit dramatic mood swings and convulsions when moving into and out of their altered states of consciousness. While in an altered state of consciousness, they report seeing, hearing, and feeling things which are not present (hallucinations) with great emotional immediacy. Occasionally, during altered states of consciousness, they may even exhibit bizarre physical changes, such as skin rashes, body swellings or even spontaneous bleeding.[23]

In Western medical practice following the work of Charcot, this kind of behavior came to be regarded as being symptomatic of a mental illness, at first called "hysteria." More recently it has been labelled dissociative disorder, and MPD is regarded as being a subtype of that mental disorder. However, this psychiatric-medical conception of the possessed as suffering something like a disease adds little to our basic psychological understanding of the phenomenon.

An alternative conception is offered by an anthropological school of thought, which views spirit possession and Multiple Personality Disorder more broadly, as culturally patterned forms of thinking and acting which regulate certain unusual mental capacities.[24] In other words, people who experience these altered states of consciousness come to comprehend and express themselves through pre-existing cultural guidelines, whether these be beliefs about witchcraft and demon possession, or beliefs about psychiatry and Multiple Personality Disorder.[25] The content of what these people experience in their altered states of consciousness is shaped by prevailing cultural explanations of their experience. Over the last several decades, since the dissemination of books and movies such as *The Three Faces of Eve* and *Sybil,* popular beliefs about multiple personality have become part of our cultural ethos. A kind of ironic cycle is set up, whereby the possessed feed back to therapists pop culture psychiatric imitations of Multiple Personality Disorder, which they learn from media stories written by therapists.

This psycho-cultural conception of the possessed does not deny that the ability to move in and out of self-induced trance states may develop in response to traumatic experiences during childhood.[26] The phenomenon probably has a complex combination of causes. Current psychiatric conceptions of Multiple Personality Disorder now suggest that the personality syndrome may result from a combination of: 1) an inherited biological capacity to easily enter trance states; 2) deeply disturbing emotional traumas most likely experienced during childhood; and 3) culturally shared learning which shapes the content of the ideas the person expresses.[27] However, therapists are still left with a difficult dilemma. Are the stories of Satanic cult survivors actual revelations of their childhood traumas, or are they mirror reflections of popular culture beliefs?

The Psychiatric Communication Network

Groupthink among Therapists
Dr. Sherrill Mulhern, an anthropologist, recently completed a two-year study in which she interviewed a sample of the most prominent MPD psychotherapists, MPD Satanic cult "survivors," and police Satan hunters. Mulhern came to the conclusion that the key factor in the acceptance of Satanic cult "survivor" stories is the preconception of psychotherapists to accept them in response to group conformity pressures.

> Preliminary findings underscored the paramount importance of training seminars for the 'conversion' of perplexed therapists into "believers." These conferences were organized ostensibly

to educate therapists and CPS [child protection service] workers
in the dangers of ritual abuse. A careful review of the most
popular facilities revealed that *believing in the phenomena was
the principle unifying criteria.* Some of the most respected
specialists in child sexual abuse presented alongside cult "experts" whose erudition was illuminated essentially by their
fervent Christian religious beliefs and adult "survivors" who
"recalled" early childhood cult tortures during therapy, generally for multiple personality disorder. The memories of the
survivors were consistently offered in lieu of proof of the
existence of elusive cults.[28]

How did so many educated professionals come to believe
the Satanic cult stories of their patients? A possible explanation
is that these psychiatrists, psychologists, and social workers
came to accept the Satanic cult stories in a manner essentially
similar to the group conformity process that people in a
community come to accept Satanic cult rumor stories. This
process has been termed "groupthink" by the social psychologist, Irving Janis.[29]

The social process of groupthink is a collective response to
conformity pressures operating within communication networks and groups which are somewhat closed to the influence of
external sources and, thus, closed to the influence of alternative
beliefs. Groupthink can be seen to operate in religious groups,
therapy groups, and even corporate bureaucracies, groups in
which the need to maintain cooperative interaction between
members creates social pressures to conform. These pressures,
in turn, suppress critical analysis of, skepticism of, and dispute
about prevailing beliefs. The desire of participants to preserve
friendly relationships among themselves inhibits their expression of points of view that deviate from informally accepted
group norms. Participants who attempt to bring up issues that
might cause internal bickering and conflict are subtly ostracized
or chastised for their disloyalty. The process works upon
people's perception of reality. Members who might privately consider unacceptable beliefs, begin to doubt their own
thinking and change their beliefs to fit into the reality constructed by the group. As a result of groupthink, critical
thinking and reality testing are repressed by the pressures for

group solidarity. The process of groupthink is by no means unusual or rare. Many of us have been members of groups in which this process operates.

The essence of the dilemma is that MPD psychotherapists are faced with an ambiguous problem in need of a clear explanation. There is no clear understanding of the nature and causes of Multiple Personality Disorder. Even its existence as a distinct and specific mental disorder is a matter of serious dispute.[30] It is frustrating for therapists to try to help people in evident emotional pain, without an adequate explanation for their distress. The Satanic cult legend serves as a substitute for "hard news", that is, a substitute for a decisive discovery of a cause for the ambiguous symptoms of Multiple Personality Disorder.

The interaction of psychotherapists and their MPD patients is symbiotic in that both need each other to explain ambiguity. The Satanic cult "survivor" stories offer both of them an explanation for the experience of Multiple Personality Disorder. There is good evidence that MPD patients have a chameleon-like, manipulative personality and feed therapists the kind of stories they feel therapists want to hear.[31]

Bizarre Satanic cult stories are easily pieced together by MPD patients. They can get them: from traditional rural folklore about black magic, witches, and Devil worship; from newspaper articles reporting Satanic cult rumor stories; from popular culture entertainments like tabloid newspapers and horror movies; and, of course, from the speeches and books of other self-proclaimed survivors. This accounts for similarities between the stories of patients who don't know one another and may even live in different countries. The psychiatric network is now transmitting the Satanic cult legend from the U.S. to England and Holland.[32]

The "survivor" stories were first given credibility when leading MPD psychiatric authorities publicly professed belief in their plausibility. This happened at the first national conference of the International Society for the Study of Multiple Personality Disorder, in 1984. Once authority figures lent credibility to the stories, the process of consensual validation, operating through the psychiatric communication network, reinforced the credibility of the stories. In this network, the normal open and public scientific criticism and dispute is discouraged. The rationale is that this is necessary to protect the "survivors" from supposed dangers of the Satanic cult conspiracy. As a result, this communication network operates like a closed community of believers, paradoxically, much like a religious cult. The discouragement of normal, critical scientific discourse is expressed even in conference presentations by therapists:

> I don't want more survivors going into clinicians' offices feeling again that they are being re-abused by the mental health profession. If you do not believe that this could possibly happen, do not work with this issue. We don't want you a part of this because it is simply going to make the issue be more confounded and more difficult.[33]

Many psychotherapists in this communication network now accept the Satanic cult stories on the basis of faith alone. Traditional religious therapists, in particular, have an ideological receptivity to the Satanic cult stories and have become committed to their dissemination. Because of their ideological preconceptions, they are not likely to regard the stories with cautious professional skepticism, especially in the face of group conformity pressure from colleagues. The "survivor" stories have now attained the status of a taken-for-granted reality in the MPD psychiatric communication network. This is so, even though many therapists continue to express doubts about the stories.[34] Groupthink is a process of collective behavior which neutralizes individual expressions of dissent.

The Dissemination of "Survivor" Stories

By the mid-1980s, an increasing number of psychiatric patients were being diagnosed as having Multiple Personality Disorder. In the period between 1970 and 1981, a total of seventy-nine cases of MPD were identified worldwide; while in contrast, over the preceding twenty-five years, only eight cases were confirmed.[35] An increasing number of these MPD patients were reporting Satanic cult survivor stories to their psychotherapists, many of whom came to believe them.

The main agency disseminating the Satanic cult legend to the psychiatric profession as a whole is the International Society for the Study of Multiple Personality and Dissociation, which sponsors national and regional conferences on Multiple Personality Disorder.[36] These conferences regularly include lectures and professional training sessions about Satanic cult ritual abuse. Most of the papers from these conferences are never published. When distributed to those who attend, they are usually marked "not for distribution or reproduction." Therefore, they are not easily available for scientific examination and criticism. Nevertheless, some of these unpublished conference papers are photocopied and eventually find their way into the hands of police agencies, which use them as authoritative "evidence" of Satanic cult crime. (For example, I obtained one such paper from a policeman, from a remote rural area, who had attended a police training seminar on Satanic cult crime.[37])

Both former MPD patients who claim to be survivors and their believing therapists have been networking extensively. They disseminate the Satanic cult stories at various kinds of meetings: training seminars about ritual child abuse for mental health workers; police conferences about occult crime; and even gatherings sponsored by fundamentalist religious groups.[38] At these meetings, the former MPD patients and their therapists are presented as authoritative experts on Satanic cult crime and torture. Special hospital units have even been set up in several cities for the treatment of MPD survivors of Satanic cult "ritual abuse."[39] These hospital units also provide lectures and training for therapists, counselors, police, and other professionals in how to identify signs of criminal Satanism, in order to help victims of "ritual abuse."

Believing therapists have been articulating the Satanic cult legend in great detail for years, since the mid-1980s, without publishing any empirical research findings in juried scientific journals where the findings can be subjected to scientific cross-examination. These therapists' articulation of the Satanic cult legend, embodying concepts such as cult "brainwashing" techniques, conditioning, symbolic "cues" for subconscious responses, and conspiratorial organization, now functions as an elaborate substitute for a genuine scientific theory based upon verifiable empirical data.

Several eminent therapists have publicly endorsed the conspiracy theory of Satanism. One such person is Dr. Bennett Braun, Director of the Dissociative Disorders Program at Rush Presbyterian-St. Lukes Medical Center in Chicago, who has publicly stated his belief that:

> We are working with a national-international type organization that's got a structure somewhat similar to the Communist cell structure, where it goes from local small groups to local consuls, regional consuls, district consuls, national consuls and they have meetings at different times.[40]

Illustration: A Psychiatric Seminar about Satanic Cult "Survivors"
The following is a report of my participant observation study of the transmission of the Satanic cult legend at a psychiatric seminar. The six-hour seminar was titled "Culture, Cults and Psychotherapy: Exploring Satanic and Other Cult Behavior."[41] It was sponsored by Harding Hospital, of Worthington, Ohio, a suburb of Columbus, and took place in March 1990. The main speakers were Maribeth Kaye, a social worker, and Lawrence Klein, a clinical psychologist. They each presented "information" about Satanic cults and the ritual torture of children. The structure of the seminar did not allow the audience to critically cross-examine speakers or to engage in dialogue with them. Members of the rather large audience had to submit questions in writing. The speakers responded to some of them at the end of each session.

There were 370 people in attendance, at a fee of seventy dollars per person. An official count of professionals in the audience listed ninety social workers, seventy-two nurses, fifty psychiatrists, forty psychologists, and seventy clergymen and counselors. Continuing education credit was offered to the psychologists who attended via the American Psychological Association.

Kaye and Klein presented an elaborate description of Satanism and Satanic cults, including their ancient origin, the use of torture and sexual abuse of children to "brainwash" them, the use of secret symbolic cues to trigger programmed behavior in members, the recruitment of members, the levels of membership, and their political-ideological goals.

According to Klein and Kaye, organized Satanic cults, dedicated to the worship of Satan and evil, have existed as a secret "countercultural religion" since ancient times. Klein and Kaye claimed that membership is transmitted primarily through families. Sexual child abuse and torture is deliberately employed by Satanist families as a technique to brainwash and program children to confuse evil with virtue, so that they will follow instructions to commit Satanic evil acts without feeling any guilt. However, Satanists also attempt to recruit members by getting young people involved in occult, black magic practices. Klein and Kaye claimed that through a process of increasing involvement and manipulated commitment, Satanists gradually assimilate recruits into deeper circles of this secret society. By this means, teenage dabblers in black magic are recruited into more secretive witchcraft cults, from which even more secretive hard-core Satanic conspirators are recruited, usually only after proving themselves by arbitrarily murdering some stranger. Hard-core Satanists, they said, are involved in a variety of nefarious criminal activities, such as child pornography, "snuff" pornography films, and the international drug trade. An international network of very secretive, hard-core Satanic cults are linked together in pursuit of Satanic ideological goals. These secret Satanists try to infiltrate the higher levels of the power structure in all societies, in order to undermine the moral order. The ultimate goal of the international Satanic conspiracy is to create international chaos in order to allow Satan to take over the world.

The main source of evidence cited by Kaye and Klein for all of this elaborate description was the testimony of MPD patients.

When Klein was asked, in a written question, to cite some external corroborating evidence for a Satanic cult conspiracy, he candidly admitted that there was none and said that all the evidence is circumstantial. He referred to several pop culture, "true crime" books about Satanism as useful sources of information. Then he asked members of the audience to raise their hands if they had encountered cases of "ritual abuse" in their practices (without defining what he meant by the term). About two-thirds of the audience raised their hands. There was no further discussion of the issue. (This was an obvious group conformity pressure technique, which is part of the process of groupthink.)

In one of her presentations, Kaye offered as evidence of Satanic influences, photographic slides of drawings made by MPD patients. Her basis for treating the drawings as evidence was the supposed Satanic symbolism she found in them. She also offered slides of odd paraphernalia that she claimed were Satanic, black magic artifacts and symbolic cues used to trigger programmed behavior in MPD sufferers. At one point, Kaye referred to the film "The Manchurian Candidate" as "an excellent example of how mind control operates." In a written question, Kaye was asked if she had any external corroborating evidence to verify the Satanic cult stories of her MPD patients. She responded, "A good therapist can tell whether or not a client is truthful by the internal consistency of what the client says."[42] She also noted that since the relatives of the patient are involved in a criminal conspiracy, they would be expected to deny the stories told by people who they victimize.

I was interested in how these stories were being received by the audience, so I asked the people sitting on each side of me about their reactions. They told me that what they heard was difficult for them to believe and that they would like to see some hard evidence. However, during a conversation at lunchtime, I found quite a different reaction. A psychiatric nurse who worked at Harding Hospital was seated beside me. I asked her if she believed what the presenters had reported about Satanic cults, including the idea of an international network of criminal Satanists. She responded, "Definitely!" I then asked her how she could be so certain that Kaye and Klein's presentation was true? What she told me reveals the crux of the whole Satanic cult phenomenon. She quite candidly said that the existence of Satanism confirms her belief in God. Being a bit mystified by this response, I asked, "Why?" She said, "Anyone who is a Christian and believes in God, must also believe in the existence of Satan. Satanists believe in Satan and work for him, just like people who believe in God work for God. So I know that God and goodness really exist."

At the closing of the conference, members of the audience could participate in small group "debriefing sessions" with staff members of Harding Hospital. The discussion group I joined included Dr. Ellen Mosley, a psychiatrist at Harding Hospital, and her psychiatric intern. It also included two mothers concerned about Satanism among teenagers in their town. One of the mothers told the group that her son had been "taken" by Satan and Satanism. When we were asked about our reactions to the presentation, I cited the need for hard evidence to confirm the MPD patients' stories about Satanic cults. Dr. Mosley told me that she treats many MPD patients and believes their stories. "You would also," she said, "if you saw the evidence right in front of you." She referred to her patients' evident emotional pain upon recalling what happened to them. She said that the internal consistency of their stories proves that they are true. When I pressed her for external corroborating evidence of a Satanic cult conspiracy, she referred to the Bible as evidence and said, "Isn't that good enough?" Her psychiatric intern then told the group that she believed that MPD patients "were possessed by the Devil and only exorcism could really help them."

Another Hoax in the Name of Science

There have been few attempts to thoroughly investigate the claims of a Satanic cult "survivor." The only detailed investigation on record is one carried out by reporters, for the evangelical Christian magazine *Cornerstone,* who investigated the claims of Laurel Willson.[43] Ms. Willson, who is more widely known by her pen name of Lauren Stratford, published her story in the book *Satan's Underground*.[44] She has been featured on several national TV talk shows about Satanism, including the celebrated Geraldo Rivera "Special" on the issue, which attracted one of the largest audiences in television history.[45] Her book is frequently cited in the conference papers of eminent therapists as evidence, and she has spoken widely as an expert witness to Satanic cult crime.

The reporters found her story to be riddled with contradictions of fact and to be, essentially, a hoax. For example, she claims to have given birth to three children as a Satanic cult breeder during her teens and early twenties, but not one of her relatives, friends, or teachers could confirm seeing her pregnant.[46] She claims that she was able to escape from a Satanic pornography ring after her father's death in 1983, yet the fact is that her father died in 1965. Many of the people interviewed, people who knew her, said that she was a deeply disturbed young woman, given to telling fantastic tales. As a result of the *Cornerstone* magazine investigation, the publisher of Stratford's book withdrew it from sale.[47]

Satanic cult "survivor" stories are being disseminated through the communication network of psychotherapists working with Multiple Personality Disorder patients and, furthermore, are reaching a much broader audience of professionals concerned about child abuse. These stories have been legitimized by some leading psychiatric authorities specializing in the study of MPD, as well as some authorities specializing in the study of child abuse.[48] As a result, Satanic cult "survivor" stories have adulterated the scientific study of child abuse, incest, and therapy for these deeply disturbing experiences.

Why have these stories spread so rapidly among normally careful professionals, who are supposedly informed by science? Part of the answer lies in the process of groupthink. Another part of the answer may be that these stories, like the Catholic convent survivor stories before them, serve as propaganda vehicles for ideological interests. The survivor stories reflect the ideological preconceptions of many religious fundamentalists and conservatives. Many of them, today, work as Christian counselors and Christian therapists. The survivor stories also stimulate the outrage of many ideological child advocates and feminists, who are concerned about the concealment of sexual abuse in male dominated society. The Satanic cult legend is, thus, able to join together normally antagonistic secular and sacred definitions of social "evils" and their differing proponents.

Chapter Six
Satanism and Alleged Threats to Children

Magistrates from the town, church members, leading people, and people of all sorts, flocked to witness the awful power of Satan, as displayed in the tortures and contortions of the "afflicted children;" . . . *The aspect of the evidence rather favors the supposition, that the girls originally had no design of accusing, or bringing injury upon any one. But the ministers at Parris's house, physicians and others, began the work of destruction by pronouncing the opinion that they were bewitched.*

Charles W. Upham,
Salem Witchcraft, 1867[1]

The Salem witchcraft scare was ignited by the unexplainable suffering of teenage girls, suffering to which professional authorities, ministers, and physicians, attributed a frightening meaning. So too, the contemporary Satanism scare was sparked by the unexplainable suffering of children that was given a frightening interpretation by some professional authorities. The gathering storm of a new witch hunt is being propelled by the same social forces; once again imaginings of a conspiratorial menace are being called up out of the dark shadows of the mind. Times have changed perhaps, but fear running rampant among a people always has the same terrible consequences.

In this chapter, we will examine, in the light of scientific research which can allow us to distinguish truth from falsehood in these claims, fear-provoking claims about how Satanism threatens our children.

Claims about Child Sexual Abuse by Satanists

The most alarming claims about threats to children are those which link Satanism with the sexual molestation of children. The Office of Criminal Justice Planning of the State of California published a special report in 1990, titled "Occult Crime: A Law Enforcement Primer,"[2] which presents claims about Satanic cult ritual child abuse made by several prominent professionals. These claims are very similar to those being made across America in popular magazine articles, on television talk shows, at police and social work conferences, and in local neighborhood rumors.

> Dr. Bennett Braun has personally worked with over 70 adults with Multiple Personality Disorder (MPD) and has conducted two recent studies on data collected from 40 states. He estimates that of the approximate 200,000 Americans who suffer from MPD, up to one-fourth, 50,000, could be victims of Satanic Ritual Abuse.[3]

> Psychiatrist Roland Summit, whose subspeciality is child sexual abuse, calls ritual abuse of children "the most serious threat to children and to society that we must face in our lifetime." Dr. Summit's experiences point to "no less than 1,000 children who stated their involvement in ritualistic systems."[4]

> Dr. Lawrence Pazder, psychiatrist, describes the motives and pervasiveness of ritualized abusers who are "normal-looking and carry on normal lives. They are members of every strata of society which they have carefully infiltrated. Any position of societal power or influence should be seen as a target for infiltration. The perpetrators have masses of money available. Many have impeccable credentials—doctors, ministers, professionals of every kind."[5]

An organization called "Believe the Children" is a volunteer group of parents, dedicated to the dissemination of information about the ritual sexual abuse of children. One of its pieces of "information," titled "Characteristics of Schools in which Satanic Ritual Abuse Occurs," contains the following claim.

> Satanic ritual abusers tend to infiltrate preschools in clusters, by geographic area. As in the case of the South Bay, in which 7

offending preschools were involved in a given area. Currently, we are aware of clusters of offending schools in the Newbury Park, Whittier, and Riverside areas.[6]

A similarly alarming claim is made in a report called "Ritual Abuse," put together by The Ritual Abuse Task Force of The Los Angeles County Commission For Women. This report is handed out at many police and social work conferences on ritual abuse across the country.

> Ritual abuse has also occurred, without parents knowing, at preschools, day-care centers, churches, summer camps, and at the hands of baby-sitters and neighbors. The ritual abuse in such an institutional setting is not incidental to its operation, but it is in fact intrinsic to it, the very reason for its existence. Children are subjected to sexual abuse, ritual intimidation to terrorize them into silence, and ritual indoctrination to convert them to the belief or worship system of the group.[7]

Claims like these have evoked public outrage about the victimization of innocent children and have ignited a moral crusade against secretive, conspiratorial child molesters.

The Ambiguous Meaning of the Phrase "Ritual Abuse"
Rumors of Satanic cult ritual abuse of children arose from the "survivor" stories of Multiple Personality Disorder patients, beginning with the publication of *Michelle Remembers* in 1980, and spread rapidly after the allegations of Satanism in the McMartin Preschool case in 1983. By the end of the 1980s, the concept of ritual abuse had become a taken-for-granted reality among many police officers, journalists, therapists, and social workers. The two-word prefix "Satanic cult" was quickly dropped, however, from the phrase "ritual abuse," in order to make it more acceptable to secular audiences such as trial juries, who might reject Satanic conspiracy theories as being too bizarre to be credible.

The concept of ritual abuse is now at the center of heated controversy in law enforcement and in the helping professions. Before adequate behavioral science research can be done and before any reliable police investigation can be conducted, the concept needs to be clearly defined. Unfortunately, the term is ambiguous. It is unclear exactly what behavior constitutes ritual abuse, whether for the purposes of scientific research or police investigations. There are many meanings given to the term "ritual abuse" and most are burdened with unspoken connotations about Satanism.

The California state criminal justice report on "occult crime," for example, defines ritualistic abuse as: "repeated physical, sexual, psychological and/or spiritual abuse which utilizes rituals."[8] Certainly, when we start talking about "spiritual abuse," we are on very shaky ground if we need to specify acts which might be illegal and scientifically verifiable in careful research.

A more elaborate definition appears in some recent articles in professional journals. For example, Susan Kelley, a psychiatric nurse, defines ritualistic abuse as follows.

> Ritualistic abuse refers to the systematic and repetitive sexual, physical, and psychological abuse of children by adults engaged in cult worship. The purpose of ritualistic abuse is to induce a religious or mystical experience for adult participants. Perpetrators of ritualistic abuse involve children in group religious practices and ceremonies that often include the ingestion of human excrement, semen, or blood; witnessing the mutilation of animals; threats with supernatural or magical powers; ingestion of drugs; and use of songs or chants. The child victims are threatened with supernatural powers and physical harm to prevent disclosure of the ritualistic activities. For example, children may be threatened that the devil or demons will harm them.[9]

However, Kenneth Lanning, head of the FBI's Behavioral Science Unit, points out the inherent ambiguities in attempts to construct a new category of harm done to children in the context of ritualistic activity. Lanning suggests that police investigation and scientific research need to focus upon concrete acts of physical, sexual, or emotional harm, rather than upon the social context of those acts (e.g. rituals).

> The author has been unable to precisely define ritualistic abuse and prefers not to use the term. It is confusing, misleading and counterproductive. . . .

When a victim describes and investigation corroborates what sounds like ritualistic activity, several possibilities must be considered. The ritualistic activity may be part of the excessive religiosity of a mentally ill, psychotic offender. It may be a misunderstood part of sexual ritualism. The ritualistic activity may be incidental to any real abuse. The offender may be involved in ritualistic activity with a child and also may be abusing a child, but one may have little or nothing to do with the other.[10]

At the core of allegations of ritual abuse are accusations of child sexual abuse and that is what really evokes the deepest sense of outrage. Unfortunately, the term "sexual abuse" itself is a rather broad rubric. Sexual abuse of children may be defined as the use of violence, threats, deception, or authority by an adult to encourage a child to be a partner in sexual activity. It may include: 1) incest between adult relatives and their children; 2) the sexual molestation of children by adult strangers; and 3) the use of children in pornography or prostitution.[11] In other words, studies of collected cases of alleged ritual abuse are confused by the cross-classification of many different types of possible sexual exploitation of children.

Research on Ritual Sexual Abuse Allegations

Conspiracy theories are very seductive for people who desire simple and easy explanations for complex social problems. They appeal particularly to people who are anxious and fearful about ambiguous dangers in society. Conspiracy theories are impossible to disprove, because one can never prove the non-existence of an elaborate conspiracy. Conspiracy believers will always find "signs" of conspiracy; even the absence of evidence is taken as a "sign" of a conspiratorial cover-up.

There is simply no corroborating evidence for the existence of an organized network of Satanic cults whose members sexually molest children in order to brainwash them into a Satanic ideology. Instead of presuming that ritual abuse allegations arise from the behavior of Satanic conspirators, we need to shift our focus in order to be able to see that the allegations arise from a national pattern of collective behavior. As a response to collective behavior, ritual abuse allegations are part of the contemporary legend about Satanic cults. They are "atrocity stories," spread across the country by the mass media and by communication networks of groups concerned about child abuse. One effect is "mass contagion," in which children in different parts of the country report very similar stories of Satanic ritualism. The question we need to ask is this: What are the social dynamics which lead to allegations of ritual abuse made by children?

A journalist who has investigated many cases of alleged ritual abuse, Debbie Nathan, offered a conclusion about these allegations in an award winning article titled "The Ritual Sex Abuse Hoax." It stands as perhaps the best summary of ritual abuse investigations.

> Investigations usually began because of vague medical symptoms or after an upper-middle class child did something inappropriately sexual. Then, even though most sexual abuse occurs within the family, investigators immediately directed their inquiries outside the home. Sometimes they suspected community sex rings, but most often they focused upon elite child care centers. The first allegation sometimes seemed plausible. But in remarkable departures from traditional forensics, police, social workers, doctors and therapists badgered children to name more victims and perpetrators, ignoring answers that contradicted a ritual abuse scenario. As a result, many men were charged; but women were too, and this was especially shocking, since women have not been thought of as child molesters, much less sex torturers.
>
> From 1984 to 1989, some 100 people nationwide were charged with ritual sex abuse; of those, 50 or so were tried and convicted, with no evidence but testimony from children, parents, "experts" expounding on how the children acted traumatized and doctors talking about tiny white lines on anuses or bumps on hymens—"signs" of abuse" that later research would show appear on nonabused children.[12]

As Nathan indicates, the moral crusade against ritual abuse has resulted in a zealous rush to judgment, in which the lives of innocent people have been ruined. In many prominent cases, such as those in Bakersfield, California and Jordan, Minnesota, people who were convicted of ritual sex abuse have had their convictions overturned upon appeal. There is mounting evidence, gathered from reports about specific cases, that many innocent people have been accused, put on trial, and even convicted of ritual abuse.[13] Unfortunately, no national survey of the number of such miscarriages of justice is yet available. However, some recent studies suggest that there are a large number.[14]

It is likely that the Satanism scare will lead to an increasing number of allegations of ritual abuse. The American Bar Association's Center on Children and the Law is conducting a survey of county prosecutors, to obtain an estimate of the national incidence of different types of cases of child abuse. The survey is not yet published, but as of early 1993, the data indicated that 27 percent of county prosecutors have handled cases involving "ritualistic or satanic child abuse."[15] If these preliminary findings are representative of the eventual survey conclusion, that would mean that the courts across the country are now dealing with a great number of accusations of ritual abuse.

A ritual child abuse case featured on a PBS "Frontline" television documentary titled "Innocence Lost" (first broadcast on May 7, 1991) illustrates the tragic results of the Satanic cult scare.[16] In the small town of Edenton, North Carolina, in the spring of 1989, twenty-nine children claimed to have been sexually molested at a day-care center, in bizarre rituals sometimes by groups of adults. The initial allegations referred to ritual activities, such as the killing of babies and animals, that took place in the presence of the children.[17] The main social worker in the case, who helped to bring out the children's allegations of ritual abuse, has been active in lecturing about Satanic cult ritual abuse.[18] Two men and five women were arrested and charged with child molestation. They included the married couple who owned the day-care center, three women child-care workers, and two other residents of the town. The bail was set so high that several of the defendants could not afford to pay it and spent more than two years in prison awaiting trial. Two of the employees were young mothers, whose incarceration in prison took them away from their children. On April 23, 1992, the male owner of the child-care center, Robert F. Kelly, was convicted and sentenced to life imprisonment.

Allegations of Ritual Sexual Abuse against Women

An estimate of the extent of ritual abuse allegations can be found in research studies which attempt to determine the national incidence of child sexual abuse. The best known and most commonly cited study of this kind is one done by sociologist David Finkelhor and published in a book titled *Nursery Crimes*.[19] The study focusses upon allegations of sexual abuse in day-care centers across the country, from 1983 to 1985. It collected information, mainly from child protection services, about 270 cases which these agencies regarded as being "substantiated," meaning that these agencies considered the allegations to be true. This, of course, did not mean that any legal charges were necessarily filed in court. Actually, fewer than a third of the cases were prosecuted, and less than a tenth of those resulted in guilty pleas or convictions. (The famous McMartin case, for example, which involved bizarre allegations against the seven original defendants but resulted in no convictions, was one of the cases included.) It is unfortunate that the Finkelhor study is often misunderstood and cited as being a study of the actual incidence of sexual abuse in child-care centers.

The Finkelhor study identified thirty-six cases of alleged ritual abuse in day-care centers. These constituted 13 percent of the total cases of sexual abuse. Curiously, women were the accused sexual abusers in all of these ritual abuse cases, and in some of them, women alone, without male associates, were the accused perpetrators. This finding alone throws doubt on the validity of ritual abuse allegations.

Research on sexual behavior has found that it is extremely rare for women, especially without the coercive influence of male accomplices, to sexually molest very young children.[20] It is especially rare for women to sexually molest children outside of the family, and particularly rare for women to sexually exploit children of both sexes indiscriminately. A study of 2,372 cases of child sexual abuse "substantiated" by the Iowa State Department of Human Services for the years 1985 and 1986, for example, found that 86.5 percent of the cases in all social settings involved male perpetrators in institutional settings, such as child-care centers. Males were twenty-four times more likely than females to be the accused perpetrators.[21]

The Social Creation of Ritual Abuse Allegations

The original accounts of ritual child abuse came from the Satanic cult "survivor" stories of MPD patients, as conveyed by the therapists who believe their stories. The book *Michelle Remembers* by Smith and Pazder, and the still unpublished conference paper by Marybeth Kaye and Lawrence Klein (described in the previous chapter) are the most frequently cited sources of eyewitness accounts, presented as evidence in professional journal articles about ritual abuse.[22] This is so, even though these sources are, at best, works of imaginative speculation rather than sources of carefully collected, verifiable information.

Later accounts of ritual abuse came from the allegations of children who described being ritually abused, most commonly in day-care centers. If these children's allegations of ritual abuse are not true, what else could possibly account for their detailed recounting of intimate sexual acts, accompanied by bizarre rituals, often involving such behavior as the killing of animals and babies, drinking of blood and urine, and transportation to graveyards?

In order to understand these stories, we need to shift the focus of our attention from the presumed motives of the children (meaning their honesty or dishonesty) to the observable interactive social process which gives rise to the children's stories. In other words, when we examine the interactions between child protection workers, who may be believers in ritual abuse, and the children whom they are questioning, we can understand how the stories may be socially manufactured in a process of joint story-telling. The real issue isn't whether or not children's stories of ritual sex abuse are honest accounts or lies, but whether or not the stories are verifiable. We need only recall that the original charges of witchcraft in Salem were made by young girls who were carried away by group hysteria.

This interaction process whereby children's false stories of sexual abuse are socially created is described in detail by psychiatrist Lee Coleman and attorney Patrick Clancy, both of whom have had considerable experience dealing with cases of child sexual molestation. It was published in a bench mark report in a law journal, in an article titled "False Allegations of Child Sexual Abuse."[23]

> In our experience, which adds up to hundreds of allegations and about fifteen hundred hours of audio- or videotaped interviews with children being investigated for possible molestation, children quite regularly make allegations that can be factually proven not to be true. When this happens, it is rare for the child to be the true initiator of the false statements. In most cases, the child's false statements are the product of an interviewing style that leads the child gradually to construct a mental picture of abuse. This picture becomes the child's "memory." The result can be disastrous, not only for the justice process, but also for the child's emotional well-being . . .
>
> It is common practice for police or child protection investigators to refer a child for therapy at the very outset of an investigation. The stated purpose is either to help the child disclose information about abuse or to help the child with the trauma secondary to abuse.
>
> If the child is a true molestation victim, both of these purposes may be fulfilled with no harm done to the truth-seeking process. But, if the child has not been abused, such therapy can have a profoundly contaminating impact. Week after week, the child is questioned about abuse and encouraged to "tell the secret." In our experience, children may "learn" in such sessions that they are in danger and may develop major fears and anxieties. They may learn to believe they were abused and gradually construct the details. They may come to believe in these inventions with all the sincerity that real events would call forth.[24]

Coleman and Clancy point out that child protection workers are not expected to be impartial investigators searching for evidence of wrongdoing. Instead, they are advocates for children and commonly act on the presumption that children have been victimized in some way whenever allegations have been made by parents, or neighbors, or even sometimes by anonymous telephone callers.

Once they are drawn into the child protection system, children are caught in a contradictory Catch-22 situation. If the child denies being involved in sexual acts, that is taken as evidence that the child is repressing his or her memories of terrifying abuse that the child protection worker is morally responsible to bring out, gradually and carefully. If the child expresses anxiety, the anxiety is regarded as evidence of repressed memories, rather than anxiety due to being repeatedly interrogated by unfamiliar child protection workers and police.[25]

Coleman and Clancy's examination of videotapes of the interaction between therapists and children being interviewed found that overzealous child advocates often use leading questions, cuing of desired responses, praise for desired answers, and manipulated fantasy play to gradually implant ideas about sex and about Satanic rituals in the communication process between the child and therapist.[26]

Social psychologists call this process "priming".[27] The research on priming indicates that it is most likely to happen when an authority figure questions a child who is anxious and highly suggestible. The process isn't necessarily conscious and deliberate. If a child protection worker inadvertently shapes the discourse around their preconceptions about ritual sex abuse, priming can easily occur.

When overzealous therapists prime the discourse between themselves and children, they may gradually implant reconstituted "memories" of events that get shaped by the subsequent discourse. These pseudo-memories may then become reinforced by later conversations between the child and parents, other children, and police. If these other people frequently reaffirm the pseudo-memories of ritual abuse, they may become subjectively "real" events in the memory of the child. In this way, it is possible for children to "remember" events which never occurred. Much research suggests that childhood memories are largely a product of language learning structured by the discourse between the child and other people.[28]

Personal memories are, to a considerable extent, rooted in the collective memories of groups. For example, our memories of our early childhood experiences are commonly filtered through the memories of our parents and relatives, who recall for us incidents in our early life. When we try to recall whether our memories from childhood are products of events our parents described to us (perhaps while reviewing photo albums with us), or whether we recall them as direct memories of events, it may not be possible to recall the actual origins of the memories.

Contrary to popular belief, eyewitness accounts are not invariably accurate. People's minds don't work like photographic cameras. Our memories of events can be distorted by severe anxiety, by our preconceptions to see what we expect to see, by the power of suggestion from others, and by contamination from memories filled in since the original event.[29]

In some cases, real sexual abuse is confounded by children's stories of bizarre happenings. Priming by poorly trained therapists is not the only source of distortion. Several additional explanations for children's bizarre stories of ritual sexual molestation are suggested by the FBI's Kenneth Lanning, who has studied many cases of alleged ritual abuse since they emerged in 1983.[30] In some cases, the traumatic fears of children in response to actual sexual abuse in their homes may produce elaborate fantasies about events in day-care. In other cases of actual sexual abuse, for example, child molesters may deliberately use threats of magic spells, witches, and demons, in order to intimidate the children; but not as part of any commitment to a Satanic ideology. Child molesters may be familiar, as are most people today, with the Satanic cult legend, and appropriate it for their own exploitive use.

Sometimes children's stories of Satanic cult ritual abuse are outright lies fabricated by the children with the assistance of adults with a score to settle. Evidence comes from some cases in which children have recanted their stories. In one such case in 1989, four brothers, who had appeared on the "Geraldo" TV show to testify about Satanic ritual abuse, recanted accusations that they had made against their mother and her boyfriend.[31] The allegations of the boys included accusations of killing babies and drinking their blood. It appeared that the boys' divorced father had coached the boys to tell the same fabricated stories. In another case, in England in 1991, two sisters admitted under cross-examination in court that they had lied about being sexually abused in Devil-worshipping rituals.[32] Five people, including the girls' parents, had been arrested on the basis of the accusations of the older sister, age ten. The girl admitted in court to making up the stories, which included, once again, the killing of babies and being forced to eat their flesh. The girl said that she had fabricated the stories to please her grandmother, with whom the girls had been sent to live after their parents had separated. Cases such as these, where children recant stories of Satanic cult torture, are given much less attention in newspaper reports than are the initial atrocity stories of ritual abuse.

The Collective Behavior Process in Ritual Abuse Scares

The Role of Communication Networks

The moral crusade against "ritual" abuse is likely to persist for a long time to come. The reason for its persistence is that the moral crusade has become very well organized.

Volunteer associations of parents, with chapters in several cities, educate the public about "ritual" abuse by disseminating claims about it through the mass media, and lobby child protection workers to become concerned about it. A variety of businesses now produce police training manuals, social work training videotapes, and reports about "ritual" abuse.

Conferences and training workshops on "ritual" abuse for police and child protection workers function as organizing agencies; they recruit more and more professionals to the moral crusade, including social workers, psychiatrists, psychologists, physicians, and police. These professionals then become "experts" on "ritual" abuse and disseminate claims about the Satanic cult legend on the local level, where they alert people to the so-called signs of "ritual" abuse in public speeches and small town newspaper articles. As a result, more and more "signs" are detected and allegations made. In other words, there is now a vast communication network which disseminates elaborate assumptions about "ritual" abuse, even though there is an absence of scientific and law enforcement evidence to verify those claims.

The Role of the Mass Media

Another reason for the persistence of allegations of "ritual" abuse is that they provide sensational atrocity stories for the mass media. Small town newspapers are particularly likely simply to report the stories of bizarre "Satanic" activities, without much skepticism or critical analysis.

The McMartin Preschool case offers an excellent example of the social dynamics of media sensationalism. The case began with proliferating allegations of hundreds of children being subjected over a period of years to rape, anal, oral, and group sexual activity, pornography sessions, naked games, animal mutilations, baby killings, cannibalism, trips to secret tunnels, and transportation to distant places, sometimes by airplane— all done in a context of Satanic rituals.

The Los Angeles Times published a detailed analysis of the media's coverage of the case, including its own reporting.[33] Its conclusions apply equally well to similar cases, which arise continually in other locations and which do not receive national attention.

> More than most big stories, McMartin at times exposed basic flaws in the way the contemporary news organizations function. Pack journalism. Laziness. Superficiality. Cozy relationships with prosecutors. A competitive zeal that sends reporters off in a frantic search to be the first with the latest shocking allegation, responsible journalism be damned. A tradition that often discourages reporters from raising key questions if they aren't first brought up by the principals in a story.
>
> In the early months of the case in particular, reporters and

editors often abandoned two of their most cherished and widely trumpeted traditions—fairness and skepticism. As most reporters now sheepishly admit—and as the record clearly shows—the media frequently plunged into hysteria, sensationalism and what one editor calls "a lynch mob syndrome".[34]

Media sensationalism helps to spread rumor stories about Satanic cult crime from one location to another. Research on rumors has found that people tend to recall the most sensational aspects of news reports and forget later published denials.[35] In this way, the sensational reports provide a plausible scenario for similar rumors to pop up sometimes years later, in distant locations. After the initial sensational reporting about the McMartin case, for example, eight other preschools in the area were identified as being centers of Satanic cult activity; shortly thereafter, over one hundred preschools across the country became targets of similar allegations and police investigations.[36]

The Ritual Abuse Hoax

The ritual abuse scare is the social creation of a late twentieth-century witch hunt. There is no verifiable evidence for claims about a Satanic cult ritual abuse conspiracy. However, there is abundant evidence that an increasing number of moral crusaders are creating a form of deviant behavior, which exists only in their preconceptions. The victims of this rush to judgment include children who are traumatized by the emotional over-reaction and repeated interrogations by well-meaning child protection workers. The victims include children who are taken away from parents who have been falsely accused of ritual sex abuse. Victims also include the parents who are imprisoned and often held with exorbitantly high bail for months before going to trial.

These allegations of Satanic cult ritual sex abuse also distort and confuse investigations of cases in which real sexual abuse has occurred, often resulting in such cases being thrown out of court.

Illustration: The Ritual Abuse Scare in England

In the fall and winter of 1990, a case of alleged ritual abuse created sensational newspaper stories in England, making headlines throughout that country. The case clearly illustrates the way that the collective behavior of the Satanic cult scare gives rise to a witch hunt for ritual sex abusers of children.

The case began on June 14, 1990, in Rochdale, a suburb of Manchester, when seventeen children were suddenly taken away from their parents by police and social workers.[37] An initial complaint came from the teachers of one six-year-old boy, who they said was telling bizarre stories of black magic and the killing of babies. The children were made wards of the court and put in foster care, without parental visits allowed, while child protection workers conducted weeks of questioning of the children. After lengthy questioning, the social workers charged that the children were all victims of a secret Satanic cult which had abused them in sexual rituals. At first, the charges against the parents created the usual furor of sensational news reports, emphasizing the allegations of sex, sadism, and occult religion.

However, after some more thorough investigative reporting, the attitude of the news reports and that of law enforcement agencies shifted toward concern about the parents and their children having been taken from them, perhaps unjustly by bureaucratic agents of government.[38] A judicial inquiry was commissioned to investigate the charges, and the practices of the social workers as well. The judge heading the official inquiry rendered his decision on March 8, 1991, to return the children back to their parents. He severely criticized the practices of the local police and social workers for needlessly traumatizing the children by removing them from their parents.[39] Rochdale's director of social services resigned immediately in disgrace, and an official government investigation of the handling of sexual abuse allegations began.

The thorough investigative reporting of several newspapers, particularly *The Independent,* revealed the social dynamics which led to the creation of allegations of ritual abuse in Rochdale. Initially, in 1988, several social workers with a Christian fundamentalist charity became concerned about ritual abuse after reading some American materials about the so-called signs of ritual abuse. Some of them went to the U.S. for training in how to identify ritual abuse. Later, back in England, they organized several conferences on the topic for September

1989, which helped to popularize the Satanic cult conspiracy theory of ritual abuse. American "experts" in ritual abuse, Chicago police detective Robert "Jerry" Simandl and "ritual" abuse counselor Pamala Klein, were brought in as guest speakers. The English social workers felt that the Americans were more informed about how to uncover these crimes. The social workers then went about "uncovering" cases of ritual abuse in England—by interrogating the children of Rochdale and priming them with their preconceptions about Satanism and sexual abuse.

Some of the children's stories were traced by investigative journalists and police detectives, to child protection workers who had attended the conference, and from them back to Simandl and Klein. The newspapers reported, for example, that these American "experts" had claimed that babies in the U.S. were being cooked by Satanists, in microwave ovens. Similar bizarre stories were heard shortly thereafter, from the mouths of children, interviewed intensively by the child protection workers.[40] A report in *The Independent* summarized the origins of the Satanic cult ritual abuse scare in England.

> The panic spread to Britain early in 1988 through several channels including the evangelical Christian movement, in books, testimonials of survivors and "Deliverance" ministries, and through "experts" from the U.S. who spread the message here, in newspapers and on conference circuits.
>
> Once here, the stories have been spread by Christian organizations such as the Association of Christian Psychiatrists and the Social Workers of the Christian Fellowship, by churches, anti-occult campaigners and by born-again "survivors" of Satanic abuse.[41]

The 1991–92 San Diego Ritual Abuse Scare

The San Diego county Child Protection Services department faces a series of inquiries in the face of widespread complaints that social workers abused parents' rights in removing children from families. The incidents, involving

at least three families, resulted from the implementation of
a Ritual Abuse Task Force's guidelines to identify and treat
children being abused by multigenerational satanists. A
56-page booklet, "Ritual Abuse—Treatment, Intervention
and Safety Guidelines," was put together by a team of local
psychiatrists and social workers and released by the county
commission on Children and Youth in September 1991.

Even before the booklet's release, Sue Plante, the
department's expert on ritual abuse and an author of the
guidelines, had been hard at work on the case of "Bill and
Betty Jones" (pseudonyms). In early July, a therapist called
a San Diego child abuse hot line and said that one of the
Jones's adult daughters, "Mary Jones" (also a pseudonym),
had told him that her parents had involved her and other
children in Satanic rituals while they were youngsters.
When interviewed by Plante, Mary confirmed that her
family had been part of "a large Satanic cult during the
1960s that had practiced bizarre sexual rituals and human
sacrifices." Among other charges, Mary claimed that she
had been tied to a stake and raped repeatedly by the cult,
and that when she gave birth to a baby, her mother
immediately cut it in half during a ritual. Plante located
Mary Jones's parents in San Diego and found that they had
become legal guardians of three of their grandchildren,
when another of their children suffered manic-depressive
disorder.

Early in August, Plante entered the house without
warning and began looking under the children's clothing
for signs of abuse. Discovered and warned by Bill Jones to
leave or he would call the police, she allegedly said, "Go
ahead. . . . You'll find out who I am and what I can do." On
August 22, she returned with three patrol cars of police
and removed the three children from the house. Plante was
suspicious of a scar on one boy's stomach, even though the
Joneses produced medical records that it was from an
operation performed at a local hospital to correct a bowel
obstruction. "Satanists," she explained, "sometimes cut
open young children and then tell them that they are
placing a bomb or a live rat in the wound. The children are
warned that the bomb will explode or the rat will come out
if they reveal details of the cult."

The children denied suffering any abuse, but Jean Campbell, a La Jolla psychologist, found symptoms of fear and anxiety. The 12 year-old girl, she said, "came across as an ideal teenager in a too-good-to-be-true sense." The 10 year-old boy dreamed about "a ghost in the bathroom [who] took his voice." He also talked about "devils and angels, people going to heaven or hell, and fear about his grandmother dying," all elements "suggestive of ritual material." When the 8 year-old girl was told that a physical exam suggested sexual abuse, she "became very upset and burst into tears, exclaiming, "I didn't have bad touching." But when she later asked, "How do they tell if you have bad touching?", the psychologist felt this was "like a tacit acknowledgment that abuse had occurred." She recommended that the children be completely isolated from their family for six months and given twice-weekly therapy sessions: "Given positive therapeutic conditions," she expected that the two younger children, at least, would eventually "be able to disclose."

Bill and Betty Jones's letters to the children were confiscated by Plante, who found "subliminal Satanic messages" in them. They were allowed to send a birthday card to the 8 year-old, provided it did not have animals or clowns on it, "because those were potential cult symbols, too." On October 4, the children's father was allowed to visit them briefly, but he was warned by Plante not to hug the children, for fear that he might whisper in their ears. He also was told not to make any reference to time, and Plante told him, "if you touch your nose or touch your ears, we are going to end the meeting." Such actions, she explained, were "possible cult signals they might be using to control the children."

At the insistence of the family's attorney, the children were examined by a second psychologist, who found no signs of ritual abuse, and when photographs of the 8 year-old's genitals were viewed by a nationally respected child abuse expert, he found no abnormalities: "I would use this picture to teach what normals look like." At this point, the county sent a deputy counsel to interview Mary Jones, and he found that she was collecting state disability for mental illness, having been diagnosed as a schizophrenic. Although prescribed several anti-psychotic drugs, she was refusing to take any of them and instead had joined a support group for adult molestation victims. The county dropped the case on October 23 [1991] and returned the children to the Joneses.

Sue Plante was also involved in a number of other cases, one in which police cars tailed and pulled over a San Diego mother to take away her children, [age] 3 and 5. The raid, evidently, was timed three days before the fall equinox, a "Satanic holiday," when the younger child was to be used as a human sacrifice. Besides the memories of the mother's younger sister, another diagnosed schizophrenic, social workers noted that her father owned a boat named "Witch Way."

A series of front-page articles in the *San Diego Union* brought more than 350 additional complaints from parents who had been accused of Satanism or had children taken away for questionable medical examinations. Further research revealed that as early as November 6, 1990, supervisors had noted a rising number of complaints from parents about unsubstantiated child abuse accusations and had called for an immediate review of the department. Much of the social worker's information had come from training videotapes, featuring Roberta Sachs and Pamala Klein and produced by Cavalcade Productions of Ukiah, CA. Rosie Waterhouse of *The Independent* confirmed that the same tapes had been used to prepare social workers at Rochdale, Nottingham, and the Orkney Islands.

After a stormy public town hall meeting with parents on January 30 [1992], the director of the Department of Social Services announced that an ombudsman would be appointed to handle complaints and expedite return of children to families. One social worker present admitted, "We . . . screwed up . . .". A grand jury investigation into faking of medical reports is pending.

Excerpted from *FOAFtale News: The Newsletter of the International Society for Contemporary Legend Research*, March 1992, pp. 6–7; Bill Ellis, Editor. (Summary of news reports published in the *San Diego Union*, Nov. 8, 1991; Jan. 19; Jan. 29; Jan. 29; Jan. 31, 1992.)

Claims about Kidnappings, Missing Children, and Ritual Murders

Probably nothing is more frightening to parents than to hear stories about children who are kidnapped and murdered by strangers. Public opinion polls conducted since the early 1980s have found that a high proportion of parents consider the chances of their children being kidnapped by strangers to be very serious and increasing.[42] A public opinion poll done in Illinois in 1986, for example, reported that 89 percent of Illinois parents considered the problem of child kidnappings by strangers to be either "very" serious or "quite" serious.[43] Claims about Satanic cults which kidnap and murder thousands of children have become more plausible to many parents, who are already worried about the dangers of kidnapping. Thus, the anxieties generated by the "missing children" hysteria of the 1980s enabled the ancient Satanic cult legend about kidnapping and ritual murder to surface once again.

Exaggerated claims about Satanic cult kidnappings come primarily, but not exclusively, from fundamentalist religious sources. For example, Reverend Bob Larson, a prominent fundamentalist minister and host of a daily religious radio talk show ("heard by millions"), makes the following claim in his 1989 book, *Satanism: The Seduction of America's Youth.*

> The defilement of children is important to Satanists. The more helpless the victim, the greater proof of their devotion to the devil. They also believe that the more pure the sacrifice for Satan, the more power they obtain from the god of darkness. Innocent children and guiltless babies are perfect victims. Officer Mitch White of the Beaumont, California Police Department estimates that 95 percent of all missing children are victims of occult related abductions.[44]

Evangelist Jerry Johnston, who is often a guest on religious radio programs and a freqently invited speaker to high school audiences around the country, makes similar claims. In his 1989 book, *The Edge of Evil: The Rise of Satanism in North America,* he offers the following assertion.

> They are internationally located throughout the world [hardcore satanic cults]. Perhaps more organized than the mafia, they are

known to kill, abduct and brainwash ever so secretly. Dr. Al Carlisle of the Utah State Prison System has estimated that between forty and sixty thousand human beings are killed through ritual homicides in the United States each year. This statistic is based upon an estimated number of satanists at the level where they commit ritual sacrifices times the frequency with which these would be done during a satanic calendar year.[45]

Larson and Johnston both attempt to give secular credibility to their claims by referring to the assertions of local law enforcement officials. This is a common tactic of religious Satan hunters today. It is easy to find exaggerated assertions about Satanic cult crime from the ranks of local law enforcement authorities, many of whom share conservative religious ideology and use it, rather than scientific criminology, as a basis for their assertions about crime.[46] One research study, for example, found that police who are "true believers" in the Satanic cult conspiracy and often present public lectures on ritualistic crime are also more likely to be traditionally religious.[47]

An excerpt from a 1987 article about "occult crime" by Salt Lake City Patrolman Jim Bryant, published in the magazine *Police Marksman* illustrates the point.

> Another aspect of occult crimes . . . is the possible connection between the occult and the tremendous number of missing children who have never been found. As I mentioned, children are perceived by some occultists to be a source of an extraordinary amount of power. In order to release that power, the child must either be sacrificed at some point or ritually abused. . . . A whole year dedicated to "The Feast of the Beast," in which sacrifices are believed by some to be mandatory in the practice of some occult beliefs, just happened to coincide with record numbers of children being reported missing.[48]

These claims about the ritual murder of children have also been taken up by some prominent child advocates, such as Kenneth Wooden. Wooden gave a speech to a conference on child victims of crime in Olean, New York, during the time of the widespread rumor-panic over western New York, in April

1988. He claimed that: "Twenty-five percent of all unsolved murders are ritualistic in nature and the victims are children and women."[49] Wooden has been particularly influential in spreading the Satanic cult scare to a national audience. In a letter to the editor in the *New York Times,* in October 1988, in response to widespread criticism of a Geraldo Rivera TV special on Satanism, Wooden noted:

> In 1984, I Investigated and was coproducer for the first news story on Satanism (ABC, "20/20"). I again investigated cult crimes for the Rivera special. During the four-year span, violent ritual crimes had escalated tremendously.[50]

Research on the Kidnapping of Children

The generic term "missing children" emerged as a label for a social problem in the early 1980s, as Americans were constantly being exposed to information about children whose whereabouts were unknown to a parent.[51] These reminders about the problem were printed everywhere: on milk cartons and shopping bags, on posters in public places and even on highway billboards. This burst of national concern followed from a series of incidents which received national attention. In 1979, a six-year-old boy, Etan Patz, disappeared one morning after leaving for school and was never heard from again. Then, in 1981, Adam Walsh, another six year-old boy disappeared from a shopping mall and was later found murdered. The case received a great deal of national media coverage, prompting a flurry of newspaper and magazine articles about "stolen children."[52] The case of Adam Walsh became the subject of an influential television docu-drama in 1983 and eventually led to federal attention being given to the missing children problem. In 1984, the federal government funded The National Center for Missing and Exploited Children, a private organization designed to collect reliable national information about missing children and to publicize that information.

Unfortunately, the term "missing children" can be misleading, because it covers a rather broad range of different situations. The rubric includes: abductions by family members, as in divorce cases; children who have run away from home; children who have been abandoned or thrown out of their homes by their parents; children who have become temporarily lost through some accident; as well as children who have been abducted by strangers. When Satanic conspiracy theorists refer broadly to "missing children," they evoke the stereotype of children kidnapped by strangers and, intentionally or not, they can mislead an audience about the extent of kidnappings.

Scientifically reliable data about various specific kinds of missing children situations has not been easy to obtain, until quite recently. There is no federal agency whose job it is to regularly collect and analyze information about missing children from all communities across the country. There is the added confusion of differing laws in each of the fifty states, with their varying definitions of such crimes as kidnapping and abduction by relatives. Another difficulty is that some kinds of missing children (e. g. runaway and throwaway children) often don't get reported to any official agency. In the absence of reliable data, exaggerated claims about the numbers of children kidnapped by strangers were easily made.[53] It was widely reported in the mass media that there were an estimated fifty thousand "missing children," or even fifty thousand "abductions" of children each year.[54] These reports lent credibility to conspiracy theorists, who were quick to see some kind of organized menace to the safety of our children.

In 1990, the U.S. Department of Justice published a careful and thorough study of reliable data on missing children.[55] The study developed estimates from five sources of data, including that from FBI records, a sample of local police records, a sample of community agencies, a sample of juvenile facilities, and a national telephone survey of households. The study estimated that, for the year 1988, the number of "stereotypical kidnappings" of children by strangers was between 200 and 300. In comparison, the study estimated that abductions of a child by a family member, with intent to conceal the whereabouts of the child, in the same year amounted to about 163,200. The study also estimated that the annual number of children who were kidnapped and murdered by strangers was between 43 and 147 annually, for the years 1976 to 1987, according to FBI records. Another research study, using different sources of data, came up with a similar estimate of the annual number of children kidnapped and murdered by strangers, between 52 and 158.[56] Teenagers (aged ten to seventeen), rather than young children, accounted for the bulk of the victims. These statistics are depressing because of the horror of the crimes involved, but they do suggest, at least, that there exists no widespread, organized conspiracy to kidnap and murder our children.

It is unlikely that research evidence of any kind will deter the conspiracy theorists from making exaggerated claims. They can still claim that runaway teenagers are being murdered and that their remains are made to disappear. They will cite specific atrocity stories, in which some psychopath kills children and proclaims himself to be a "Satanist." However, the burden of proof should always be upon those people making alarmist claims about secret, conspiratorial threats. These claims-makers are also dangerous. They can provoke needless fear and runaway witch hunts; this leads to making innocent people the victims of hysteria. They are like alarmists who yell "fire" in a crowded theatre.

The Collective Behavior Process in Satanic Cult Kidnapping Scares

The Role of Communication Networks

Claims that Satanic cults are kidnapping and ritually murdering our children are being disseminated across American society through several different communication networks. These claims are spread through the fundamentalist network via Christian books, articles in denominational magazines, church newsletters, Christian radio programs, and public lectures by evangelists about the dangers of "Satanism" to our youth. They are also being spread by local police Satan hunters via conferences on ritualistic or occult crime and articles in police magazines.

Police Sergeant Greg Hill, for example, travels around the country speaking about the "missing children" problem to police and school groups, on behalf of the Lost Child Network, an organization he helped to found. In a newspaper report on a school sponsored community meeting in Wichita, where he spoke, he was quoted as claiming that "many missing children are victims of ritualistic kidnappings and murders."[57] To emphasize the seriousness of the problem, he showed a film of police removing the body parts of a fifteen-year-old girl who had been murdered and dismembered, supposedly by Satanists. "That's one of the things we're trying to get out to school officials. This is not just something happening in the movies," Hill is quoted as saying. Similar claims are also being disseminated by child protection workers to professionals at conferences on Satanic ritual child abuse.

The dissemination process has led to widespread public belief in the existence of well-organized and dangerous Satanic "cults," even in the absence of any confirming evidence. When people hear these claims repeated over and over again, from sources in different communication networks, the stories gain additional credibility through the consensual validation of reality.

The Role of the Mass Media

Claims about Satanic cult kidnappings are most likely to appear in local news articles, where local claims-makers are quoted as offering a Satanic cult explanation for a missing child. These claims are often treated without any journalistic critical analysis, as simply being part of the story. It is common for local newspapers to flag these stories with sensational headlines like "Child Kidnapped by Satanists." Equally often, newspapers do not follow up with corrections to false claims, because such corrections are not regarded as being a story.

One such case, for example, led to the notorious Toledo dig which received national media attention in 1985 (described in Chapter Four above). The case was that of Charity Freeman, a seven-year-old girl who was reported missing by her mother, in Lucas County, Ohio, in 1982. Wild rumors and allegations circulated that the girl had been kidnapped and sacrificed by a Satanic cult. These led to the famous diggings, initiated by Sheriff Telb, in 1985. Charity was finally found by the FBI in 1988, at the age of thirteen, living with her grandfather in Huntington Beach, California. The *grandfather* had abducted her and *not* a Satanic cult.[58] Nevertheless, what lingers like a latent image in the memories of many fearful parents are the newspaper headlines and quoted allegations about Satanic cult kidnappings.

The most notorious Satanic cult kidnapping story was that of the Matamoros murders, which was initially presented in some mass media coverage as a case of Satanic cult ritual sacrifice rather than as drug gang murders. These media presentations are picked up by Satan hunters and used to provide credibility for their claims.

Illustration: The Baby-Parts Contemporary Legend

The collective behavior process through which Satanic cult kidnapping stories are disseminated and believed is not unusual. Research findings about similar contemporary legends concerning organized conspiracies to kidnap and murder children illustrate the social dynamics whereby sensational claims are transformed into conventional "truths."

Alarming rumors spread across Latin America beginning in 1987, claiming that children were being kidnapped and butchered, so that their body parts could be used as organ transplants by wealthy Americans.[59] The story first surfaced officially in a newspaper report in Honduras, in January 1987. The newspaper presented testimony from police and social workers that children were being sold by poverty-stricken Honduran mothers to secret criminal organizations and sometimes the children were even being kidnapped. Then, the children were sold to wealthy Americans, who dismembered them and used their organs for medical transplants.

Shortly thereafter, similar newspaper reports appeared in several other Latin American countries, including Guatemala and Paraguay, all of the reports claiming to have discovered clandestine agencies selling kidnapped children to wealthy Americans for their body parts. These reports came from countries which were thousands of miles apart and that seemed to lend credibility to the kidnapping stories. For many people, the reports seemed to confirm the existence of an elaborate network of criminals kidnapping children for their body parts. The very idea was so repulsive that it quickly caused widespread outrage across Latin America.

The reports of a commerce in baby-parts were also quickly picked up by newspapers in Europe. A resolution to condemn the practice was even brought before the Parliament of the European Common Market in May 1987, by leftist representatives who believed the story. Although the resolution failed to pass, it did provoke widespread attention to "the problem." Communist and leftist newspapers around the world condemned the commerce in baby-parts as one more example of the evils of American capitalism unfettered by any moral values.

There were few reports about the story in the American news media, because, as it might be expected, here it was regarded as being beyond belief. However, the United States Information Agency did try to actively counteract the baby-parts story with attempts to demonstrate that the stories were fabrications based only upon false testimonies, misinformation, and distortions of real incidents, which were being used in ideological propaganda. Nevertheless, the baby-parts story became social reality for many people in Latin America and Europe. Efforts to deny the story simply served to reinforce the preconceptions of leftist believers that wealthy Americans had something to hide. Today, it survives in the memories of many millions of people, as something that really happened.

Conclusions

The dark imaginings of Satanic cult crime against children has been constructed out of false testimonies, misinformation, and distortions of real incidents.

In one of the first major historical studies of the Salem witchcraft trials published in 1867, Charles W. Upham, a mayor and Congressman from Salem, wrote the following perceptive observation of the essence of what gave rise to the witch hunt. It applies equally to what is happening once again in America.

> There is nothing more mysterious than the self-deluding power of the human mind, and there never were scenes in which it was more clearly displayed than the witchcraft persecutions. Honest men testified, with perfect confidence and sincerity, to the most absurd impossibilities; while those who thought themselves victims of diabolical influence would actually exhibit, in their corporeal frames, all the appropriate symptoms of the sufferings their imaginations had brought upon them.[60]

We often assume, too easily, that the worst of human maliciousness arises from the pathological minds of a few vicious personalities, who feed their selfish desires by preying upon others. Much more than we would admit, however, the worst injustices arise from the fear and hate felt by quite normal and decent people, acting in protective support of each other.

Chapter Seven
Satanism and Teenage Crime

I and the public know
What all schoolchildren learn,
Those to whom evil is done
Do evil in return.

W. H. Auden.[1]

Claims about Teenage Satanism

Perhaps the most widely accepted claims about Satanism are claims about *teenage* involvement in Satanic cult activity. These claims are being disseminated across the country by various groups which are concerned about teenagers and their possible involvement in crime. Local police spread claims about teenage ritualistic crime in police conferences, in lectures to community groups, and in police magazines. Child protection social workers spread the claims in conferences about the problems of youth. Anti-cult organizations spread the claims at conferences about teenage involvement in religious cults. A host of religious evangelists spread the claims at church and community meetings about teenage Satanism.

The particular claims vary, but there are many consistent

assertions. Teenagers are generally said to be drawn gradually into an interest in occult ritual activity through a prior interest in heavy metal rock music, *Dungeons and Dragons* fantasy games, and books on occult magic. Some claims-makers also assert that secretive adult Satanists encourage these teenagers into deeper involvement in black magic ritualism and Satanic beliefs. It is commonly asserted that once teenagers become obsessed with Satanic magic and Devil worship, they are driven to commit increasingly serious anti-social acts, such as abusing drugs, vandalizing churches and cemeteries, and killing animals in ritual sacrifices. It is also commonly claimed that some of these teenage Satanists become so disturbed that they commit suicide and even murder. Some claims-makers assert that adult Satanists recruit new members into their secret criminal organizations from among teenagers in these "Satanic cults."

In her book, *The Devil's Web*, Pat Pulling, for example, offers a brief synopsis of these claims about teenage Satanism.

> Law enforcement officials and mental health professionals now recognize the fact that adolescent occult involvement is progressive. The child who is obsessed with occult entertainment may not stop there, but he often moves on to satanic graffiti and cemetery vandalism. From that point, he easily moves into grave robbing for items needed for occult rituals, and he is just a step away from blood-letting. Blood-letting begins with animal killings and mutilations and progresses to murder if intervention does not take place.[2]

Some claims-makers have developed elaborate explanations of stages and types of teenage Satanism; all are constructed without any basis in systematic empirical research data. In a police magazine, Dr. Ronald Holmes, a professor of criminal justice at the University of Louisville, for example, offers a scheme for identifying the progressive involvement of teenagers in Satanism. While he admits in the article that there exists little reliable knowledge about the matter, he nevertheless fabricates an elaborate description of the stages of teenage Satanism. His underlying assumption is that teenagers learn Satanism much like someone learns a strange new religion.

Stage 1. The youth in the occult is immediately drawn into the world of black magic and the worship of the devil because he is told that great worldly power and temporary glory will be his for the asking. . . .

Stage 2. In this second stage, the initiate is now exposed to Satanic philosophies and becomes one with the demonic belief system. . . . This new member learns the prayers, spells, doctrines, dogmas of the faith, holidays, rituals, and the importance of being baptized in the blood of Satan. . . .

Stage 3. Now that the youth has progressed into the world of the Satanic, he is now accepted into the secret and religious ceremonies of the coven. He learns the various sabbats and the reasons for their celebrations. He participates in the sacrifice for Lucifer. . . . The Satanist at this level of participation and sophistication with the occult understands the proper animals for sacrifice. . . .

One sacrifice that the new member into Satanism may become involved with is the human sacrifice. At this stage the member becomes acutely aware that humans are indeed sacrificed for the devil, and the form of sacrifice will take two forms: blood or fire. . . .

Stage 4. In the final stage of total involvement in Satanism, the young person becomes firmly committed to the occult lifestyle. . . .

In the sabbats, the initiate is intimately involved in sexual orgies which are often an integral part of the worship ceremonies. Obviously, for the seriously disenfranchised members of the youth subculture, this can be a powerful drawing force into full membership.[3]

Teenage Satanism is linked to the secret Satanic cult conspiracy theory by claims that adults from secret Satanic groups operate as the guiding hand behind this indoctrination into Satanism. In this way, claims about teenage Satanism are incorporated into the broader Satanic cult legend, and given apparent credibility with other atrocity claims about ritual child abuse, missing children, ritual child sacrifice, and serial murder. The president of the Cult Awareness Council of Houston, Texas, for example, was quoted in a professional journal about family related violence, as making these claims at a seminar concerned with ritual child abuse and teenage

Satanism.[4] According to the report about the seminar, she claimed that:

> Adult satanists . . . provide an abandoned house for recruits where they engage in drugs, and sex, and listen to allegedly satanic, "heavy metal" music. . . . Initially, this is fun for the adolescents. Then, over time, and often while under the influence of some drugs, the recruits are encouraged to engage in various sexual behaviors. While the adolescents are engaging in sexual behaviors, and often unbeknownst to them, tapes of their activities are made. These tapes can be marketed as pornography, or they can be used to threaten or blackmail the adolescents into staying with the cult.[5]

When the average parent reads such assertions in local newspaper reports about teenage cemetery vandalism or animal mutilation, especially when the claims are made by so-called "experts" in teenage Satanism, they can easily be moved to fear that there is some grain of truth in the claims. Then, when they see strange symbolic graffiti on walls in their town, and teenagers in strange clothing displaying some of the same symbols, they can easily conclude that there is an epidemic of teenagers becoming involved in another new bizarre form of anti-social aggression, perhaps under the influence of adult, organized criminals.

Teenage Behavior Labelled as Satanism

There is an alternative way of understanding the meanings of teenage behavior mistakenly labelled as Satanism. If we put to use reliable research about teenage behavior, we can see that what gets labelled "Satanic activity" by the claims-makers is a diverse collection of activities, including adolescent legend trips, teenage fad behavior, malicious teenage delinquency, and pseudo-Satanism among groups of psychologically disturbed adolescents. When these diverse activities are lumped together and viewed through the distorting lens of belief in the Satanic cult legend, they are misinterpreted as evidence of teenage

Satanism. Teenagers engaged in these activities do not constitute a cult or a religion, any more than a motorcycle gang
constitutes a cult or the hippie counterculture a religion.

Adolescent Legend Trips

The graffiti, cemetery vandalism, and "altar" sites usually
mistaken for evidence of teenage Satanism are most often
simply remnants of adolescent legend trips. Research about this
widely practiced teenage custom can be found in the writings of
folklore scholars, particularly in the work of Bill Ellis.[6] Few
psychologists or sociologists have studied the activity, perhaps
because the behavior has been treated as unimportant pranks of
rural and small town teenagers.

Contemporary folklore research has adopted the systematic
methods of behavioral scientists to investigate orally transmitted traditions, such as children's games and stories, supersti-
tions, proverbs and riddles, local legends, and recurrent rumor
stories called "urban legends."[7] Folklore research is no longer
the mere collection of quaint old tales and ancient myths. Some
folklore scholars have turned their attention to the orally
transmitted customs of adolescents, which they have investigated much like anthropologists doing field studies of tribal
peoples.

An adolescent legend trip involves the testing of a local
legend about a scary supernatural site or paranormal incident.[8]
The local legend may focus upon a supposedly haunted house
or cemetery, or a site supposedly frequented by a witch. Often,
parts of a local legend are used like a script for a re-enacted
performance of the legend; for example, the legend might be
about a ghost called up from the dead, or a witch's ritual in the
woods. Legend trips are in some ways similar to the ghost
stories told and acted out around campfires during evenings at
summer camp.

A legend trip is a form of recreational entertainment. Even
when magic spells are chanted or rituals performed, as they
often are, the behavior is not an expression of any genuine belief
in supernatural or paranormal powers. It is not in any way a
religious practice. Instead, a legend trip, in order to be enjoyed,

requires merely the temporary suspension of disbelief. This is much like what happens when people watch a supernatural horror movie in order to be frightened and amused. Too much skepticism and critical thinking makes the experience seem a bit ridiculous.

There are a great variety of these local supernatural legends. Bill Ellis offers a summary of some themes.

> Babies are especially popular victims of the accidents or murders that provide the background for legend-trips. They are often associated with a "Cry Baby Bridge," where their mothers murdered them or where they were flung out the window of a crashing car into the path of an oncoming locomotive. Decapitated ghosts, usually looking for their lost heads, also show up frequently. The headless horseman still rides near Cincinnati, but near Sandusky, Ohio, he has become a headless motorcycle man, his head cut off by piano wire stretched across the road, and near Cleveland the ghost is a headless little old lady in a Yellow Volkswagen. Headless women are twice as popular as headless men, and usually prowl bridges where they died in crashes or were murdered.[9]

A legend trip is a clandestine group activity, in which the presence of any adult is definitely not desired. One reason is that a legend trip functions as a kind of ritual for adolescents to prove their courage, much like some Indian adolescents used to prove their bravery by stealing horses from another Indian tribe.[9] Another reason is that a legend trip usually involves deliberately transgressing the rules of adult society and even breaking laws, in order to enhance the exciting risk of danger.[11] Adolescent legend trips are usually designed to shock and offend adult sensibilities. They are a way of "playing chicken," so that adolescents can test their anxieties about challenging adult authority. In a sense, adults are the other "tribe" for teenagers on a legend trip.

Legend Trips and Juvenile Delinquency

Adolescent legend trips sometimes, but not always, involve such crimes as trespassing on private property, defacing property with graffiti, vandalism, underage drinking, and in more recent years, the use of illegal drugs. Sexual activity may also occur, when boys make use of the frightening situation to provoke girls' desires for closer contact. This may sometimes be a hidden agenda when boys bring their girlfriends along on a legend trip.

Teenagers who take part in legend trips, however, are usually not habitual delinquents. They don't normally pursue a criminal life-style of aggressive, anti-social behavior. The crimes which may take place during legend trips are used to heighten tension. Breaking adult rules is part of the scripting of an exciting legend trip, rather than an expression of the supposed anti-social personalities of a few adolescents.

The research on adolescent legend trips indicates that these activities occur across the country. There are thousands of local legends about supernatural or paranormal happenings.[12] In Ohio alone, for example, 175 locations of legend trips have been identified by folklore researchers.[13] They occur in rural, small town, and suburban areas. (These are also the areas where almost all incidents of so-called teenage Satanism are reported in local newspapers.) The age level of teenagers involved in legend trips, according to the research, tends to be between twelve and eighteen, with participants more likely to be in their later teens.[14] There are no records of Afro-American youth participating in legend trips, so the activity may be a cultural inheritance of people from Europe. The percentage of teenagers who experience a legend trip at least once is unknown, because there is no national survey of this activity. However, several localized studies indicate that between 14 percent and 28 percent of teenagers have participated in a legend trip.[15] These activities have been going on for generations, long before the current Satanic cult scare.

The remnants of adolescent legend trips are commonly mistaken by police "experts" on ritualistic crime, local clergymen, and newspaper reporters, for indicators of teenage Satanism or Satanic cult activity. What is seen as an "altar" for a Satanic sacrifice, may really have been a makeshift altar or a campfire site for a legend trip. "Satanic" graffiti spray-painted on the walls inside an abandoned old house, or on trees in a secluded wooded area, may really be the ersatz magical inscriptions necessary for an exciting legend trip. Similarly, more serious remnants of juvenile delinquency, such as mutilated animals and vandalized cemeteries, are commonly products of legend trips.[16]

When teenagers sometimes leave behind symbols widely regarded as being Satanic, they have a new and rather effective way of shocking adults, particularly adults in communities where many people believe that Satan is a being, prowling the world in search of souls. Some teenagers may now act out a parody of Satanic cult activity, in order to shock adults who read about their delinquent antics in the local newspaper and take it very seriously as evidence of dangerous Satanists in the area. Photographs in newspapers of graffiti symbols on overturned tombstones are easily seen by adults through the distorting lens of preconceptions about teenage Satanism.

Juvenile Delinquents Involved in Pseudo-Satanism

In 1990, the Michigan State Police conducted a careful survey of "occult-related" crimes reported by law enforcement agencies in that state.[17] Only 22 percent of the responding agencies reported having investigated any "occult-related" crimes, much less than popular concern in rural areas and small towns might suggest. The vast majority of these crimes, 74 percent, involved graffiti, vandalism, the mutilation and killing of domestic or farm animals, and cemetery desecrations. (Only 1 percent involved homicides.) Almost all of the people who committed "occult-related" crimes were young, white males. Only 8 percent of the offenders were over the age of twenty-five and most were teenagers.

Inquiries about the offenders' training in occult matters revealed that in almost all cases the offenders were self-taught from sources that included friends, heavy metal rock music, movies, magazines, and books. In other words, so-called occult-related crime is primarily a matter of petty juvenile crime. Most importantly, the study concluded that the occult practices and paraphernalia in these kinds of crimes are a "red herring across the trail, distracting the investigator from real issues or motives in the case."[18]

Many "occult-related" juvenile crimes are products of adolescent legend trips. However, additional circumstances also account for "occult-related" juvenile delinquency. We can get a better understanding of what is happening, if we carefully examine the reliable research about pseudo-Satanist juvenile delinquents in the broader context of what we know about teenage crime in general.

In behavioral science, attempts to understand aggressive criminal behavior have led to the identification of two basic kinds of factors which contribute to such behavior: 1) personality dispositions toward deviant (meaning rule-breaking) aggressive behavior; and 2) group influences upon the person from participation in deviant subcultures which promote criminal behavior.

The beliefs and values which a person uses to justify (to excuse) their aggressive and criminal behavior is usually learned and strengthened in a deviant group subculture. Criminologists refer to these beliefs and values as a "deviant ideology." A deviant ideology functions to neutralize possible feelings of guilt. No particular beliefs are intrinsically deviant. Satanic beliefs can be used as a deviant ideology to justify aggression. So can beliefs about masculine ("Macho") pride. Even beliefs about God, Christ, or the Bible can be used as a deviant ideology by some people to justify their aggressive acts.

When people justify murder in terms of their personal Christian beliefs, we don't attribute the cause to the Christian religion. Instead, we seek the causes of their aggression in their particular personality dispositions and group influences. We must do the same when we learn about some vicious act of aggression committed by a teenager, who justifies what he or she has done by referring to some self-taught Satanist beliefs. It is misleading to focus too much attention on the excuse of Satanist beliefs, no matter how repulsive we may find them.

The ritual acts and group beliefs of these delinquents does not constitute a religion anymore than do the ritual acts and group beliefs of teenage gang members, or than those of the Ku Klux Klan. Almost all teenagers who even profess to be Satanists lack any elaborate belief system focussed upon Devil worship. Instead, they have fabricated a deviant ideology in order to: justify their underlying personality dispositions to express aggressive hostility; or justify rebellion from adult social restrictions; or obtain public noteriety. This is what I mean when I refer to teenagers as "pseudo-Satanist" delinquents rather than as "teenage Satanists."

Research Findings about Pseudo-Satanist Delinquents

There are very few genuinely scientific studies of teenage pseudo-Satanists. At this point, the most careful study of these juvenile delinquents has been done by Kelly Richard Damphousse, in 1991.[19] Damphousse studied 55 juvenile delinquents involved in some degree of "Devil worship," and compared them with 475 juvenile delinquents who were not involved in such activity. All of the teenagers were incarcerated at the Texas Youth Commission Reception Center, in Brownwood, Texas.

All of them were interviewed using a sixty-one-page questionnaire about their drug use, delinquent behavior, school activities, family and peer relationships, and personality, as well as their involvement in Satanism. Damphousse identified the teenagers who were involved in "Satanism," by means of their own admission that they had taken part, at least once, in some kind of "formal ceremony to worship Satan or the devil."[20] The information was then carefully analyzed, using statistical techniques to compare the two samples of juvenile delinquents.

The pseudo-Satanist juvenile delinquents differed from the other juvenile delinquents in several ways. 1) They were more likely to be white, rather than Afro-American. 2) They were more likely to be from middle class backgrounds, rather than working class or poor backgrounds. 3) They were more likely to have high intelligence scores on an I.Q. test, rather than average scores. 4) They were more likely to heavily use hallucinogenic drugs, rather than other kinds of drugs, such as cocaine or heroin, or no drugs. 5) They were more likely to feel that they had little power or control over their lives, rather than see themselves as having some degree of control over lives. 6) Finally, they were just as likely to be females as males, rather than mostly males. In other ways, the two sets of juvenile delinquents were similar. The research also found that the delinquents who participated in Satanic ceremonies, did so as part of a group activity, indicating that they were not social loners as is popularly believed.

In other words, white, middle class, highly intelligent teenagers, who have a high need for control in their lives, are those who are most likely to justify their criminal activity in terms of a Satanist deviant ideology. It is important to keep in mind that these findings apply only to imprisoned pseudo-Satanist delinquents. So, we can't be sure how widely they can be applied to pseudo-Satanist delinquents who have not been arrested and imprisoned.

Damphousse also sought to determine whether this pseudo-Satanist juvenile delinquency develops through some special circumstances. He could not find any truly unique circumstances. In terms of family relationships, peer group attachment, alienation from school, and personal problems, the pseudo-Satanist delinquents had backgrounds similar to those of other delinquents. Therefore, Damphousse concluded that teenagers become involved in pseudo-Satanist delinquency through essentially the same circumstances as other juvenile delinquents.[21]

A Psychological Analysis of Pseudo-Satanist Delinquency

If we expect to be able to deal effectively with teenagers who commit crimes attributed to pseudo-Satanism, we must first have an accurate appraisal of the underlying psychological causes of such criminal behavior. Explaining such behavior as being a product of religious "cult" brainwashing and the influence of evil religious beliefs is dramatic, but entirely misleading. The behavior of teenagers engaged in pseudo-

Satanism needs to be understood in the context of what we know about juvenile delinquency.

There is no single, comprehensive explanation of juvenile delinquency, nor can there ever be one. The criminal behavior in this catch-all category includes everything from truancy to murder. Therefore, we need to focus upon understanding specific forms of criminal behavior. Almost all of the crimes attributed to teenage pseudo-Satanists involve vandalism of cemeteries, churches and abandoned old houses, and the mutilation and killing of animals. Therefore, we need to ask about what satisfactions are obtained by young people through these kinds of behaviors. Simply calling the behavior "irrational" is meaningless circular logic and gets nowhere toward any understanding.

Some psychological insight into teenage pseudo-Satanist delinquency can be gleaned from a study of a small number of emotionally disturbed teens who were patients in a psychiatric clinic affiliated with a university in Canada.[22] The study collected information form therapy sessions given to eight adolescents, ages thirteen to sixteen, who were in treatment for a variety anxiety-related disorders and aggressive behaviors. It is not surprising, considering that they were admitted for psychotherapy, that most of them came from disrupted, dysfunctional families, or that most were involved in aggressive crimes against property. Six of the eight were heavy users of hallucinogenic drugs before they developed any interest in Satanism, and none of them were involved in any kind of Satanic religious organization. The "Satanism" of these youths consisted of making Satanic drawings and listening to heavy metal rock music (all eight), to participation in makeshift "Black Masses" (seven), to the sacrifice of small animals (two).

Another series of case studies offers several sensitive portraits of emotionally disturbed teenagers who used magic ritualism to deal with their psychological problems. One case is that of a sixteen-year-old, who was undergoing psychotherapy for recurrent depression, severe identity problems (borderline personality disorder), and the abuse of hallucinogenic drugs.[23] The youth first became involved with Satanic ritualism, at the age of eleven, after attending a "Satanic mass" with some friends. The most common ritual that he engaged in was one of his own creation, which he called making proposals. In this ritual, he concentrated his thoughts on making a request to the Devil to harm someone through his use of mental telepathy. The teenager developed elaborate beliefs around this supposedly magical ritual, involving calling up spirits and demons. The therapist suggested that the boy relied upon this magical thinking and ritualism in order to obtain feelings of power and control in his life.

When the claims-makers focus our attention upon so-called Satanic beliefs, symbols, and rituals, they deflect our attention away from the real underlying problems of teenagers involved in pseudo-Satanism. It is much more useful to find out why so many emotionally disturbed and delinquent teenagers suffer from severe feelings of powerlessness and feelings of hostility. That should be the focus of our concern.

The Rewards of Vandalism and Black Magic

A very useful understanding of the satisfactions gained from vandalism can be found in the book *The Seductions of Crime,* by Jack Katz, a sociologist specialized in research on deviant behavior.[24] Katz used self-reported biographical descriptions from people who committed crimes, in an effort to determine the meaning the criminal behavior has to the people who actually engaged in that behavior (in contrast to taking for granted the meanings that are attributed to the crimes by victims or law enforcement officials). Katz's exposition of the satisfactions of vandalism demonstrates that the goals are symbolic and emotional, and largely function to enhance the vandal's feelings of power in being able to engage in such deviant behavior (rule-breaking).

The vandal doesn't obtain any material benefit from the behavior, and the evidence of the crime is always deliberately left behind. The main satisfaction found in vandalism by those who engage in it is the excitement of playing a kind of game, in which the challenge is to "get away with something" forbidden. When the vandal "gets away with it," he can feel a sense of accomplishing something which requires risk. Because the vandal subjectively defines his behavior in this way, it can also provide a feeling of self-affirmation, a sense of uniqueness and distinctiveness. (It is the feeling of "I am somebody.")

Secondly, the behavior is an attack on the moral order of society and, thus, provides an outlet for feelings of hostility toward conventional society. Vandalism can be especially exciting if the objects of desecration are commonly defined as being sacred, as is the case with graves and churches. In such cases, the "forbiddenness" of the act of vandalism is heightened. Vandalism is the projection onto a public screen, of a negative, deliberately offensive identity, demanding attention. Finally, vandalism functions as an act which enhances group bonding, as adolescents share in a kind of secret, conspiratorial team effort.

The practice of Satanic black magic rituals doesn't cause teenagers to engage in vandalism and animal mutilation. Instead, such activity is drawn from the same package of subjective meanings. Makeshift black magic rituals offer the excitement of getting away with socially tabooed, deviant behavior, assaulting the moral order of conventional society, and bonding adolescents together in a secret, forbidden activity. The black magic rituals provide teenagers, who suffer from severe feelings of powerlessness, with an ersatz sense of empowerment. Their feelings of empowerment are heightened when teenagers take the magic rituals seriously, as if the rituals actually provide them with some kind of power to shape their social environment. If disapproving adults also take the magic rituals seriously, in either fear or anger, rather than ridicule them, those adults inadvertently reinforce the teenagers' attraction to black magic.

The Development of a Deviant Identity
If we are really to understand these adolescents, we must first comprehend how someone can find emotional satisfaction in strongly condemned deviant behavior. How can a person feel *good* about being *bad?* How can a deliberately offensive identity be satisfying to some teenagers, or even adults for that matter?

Another research study of teenagers involved in vandalism

offers some insight into how adolescents can develop a self-concept centered upon the satisfactions of deviant behavior.

> Once the boys acquired an image of themselves as deviants, they selected new friends who affirmed that self-image. As that self-conception became more firmly entrenched, they also became willing to try new and more extreme deviances. With their growing alienation came freer expression of disrespect and hostility for the representatives of the legitimate society. The disrespect increased the community's negativism, perpetuating the entire process of commitment to deviance.[25]

Sociologists call this gradual process, the development of a *deviant identity*. Deviant identities emerge out of the meanings people attribute to their own behavior, which in turn, may bear the mark of other people's reactions to deviant behavior. Deviant identities are, in a basic sense, chosen by the people themselves and are not simply the by-products of the detrimental influences of other people. Nevertheless, the condemnation of other people weighs heavily on the development of anyone's self-perception.

The process of acquiring a deviant identity can begin at a very early age, long before adolescents become involved in any serious criminal activity. A child's self-concept of being a "bad kid" emerges gradually, as a result of experiencing constant humiliations, insults, and rejection at the hands of others. There is abundant research evidence showing that aggressive teenage delinquents experience more frequent humiliations to their self-esteem during childhood than do non-delinquents, from parents, peers, and school teachers.[26] The feelings of being shamed are projected outward in constant hostility and anger.

Children with the self-image of being a bad kid experience the pain of feeling shame in their own eyes, to be sure. However, such self-images also offer certain potential emotional satisfactions.[27] This helps to account for their tenacity. Bad kids get a lot of attention, which is preferable to being ignored. Bad kids attract a circle of friends with similar self-concepts, which is preferable to being socially isolated. Bad kids also often have the power to scare "good kids" simply by their reputations. (There should be no illusions here; many "bad kids" are downright nasty, malicious, and even sadistic.) Ultimately, choosing the self-image of being a bad kid is preferable to having an ambiguous, ill-defined identity.

An Evil Self-Concept

In a few children, the self-concept of being a bad kid can go to an extreme, such as when children regard themselves as being "evil" people. This is most likely to happen when children have authoritarian, punitive parents, who use religious threats to humiliate and control them.[28] Michael Beck, a psychotherapist, has written about his own inner experience of having an "evil" self-concept as a child.

> I lived in constant dread of committing a mortal sin and dying without being forgiven. . . . Imagine yourself as being in some precarious position . . . and not knowing quite how you got there. Unrelieved dread leaves its indelible impression, and since anxiety generalizes, one grows apprehensive that things not evil are indeed evil merely because one becomes anxious about them.
>
> This is a particularly taxing issue during adolescence, when one is constantly preoccupied with sex. It is a mortal sin to think about sex. The prescription for handling sexual impulses is suppression. Since, whatever is suppressed intensifies and seeks expression, one is forced to handle a sticky wicket—so to speak.[29]

Beck goes on to explain how some people who develop an "evil" self-image can lead themselves to believe that their behavior is being controlled by the Devil.

> With even more damaged patients who think they are evil, the issue of their ability to deal with anger becomes a priority. They often turn anger against themselves. The extreme is the patient who becomes totally or partially identified with evil and feels that she or he is either Jesus Christ or the devil, or possibly believes the devil is controlling him or her.[30]

These observations by Beck that some people have a self-concept of being "evil" provide insight into why some teenage delinquents may be drawn to Satanic beliefs, in order to justify their aggressive behavior. Adolescents who see themselves as being "evil," create a psychological environment consistent with their self-concept. They see the world as they see themselves, a place where malicious evil is more genuine than compassion.

A therapist's description of a seventeen-year-old girl involved in pseudo-Satanism illustrates the point.

> Christina was also using satanism to rebel against her parents' religion. She did not keep her satanism a secret from her family. When her mother asked her directly about her satanic beliefs, Christina told her mother that there was nothing good in the world and that was why she liked satanism.[31]

It is quite likely that a great many pseudo-Satanist teenagers are rebelling from an overly restrictive, traditional religious family background which emphasizes that the world is an evil place. The possibility needs to be investigated.

Social Influences upon Teenage Pseudo-Satanism

Many of the claims-makers assert that average adolescents can suddenly be transformed into hostile, aggressive delinquents, simply by their becoming involved in Satanic ritualism. This kind of claim appears to suggest that some kind of religious conversion process is at work, very similar perhaps to the process of becoming a "born-again" Christian and giving up one's past sinful ways, only with a reverse conversion from virtue to sinfulness. The claim has dramatic appeal. However, it is entirely inconsistent with what we know about the development of juvenile delinquency.

Most of the claims-makers also insist on viewing teenage pseudo-Satanism as being primarily a form of religious behavior, albeit in pursuit of evil religious beliefs. This model of thinking about teenage pseudo-Satanism as a process of religious conversion logically leads to an emphasis upon Satanic beliefs and magic rituals as the cause of the aggressive and criminal behavior. So, it is not surprising that one hears an elaborate presentation of purported Satanic symbols, religious beliefs, and black magic rituals at public seminars about youth involved in Satanism, while one hears very little about the psychology and sociology of juvenile delinquency.[32]

Much is also made about the supposed influence of Anton LaVey's Church of Satan in drawing teenagers into Satanism, primarily through their reading of his book, *The Satanic Bible*.[33] Some of the claims-makers also assert that a secret conspiracy of adult Satanists are recruiting young people into Satanism, operating as secret cults across the country. Again, this assertion appears to be drawn from a religious model of thinking. The analogy applied here is one in which adult proselytizers recruit youth in psychological crisis to their religion. However, there is simply no evidence for this kind of speculation. The claims-makers are weaving a tapestry out of their own imaginations and fears.

The Social Dynamics of a Self-Fulfilling Prophecy

What social influences can account for the increasing use of Satanic beliefs by some teenagers as a deviant ideology to justify aggressive and criminal behavior? One social process at work is that of the self-fulfilling prophecy. The more attention given to the dangers of "Satanism" among youth, the more curious aggression-prone teenagers become about it, and the more some of them dabble in makeshift black magic.

The social process is similar to that which led to the rapid increase in the "hippie" subculture during the mid-1960s. The small number of strange countercultural youth in Haight-Ashbury were given sensationalized attention in the mass media. It was a dramatic story. Then, as the mass media reports were imitated by young people in other cities, the numbers of would-be "hippies" grew rapidly. Once they were widely condemned in public presentations, they were imitated by even more rebellious youth. (Remember the billboards urging teenagers to "get a haircut"?)

This does not imply that the mass media created teenage pseudo-Satanism. It didn't. Certainly, much of the newspaper sensationalism contributed to its spread. Paradoxically, most of the attention was drawn to it by local police, social workers, and clergymen, in their public lectures condemning teenage Satanism. What this self-fulfilling prophecy means is that a society often gets the kinds of deviants it fears and condemns most.

The Satanic Symbolism Fad among Teenagers

With all of the publicity condemning certain symbols as being Satanic, it was inevitable that many teenagers would adopt those same symbols as a way of "shocking" adult authorities. Using so-called Satanic symbolism has become a fad among many teenagers. This is neither new nor surprising. Adolescents have a way of finding exactly those things which will disturb adults the most. This is especially the case during the early teenage years when they are striving to exert their independence from adult authority. Many teenage rebels are now affixing these taboo symbols on their clothes, scribbling them on their school notebooks, drawing them on their arms, and spraying them on walls, along with other messages offensive to adult sensibilities. These decorative insults do not, of course, constitute any kind of Devil worship, but the fad can lead a few curious teenagers toward an interest in makeshift black magic.

Once a young person develops an interest in things "Satanic," he or she can learn a lot about the so-called arts of black magic by simply visiting the local library. It is easy for a teenager to put together a concoction of "Satanic beliefs" from newspaper articles, from popular folklore, from horror movies, and even from what is learned in church about the Devil. He or she doesn't need to read *The Satanic Bible.*

It is highly unlikely that teenage pseudo-Satanists have any contact with organized Satanic religious groups, and it is very far-fetched to claim that criminals are recruiting teenagers into a secret Satanic Mafia. Such claims are similar to those made in the 1960s by some public officials, that the Communists were responsible for organizing college student radicals. In reality, of course, most student radicals put together their bits and pieces of social philosophy mainly through conversations between themselves. Very few of them read any books by Marx or Lenin, which they regarded as being quite tedious. Similarly, it is unlikely that many of today's pseudo-Satanist teenagers read much complicated occult theology.

The Rootlessness of Many Teenagers

It is a matter of speculation why so many teenagers today have feelings of powerlessness, but it may well be because so many teenagers today are rootless. I suspect that one of the circumstances which draws together bands of adolescents into pseudo-Satanic ritualism in search of power over their fate is their alienation from stable family and friendship groups. Rootlessness is commonplace among lower class adolescents who live in urban poverty. However, similar conditions are also being experienced by more and more middle class adolescents.

The criminologist Gwynn Nettler suggests that advanced, industrial societies are producing more and more unwanted youth from fragmented families, youth who are disconnected from stabilizing adult influences.[34] Many of these youth account for the seemingly senseless crimes of aggression which plague modern community life.

Connectedness to caring intimates is one of the prerequisites for adequate self-esteem, for having a self-image as an appreciated, unique, and "good" person.[35] I believe that those middle class teenagers who are most likely to be drawn into pseudo-Satanism are those who are disconnected from loving and caring parents and/or are ostracized from conventional middle class peers at school. They are likely to experience themselves as inhabiting a hostile, uncaring world, in which people's maliciousness is more real than their love. For them, evil is more real than goodness.

What Can Be Done to Help Teenagers?

Teenage pseudo-Satanism presents a problem for many parents and communities. Beyond understanding it, what can be done?

It is likely to be self-defeating to attract a lot of public attention to the supposed dangers of teenage pseudo-Satanism. When so-called experts in teenage Satanism are brought into communities to lecture at schools and churches, one unintended effect is that they provoke curiosity about Satanism among hostile, marginalized adolescents. Ironically, these "experts" even provide youthful rebels with the Satanic symbolism, rituals, and beliefs, which they use to fabricate new ways to shock adult authorities.

A report about claims concerning teenage Satanism designed for teachers and school administrators sums up the basic findings of this chapter and the kind of recommendations most useful for schools.

> . . . it appears that Satanic beliefs, when coupled with deviancy is an outcome of something more basic. In most cases, both the Satanic beliefs and the deviancy are symptoms of more fundamental personal problems. A symptom is not a cause. Thus, personal problems, rather than Satanic beliefs, should be the target for school or community intervention.
>
> In fact, any school intervention which narrowly defines its purpose as an effort to purge Satanic beliefs from the student body is inappropriate. Such activity is more likely to make Satanism attractive. A far more prudent choice is for schools to build programs designed to help overcome personal problems such as substance abuse, academic failure, low self-esteem, child abuse, suicidal tendencies, or a pervasive sense of alientation. Inappropriate concerns over Satanic activity may serve to distract educators from developing programs which address serious problems known to affect many students.[36]

It would be useful for community agencies to develop youth programs aimed at enhancing the self-esteem of socially ostracized and alienated, middle class adolescents. The state of California is already developing such a program.[37] However, it is extremely difficult for social agencies to provide intimacy and genuine caring when these comforts are lacking from parents and peer groups.

Some teenagers who aspire to be Satanists are responding with rage to their own self-hatred. It is a self-hatred born out of lives empty of the love which heals. Perhaps the most malignant evil of our time is the harm caused by neglect and indifference, in societies offering abundant material satisfactions at the cost of poverty in human relatedness.

Chapter Eight
Searching for Satanism in Schools, Books, Music, and Games

The witch-hunt was a perverse manifestation of the panic which set in among all classes when the balance began to turn toward greater individual freedom.

The witch-hunt was not, however, a mere repression. It was also, and as importantly, a long overdue opportunity for everyone so inclined to express publicly his guilt and sins, under the cover of accusations against the victims.

Arthur Miller, *The Crucible*[1]

The Search for Subversive Satanic Influences

Moral crusades against newly perceived forms of deviance are aimed at redefining the moral boundaries between good and evil in behavior. They arise out of moral conflicts in a society, when contending social groups each seek to implement their own visions of a moral society.

The current moral crusade against Satanism arises out of social changes which affect children, or at least, out of changes believed to affect the well-being of children. The Red Scare of the 1950s was propelled by concerns about national security. Similarly, the Satanic cult scare is fueled by fears about the security of our children. Parents fear child molesters and drug dealers, violent teenage gangs and teenage suicide, to be sure.

However, the deepest fear of parents is that their children may "go wrong," due to "outside" influences over which parents have little control: influences from their childrens' peer group, teachers, and the mass media.

This chapter documents the widespread threats to civil liberties and to personal safety which have resulted from the Satanic cult scare. It examines censorship campaigns aimed at school books, libraries, rock music, and fantasy role-playing games. It also documents the physical and social harassment of individuals, which results from Satanic cult rumors.

Searching for Satanism in Schoolbooks and Libraries

"The school year of 1990–91 marked the single worst years for school censorship in the history of our research," reports Arthur J. Kopp, president of People for the American Way, a national organization which studies censorship of books and other educational materials.[2] According to a national survey of censorship incidents done by that organization, over half of the censorship attempts now involve accusations about purported Satanic or occult content of books.

One disturbing expression of the Satanic cult scare involves attempts to censor books. Censorship campaigns are being nationally orchestrated by organizations having a Christian fundamentalist and conservative political agenda.[3] The primary targets are school textbooks, school library books, and public library books. Other targets include symbols on clothes worn by school students, such as the peace symbol, and school celebrations, such as Halloween, which these groups regard as having occult or Satanic meaning.[4]

The Campaign against the Impressions Reading Curriculum
The most common target of censorship attempts is the *Impressions* reading curriculum. The *Impressions* curriculum is a series of literature studies designed for elementary school children, published by Harcourt, Brace, Jovanovich. It is being used in about fifteen hundred schools in thirty-four states.[5]

The curriculum is under attack by groups which claim that it encourages occult practices, Satanism, violence, cannibalism, and relativism.[6] These claims are being promoted by several national fundamentalist and conservative organizations through articles in their publications and through financial support for law suits.[7] The organizations include Reverend Donald Wildmon's American Family Association, Dr. James Dobson's Focus on the Family, the National Association of Christian Educators, Phyllis Schlafly's Eagle Forum, and the Traditional Values Coalition.[8]

Many local parents and citizens groups have been informed about *Impressions* by the publications of these organizations, which also provide guidance in tactics of organizing local opposition to the curriculum. Many concerned parents, of course, are not members of any national organization and may not have even heard of such organizations, but are simply drawn into the struggle when they learn about and believe the accusations made against the curriculum. In some local school districts, organized efforts to remove the *Impressions* curriculum have generated heated community feelings and angry recriminations, as happened in Yucaipa, California, for example.[9]

One of the national organizations most active in attacking the *Impressions* curriculum is Focus on the Family, which has recently published several articles about it in its *Citizen* magazine.[10] The magazine is sent out to about 300,000 subscribers, so it reaches a wide audience of parents. In a 1990 article published in that magazine, titled "Nightmarish Textbooks Await Your Kids," the author links the curriculum to concerns about Satanism in the following way.

> Experts are especially troubled by "Impressions'" overtly occultic messages. . . .
> San Jose, Calif., police officer Thomas C. Jensen, who investigates occult crimes and is considered an occult crime specialist, said he sees the result of children who are exposed to the kind of violence and fear portrayed in "Impressions."
> "This does affect children," he said. "I see how it affects them when they get older in criminal activity."

Jensen said "Impressions" contains rituals and symbols used in Wicca, a witchcraft religion; Satanism; and Santeria, a blend of the Aruba (sic) religion of Africa and Catholicism.

"By having the children sit in a circle and chant or prepare a spell that would send them somewhere or change them into something else, kids are participating in ritualistic activities in the classroom," Jensen said.[11]

The campaign to ban the *Impressions* curriculum has been successful in some locations. State school boards in Georgia, Mississippi, North Carolina, and Oklahoma decided to reject funding for its use in local school districts.[12] According to the publisher, the curriculum was being challenged by citizens groups in four hundred local school districts during the spring of 1991, and formal law suits were filed in thirty-four of these districts.[13]

These kinds of controversial law suits can be costly and demoralizing for local school districts, especially when they need to defend themselves against well-financed attacks of national organizations. The American Family Association, for example, is supporting a civil suit seeking $1.16 million in damages from the Willard, Ohio, school board, claiming that the *Impressions* instruction violates some children's free exercise of religion, by forcing them to participate in occult religious rituals.[14] Several other similar suits have been brought and the numbers can be expected to increase as the issue attains wider public awareness.

Illustration: An Attempt at Censorship

A struggle over the *Impressions* curriculum arose near this author's home community. The case illustrates the way in which one element of the Satanism scare is disseminated in rumor-stories and erupts in scattered incidents of collective behavior across the country. It illustrates how national organizations are able play upon the worries of local parents about the mental health of their children.

The controversy started when about fourteen parents organized opposition to the introduction of the *Impressions* curriculum in the Southwestern School District of Lakewood, New

York, a suburb of Jamestown.[15] The curriculum was introduced as a pilot program in the second and third grades of the district and the school system had to decide whether or not to continue with it. The protesting parents were led by a couple who described themselves as being "fundamentalist Baptists and born-again Christians."[16] Their criticism of the *Impressions* curriculum relied upon the article from *Focus on the Family– Citizen* magazine previously noted, as their primary source of information about it. In a guest editorial that one of the parents wrote for the local Jamestown newspaper, for example, the parent copied sections of the article, practically word for word.[17] However, few of the parents had ever asked for and taken home copies of the curriculum to study it.[18] The parents group organized community meetings about the curriculum, and even circulated a petition of protest through churches in the local area, obtaining over five hundred signatures.[19]

The protesting parents asserted that they were concerned about themes of "despair, mutilation, occultism and witch-craft" in the curriculum.[20] However, worries about Satanism seemed to be the key underlying concern. For example, the fundamentalist couple who led the group was quoted in several newspaper articles as referring to the threat of Satanism. Their words reveal the kind of beliefs shared by people who are caught up in the Satanism scare.

> We believe there is a desensitization effect here. . . . Pretty soon, casting and chanting spells will seem so commonplace to kids that, when they're confronted with the advances of satanic groups on a darker level, it will seem more acceptable. . . .
>
> What we're saying is that the recurring themes—the chants, the violence and the fear—will help to develop phobias and fears in the kids.
>
> And his wife added: Throughout the curriculum, it's a pattern that builds and builds, and that's how Satanism enters the minds of our children.[21]

The wife was also quoted in another news report as saying:

> We want to trust our teachers, but it only takes one teacher to teach Satan and ruin a child.[22]

Satanism, in this kind of thinking, is a package, into which all manners of seductive evils are thrown. These parents' thinking is much like that of the parents of the 1950s who were similar politically conservative fundamentalists who searched for subversive Communist influences in the schoolbooks of children and always found some. The irony is that in our times, with the demise of the Communist threat, we are once again back to hunting for witches.

However, maybe some Americans have learned from our past, not to surrender too easily to the witch hunters. The school board of the Southwestern School District voted to continue using the *Impressions* curriculum. It now appears that a majority of parents in that school district agree with the decision.

Attempts to Censor Library Books

People for the American Way, in its 1990–91 survey, "Attacks on the Freedom to Learn," reported that charges of Satanic, occult, and New Age content had emerged in 1990, as the most common accusations of would-be censors of educational materials.[23] These charges have now replaced accusations of "secular humanism," profanity, and sexual explicitness. In most cases, these objections come from organized fundamentalist Christian groups.

The censorship campaigns are directed primarily at school libraries. However, they also extend to public libraries and involve attempts to stop the circulation of specific books. Most such attempts have been unsuccessful, but even so, they are likely to have the "chilling effect" of encouraging self-censorship by small town and school librarians.

The American Library Association regularly monitors attempts to censor library books. The Association reports that there have been an increasing number of attempts over the last several years to get libraries to stop circulating books on topics which some citizens, mainly fundamentalists, regard as promoting so-called occult religion and Satanism. These books include traditional folk stories and fairy tales about witches, demons, ghosts, and the like, books about the history and the nature of witchcraft and magic, and even books of Halloween stories. There are no national surveys of these incidents. However, a survey done by the Florida Library Association in 1989 found that these kind of books were the third most common target of complaints, especially when the books were designed for young readers.[24]

Police Requests for Names of Library Users

In recent years, there have been several newspaper reports about police requests of libraries to supply them with lists of people who check out books on occult topics and witchcraft. In one case, for example, police in Defiance County, Ohio, requested that a local library give them a list of the names of people who had checked out books on witchcraft. The police wanted to use the list to help them in their investigation of rumors about witchcraft rituals, which were alleged to be taking place in the area. The library refused to do so because it was contrary to library policy.[25]

In another case, New York City police searching for a serial murderer, the "Zodiac killer," were able to obtain library records of people who checked out "occult" literature. The action led to the questioning and fingerprinting of a young, white stockbroker, even though the killer had been identified as being a Black person.[26]

Unfortunately, many states do not have laws which protect library records from public scrutiny. The danger here comes from the great number of local police Satan hunters in small towns, who are caught up in the Satanic cult scare and go on fishing trips in search of ritualistic criminals.[27]

Searching for Satanism in Rock Music

Part of the Satanic cult legend includes the assertion that Satanists are influencing children and teenagers through messages embedded in entertainment media, particularly in heavy metal rock music. The appellation "heavy metal" is often used indiscriminately, as a critical judgment applied to any rock music which seems to be composed largely of a lot of shouting and acoustical distortions of sound. The music appeals most commonly, but not exclusively, to white, working-class teenage males, living in suburbs and small towns, who don't plan to pursue a college education and who usually have diminished job opportunities.[28]

It is sometimes a bit uncertain just what music fits the stylistic category of heavy metal rock. A scholarly music historian of rock describes heavy metal music in the following way.

> Musically, heavy metal began as an exaggeration of the hard rock side of the mainstream. If hard rock was loud, heavy metal was louder; if hard rock was simple and repetitive, heavy metal was simpler and more repetitive; if hard rock singers shouted, heavy metal singers screamed; if hard rockers experimented with electronic distortion and feedback, heavy metalers distorted everything; if hard rock favored long instrumental improvisations, heavy metal offered longer, louder, and more dazzling instrumental solos . . . [29] Because the shock factor has become an integral part of heavy metal, many of the bands have become increasingly overt in their references to sex and drugs and have dwelled on violence and overt and extreme forms of rebellion. The high, screaming vocals of heavy-metal groups are often mixed just slightly above the instrumental accompaniment, making the lyrics even more obscure. A fascination with the occult and the macabre has led some to satanic themes.[30]

In the 1970s and early 1980s, heavy metal rock music was generally ignored by rock music radio stations and was available to teenagers primarily through record sales and at rock music concerts. However, by the late 1980s, heavy metal music was increasingly played on FM radio stations and MTV, and as a result, it was able to attract a much wider audience.[31] With the increased visibility, some of the bands were able to sell millions of record albums.[32]

Heavy metal rock music eventually attained formal recognition in the entertainment industry, when the Grammy Awards set up a special category for it. Some prominent heavy metal bands include: Guns and Roses, Van Halen, Motley Crüe, Bon

Jovi, Ratt, Kiss, Metallica, and Megadeth from the United States; Black Sabbath, Iron Maiden, Def Leppard, and Judas Priest, from England; and AC/DC, from Australia.[33]

The Claims about Heavy Metal Rock Music

The claims-makers assert that audible and subliminal messages in heavy metal rock motivate frequent listeners to commit suicide, or to commit other acts of aggression.[34] It is also claimed that these messages have the effect of brainwashing innocent youth into becoming criminal Satanists. As a result, these claims have become ammunition in local censorship campaigns directed against these entertainments.

Dr. Paul King, a psychiatrist, for example, studied the music preferences of emotionally disturbed teenage patients in a Memphis, Tennessee, hospital. He found that among about two hundred teenagers, ages thirteen to seventeen, who were hospitalized for drug dependence, about 60 percent chose heavy metal music as their first choice for listening, and high percentages of them were also involved in violence, stealing, and sexual activity.[35] He offers the following erroneous conclusions about the supposed effects of heavy metal rock music on teenage listeners.

> The attraction of heavy metal music is its message that a higher power controls the world, and that that power is hate—often personified by Satan. Hopeless, troubled youngsters can sink their teeth into this philosophy, so they can crank up the music, tattoo or carve in their body a symbol of Satan, and do drugs, all of which makes them feel powerful and in charge. . . . As they wander in and out of reality, they hear songs that glorify the occult and Satan. . . .[36]
>
> Although the relationship of heavy metal music to drug use and suicide is speculative, further epidemiological research is warranted, because material that speaks directly to young people about sex, violence, and suicide may well be a serious public health problem.[37]
>
> Heavy metal music represents a public health problem for youngsters that is serious enough to warrant some type of control.[38]

There is no doubt that some heavy metal rock music contains lyrics about the Devil, and that much of it contains imagery of aggressive masculinity and blatant sexuality.[39] However, the central issue isn't whether or not heavy metal rock music is offensive to some people's moral values, but whether or not specific contents of the music has the ability to motivate people to commit suicide or other criminally aggressive behavior. (Some people, for example, react to *Rambo*-type war movies with feelings of moral revulsion, but that does not mean that these violent movies can cause some people to commit acts of physical aggression.) Most people who are not carefully trained in scientific research methods and analysis find it very difficult to psychologically separate their personal moral judgment from their evaluation of the possible dangerous effects of a phenomenon. The problem is one of parallelism in thinking: "evil things cause evil deeds."

Most so-called studies of Satanism in heavy metal music, such as the one done by Dr. King, rely upon unrepresentative, selected cases or groups of juvenile delinquents, and observe that the delinquents prefer to listen to heavy metal music, frequently use illegal drugs and alcohol, engage in promiscuous sexual behavior, dabble in some kind of pseudo-Satanic ritualism or graffiti writing, and frequently express themselves in various kinds of aggressive behavior, such as vandalism or physical assault. Then, these "studies" confuse correlation with cause-and-effect association, by inferring that the heavy metal music is a contributing cause of the other deviant behavior. In contrast, most social psychologists would be quick to spot the behavioral syndrome whereby these delinquents' long-term aggressive dispositions shape their preferences for symbols of hostile expression.[40]

It is a common mistake to confuse a correlation between two things and a cause-and-effect relationship between them, but one which needs to be avoided in serious scientific research. This is especially true when we examine claims about the psychological effects of mass media entertainments. One research project, for example, found that people in bars drink faster in response to slow country music than in response to music with a faster tempo.[41] Obviously, it would be a mistake to jump to the conclusion that country music causes alcohol abuse. (The researchers concluded that heavy drinkers who enjoy country music simply prefer slow country music as a context for drinking.)

The Dissemination of Claims about Satanism in Rock Music

The claims about the criminogenic influences of Satanism in rock music are part of the ongoing agenda of many organizations designed to protect children from malicious influences in the entertainment media. The Parents' Music Resource Center, for example, sells a "Satanism Research Packet" for fifteen dollars, containing "clippings of crimes connected with Satanism and heavy metal music." The Cult Awareness Network offers a similar package of materials. Lectures about Satanism in rock music, complete with slide shows of loathsome-looking rock music groups, are a featured part of many public service crime seminars about "Satanism and Youth," offered across the country by police Satan hunters and Christian evangelists. Some influential public figures have even lent credibility to these claims, as did Cardinal O'Connor of New York in March 1990, when he warned that some rock music can lead to "demonic possession and even suicide."[42]

Illustration: A Police Training Seminar about Satanism

I attended a police training seminar in April 1989, titled, "The Identification and Investigation of Satanic and Cult Related Crime Scenes," sponsored by the New York State Crime Prevention Coalition. The featured speaker was Detective Paul Hart, who is a juvenile crime officer in Jefferson Township, New Jersey, a distant suburb of the metropolitan region of New York City. Hart was the chief investigator of the much publicized Tommy Sullivan case.

Tommy Sullivan was a fourteen-year-old, who killed his mother in a fit of rage by stabbing her several dozen times, mutilated her body, set fire to his house, and then committed suicide by slashing his wrist and his throat. According to newspaper reports, Tommy had no apparent problems until a month before the crime, when he began reading about the occult and Satanism.[43] The case has been widely cited in newspaper and magazine articles as an example of teenage violence due to the influence of Satanism.[44]

The audience at the seminar was composed mainly of small town police and a scattering of citizens concerned with crime prevention. According to Detective Hart, his presentation was "designed to address the fact that there is evidence that teens and adolescents are becoming involved with Satanism and have acted-out in violent ways."[45] He documented this rather ambiguous conclusion with a video of excerpts from Geraldo Rivera's TV Special, "Exposing Satan's Underground," and a slide show of bizarre rock musicians and readings of aggressive rock music lyrics, followed by slides showing the gruesome results of Tommy's outbreak of violence. Detective Hart emphasized repeatedly that Satanism in heavy metal rock music and *Dungeons and Dragons* games "play a role" in violent crimes. I may have misunderstood, but it seemed to me that Detective Hart was implying a causative link between Satanic imagery and violent crime.

Detective Hart told the audience that Tommy came from a very religious Catholic family and had no history of troublesome behavior. Hart then presented some "evidence" to show how Tommy's mind was influenced by Satanism. He displayed Tommy's drawings of Satanic symbolism, rock musicians, and horror scenes. He noted Tommy's interest in heavy metal music (although he was careful to caution that "the music is only a symptom, not a cause"). He cited an incident, in which Tommy told one of his friends that he had had a vision of the Devil telling him to kill his parents. Detective Hart also showed a note by Tommy, found in his room, in which he wrote a kind of compact with the Devil to kill his parents.

In my private conversations with Detective Hart, I found him to be a genuinely caring, concerned, and reasonable person, committed to helping teenagers. Hart offered me the disclaimer that he was "not a psychologist" when I asked for psychological background information about Tommy Sullivan. Then, Hart gave me a very perceptive psychological evaluation of the case. He remarked that Tommy must have been developing a lot of inner rage for a long time before his violent outburst. He told me that Tommy's mother was very controlling, and that his father was very distant and aloof from family problems. He suggested that "this kid had very little control over his own life." As one illustration, Hart said Tommy "was forced to attend a Catholic school against his wishes." Hart also said that Tommy's mother was "almost fanatical" in her Catholicism. When I asked him, if he believed that Tommy's interest in Satanism caused his violent aggression, Hart told me that "the interest in Satanism was probably a symptom of much deeper psychological problems."

Yet, Hart spent much of his three-hour presentation describing the lyrics and bizarre antics of heavy metal rock music bands. I don't know why he neglected to describe the crucial details of Tommy Sullivan's family situation, as he had done in his private conversation with me.

The evidence indicated to me that Tommy was indeed a very deeply disturbed youth who had developed an evil self-image, a manifestation of severe low self-esteem. This kind of self-concept is found by psychotherapists in people who experienced rigid parental control through oppressive guilt-mongering and constant criticism, justified by a personal distortion of some kind of punitive religious belief system.[46]

Illustration: A Church Revival Meeting about Satanism

Quite a different kind of public presentation about Satanism took place at a church revival I attended during February 1989. The subject of the "lecture" was billed as "Rock and the Media," offered by Mike Adams of Mike Adams Ministries, from Tulsa, Oklahoma. Mike Adams had previously had a career in radio broadcasting and has since become a consultant for Christian radio. He travels around the country speaking about the entertainment media. His visit to my area was sponsored by The Full Gospel Businessmen's Fellowship International. He spoke at seven local churches which I recognized as being fundamentalist churches.

Mike Adams's presentation started out with a slide show

depicting various groups of rock singers, whose appearances were certainly demonic enough to allow them to fit into a Halloween masquerade party. Throughout the long slide show, Adams repeated the message, "Satan is attempting to capture the souls of our youth through rock and roll music." He went through a litany of claims about how rock musicians promote drug addiction, sexual orgies, and violence. Adams claimed, for example, that "70 percent of all rock musicians are homosexuals." He also claimed that "many hundreds of teenagers commit suicide each year because of the Satanic influence of rock music." Adams didn't make any fine distinctions between different styles of rock music.

Adams even made many extremist assertions about religion. For example, Adams asserted that, "any religion which does not accept Jesus Christ as the path to salvation is a false religion," and that "many so-called churches today are no longer teaching the Christian religion." He told the audience that, "if you don't accept Jesus Christ as your savior by the day you die, you will go to hell. You are either serving God or serving Satan. There is no middle ground."

In relating Satanism to the entertainment media, Mike Adams was similarly unequivocal in stating that, "the people who control the media are serving Satan." He claimed, for example, that, "John Denver is serving Satan's cause, because Denver says that all religions have some good in them." Adams's bottom line message was that we are now in "the final days," during which Satan is trying to foment anarchy and confusion in society, primarily through the use of the entertainment media.

It was an emotion-packed presentation. At the end of Adams's speech, regretful sinners were asked to come up front, to be saved by the laying-on of Adams's hands. Six adults and one child responded to the call.

Legal Cases Involving Heavy Metal Music

The most famous case in which these claims were taken to court was that involving the Judas Priest band, an English heavy metal rock music group. The trial took place in Reno, Nevada, during the summer of 1990. The case centered on a tragic incident in which two youths, ages eighteen and twenty, shot themselves on December 23, 1985, after drinking heavily, smoking marijuana, and listening for hours to the music of the Judas Priest band. One of the youths died immediately and the other died three years later from complications due to his self-inflicted wound.

The parents of the youths took the rock band to court, in a $6.2 million suit, claiming that their children were driven to attempt suicide as a result of subliminal messages in the music of the band's "Stained Class" album. They charged the Judas Priest group, the record distributor, CBS Inc., and the band's English production company with selling a dangerous product, without adequate warning labels to that effect.[47] In this way, the plaintiffs sought to circumvent previous court rulings, which held that similar "heavy metal" music lyrics were protected as free speech by the First Amendment. (One such case was brought against the English singer, Ozzy Osbourne, in Los Angeles in 1986.)

The trial focussed on the issues of whether or not there were self-destructive subliminal messages in the music, and whether or not subliminal messages can motivate people to commit suicide. After a trial lasting five weeks, the judge ruled in favor of the defendants, finding that there was no intentional subliminal message of any kind in the disputed record album of the Judas Priest band. He also ruled that the plaintiffs had not proven the destructive effects of subliminal messages.[48]

Local Newspaper Reports about Satanism in Rock Music

Most claims about suicide motivated by Satanism in heavy metal music are never brought to court. Instead, they only go as far as speculation in local newspapers about specific incidents. One such incident, for example, was that of grandparents who publicly blamed the suicide of their twenty-two-year-old grandson on his listening to the music of the band Metallica, even though the boy had spent years wandering the streets, was a heavy drug abuser, and was in and out of detention centers across the country. According to the newspaper report, the grandparents made the connection between their grandson's suicide and the Judas Priest case in arriving at their conclusion that it was the music which prompted his suicide.[49]

What this news article demonstrates is that the Satanic cult legend will persist and grow, regardless of what happens in court. Research on the rumor transmission process has found that people tend to selectively remember the emotionally dramatic aspects of newspaper stories many years later, rather than more mundane facts, such as scientific disclaimers or trial outcomes.[50]

Research about the Influence of Rock Music

Some behavioral science research has investigated the claims about aggression-producing influences in popular music. Two social psychologists conducted an elaborate series of experiments to test listeners' abilities to perceive messages with the words recorded backwards and embedded in popular music.[51] This was done to test the so-called "back masking" of supposedly subliminal messages, which the claims-makers assert motivate aggression. They found no evidence that various embedded messages served to prompt any actions suggested by the messages. Instead, what they did find was that the preconceptions held by individual listeners shaped the meanings each attributed to the embedded messages. This finding is supported in another research study, which investigated whether or not listeners could decipher unintelligible messages in parts of rock music played backwards.[52] Subjects who received the experimenter's suggestion to listen for "Satanic messages" hidden in the music were significantly more likely to believe that they heard them. In contrast, subjects who did not receive the suggestion were not likely to attribute any intelligible meanings to the sounds they heard. The research on "hidden messages" in popular music indicates that people hear what their preconceptions lead them to hear.

Two sociologists studied the music listening habits of a large sample of high school students and found that the music preferences of most of the teenagers was determined not by the lyrics, but by the beat of the music and its overall sound.[53] They also found that the teenagers commonly misinterpreted the messages in the lyrics of the music, including references to sex, violence, drugs, and Satanism. Instead, they found that teenagers' understanding of meanings of the lyrics is usually based upon ideas they learn external to the music itself from their teen subculture and media publicity.

In brief, most teenagers seem to pay little attention to the exact wording of rock songs and attribute meanings to the messages, based upon their socially constructed preconceptions. Those preconceptions are likely to reflect the particular teenage subculture they share with their clique of friends.[54] If a teenager's friendship clique values symbols of aggression, he or she is likely to find them in the kind of music they prefer to listen to regularly.

Teenage Aggression and the Entertainment Media
There is a more fundamental issue in this controversy. That involves the question of whether entertainment media shapes aggressive attitudes and behavior of consumers, or whether it simply reflects the aggressive personality predispositions of particular consumers, who selectively seek out media with aggressive content. The consensus of research specialists is that media can reinforce the aggressive predispositions of some teenagers, in some circumstances, and that such effects depend greatly upon the simultaneous encouragement of aggression in conversation with family and friends.[55] This principle can be applied to heavy metal rock music, but it can also be applied to *Rambo*-type war movies, "slasher" horror movies, and even aggressive sports, like football, enjoyed by many teenagers.[56]

Research on the relation between media and personality has found that people must first have the motivation to seek out and select that kind of content which offers them some kind of emotional satisfaction.[57] Violent action movies, for example, attract people who find fantasy violence emotionally satisfying. Romantic love movies, in contrast, attract people who find fantasy love satisfying.

In conclusion, it would seem that the aggressive predispositions of some teenagers leads them to seek out symbols of aggression in specific types of rock music, much like any consumer seeks out what they most appreciate in the entertainment media. However, the key factors in the aggressive behavior of some teenagers include having a personality with an aggressive predisposition and receiving encouragement of aggressive behavior from family and friends, rather than the content of the music the teenagers happen to prefer.

Searching for Satanism in *Dungeons and Dragons* Games

Dungeons and Dragons is a role-playing game, in which the players create an imaginary environment populated by hostile creatures and various hazards through which they must maneuver. The game stresses cooperation between game players in dealing with the hazards, rather than competition, and doesn't have winners and losers. The rules of the game are set by the particular roles of fantasy characters chosen by each player and by a facilitator, called a "Dungeon Master," who organizes a series of adventures. The game characters are drawn loosely from magical-fantasy literature and medieval folklore. Movements and events are determined by a throw of the dice. The players use their imaginations cooperatively to deal with the hazards structured by the Dungeon Master.

There have been over 10 million copies of the *Dungeons and Dragons* (*D&D*) game sold around the world. There are many more millions of similar games, considering that there are many other games that imitate the *D & D* role-playing format.[58] The manufacturer of the game estimates that about 4 million people play *Dungeons and Dragons* with some regularity.[59]

Claims that *Dungeons and Dragons* games influence teenagers to commit suicide and other acts of aggression appear to have originated from one case. Pat Pulling, a mother of a teenager who committed suicide in June 1982, believed that her son's involvement in playing *D & D* games was the cause of the tragedy and turned her beliefs into a moral crusade against the game.[60] Pulling filed suit against the principal of the youth's high school, claiming 1) that the school was responsible for the suicide because the games were played there as an organized school activity and 2) that the games caused his death. However, the judge in the case dismissed the lawsuit.[61]

The Dissemination of Claims about *Dungeons and Dragons* Games

Pulling also built an organization to alert parents to the supposed dangers of *D & D* games and to work for their exclusion from school functions. The organization goes by the acronym B.A.D.D. (for Bothered About Dungeons and Dragons). Pulling and B.A.D.D. are now concerned with combating a wide range of supposed Satanic influences in society and the organization sponsors law enforcement seminars to fight "ritualistic" crime.[62] A publication from B.A.D.D. provides a list of teenage suicides in which *D & D* games are supposedly "one common denominator" and a list of school districts around the country which have "removed *D & D*" games as a school sponsored activity.[63] The supposed link between criminal Satanism and *D & D* games is particularly believable for religious fundamentalists, who object to the "occult" play-language in the games.

Most, but not all, of the organized opposition to *Dungeons and Dragons* games comes from fundamentalist Christian groups. In addition to B.A.D.D, some of these organizations are: the National Coalition on Television Violence, Media Spotlight, Chick Publications, Pro-Family Forum, Christian Life Ministries, and The Daughters of St. Paul.[64]

Bob Larson, the radio evangelist, writes about the malevolent influence of *Dungeons and Dragons* games in his book, *Satanism: The Seduction of America's Youth*. His views are typical of fundamentalist criticism of the games, and highlight the probable reason *D & D* games are singled out for such vehement attacks by most of the groups which object to the games.

> The occult overtones of D & D are so explicit that virtually nothing in the world of Satanism is omitted. Players are told how to have their characters commune with nature spirits, consult

crystal balls filled with human blood, and conjure the Egyptian deities that Moses opposed. . . .[65]

Christian teaching underscores many objections to D & D, including the command to ignore evil imaginations and avoid "every thing that exalts itself against the knowledge of God, bringing every thought into captivity to obedience of Christ." . . .

The link with Satanism occurs when players use symbols and protective inscriptions associated with witchcraft and the occult.[66]

Many religious conservatives embroider their underlying moral objections to the games with a seemingly pragmatic, secular rationale, thereby making their criticism more credible to people who do not share their religious ideology. In her book, *The Devil's Web*, Pat Pulling emphasizes a primarily secular rationale for opposing *D & D* games, although the underlying moral objections to the symbolic (religious-like) imagery is apparent. (One has only to wonder, if the game were a war game between Americans and "the Evil Empire," whether the underlying hostility toward the game would be the same.) The gist of Pulling's argument is that: "D & D is limited only by the players' imaginations. For those with particularly vivid imaginations, the game can become a mystical experience, consuming, addictive and potentially dangerous."[67] Then, Pulling goes on to quote authority figures, who lend credibility to her beliefs. For example, she notes that: "Dr. Thomas Radecki, M.D., chairman of the National Coalition on Television Violence, has stated, 'There is no doubt in my mind that the game Dungeons & Dragons is causing young men to kill themselves and others.' "[68]

Claims about the criminogenic influence of *Dungeons and Dragons* games, like similar claims about heavy metal music, are both standard parts of police seminars on "occult" or "ritualistic" crime and Satanism.[69] It is alleged that the fantasy game leads some unsuspecting youth into occult beliefs, then into black magic and Satanic ritualism, and eventually into ritualistic crimes, such as the vandalism of churches and even ritual murder. These claims are also disseminated around the country by fundamentalist evangelists who lecture about "Satanism and Youth." In many areas of the country, the claims have become a part of conventional wisdom.

One result is that small town newspapers sometimes refer to claims about *D & D* games in reports about a local suicide or other act of juvenile aggression. In a recent case in Virginia Beach, for example, a sixteen-year-old was arrested for the gruesome murder of two young boys, a seven-year-old and a nine-year-old, with whom he played *Dungeons and Dragons.*[70] The local news report on the case emphasized the confessed murderer's involvement in *D & D* games, implying that the games could somehow account for the murders.

Research about *Dungeons and Dragons* Games

It can't automatically be assumed that fantasy role-playing games have any significant effects on players, any more than card games or chess. There are few, if any, scientific studies of the psychological effects of fantasy role-playing games such as *Dungeons and Dragons.* Therefore, claims about the supposed criminogenic influences of *D & D* games must be regarded as sheer speculation.

One study of the interaction of a group of pre-teenage boys who were "hyperactive" and sometimes aggressive before they began playing *D & D* games, concluded that the games fostered cooperative, helping relationships between the boys.[71] Another research study used a psychological test to investigate emotional stability in a sample of sixty-eight frequent *D & D* players, about one-third of whom were teenagers, the remainder being older. The study found that the *D & D* players had "a healthy psychological profile" and there was no evidence of emotional instability correlated with playing the game.[72] Several studies of the effects of fantasy role-playing activities on young children found that such activities help children to develop their abilities for creative imagination in thinking.[73] The effect is analogous to the way physical exercise helps to improve physical performance.

Concerning claims that *D & D* games foment violent aggressiveness in teenagers who were not previously aggressive, the same principles apply as would apply to any form of entertainment. Teenagers who have a hostile, aggressive personality will take that personality into the games they play. If they didn't play *D & D* games, they would simply find another outlet for their aggressive predisposition.

A major analysis of the claims against *D & D* games came to the following conclusion.

> What all of these studies indicate, then, is that the involvement in fantasy role-playing games seems unrelated to the allegedly more maleficent outcomes of gaming claimed by crusading groups. Some research findings, in fact, indicate precisely the opposite, that fantasy play in general, and possibly even D & D, is developmentally beneficial for the children who participate.[74]

It would appear that the attack on *Dungeons and Dragons* games arises from ideological preconceptions and have no basis in fact.

Searching for Secret Satanists in Local Communities

Threats of Physical Assault

There is evidence from newspaper reports that Satanic cult rumors create a climate of fear and hostility in some rural areas, which makes it easy to justify violence against individuals and groups misperceived as being dangerous Satanists. The following incidents illustrate threats of physical assault due to the Satanic cult scare.

In March 1990, police in rural Dillsburg, Pennsylvania, intercepted a group of teenagers on the way to attack "Satanists" at a rumored ritual meeting site. The group consisted of five boys and two girls, between the ages of fifteen and seventeen. The teenagers' truck was stopped by police patrolling a mountainous area south of Harrisburg, which was rumored to be an area for Satanic cult meetings. The police searched the truck after they noticed two gun barrels sticking out from under a blanket. They found the group armed with two homemade napalm bombs, four shotguns, boxes of ammunition, knives, and clubs. The teenagers told police that they were out to disrupt a meeting of "Satanists" because they wanted to take a stand against "Devil worshippers." Rumors had been circulating in the area for some time that a group of other local teenagers were involved in Devil worship.[75]

During August 1990, in rural Beulah, North Dakota, two armed men were arrested and charged by police with conspiring to murder a sixty-one-year-old woman, who they believed was a witch. Rumors had been circulating in the area that the woman was involved in witchcraft and that her guesthouse was a meeting place for secret rituals. The two men hatched the murder plot while drinking at a local bar, after deciding "they were going to eliminate the problem."[76]

In October 1988, police in the village of Cobleskill, New York, learned from local "informants" that a meeting of a Satanic cult would take place on Halloween night, during which a human sacrifice was planned. The police rushed with guns drawn into a large gathering of people in a field, about ten miles outside of the village. The participants were dressed in black robes, were carrying candles and chanting. The police quickly determined that the gathering was a Halloween costume party spoof of a Black Mass, consisting of fifty to seventy-five college students, organized by a college professor from State University of New York College at Cobleskill.[77]

During a Satanic cult rumor-panic in eastern Kentucky in September 1988, a photographer working on a grant from the Kentucky Arts Council to photograph school children had to flee for her safety from the village of Irvine. While seeking children to photograph, local rumors accused her of photographing "blond, blue-eyed" potential child victims for ritual sacrifice by Devil worshippers. She was forced to leave town hurriedly after a school principal, with whom she had arranged a meeting, chased her out of the school, shouting insults and threats at her.[78]

Social and Economic Harassment
There is evidence from newspaper reports that Satanic cult rumors have sometimes led to the social and economic harass-

ment of individuals and groups. The following are a few incidents which exemplify such harassment.

A 1989 civil suit in Bay City, Michigan, illustrates the ways in which Satanic cult rumors can victimize teenagers accused in gossip of being Satanists. Two teenage sisters, one in eighth grade and the other in tenth grade, had to leave their school system because they were victims of social harassment sparked by rumor accusations that they were members of a Satanic cult. The father of the two girls, who happened to be a lawyer, brought suit against a school principal, a teacher, and the school district superintendent, charging them with subjecting the girls to an arbitrary public investigation and official surveillance which resulted in their social ostracism. The investigation was prompted when several students told the principal that the girls were members of a Satanic cult which practiced animal sacrifice and planned to murder a popular student. This occurred in October 1988, coincident with the broadcast of Geraldo Rivera's "Special" television show, "Exposing Satan's Underground." The principal requested an investigation by the state police, who searched the teenagers' school lockers and found drawings, poetry, and song lyrics.[79]

In Montezuma Creek, Utah, in November 1988, a group of parents took their allegations that a school counselor was involved in Satanism, to the San Juan School District Board of Education. The parents held their children home from school for two days, forcing the school to close. The parents alleged that the counselor, who was a Ph.D. in philosophy, had written an unsigned document "containing Satanic references" and was trying to influence students with his philosophical ideas. In response, the school board decided to remove the counselor from his duties at the school and to hold a formal investigation of the allegations, stating that the counselor had lost his credibility in the community. Rumors about Satanism had been circulating in the area, focussed upon a trading post of which the counselor was a part owner.[80]

The research of this author found that during the Satanic cult rumor-panic in Jamestown, in western New York State in May 1988, about a dozen teenagers received a continuous barrage of telephone death threats from anonymous strangers. Rumors had been widely circulating in the area for weeks, that a Satanic cult planned to kidnap and sacrifice a blond, blue-eyed, virgin. These teenagers were misrepresented by rumors to be members of the alleged Satanic cult because of their unusual countercultural clothing and appearance at a time when relatively few teenagers in this small town area had a similar non-conformist appearance. Fortunately, local police actively tried to diffuse the growing tension in the community by meeting with social workers, school counselors, and other concerned professionals, together with some of the accused teenagers. However, that did not prevent the vandalism and destruction of $2,000 worth of musical equipment at a warehouse where many of these teenagers listened to local rock music bands practice. The warehouse was rumored to be a meeting place for Satanic cult rituals.

Conclusion

Playwright Arthur Miller suggests in *The Crucible* that a witch hunt is, in part, motivated by guilt and projection of "sins." There is plenty of guilt among parents today and it is guilt related to those precise objects of their resentment. There is the guilt of mothers over leaving their children at child-care centers. There is the guilt of parents who have little time to spend talking with their children, or supervising them, because both parents are working full-time. There is the guilt of parents who are reluctant to use their authority to guide their childrens' choice of entertainments and friends.

This is why the ideological targets of the Satanism witch hunters are things which are believed to shape the minds of children: child-care centers, schoolbooks, popular music, and even games.

Chapter Nine
The Moral Crisis in American Society

> *At the apparent zenith of its triumph, its enemies confounded, America seems headed for disaster. What may seem hyperbole is only to repeat what I hear on every side. The country is visibly decaying. I do not know anyone who sees a bright future for it.*
>
> Robert Heilbroner (1991)[1]

Disruption and Stress in Family Relationships
Social change since the 1960s has produced widespread disruption in family relationships. There have been rapid changes in gender roles and in the conditions of child-rearing. These accelerating changes have precipitated widespread tensions and conflict in the relations between men and women, between husbands and wives, and between parents and their children. Marital conflict and divorce have skyrocketed. Parenting has become more difficult and problematic. Children now experience more stresses in their lives and more disruptions of stable bonds with parents. Many people, adults and children, are now left with less emotional support from others. A great many people have become socially isolated.

A glance at some research findings tells the story of this vast rupture and dislocation in the intimate bonds between people and the resulting stress in the private sphere of social life. All these changes and their consequences have been greater in the United States than in any other advanced, industrial society, even though other societies are also undergoing similar social changes.

Indicators of Disruption and Stress in Family Relationships
1. More people are experiencing broken marital bonds.

The divorce rate, after reaching a plateau in the early 1980s, began to accelerate again. A major analysis of the current divorce rate estimates that two-thirds of all first marriages will eventually end in divorce or separation. Divorce rates for second marriages are even higher. As a result, a majority of Americans sometime shortly after the year 2000 will have experienced the disruption of divorce.[2] Accumulating research evidence indicates that divorce causes lasting stress in the lives of many adults, especially those who have experienced more than two divorces.[3]

2. More children are experiencing broken bonds with parents.

In 1988, 49 percent of American children under the age of eighteen were not living with both of their biological parents. Current projections made by family researchers indicate that between sixty and seventy percent of all white children who were born in 1990 will experience the divorce or separation of their parents and live in a single-parent household for a period of time, before they reach the age of eighteen.[4]

3. More children must adjust to living with step-parents.

Currently, about 40 percent of all marriages which occur in a year are remarriages for one or both partners. By the year 2000, well over half of all children under eighteen will be living with step-parents, rather than with their two biological parents.[5]

4. Divorce of parents causes lasting stress for many children.

Accumulating research findings about the effects of marital conflict and divorce on developing children indicate that divorce causes long-lasting, unresolved emotional problems for many children which may last into adulthood.[6] A national survey of children's health and well-being published in 1991, for example, found that: "children living with single mothers or with mothers and stepfathers were more likely than those living with both biological parents to have repeated a grade of school, to have been expelled, [and] to have been treated for emotional or behavioral problems in the year preceding the interview."[7] This research and other studies have found that children of divorced parents are more likely to suffer from stress-related disorders, such as depression, anxiety, aggressive behavior, frequent headaches and asthma.

5. Being a parent is increasingly stressful.

According to research findings, parenting is becoming increasingly stressful. Data from a national study of mental health, for example, found that between 1957 and 1976, parents reported increasing worries about their children and decreasing satisfaction with the role of being a parent.[8]

6. Being a child is increasingly stressful.

Research compiled from several national surveys finds increasing indicators of stress among children and teenagers since the 1960s. The data for this conclusion comes from the reports of parents, school teachers, and psychotherapists.[9] According to one national survey, for example, the percentage of parents who reported that their child had experienced something seriously disturbing, increased from 27 percent in 1963 to 37 percent in 1976.[10] The most commonly reported disturbing experience was serious marital conflict.

One measure of stress in people's lives is whether they have serious thoughts of suicide. A recent national mental health survey of adolescents found that "25% of boys and 42% of girls reported that they had, at some time in their lives, seriously considered committing suicide."[11]

The Gap between the Ideal and the Real

The social changes of recent decades have largely removed the degrading social stigma of being a divorced person or the child of divorced parents or a single parent. However, these changes could not remove the painful stress caused by the rupture of intimate relations. The social changes also did not lessen the desires of Americans to find ideal, stable, permanent bonds of intimacy in family life.

Public opinion polls reveal that the cultural ideals of Americans about family life have not changed. A national opinion public poll by the Roper organization in 1987, for example, found that nine out of ten Americans regarded being a good parent and having a happy marriage as "very important" elements of success in life.[12] A 1986 poll commissioned by Ethan Allen, Inc. also found that nine out of ten Americans regarded their family as being the most, or one of the most, important element(s) in their lives.[13] American youth are no less insistent on the ideal of finding a stable and satisfying family life. A national survey of college freshman in 1986, for example, found that two-thirds of them regarded raising a family to be very important or essential to satisfaction in life.[14]

The essential point is this: despite the increased acceptance of divorce in cases of unhappy marriage, most Americans retain the ideal of finding intimacy in permanent bonds of family relationships. Americans still seek lasting bonds of love in marriage, and believe that a two-parent, continuing family is the best environment in which to raise children. They resist accepting these intimate attachments as being inevitably temporary and transient. The gap between the ideal and the real in the private sphere of life is, increasingly, causing intolerable stress for a great many Americans.

The Family under Assault by Social Problems

Intimate bonds in family relations have become increasingly fragile, in part because Americans today expect more out of the family than did their ancestors. They now expect to find intimate communication, companionship, expressions of affection, and the sharing of child-rearing and household tasks. Social change has isolated marriage partners from the possibility of finding these satisfactions with their grandparents and brothers and sisters, who now live distant from them. Marriage partners now have only each other to count upon. They expect more out of marriage because they have little alternative.

At the same time, stable family life is threatened by social problems external to the family, which puts even greater burdens upon family relations. Families today live in a social environment which poses more problems for parents and children than it did for the families of their parents and grandparents.

A great number of parents express the opinion that "it is much more difficult to raise children in today's world." A national Louis Harris poll in 1987 found that "74% of the American people are convinced that the problems affecting children have grown worse compared with what they were when they themselves were young."[15]

Parents today must worry about their teenage children ruining their lives if they use dangerous drugs, such as cocaine, "crack," and heroin. Even when the worry is exaggerated, as is often the case, the fear simply adds to parental anxieties. Another parental worry is added in a society where one out of every ten teenage girls gets pregnant, usually unintentionally.[16] Many parents now worry about teenage suicide and suicide attempts (even if needlessly), not surprisingly since suicide has become the second most common cause of adolescent deaths after accidents.[17] The increased violence between teenage gangs is another source of anxiety for parents, especially those living in areas touched by the epidemic of violence. The increased disorder in schools and the declining quality of education adds even more parental stress. In 1987, a national poll revealed that 60 percent of Americans felt that their children were not getting and adequate education.[18]

The Family and Economic Dislocation

On top of all these social problems tearing away at the fabric of family bonds, many families must now deal with the destructive effects of economic dislocation resulting from vast changes in the American economy. Several major economic studies indicate that the average young family with children was more exposed to financial problems in the late 1980s, than any time since the Depression of the 1930s.[19] The economic stress hits most hard those young parents, including single mothers and male heads of households, who have inadequate education to keep up with the skills needed in a changing occupational structure.[20]

The people most affected by the changes are young blue-collar workers, who can no longer aspire to find the kinds of jobs which provided their parents with a home of their own and a reasonably comfortable living. A detailed economic analysis done by the Economic Policy Institute found that: "In 1987, the average family headed by someone between the ages of 25 and 34 had an income 9% lower than their counterparts in 1973."[21] The loss of well paid manufacturing jobs and their replacement, to some extent, by so-called "service jobs" has resulted in a substantial decrease in hourly wages for a great many young blue-collar workers.[22] There is an abundant amount of research which indicates that financial distress in families, caused by loss of jobs and underemployment, commonly produces increased conflict in marital and family relationships.[23]

The Moral Crisis in American Society

Americans' Belief in the Moral Decline of Society

A shared belief in the "moral decline" of one's society is a kind of global expression of discontent. The belief is held by people with quite different values, religious traditionalists and modernists, political conservatives and liberals, each harboring different complaints and each proposing very different solutions. What the global expression asserts is essentially that "something is very wrong" with the value priorities which guide everyday life in American society.

A shared belief in the moral decline of society is a collective perception rather than something that can be measured by any absolute indicators. Nevertheless, when people collectively believe something to be real, it has real consequences in their behavior. The perception arises from a sense of relative deprivation rather than any absolute comparison with the past. It may be argued that the amount of moral corruption has been consistent throughout American history. However, that argument misses the point that the *perception* of moral decline is widespread, even though it may not be accurate.

There is evidence from opinion polls that a great number of Americans feel that "something is very wrong" with the moral condition of American society. The Gallup Organization, for example, asked about people's opinions of the state of moral values in national opinion polls over several decades, with the question: "On the whole, would you say you are satisfied or dissatisfied with the honesty and standards of behavior of people in this country today?" The percentage of people expressing dissatisfaction was 58 percent in 1963, 72 percent in 1973 and 63 percent in 1986.[24] Then, in 1987, the percentage of Americans who expressed dissatisfaction with standards of behavior in the country shot up to 71 percent, about the point it reached during the time of the Watergate scandal.[25]

A national opinion poll done in 1989 for *Parents* magazine found that 75 percent of Americans felt that ethical standards in the country had gotten worse over the last few decades.[26] The widespread perception of moral corruption in American society is painfully distressing for many parents today. They are worried about teaching decent ethical values to their children and resent having to fight a rising tide of revelations about deception and dishonesty in the highest places of power and prestige.

In the late 1980s, news reports of widespread corruption among national political leaders, heads of huge financial enterprises, sports heroes, and even among prominent televangelists probably aggravated the general sentiment that "something is very wrong" with moral-value standards in American society. However, belief in the moral decline of American society is not simply a reaction to passing events. The belief has been held by a majority of Americans for decades.

The Gap between the Ideal and the Real

One of the causes of people's perception of moral decline in American society is the widening gap between the ideal and the real, the gap between publicly preached ideals and people's experience of actual practice.

People, like Americans, who are simultaneously inclined toward puritan moralism in public preachments and the pragmatic pursuit of self-interest in personal concerns, are particularly susceptible to the dilemmas of hypocrisy. Americans tend to get trapped in the dialectic between extremist moral puritans on one side of their culture, and self-centered, amoral "pragmatists" on the other side. The common result is that pretension is more important than substance in behavior. Good "PR" (public relations) is more important for leaders and organizations than their actual conduct. As the conventional wisdom of national politicians goes: "the appearance of honesty is more important than honesty itself."

What is perceived by Americans in their worries about moral decline is the growing moral corruption in society. "Moral corruption" has a special meaning in this context. Moral corruption consists of a kind of lying, in which people's self-presentation differs greatly from their private practice. It may involve outright lying, cheating, breaches of trust, and public relations manipulation of the truth. Moral corruption is essentially dishonesty. That is why public opinion poll questions about the level of honesty in American society get right to the heart of the matter.

The existence of pervasive lying in a society is not reducible to the psychology of individual lying. The issue isn't that "people are never perfect," and practical considerations make it often necessary for people "to shade the truth a bit." Pervasive moral corruption is a sociological phenomenon. When various kinds of lying become commonplace in human relationships, it becomes increasingly necessary: to cover up the truth; to rely upon pretension; and to lie even further to conceal a shameful truth. When lying gets taken for granted as part of self-presentation in a society, it inevitably spreads from one aspect of life to another, from the public sphere to the private sphere. When deception becomes a commonplace practice in a society, it destroys the bonds of trust between people and the collective trust in the institutions of society.[27] When the glue of social trust is destroyed, people begin to suspect that deception and conspiracies are permeating society.

In the experience of the average American today, the moral corruption of society is encountered throughout the institutions of American society. In recent decades, Americans have encountered lying on a grand scale in national politics. The self-righteous lying of Oliver North, Admiral Poindexter, and President Reagan about selling arms to the Iranians in exchange for the desired release of American hostages and the illegal sale of arms to the Nicaraguan "contras" is a dramatic example. Washington, D.C. mayor Marion Barry's more mundane lies about his drug use is another. A great many Americans now simply regard politicians as being liars and are sadly reluctant to believe them, even when they speak the truth.

The newspapers report one case after another of fraud (a form of lying) among multi-millionaires in the Savings and Loan scandal and the various Wall Street scandals. In organized religion, Americans have followed media reports of the lying of Reverend Jim Bakker (financial fraud and perhaps also rape) and Reverend Jimmy Swaggert (using prostitutes while preaching about sinful sex). In national sports, Americans experienced the lies of Pete Rose (about his gambling and tax evasion), Ben Johnson (about his illegal use of steroids), and the lies of lesser sports idols about their use of cocaine. In the field of journalism, a Pulitzer prize–winning story about children using drugs, published in the prestigious *Washington Post* was later found to be a total fabrication. Even in the field of science, Americans now read about cases of fraudulent research studies. Yet, these are only examples on the national level of the kinds of public moral corruption that Americans find closer to home, in their own local communities.

For an example closer to home, consider that recent re-search reveals student cheating has become commonplace; at the same time Americans must worry about their children learning adequate skills in school. Several studies have found, for example, that between one-third and one-half of high school and college students regularly "cheat" their way through school, by doing such things as cheating on tests and copying the work of other students to hand in to class.[28] Today, many students who cheat are proud of their cleverness, and angry, rather than embarrassed, about receiving any punishment when caught. This ought not be surprising. Young people are merely following the public role-models of "successful" political leaders, sports idols, and popular entertainers. The concern for American society is that people who learn to cheat their way through life will also rely upon cheating in their work and family life.

A great many parents and teachers today express concern about the prevailing moral values of children. Recent research indicates that serious concern for the moral values of America's children is warranted. In 1990, Louis Harris and Associates published a survey of the moral attitudes of a sample of five thousand elementary and high school children.[29] The survey found that 65 percent of high school students admitted that they would cheat on an important examination if they had a chance to do so; 53 percent would lie to protect a friend who vandalized school property. An absence of parental guidance was evident in the children's responses to the survey: 41 percent of the children reported that their behavior usually goes unpunished by their parents if they do something wrong. The survey found that the older children became, the more likely they were to justify lying and cheating. The study's research director said, in a newspaper interview, that there is "reason for despair," because few people and institutions, including parents, schools, and churches, seem to be taking the moral education of our children seriously.[30]

Value Conflicts in American Culture

Another reason for the widespread perception of moral decline in American society is hidden cultural conflict, which is much more intense in the U.S. than it is in European societies. American society is going through many of the same social changes that are creating newly emergent values in all post-industrial societies.[31] These newer values clash with older, traditional values, thus causing a lot of cultural contradictions and value conflicts.

The newer, modernist values tend to emphasize autonomy and internal self-control in personal conduct, plus freedom from unnecessary external constraints and tolerance for individual differences in social relationships. Traditional values, in contrast, tend to emphasize responsibility and loyalty to family, religion, and nation, and obedience to traditional authority in these groups. In essence, the contradiction is between the goals of personal fulfillment and responsibility to others, personal freedom versus compliance to established authority. This cultural contradiction is certainly nothing new. However, underlying structural changes in industrial societies have served to widen the breach between these two equally necessary requirements for social life.

The contradictions between these two general value orientations in American culture are played out in conflicts over many "trip-wire" social issues, such as abortion, the rights of homosexuals, social policies regarding the AIDS epidemic, the role of women in the family and workplace, government funded day-care, prayer in public schools, the differences between art and pornography, multiculturalism in public school education, and the meaning of patriotism. These issues of symbolic value conflict have dominated American politics since the 1960s. The situation has been termed a "cultural civil war."[32] Its seriousness can easily be underestimated, because the aggressive hostility is expressed in political struggle rather than in violence.

The Republican Party presidential convention of 1992 proposed making "cultural war" on cultural liberals on behalf of traditional family values. The theme didn't have the mass appeal that cultural conservatives had hoped it would. The attempt to find scapegoats, such as homosexuals and feminists, to blame for social problems in order to distract voters from economic concerns failed to light a fire.

Modernists tend to support freedom of personal choice in abortion, tolerance for homosexuals, flexible roles for women and men in family life, equal opportunity for employed men and women, and multiculturalism in education, while they tend to oppose unquestioning nationalism and mandated religious practice in any form.

Traditionalists, in contrast, tend to oppose "permissiveness" toward abortion, regard homosexuality as either sin or sickness, support traditional sex-role distinctions between men and women, prefer education to stress matters of American national pride, want more religious expression in public institutions, and condemn harsh criticism of the nation, especially in times of war, as being unpatriotic. Traditionalists tend to regard much of the social change since the 1960s as signs of increased immorality, as deviance from the expectations of religion and nation. They regard tolerance of abortion, homosexuals, open expressions of sexuality in the media, and criticism of the country, as being indulgence of sin and selfishness and they are angry about it.

Most Americans are torn between both traditional and modernist values and find themselves pulled and pushed in both directions. Americans, for example, want "family values" of responsibility to the family unit, but they also want freedom of choice for unhappily married partners to divorce. Americans want women to be free to choose a satisfying career as well as marriage, but they are reluctant to support that choice with a system of publicly funded, professional child-care services, as has been done in other countries. A majority of Americans today generally value tolerance toward diverse ethnic minorities, but they don't want to have to learn about ethnic histories of oppression in America. Americans want all their countrymen to share freedom of conscience, but they want people to stop criticizing the government when the government goes to war.

The impact these persistent cultural value conflicts have on average Americans is to create frustration and anger over their society's seeming inability to make practical compromises and go forward in dealing with basic everyday problems. As is often the case when there are basic value conflicts in a society, extremists on different sides of an issue dominate the arena of political struggle and "the tail wags the dog." The incessant subterranean conflict causes people to feel that society is blocked and powerless to deal with the practical problems of crime, economic dislocation, and the declining quality of education.

Feelings of Alienation and Powerlessness
The people who are most deeply affected by the perceived moral crisis are those Americans who hold traditional moral values. Coincidentally, a great many of them are also the same people who are under greatest stress from the economic changes in society. They are people with an inadequate education and at greatest risk of losing their jobs due to economic dislocation.[33] They are concentrated in rural and small town areas and in blue-collar areas of cities. Even though a majority of the American people are disturbed with the state of morality in society, these people are the most disturbed. On general principle, the people who benefit most from a social system and are most privileged by it, are also those who are most likely to justify the system as it is.

Pollster Louis Harris reports that feelings of alienation and powerlessness among Americans have been increasing steadily since the late 1960s.[34] In 1986, about 60 percent of Americans expressed feelings of alienation from the social order and feelings of powerlessness to make any changes for the better, compared with only about 29 percent in 1966. The people who are most likely to feel alienated are, again, those people with the least education and poorest paying jobs. It should not be surprising that as a result, more and more of these people don't bother to vote.

Louis Harris suggests that the feelings of alienation stem from people's perception of moral corruption and injustice in American society, a society in which wealthy and powerful law-breakers go unpunished.[35] Harris regards these attitudes as being quite worrisome and observes:

The price that might be paid if the alienated ever became openly hostile could be enormous, with overtones that would be traumatic. The trouble is that no one really knows what the breaking point might be for these literally millions of people. But when over 100 million adults say that they feel alienated from the establishment leadership, a national condition exists that cannot continue to be ignored.[36]

Why have "Satanists" been invented as scapegoat deviants for the social stresses and internal social conflicts which currently beset American society? Part of the answer lies in the fact that other convenient fantasy scapegoat targets, such as the Communist conspiracy to take over America, no longer fit the circumstances in late twentieth-century America. New scapegoats must be found.

A deeper explanation, however, can be found in the symbolism of Satan as the agent of evil forces and moral corruption. The symbol of Satan is a perfect metaphor for the widespread belief that American society is in moral decline. The symbolism fits perfectly into the religious and cultural heritage particular to American society; Americans have held from the beginning that America is "the promised land" for moral remnants of "old world" Europe. Americans, from the landing of the *Mayflower* onwards, have regarded their society as being more morally righteous than the nations of the decadent old world. Moralistic self-righteousness has consistently been the lens through which Americans have seen themselves as a people among peoples in the world.[37] And, as a righteous people, they have come to expect to be rewarded as a people, with abundant economic opportunities. Now, Americans may have doubts about their self-perceived national identity.

Chapter Ten
The Search for Scapegoat Deviants

There is nothing that makes us feel so good as the idea that someone else is an evildoer.
Robert Lynd[1]

The Social Construction of Imaginary Deviants

Sometimes societies invent new forms of deviance in order to have scapegoats for deep social tensions.[2] New social deviants are sometimes invented when rapid social change in a society results in widespread dislocation in people's lives, and the resulting frustration, fear, and anger, in turn, causes a great many people to seek scapegoats to blame. These scapegoats are "invented" by moral crusaders who target categories of social deviants to bear the blame for threats to a society's past way of life and its basic moral values.

The labels that a society uses to identify a new category of deviance embody socially constructed stereotypes, which are attributed to a category of people regarded as being deviant.[3]

For example, the labels "murderer," "rapist," and "child molester" convey deviant stereotypes. In reality, the actual personality patterns and behavior of people involved in these forms of deviance are quite different from the imaginary stereotypes. In some situations, socially constructed labels for newly defined forms of deviance may precede the actual existence of any behavior or persons which fit the stereotypes embodied in the labels. Such was the case of the label "heretic" in the Middle Ages and "subversive" in the 1950s.

Eventually, moral crusades and witch hunts for social deviants, such as "subversives," "heretics," "witches," or "satanists," set society on a path, whereby individuals are found who seem to confirm the stereotype embodied in the deviant label.[4] In other words, moral crusades may be aimed at deviance which does not exist, and may even create a social type of deviant which did not previously exist, by seeking out, apprehending, and punishing some people. Paradoxically, widespread witch hunts, inquisitions, purges, and persecutions function to confirm the existence of new forms of social deviance.[5]

The labels "Satanism" and "Satanic cult" are socially constructed stereotypes. In actual social usage, the label "Satanism" has vague and elastic meanings. In small town newspaper articles, the label "Satanist" is applied loosely to a wide assortment of social deviants, including: teenage vandals, animal mutilators, and gang murderers; and adult psychopathic murderers, child molesters, and vicious rapists. Similarly, the label "Satanic cult" is used to refer to such widely different groups as juvenile delinquent gangs, unconventional religious groups, and Mafia-style criminal syndicates, all of which are supposedly motivated by worship of the Devil. The point is that claims, rumors, and allegations about criminal Satanism and Satanic cults ultimately arise from people's socially constructed predisposition to find Satanism in many unrelated incidents and activities.

As a form of collective behavior, the Satanic cult scare is a moral crusade similar to the "Red Scare" of the 1950s, albeit on a much lesser scale. It is a witch hunt for moral "subversives" and criminals. There isn't any agreed upon term to describe this pattern of collective behavior. It has been called a moral crusade, a witch hunt, or mass hysteria. However, none of these terms convey the complexity and variation of the social processes involved.

The classic case is that of the European witch-hunting craze, which lasted from the fifteenth through the seventeenth century. The frequent waves of anti-Semitic persecutions, beginning in the twelfth century and continuing through the twentieth century, are another familiar set of examples. In the United States, the anti-Catholic movement of the 1840s through the 1850s and the anti-Communist witch hunts of the 1950s are other examples.

Social Conflict and the Creation of Scapegoat Deviants
When individuals build up tension from frustration, anger, and fear, they very commonly release their tension in angry attacks upon other people whom they blame for their feelings. For example, when a young husband is suddenly fired from his job, he may come home and verbally attack his wife or kick the family dog. The psychological mechanism is well known. It's called displacement or displaced aggression. We may all use it unintentionally from time to time because it temporarily reduces our feelings of tension. Similarly, when groups of people accumulate a lot of welled-up tension, the collective social process is the same. Groups seek scapegoats to blame, in part, because scapegoating temporarily reduces tension within groups.

However, the creation of scapegoat targets in a society is not only a collective extension of psychological processes. The creation of scapegoat targets tells us a lot about internal social dynamics in a society, because it is also a product of social conflict within a society.

The Search for External Enemies
Societies experiencing a lot of internal conflict and tension often seek common external enemies as a way to unify the conflicting elements within the society. The threat of an external enemy

functions to pull together conflicting parties within a society and deflects attention and activity away from their grievances against each other. It pushes them to cooperate with each other and to put less emphasis upon defining their differences. Hostility directed at a common external enemy usually causes conflicting groups to set aside, at least temporarily, their hostilities towards each other.

When a society perceives an external enemy, whether or not there exists any genuine threat to that society's security, it collectively manufactures an evil enemy image.[6] The evil enemy image is a stereotype of the enemy group, which portrays the enemy as having those qualities which are considered most immoral in that society. It is a reverse mirror image of one's own society. Onto it, we project all those qualities we most detest and condemn, the ones that violate our culture's highest values. The evil enemy is seen as having no moral scruples whatsoever.

This contrast stereotype of the evil enemy allows people to exaggerate their own virtues. In contrast to the evil enemy, they grow angel's wings. It also discourages any penetrating criticism of the society by internal dissenters, who would immediately be viewed as traitors. The stereotype of Communist "fanatics" and of the "evil empire" of Communism served this social function in American society starting in the late 1940s.[7] Other evil enemy stereotypes held by Americans have been those embodied in the labels "Japs," "Huns," and Indian "savages."

The Search for Internal Enemies
A search for internal enemies can serve the same function of providing a target for displaced aggression and a unifying force for conflicting elements in a society. This is done by defining some social category of people as being traitors to, or deviants from, the over-arching moral values of a society. When moral values are in dispute in a society, a witch hunt for moral subversives serves the purpose of clarifying and redefining the limits of moral conduct.

The internal enemy can be a useful proxy target, a stand-in, for attacks between powerful conflicting elements in a society. Conflicting groups can direct their attacks safely against the proxy target, without having to engage each other directly. Normally, a society dares not choose genuinely powerful internal enemies to function as scapegoat targets.

Research on American racism illustrates this social dynamic. American scapegoating of Black people becomes more common when there is heightened internal conflict between groups of white people in society. One research study, for example, found a high correlation between the frequency of lynchings of Blacks in the South and periods of economic stress and social conflict arising from sharp drops in the price paid to farmers for cotton.[8] Another study found greater racist behavior in areas of the country in which there was greater income inequality between white people than in areas where the income differences between whites was much less.[9] In Europe, Jews have traditionally served this unifying social function of being a proxy scapegoat target for conflicting groups of Christians.

These same conflict-unifying social functions of scapegoating are also found in small groups.[10] Research on family relationships, for example, has found that conflict-ridden marriages sometimes keep a "united front" by scapegoating a child in the family.[11] Marriage partners can displace their hostilities towards each other by blaming a child for their marital discord. The scapegoated child may actually be responsible for some disturbing behavior, but it gets exaggerated and distorted in the eyes of its parents. In some cases, the behavior may even be entirely a product of the parents' invention. Moreover, the two parents fight each other through their attacks upon the child. Thereby, on the surface at least, they may seem to be cooperating effectively. One of the consequences for the child can be emotional harm.

The fact that the internal enemy, or deviant category, need not actually exist in the society (but is instead socially constructed through the scapegoating process) is recognized by the eminent sociological theorist, Lewis Coser.

> The inner enemy who is looked for, like the outer enemy who is evoked, may actually exist: he may be a dissenter who has opposed certain aspects of group life or group action and who is

considered a potential renegade or heretic. But the inner enemy also may be "found," he may simply be invented, in order to bring about through a common hostility toward him the social solidarity which the group so badly needs . . . If men define a threat as real, although there may be little or nothing in reality to justify this belief, the threat is real in its consequences—and among these consequences is the increase in group cohesion.[12]

When a society invents an internal enemy, it creates an evil enemy image of it, much the same as that of an external enemy. The internal enemy is seen as being deviant from the basic ideals which justify the accepted organization of society. In other words, they threaten the moral order of society. They subvert the very foundations of a society. These are no ordinary criminals.

The Invention of Satanists as Internal Enemies

The Satanic cult scare arises from: deep-seated frustrations in American society; feelings of alienation and powerlessness to deal with attacks on society's moral order; and the feeling that something beyond people's control has caused "things to become very wrong."

Dangerous, criminal Satanists and Satanic cults are an "invented" internal enemy. The Satanism scare serves the unifying function of a search for evil internal enemies. This new imaginary menace is particularly useful at a time when belief in the internal threat from Communist "subversives" is no longer taken seriously. It brings together some fundamentalist Protestants and conservative Catholics who have been long-lasting conflicting parties over many issues in American society. It joins them with some secular child advocates and feminists, with whom religious traditionalists are currently in conflict over a wide range of family issues. It joins many secular police officers, social workers, and psychotherapists together with some Christian fundamentalist evangelists, groups which normally would be a bit distrustful of each other's credibility and authority.

People holding conflicting ideologies can share, for quite different reasons, the common search for the evil internal enemy and cooperate in the effort. Religious traditionalists can fight Satan's evil influences in American society and secular professionals can fight vicious criminal elements. They can each interpret the threat through the lens of their own differing ideologies. Moreover, they can attack each other through the proxy target of Satanism. They can accuse each other of subverting the moral order of society, without engaging each other directly in a way which might be disruptive to the functioning of society.

The Increasing Search for Scapegoats

The social construction of Satanists as scapegoat deviants to blame for social stress is part of a more general pattern of increased scapegoating in American society. This was already evident in the 1988 presidential race. The Bush campaign made scapegoating respectable by using the stereotype of violent Black criminals in its Willy Horton campaign ads.

There is solid evidence that the scapegoating of all kinds of groups has increased in recent years. Newspaper articles from around the country in 1990 reported an upsurge in hate crimes directed at Black people, Hispanics, and Asian-Americans.[13] A study done by the National Institute Against Prejudice and Violence at the University of Maryland found that racist incidents were reported at more than three hundred college campuses between 1987 and 1991.[14] The racist incidents included anonymous harassment messages by mail and telephone, racist fraternity pranks, and even physical assaults.

Attacks upon homosexuals and people perceived to be homosexuals have greatly increased in recent years. The number of acts of serious harassment and violence against homosexual men and women, including robberies, assaults, and murders, more than doubled between 1985 and 1987, according to reports by several agencies.[15]

Anti-Semitic scapegoating has also increased greatly. An annual survey of anti-Semitic hate crimes done by the Anti-Defamation League of the B'nai B'rith reported a sudden 12 percent increase in such crimes from 1986 to 1988, after a period of decline. In 1990, the Anti-Defamation League reported the highest number of anti-Semitic hate crimes since it began keeping records of them in 1979.[16] Anti-Semitic incidents on college campuses increased 36 percent in 1990 alone. Anti-Semitic hate crimes included the vandalism and bombing of Jewish synagogues, vandalism of Jewish cemeteries and businesses, and harassment and assaults against individual Jews.[17]

When a society relies upon scapegoating processes to manage its internal conflicts, the consequences create even more problems. The fantasy warfare prevents the people in a society from finding real solutions to real problems. It perpetuates latent, stagnating conflict, which impedes the society's ability to adapt to change. When conflicting parties don't confront each other in realistic conflict and work out practical compromises, they cannot innovate solutions to the underlying conditions which cause social stress. The submerged conflicts go on and on and the conflict-ridden society, much like a conflict-ridden family, finds itself unable to make adaptive changes.

Society and the Problem of Evil

In a sociological sense, evil always exists in a society in the form of everything which is deviant from a society's highest moral values.[18] When the basic moral values of a society are in crisis, the people of that society seek to explain what is happening to them by attributing the cause to some agent or force which embodies all the evils which are the opposite of their highest values.

In the cultural heritage of all societies, there exists a ready-made explanation of the origins and workings of the evil which threatens to undermine the most cherished values of a society. Anthropologists call this culturally inherited explanation of evil, a "demonology."[19] A demonology is usually an elaborate set of interrelated folk beliefs about the workings of evil, which may be only partly conveyed in official religious teachings.

In the demonology of Western, Christian societies, Satan and human agents who do Satan's work have been attributed as the ultimate source of evil.[20] Belief in the existence of the Devil and his (its) active involvement in human affairs tends to increase during times of social turmoil and moral crisis. The growing belief in the existence of the Devil is another symptom of the moral crisis in American society.

Over the decades since the 1960s, an increasing number of Americans resurrected a belief in the Devil as the ultimate origin of evil. Survey research found that 37 percent of Americans were certain about the existence of the Devil in 1964, and by 1973 the percentage rose to 50 percent.[21] A Gallup poll in 1990 found that 55 percent to 60 percent of Americans affirmed a belief in the Devil's existence.[22] Traditionalist Protestants, especially fundamentalists, are most likely to view the Devil as a supernatural being, actively tempting individuals into immorality. In contrast, modernist, mainline Protestants and Catholics are much more likely to regard the Devil as some kind of impersonal force.[23]

Belief in the Devil is more prevalent among Americans than it is among the peoples of any other major industrial society. In France, for example, only about 17 percent of the people affirm such a belief, while in Great Britain, the percentage is 21 percent and in Germany, it is 25 percent.[24]

Given the particular cultural heritage of Americans, so many of whom regard the Devil as an active reality in the world, it should not be surprising that "Devil worshippers" have been socially constructed as scapegoat deviants to blame for the social turmoil and moral crisis in American society. The possible existence of earthly agents of Satan is entirely consistent with the ideological fears of religious traditionalists. It does not require a great leap of faith for many of them to believe that Devil worshipping agents of Satan are at work behind much of the immorality and perversion in American society.

However, what is more curious is that many people who do not hold a traditionalist religious ideology are also swept up in the Satanic cult scare. The explanation may be that the Satanic demonology remains a powerful metaphor for the workings of evil even for some professionals, who are, after all, socialized in American culture.

Thus, secular professionals see evil in the sexual abuse of children, and some of them find it easily credible that "Satanist" Devil worshippers perpetrate such heinous crimes. Secular professionals see evil at work among teenagers who use dangerous drugs, commit acts of random violence, and or kill themselves. Some of them can easily believe that these problems are sometimes a product of "Devil worship." Police see evil at work in the acts of psychopathic murderers who kill with sadistic enjoyment. Some police officers find it quite reasonable to believe that there are hundreds of these miscreants on the loose in our society, organized into "Devil worshipping" cults that engage in ritual human sacrifice and even cannibalism.

In times of moral crisis, people believe that unbelievable evil can easily happen. When newspaper reports of moral outrage follow one after another, people are inclined to believe that even worse outrages are still to be uncovered.

Scapegoating the Shadow

There is a final element in this broad picture of the Satanism scare. The Satanism scare is all too obviously focussed upon parental anxieties about children: the allegations about ritual child abuse, the fears about teenage Satanism and potential suicide, the search for Satanic influences in children's books and games, and even the rumors about Satanic cult ritual sacrifices of children which prompt rumor-panics. All these are expressions of concern about perceived threats to children. So, it may easily be concluded that the underlying anxiety which gives such power to the contemporary Satanic cult legend derives from fears for the safety of our children. On the social psychological level of reality, that conclusion is quite convincing.

However, on a deeper, psychodynamic level of analysis, we find something quite different and a bit disturbing. We know from studies of evil enemy images and from research about the scapegoat stereotyping in small groups and in whole societies, that the evil which is perceived is a projection of those qualities people collectively condemn most strongly in themselves as a group.[25] These images of evil are capable of generating so much moral outrage because they are reverse mirror images of what people dislike most in themselves and cannot face consciously.

Furthermore, the conventional image of Satan is exactly this kind of projective mirror of the self. It enables people, individually and collectively, to project outward all their own self-perceived "sins" and shortcomings. By hating Satan, they are able to convince themselves that they need not feel guilt or responsibility for those things they most passionately condemn.

Jungian psychologists call this process "projecting one's shadow."[26] According to this theoretical notion, our "shadow" consists of all those things about ourself which are the opposite of our basic values but nevertheless are still part of our identity. Our "shadow" is everything about which we feel guilt, shame, and regret. It is hidden, in a sense, from our daily thoughts about our conduct because it is too painful to think about. So, we deny the existence of our "shadow" and condemn it by condemning the moral "evils" which most outrage us in others. The essence of this process is denial and projection. As the cliché points out: we hate most those qualities in others which we dislike most in ourselves.

The scapegoat deviance of Satanism can be viewed as a projection of serious unconscious inner conflicts in the feelings of a great many parents about how they relate to their children. As noted in Chapter Nine, there is a lot of parental guilt today. Many parents feel guilty about leaving their children at child-care centers, or about having little time to spend talking with their children, or about being reluctant to use their authority to guide their children's choice of entertainments and friends, or about feeling unable to guide the moral values of their children. Furthermore, the projected "shadow" may also reflect parental feelings of ambivalence and even hostility toward children, born out of conflicted feelings that the children they love are a stressful burden in their already stressful lives.

The essential quality of supposed Satanists is that they do evil things to children. If Satanism is a projected "shadow" for inner conflicts which are difficult to face consciously, then we Americans are telling ourselves that we regret the ways we mistreat our children.[27]

es of devil w... ...ip,

ice scare stud...

...of Satan

'Mass Hyste...

...anks, but the fascinat...
...ave with the...
...d sales'

...vate proper...
Frank Baranya...

Rumors C...se

Cult rumors

...ool's attendance
...ut he was also
...gly intelligent
...d to the...

..."You'll find..."
a kic...

...ational at...
the meeting...
A later meet...
...g and DUI la...
...roblem

...nic Rumors

...ie, but the...
...e to the problem

...d he to...
...sk afte...
...tudents
...lewoo...
...tene...
...out the acc...

weave terror

Witch-hun...

through stat...

e Chief Calv...
County Juve...
r Earl Brown
...ssure parent...
...ncerns there.

launched ov...

...ne caller said he was concern...
...about a friend in...

...the ru...

...So...h Caroli...

...ve all proved...

rumors rattle

...mci-

rumors spi...
and into oth...
Corry school...

...s be-
...r or later, the
...s the county
...Days ago,
...rie County

...stantiated.

However, Br...
really blame th...
— that's their b...
tan."

...ced in   Part of the problem is not simply

...eaching Rumors Trigg... ...ear, An...

— Rumors   als.
...ndarie...
...ua Cou...
...d school
...wn are...

...lice employee who...
...n i...
pe...
...ha...

...han-
...ne...

unnecessary dis...

Rumor Calls
Swamp Police

...lig...
...n...

rents, as have those in the near...
...estern and Panama hi...
...e parents were repo...
...youngsters hor...
...enteeism w...
...norn...

Satanis... ...exper

gives a g...

...some

warning...

...are

... officials and their Pennsylvania
...erparts have found is that the
...ve taken up a good deal of
...ors' time, caused

...cluding
...like g...
All...
sa...

...ors feed satanism fears,

...t activ...
high school
of students
...harm, ani-
...tilated, and
...occult ritu-

..."It...
are hearin...
They (rumors)...
everywhere," said a...

...ie Incidents In

...cial...

...rs of devil

...ipers in area

...unty on edge

Also a...
dinner for ho...
held on May 25. This...
with 3.5 or higher grade-...
ages will be honored.

...ree s...
...rogram
...t feels ne...
The...

...e city of C...
a smoking ordin...
one passed last...
council. "I don't
plac...

Voting aga...
busi...

...enteeism
...phone calls...
...ades sev-

...ult rumors stir up Maine towr...

...rent budget of 27 mills
...was accepted, with hopes of trimm-
ing it to 26 or 26.5 mill...

...ct for

...Eberhardt...
Police said.

...out there wa...

Satanic stories still stirring fe...

Grice also said...
expect council to l...

...a pre-

...who are unhappy over ear-...

Plate 1. [preceding page] **Montage of Actual Newspaper Headlines.**

Plate 2. **Frames from Cartoon Gospel Tract.**
Frames from the cartoon Gospel tract, "The Poor Little Witch," found at
the "hundred acre lot" in Jamestown. The story is an example of fundamentalist religious propaganda, which uses the Satanic cult conspiracy theory.
(Reproduced by permission of Chick Publications, Chino, CA.)

Plate 3.
Ritual Abuse Projective Test Picture Card.
A projective test picture card used to investigate suspected Satanic cult ritual abuse, designed for psychotherapy with children. An example of the incorporation of the Satanic cult legend into psychotherapy. (Reproduced by permission of Northwest Psychological Publishers, Inc., Redding, CA.)

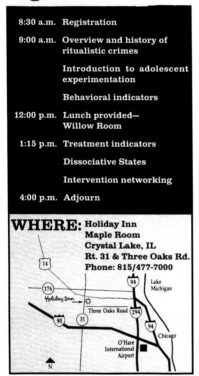

Presenters:
Robert J. Simandl
and
Pamala Klein, M.S.

Date: **Thursday, January 10, 1991**
Time: **8:30 a.m. to 4:00 p.m.**

ABOUT THE PRESENTERS

Robert "Jerry" Simandl, Youth Officer;
Jerry is a 24 year veteran of the Gang Crimes Unit of the Chicago Police Department, and an internationally recognized authority on ritualistic crime and abuse. His work has been cited by numerous publications, the media, and training videos throughout the United States. He has made presentations on levels of involvement including warning signs, investigation aspects and the nature of crimes. In addition, he is a police consultant for the Center of Childhood Trauma at Forest Hospital.

Pamala Klein, M.S., Therapist;
Pam is a therapist, based out of Chicago. She is recognized internationally as a lecturer, therapist, program developer and consultant on sexual and ritualistic abuse. Her training has been used by clinicians and law enforcement agencies. She has developed intervention programs for sexually abused children and is Clinical Program Director of the Center for Childhood Trauma at Forest Hospital.

Agenda:

8:30 a.m.	Registration
9:00 a.m.	Overview and history of ritualistic crimes
	Introduction to adolescent experimentation
	Behavioral indicators
12:00 p.m.	Lunch provided— Willow Room
1:15 p.m.	Treatment indicators
	Dissociative States
	Intervention networking
4:00 p.m.	Adjourn

WHERE: Holiday Inn
Maple Room
Crystal Lake, IL
Rt. 31 & Three Oaks Rd.
Phone: 815/477-7000

Plate 4. **Advertisement for a Ritualistic Child Abuse Seminar.** An advertisement for a seminar on ritualistic child abuse for police officers and psychotherapists. The seminar featured moral crusaders "Jerry" Simandl and Pamala Klein, whose activities helped to spread the Satanic cult scare to England. (Reproduced by permission of Forest Health Systems, Inc., Des Plaines, IL.)

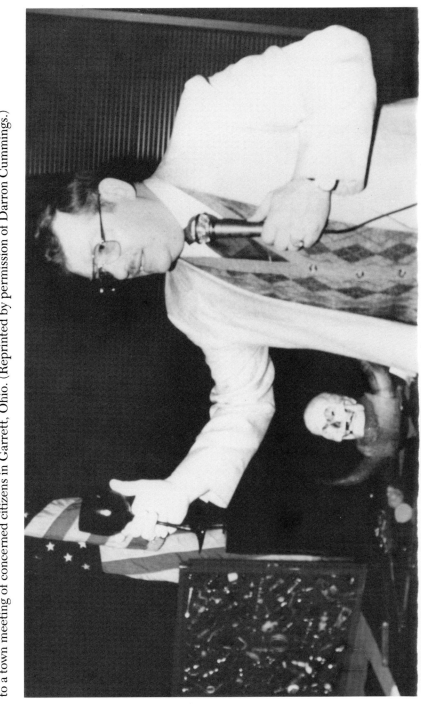

Plate 5. **Police Satan Hunter Speaking at Town Meeting.**
Many local police Satan hunters spread Satanic cult conspiracy fears across small town America. This one is speaking to a town meeting of concerned citizens in Garrett, Ohio. (Reprinted by permission of Darron Cummings.)

Plate 6. **Police Satan Hunters in Front of Alleged Satanic Graffiti.** Police Satan hunters commonly interpret teenage graffiti as a sign that local teenagers are involved in criminal Satanic cults. (Reprinted by permission of the *Fort Lauderdale Sun-Sentinel*.)

Plate 7. **Pat Pulling, a Prominent Moral Crusader.** Pat Pulling has been one of the most active moral crusaders, spreading fears of criminal Satanic cults, which she claims are trying to attract teenagers through rock music and *Dungeons and Dragons* games. (Reprinted by permission of the Richmond Newspapers, Virginia.)

Plate 8. **Early Print Showing Witches Cooking Children.** Stories about the ritual murder and cannibalism of children was one of the most common accusations against witches. Current allegations of Satanic cult ritual abuse of children replicate those stories. (Source: Francesco Mario Guazzo, *Compenium Maleficarum,* 1608.)

Plate 9. **Nineteenth-Century Engraving Depicting a Salem Witchcraft Trial.**
The social processes which underlie the current Satanic cult scare are similar to those which caused the Salem witch hunt. (This engraving by Howard Pyle is taken from *Harper's New Monthly Magazine* December 1892, and was obtained from the Peabody and Essex Museum, Salem, MA.)

Chapter Eleven
The Rhetoric of the Moral Crusade against Satanism

Mass movements can rise and spread without a belief in God, but never without belief in a devil.

Eric Hoffer,
The True Believer[1]

Moral Crusades and Moral Crusaders

In the social construction of a newly defined form of deviance, some activists must take initiative in alerting the public to the newly recognized "evil" in society. These activists strive to influence public opinion, so that the "evil" they see will also be seen by most other people in a society. In essence, these activists are propagandists for a new vision of evil, or more properly, they are moral crusaders. The moral crusaders against Satanism are simultaneously responding to, and further promoting, the Satanic cult scare, just as the anti-Communist crusaders responded to and promoted the "Red Scare" of the 1950s.

The term "moral crusader," when used in a sociological sense, is not pejorative. It refers to people who play the roles of activists in a social movement aimed at fighting a social "evil" which they perceive to exist in a society.[2] In the American past, moral crusaders have often been powerful agents in reshaping public opinion about previously unrecognized social "evils."[3] Moral crusaders in the past have included abolitionists, prohibitionists, and crusaders against white slavery. In current times, they include feminist activists fighting the exploitation of women, environmental activists fighting pollution, activists fighting against drunk driving, and activists fighting against abortion. The anti-Satanism crusade is most similar to the anti-Catholic crusade of the 1840s and the anti-Communist crusade of the 1950s.[4]

Moral crusades are not limited to any particular religious or political ideology. Liberals as well as conservatives may be activists in moral crusades. Today, environmental crusaders, for example, are trying to transform the meaning of behavior such as the dumping of chemical waste products into rivers in such a way that the behavior can be regarded as deviating from fundamental moral values. Feminist crusaders are trying to influence Americans to redefine as deviant certain forms of behavior which were previously taken for granted, such as refusing to hire people for jobs because they are women and paying women lower salaries than men for the same work. A good example of the definition and negotiation of a new form of deviance is that embodied in the label sexual harassment.

There should be no mystery about the motivations of moral crusaders. Their dedication to the cause of dramatizing previously unrecognized evil flows from humanitarian desires to help people who are afflicted by the unrecognized evil.[5] Their motivation arises from their moral values and vision of a moral society, rather than from self-interest. It is often rooted in a religious ideology, or sometimes in a secular political ideology. Contrary to popular preconceptions, the research on activists in social movements does not find any particular personality traits which distinguish such people.[6] Their antagonists, however, will see them as motivated merely by some possible self-interest, such as power or money or public adulation. It is also true that some leaders who follow in the path of moral crusaders are motivated by these base and practical considerations, but that is possible only after a moral crusade has had some success.

A moral crusade needs to be viewed as a symbolic crusade because it is a collective attempt to reaffirm, or modify, the symbolic moral values of a culture. Some moral crusades reactively attempt to reaffirm older, declining values. In contrast, other moral crusades proactively attempt to establish newly emergent values. One dangerous consequence of these symbolic crusades arises when they turn into witch hunts for deviants. Since the primary goal of these social movements is to affirm symbolic higher values, the guilt or innocence of individuals accused of deviance from those values is likely to be a less significant concern for moral crusaders.[7] Moral crusaders who are unfamiliar with the details of specific cases are likely to assume the guilt of those who are accused. In moral crusades, there is always social pressure to publicly dramatize the evil and to make symbolic examples of particular cases.

Symbolic crusades and politics are inevitably intertwined. Moral crusaders usually attempt to attack the evils they see in society by getting new laws passed to criminalize the behavior they regard as being deviant. The feminist movement, for example, is aimed at making lasting changes in some of the basic values which guide male-female relationships in everyday life, but it inevitably became political when it sought new laws to produce change.

One of the distinctive characteristics of contemporary moral crusaders is that they are compelled to validate their moral vision on the basis of scientific expertise. Today, moral crusaders seek the advice of scientific authorities to help them elaborate their claims and make them more widely persuasive. Environmental crusaders, for example, need the technical expertise of biological and physical scientists to validate their claims about the evils of environmental degradation. Most commonly, however, moral crusaders today seek the assistance of medical and psychiatric experts.[8] The moral crusade which shaped the definition of "child abuse," for example, relies heavily upon medical and psychiatric judgment about what constitutes abuse. So too, the moral crusaders against Satanism seek the assistance of mental health experts in providing credibility for their claims.

Diagram 1 presents a model of the social processes through which a moral crusade, drawing upon a contemporary legend, can lead to the social construction of deviant behavior, such as Satanic cult crime.

Moral Crusaders against Satanism

Moral crusaders against Satanism include: 1) some fundamentalist clergymen; 2) local police Satan hunters; 3) volunteers in anti-cult organizations; 4) some child protection social workers; and 5) some mental health professionals. Small town reporters and television talk show hosts commonly rely upon these moral crusaders as their primary sources of information when they quote the views of so-called experts. In doing so, the mass media disseminate their claims to a wider audience. (However, the claims don't originate in the mass media.)

These different categories of moral crusaders each have different kinds of occupational expertise, which leads them to focus their efforts upon specific evils attributed to Satanism. Fundamentalist clergymen, for example, regard Satanism as a kind of evil religious heresy, which is aimed at subverting the moral foundations of society. Anti-cult organization leaders focus their activities on fighting Satanism, which they regard as being a new kind of religious cult influence among teenagers. Police "Satan hunters" are primarily concerned with "ritualistic" crimes supposedly committed by Satanists, such as cemetery vandalism, the killing of domestic animals, the defacing of property with graffiti, child kidnappings, murders, and suicides. Child protection workers are primarily concerned about "ritual" child abuse by Satanists. Mental health professionals focus their activities upon Multiple Personality Disorder patients, who claim to have been victims during childhood of "ritual abuse" by Satanic cults.

Even though these different moral crusaders have differing primary concerns, they constantly network with each other through many agencies of contact and communication. These

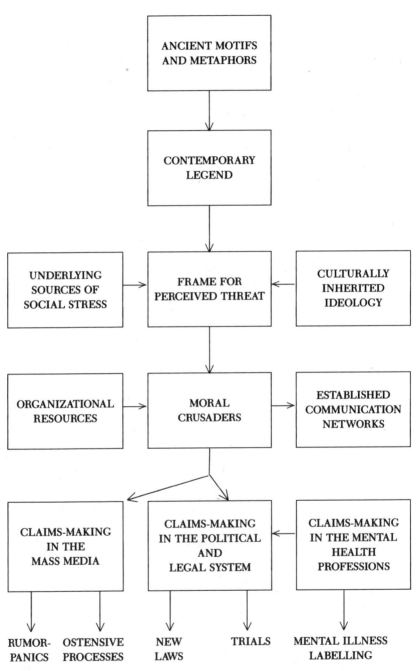

Diagram 1. Model for the Dissemination of Claims in a Moral Crusade to Socially Construct a New Form of Deviant Behavior.

agencies include police seminars on "ritualistic" crime, child protection conferences on "ritual" child abuse, professional psychiatric conferences on Multiple Personality Disorder, and community meetings in churches and schools about teenage Satanism. The networking enables the moral crusaders to assist each other by sharing the different types of professional expertise they possess. The constant networking also enables them to forge alliances and coalitions, and to share resources with each other.

Rhetorical Claims as Moral Propaganda

The claims of moral crusaders serve to construct a definition of a new form of deviance through rhetorical devices rather than through careful scientific investigation. The rhetoric of moral crusaders tends to have similar types of content, regardless of the particular kind of evil being attacked, whether it be environmental pollution, the sexual harassment of women, or pornography.[9]

Atrocity Stories

The most emotionally powerful argument of moral crusaders consists of atrocity stories. The many books, newspaper articles, television shows, and seminar presentations about the menace of Satanism rely heavily upon atrocity stories, usually offered as anecdotal evidence for the existence and dangers of Satanism. These include emotionally disturbing stories about murderers who have been publicly labelled as Satanists, such as those in the Matamoros case, Charles Manson, and Richard Ramirez, and also cases of teenagers, like Tommy Sullivan, who have supposedly killed under the influence of Satanism.

However, there is a full range of more mundane atrocity stories reported in small town newspapers and attributed to Satanists, usually by citing the authority of some local "expert" on Satanism. Stories about teenagers who commit suicide, presumably due to the influences of Satanism in heavy metal rock music and *Dungeons and Dragons* games, are examples. So are the many stories about teenage Satanists who vandalize cemeteries or kill domestic animals.

Atrocity stories paint an impressionistic picture of a growing menace in society and validate the need to take action against it. This kind of rhetoric has a powerful affect on audiences that are not prepared to be critically analytical. It is very difficult to take issue with atrocity stories because one is easily perceived by believers as minimizing the moral outrages of the atrocity.

Testimonials

Another powerful form of rhetoric involves testimonials of reformed sinners and of victims of atrocities. During every moral crusade, these kinds of people come forth to present public testimonials. Their testimony is offered as indisputable evidence of the existence of the evil, about which the general public has heretofore been unaware. In the history of anti-Semitic persecutions, there have been innumerable people who have given testimony that they saw Jews kill gentile children to use them in blood sacrifices.[10] Some of these people have claimed to be Jews or former Jews. The moral crusade against white slavery was supported by the convincing testimony of women who claimed to have been kidnapped and forced into prostitution by white slavers. During the Red Scare of the 1950s, some of the decisive "evidence" for the Communist conspiracy to take over America came from self-proclaimed former Communists.[11]

The testimony of MPD patients about their ritual abuse at the hands of secret Satanic cults needs to be seen in this light, as a predictable part of the Satanism scare. The sudden outpouring of such testimonials during the same period an abundance of other claims are being thrust forth about Satanism should be a cause for skepticism.[12]

Typologies

Another rhetorical device of moral crusaders consists of the construction of typologies of various levels of sinners. These typologies are constructed from "personal observation" rather than from any careful scientific research. Typologies serve to create the illusion that the claims-makers have accumulated so much knowledge about the evil they decry, that they can be specific about different types of personalities susceptible to the evil and most likely to engage in it. So, during the Red Scare, anti-Communist crusaders constructed the typology of hard-core Communist party members, secret Communist spies, Communist sympathizers, "fellow travellers," and Communist dupes; thus, they could fit just about anyone they wanted to attack into the typology.

In the rhetoric of the Satanic cult claims-makers, there is a nearly standard typology of Satanists and potential Satanists.[13] The types include: dabblers, self-styled Satanists, religious Satanists, generational Satanists, and hard-core criminal Satanists. Dabblers are said to be mainly teenagers getting drawn into occult interests for amusement. Self-styled Satanists are freelancers, who are said to commit serious crimes in pursuit of a Satanic ideology which they put together on their own. Religious Satanists are people involved in an organized, public Satanic religious cult (which is usually viewed as being a kind of public front for secretive criminal activity). Generational Satanists are said to be members of secret Devil-worshipping cults that are maintained through family ties and usually involved in various heinous crimes. Hard-core Satanists are supposed to be the most deeply hidden group of Devil-worshippers and consist of a conspiratorial network of criminals, some of whom have infiltrated powerful and prestigious locations in society.

Redefinition

Woven throughout the fabric of "evidence" presented by moral crusaders about the evil they wish to bring to public awareness is the constant attribution of meanings, which are designed to alter the way in which the evil behavior is perceived by nonbelievers. The persistent efforts of moral crusaders to shape public discourse around a redefinition of behavior is sometimes very obvious. The struggle of anti-abortion crusaders to redefine abortion as "baby-killing" and their mission as fighting for the right to life is one example.

In contrast, sometimes the attempt to redefine behavior is subtle and targets a multitude of activities previously seen as unrelated. The notion of "subversive" and "un-American" activities promoted by anti-Communist crusaders, for example, successfully redefined a host of activities which were not previously considered a public threat. These activities could involve anything from writing novels containing certain forbidden political themes to teaching about the ideas of Karl Marx in high school.

The moral crusaders fighting Satanism and Satanic cults are promoting a redefinition of deviance which is complex and far from obvious. The ambiguous meaning of the concept of Satanism connects many unrelated activities and redefines them in such a way as to indicate some kind of vague connection among them. The concepts of "ritualistic crime," "ritual child abuse," "teenage Satanism," and "Satanic" influences in books are cornerstones of this redefinition. These labels create the illusion of concreteness out of diverse activities, including some that may not even exist.

The label of "ritual abuse" may, as we have seen, be applied: to the alleged sexual abuse of children by so-called Satanic cults which supposedly control child-care centers; to sexual abuse that relies on make-shift ritualism to scare children into compliance; to obsessive sexual ritualism which may accompany the sexual abuse of children; or conceivably even to the use of children in emotionally painful religious rituals which involve no sexuality whatsoever.

Estimates

Another rhetorical tactic commonly employed by moral crusaders is that of making exaggerated estimates of the extent of the evil they are trying to bring to public awareness. If the evil that they are fighting is merely infrequent or isolated, their claims are not likely to attract much public concern. The evil has to be found at the doorstep of most people in order for most people, with their very busy lives, to pay any attention to the appeals of moral crusaders. Especially today, there are already a great many social problems for people to have to worry about.

Consequently, in order to compete for attention in the public arena, moral crusaders have a tendency toward rhetorical escalation.

The various attempts of anti-Communist crusaders to show the pervasiveness of the Communist threat exemplified this sort of rhetorical exaggeration. The tactic was persuasive for millions of Americans, who were led to believe that Communist "subversives" had infiltrated American society from small towns to the nation's capital. J. Edgar Hoover, for example, claimed that there was one secret Communist agent for every hundred Americans, a totally unfounded estimate which was taken quite seriously because of his position of authority.[14] Joseph McCarthy constantly made fictitious claims about the numbers of Communists in the federal government. Lesser known anti-Communist witch hunters asserted estimates of the numbers of Communists in the entertainment industry and in public school teaching. The fact that estimates of deviance are sometimes simply drawn out of thin air may not easily be recognized by a worried and unskeptical audience.

The moral crusaders against Satanism commonly employ the very same tactic of making totally unfounded estimates of the numbers of teenage Satanists, Satanic ritual child abusers, and hard-core Satanic criminals. An excellent example came from Geraldo Rivera during an episode of his television talk show focussed upon Satanism in November 1987, when he asserted that: "Estimates are that there are over one million Satanists in this country."[15] (This would suggest that there was one Satanist for every 230 non-Satanists in the country at the time.)

Even when the moral crusaders offer only vague estimates of these deviants, such as when they claim that Satanists are "everywhere," they engage in a double distortion. They employ an ambiguous label for the evil they are seeking to enumerate so that the label can be broadly applied. Satanists of some sort, just like "subversives," can then be found everywhere that Satan hunters are looking for them.

There are people involved in criminal activities who justify their crimes with some kind of make-shift ideology of Devil worship. There are a few psychopathic murderers who call themselves Satanists. There are also some people who sexually abuse children, using rituals and perhaps references to the Devil to manipulate the children. There are many teenagers involved in various forms of juvenile delinquency who are also involved in "pseudo-Satanic" practices, which they may use to justify their crimes. However, these disparate forms of deviant behavior are not part of the same package.

The rhetorical tactic of making estimates attains credibility when it comes from some kind of authority figure recognized by an audience. As part of the Satanism scare, estimates are being put forth by local police at community meetings, by clergymen at church meetings, and by psychotherapists at seminars about child abuse. These estimates are then broadcast more widely in newspaper articles by reporters who simply quote the "experts" on Satanism without providing any skeptical commentary or doing any background research.

Basic Assumptions of the Moral Crusaders

A key question for a sociologist is: How do people attribute shared meaning to an unclear, ambiguous social situation (for example, the allegations made by children and MPD patients about bizarre torture by organized groups), and then communicate that meaning in such a way that the ideas enable joint activity in a social movement? Concepts drawn from psychiatry, such as "mass hysteria," "emotional contagion," and "collective delusions" have long since proven useless in explaining the collective behavior involved in rumors, panics, and social movements.

Framing the Problem

When moral crusaders strive to arouse public awareness about a newly recognized social evil, they must be able to offer explanations of the causes of that evil and propose credible ways of getting rid of it. They must cut through the inevitable complexity and ambiguity by framing the problem in a way that can be widely comprehended. Framing the problem sets the evil within a much broader scope of moral concerns. It provides the basic interpretive assumptions through which the evil can be redefined and linked to other social evils in society.

Ambiguous situations, events, or activities are attributed meanings which justify their being labelled "Satanist," through perceptual frames for understanding evil in society. These frames are drawn from people's personal world-views. Different personal frames are connected by the demonology of the Satanic cult legend, which offers a broader explanation for the ambiguous circumstances.[16]

A frame functions like a cultural model or paradigm which organizes people's shared preconceptions. Once a new definition of deviant behavior is given a frame for interpretation, people who have little or no direct contact with that behavior can make sense of the claims about it. Most importantly, the framing of the problem in a convincing way encourages volunteers to spend some of their time, energy, and money in the joint effort of a social movement.[17] Framing a problem in a certain way can provide a context for people who are moved to do something about the problem. A shared frame for a problem also enables people from different occupations who hold different beliefs to work together with a shared definition of the situation.

The social function of framing an ambiguous problem is illustrated in the social movements concerning abortion. Activists in the Pro-Choice movement frame the issue of abortion around the model, or analogy, of elective medical surgery. In contrast, activists in the Pro-Life movement frame the issue of abortion around the model, or analogy, of the murder of infants. Dialogue between people holding these conflicting frames is nearly impossible because the basic assumptions of the two frames are so divergent. The issue of abortion is interpreted through a different world of meanings which cannot be cross-translated. Ultimately, the question of whether or not a human embryo, or fetus, is a living human being, is so complex and ambiguous, that either frame may apply. In the frame of "elective surgery," restrictions on abortion are restrictions over free choice in medical treatment. In the "infant murder" frame, restrictions on abortion are simply ways of preventing murder, and no personal desires can justify murder. It is through these divergent frames that elaborate political and religious ideologies and a host of other social issues are linked to the issue of abortion.

The Christian Religious Frame

The initial frame for the problem of Satanic cult "ritual" abuse was drawn from fundamentalist Christian religious ideology.

Christian fundamentalism is an ultra-conservative ideology, which uses a version of orthodox, evangelical Protestantism to give supernatural sanction to attacks upon contemporary social change. It is an ideological expression of a socio-cultural revitalization movement which recurs in American history at times of very rapid change and social turmoil; it is not a specific national denomination. As a social movement, it is embodied in some local churches, some Christian schools, television and radio programs, publishing companies, and political lobby organizations. Fundamentalist Protestants can usually be distinguished from other evangelicals by their belief in the imminent end of the world after which only true believers in Christ will be saved, strict biblical literalism, and a personal morality which forbids drinking, dancing, and gambling. Fundamentalists are intensely opposed to modernist-liberal theology in the churches and to any changes in traditional American cultural values and social norms. American fundamentalists share with Islamic, Hindu, and Jewish fundamentalists, a view of themselves as being under siege by the destructive ("sinful") forces of modern society, and a fierce need to defend traditional cultural patterns.

The fundamentalist crusade against Satanism can be seen as one aspect of the larger fundamentalist moral protest movement against perceived threats to traditional "family values." The Satanic cult legend focusses upon threats to children: kidnapping children for human sacrifice, the use of aborted fetuses in cannibalistic rituals, the infiltration of child-care centers by Satanic cult child abusers, the incestuous ritual sexual abuse of children to "brainwash" them into becoming future Satanists, the recruitment of teenagers into Satanic cults, and subversive attempts to spread Satanic influences among children through rock music, school books, and *Dungeons and Dragons* role-playing games. These bizarre stories are taken seriously by so many fundamentalists because they are part of a larger symbolic crusade aimed at affirming symbolic values.

Fundamentalist moral crusaders, especially clergymen, view Satanists as actual agents of Satan who are trying to spread immorality of all kinds in order to destroy the moral order of American society and hasten Satan's take-over of the world. The logic is this: if good people are working for God, then evil people must be working for Satan. Satanic cult crime is seen simply as being one manifestation of the conspiratorial work of Satan and his earthly followers. In the fundamentalist framing of the problem, "ritual" abuse is simply one more example of the growing moral corruption (especially sexual perversion) in American society by evil people who reject God and true Christianity. The assertion that organized "Devil worshippers" are infiltrating the nation's child-care centers in search of children to torture and corrupt, can be taken on faith alone, without any verification being necessary.

Fundamentalists may be particularly receptive to belief in the Satanic cult legend, not only because it seems to confirm their religious beliefs, but also because it provides an opportunity to spread their conservative socio-political ideology. Blaming Satanists for objectionable conditions in society is a useful replacement for (or complement to) fundamentalists' conspiratorial beliefs about Communists and secular humanists as evil-doers. Moreover, since many fundamentalists feel threatened by the growth of so-called "New Age" religion and by some new religious "cults," they can attack these alien beliefs as being manifestations of Satanism in society.

This frame can be found in claims-making about Satanic cult crime voiced by fundamentalist moral crusaders, including clergymen and Christian writers, of course, but also including fundamentalist police and a new breed of Christian psychotherapists, counselors, and child protection workers.

Christian psychotherapy and counseling has been one of the

most rapidly growing movements in the helping professions.[18] The movement may have been spurred by popular books, such as Dr. M. Scott Peck's *People of the Lie,* in which the Devil is explicitly portrayed as being responsible for some people's deep psychological problems.[19] This approach to people's psychological problems brings Christian ideology, sometimes dogmatically fundamentalist, into treatment procedures.

A Dallas city magazine describes the background of Christian counseling in an article about a young women who "remembered" having been a victim of Satanic cult "ritual abuse" by her parents only after being treated by a Christian therapist:

> For years, "Christian counseling" meant going to confession, or asking the pastor for help with marital problems. But in the late Seventies and early Eighties, psychologists such as James Dobson, Larry Crabb, and Paul Meier and psychiatrist Minirth began to attract the enthusiasm of the evangelical community with their integration of scriptural teachings and current methods of psychological treatment. The new approach involves Christians who are trained in psychiatry and psychology, disciplines often considered antithetical to Christianity. While the methods used by Christian psychologists are as varied as those of secular therapists, there's an emphasis on gaining insight into undesirable behavior through psychological methods, then dealing with the behavior "biblically."[20]

Therapists with an ideological Christian bent may be particularly receptive to belief in the Satanic cult legend and to find indications of Satanic "ritual abuse" in their most deeply disturbed patients.

The Social Conservative Frame

The initial frame for interpreting crimes attributed to Satanic cults has been modified by activists using a compatible conservative socio-political perspective. In this frame, so-called ritualistic crime is seen as a response to the hedonistic pursuit of pleasure and power. Satanism is seen as a response to the growing climate of moral permissiveness, which has its source in the moral anarchy of the 1960s, and which continues to be encouraged by "permissive liberals" today. It is viewed as being one more manifestation of the moral decline and corruption of American society.

This frame is most commonly found in articles and public speeches by police Satan hunters. It is also found in the book *Painted Black* by Carl Raschke, a prominent conservative intellectual.[21]

The Child Advocate Frame

Many child protection workers and therapists frame the problem of "ritual" child abuse by way of an analogy with the past hidden victimization of women and children.[22]

The child advocate's framing of the problem treats any skepticism about "ritual" abuse as simply one more attempt to discredit testimony about sexual aggression against women and children. (The contradictory fact that many of the people accused of the "ritual" sexual abuse of children are women is ignored.) A recent book about the psychological effects of incest illustrates this:

> Ritual abuse—also called cult abuse and Satanic abuse—is a phenomenon whose pervasiveness is only now becoming clear to those who deal with child sexual abuse. The chilling stories told by unrelated victims around the country are virtually identical. The truths of this abuse are so shocking to society that the victimizers are protected by our own disbelief. . . .
> Their flashbacks and memories may represent an unwanted truth, but a truth nonetheless. Believe them.[23]

This appeal demonstrates a key part of the child advocate frame for dealing with the ambiguity of "ritual" abuse allegations. It's simple: believe the children. The basic assumption is that a wall of silence and skepticism, similar to that in cases of incest, protects the Satanist perpetrators of vicious child torture. It can be found in many publications about "ritual abuse" by therapists and child protection workers. In this frame, an interest in elaborate stories about Satanism is quite secondary, and flows from a concern to protect children from one, among many, of the threats to children in contemporary society.

This frame may appear, at least superficially, to be an expression of some kind of feminist ideology. However, it is not. It only uses some of the rhetoric of feminism which touches upon perceived threats to children. It differs from a feminist ideology in the sense that it is not drawn from any broad structural critique of society, but instead, focusses upon the need to protect children from vaguely defined evil forces in society. The frame has a powerful appeal because, as was previously described, children in American society are subjects of both pretentious sentimentalization and real social neglect. It appeals to both feelings of care and guilt.

Linking Perceived Effects

A common rhetorical device used by moral crusaders seeking allies is to link the perceived dangers of the newly defined form of deviance, with other, more familiar forms of deviance in society. This enables them to attract allies from among moral crusaders and professional specialists who are fighting other forms of deviance.

So, for example, moral crusaders against pornography commonly try to link the dangerous effects of pornography with rape and aggression against women, with premarital sex, extramarital sex, and with the disintegration of the American family. The tactic has enabled religious fundamentalist anti-pornography crusaders, who regard pornography as a threat to family and religious values, to join together with some feminist moral crusaders who are trying to increase public concern about sexual aggression against women.

Similarly, environmentalist crusaders try to link the dangerous effects of dumping industrial waste products with the concerns of medical specialists about allergies and disease, with the concerns of anti-war activists about international conflict over scarce resources, and with New Age religionists who are concerned about the effects of causing an "imbalance" of spiritual power on the planet.

During its initial phase of development, the Satanism scare was promoted primarily by fundamentalist Protestant and traditionalist Catholic moral crusaders. However, by the late 1980s, the moral crusade against Satanism was no longer an isolated, traditional religionist enterprise. The initial claims about Satanism had escalated and they now linked Satanism to a vast array of social evils.

The early claims of a few police Satan hunters linked Satanism to juvenile delinquency. Later, their escalating claims linked Satanism to kidnapped and missing children, "ritual" child abuse, child pornography rings, and serial murder. These claims attracted more local police to the moral crusade. Now, at church and community meetings about Satanic crime, police Satan hunters and fundamentalist clergymen work in an alliance of mutual interest.

The claims linking teenage "dabbling" in Satanism with drugs, violence, and suicide attracted the concern of volunteers in the anti-cult movement. The anti-cult organizations had been established to fight the influence of emerging new religious groups (so-called "cults"), which were converting some young people, to the alarm of their parents. These new claims about teenage Satanism extended the mandate of the anti-cult crusaders and gave them a new lease on life in the face of waning public concern about cults. The anti-cult crusaders found it easy to redefine juvenile delinquency involving black magic hocus-pocus as a new form of religious "cult" activity.

The claims about "ritual" child sexual abuse drew some child protection workers and psychotherapists into the moral crusade. More importantly, the supposed link with child sexual abuse drew some feminists into the moral crusade against Satanism. They responded to a feminist concern about sexual aggression against women and children. Now, at seminars on "ritual" child abuse, psychotherapists and social workers offer presentations alongside anti-cult activists, police Satan hunters, and sometimes fundamentalist clergymen.

The net result is the emerging organization of a social movement, with a heterogeneous composition, supported by groups with somewhat different agendas and even different ideological orientations. However, this heterogeneity within a social movement is not unusual.[24] The social movement against the war in Vietnam, for example, was also composed of diverse groups, including ideologically New Left groups with a broad agenda for radical social change, local groups of college students organized specifically to oppose the war, church groups with a traditional pacifist morality and those having moral convictions against only unnecessary wars, and even groups of businessmen who believed that the war was harmful to the American economy. These different activists had little, if any, direct connection with each other.

The rhetoric of framing the problem of Satanism and linking its perceived effects functions to join people together in a moral crusade. They are scattered across many different occupations and different organizations, and may not even be aware of each other's activities. The moral crusade against Satanism is not a product of any deliberate plan of action or contagious emotion, but rather a product of shared perceptions of reality. The underlying social motivation derives from the human need to grasp meaning from ambiguous experience. Research is needed to investigate the claims-makers, and not only their claims.

Conclusions

How could a search for imaginary deviants arise in a society? In the past, inquisitions and purges of scapegoat deviants such as witches, heretics, and various kinds of "subversives" have occurred all too often, during periods of economic and moral crises. The conventional explanation for these collective searches for scapegoat deviants is that they are products of irrational and contagious mass hysteria. This psychiatric explanation erroneously reduces collective behavior to personal mental disorders. However, a moral crusade is not a product of personal irrational fears and fantasies. Collective behavior cannot be reduced to individual personality traits and personal motives.

This chapter argues that moral crusades against imaginary

deviants are not the products of mental disorders or superstitious medieval minds. Instead, moral crusades arise when quite rational and decent people get caught up in an organized effort to deal with problems of everyday life, problems which have uncertain, ambiguous, and complex causes. Individual activists become involved in organized efforts to attack specific evils, each in their own sphere of concern, usually unaware of the broad scope of the collective organizing process going on.

Diagram 2 offers a schematic model for understanding the collective behavior of the Satanic cult scare. It offers an understanding of how a contemporary legend has been used in the moral crusade against Satanic cult crime.

The moral crusade against Satanism arises out of the moral crisis in American society and expresses a need to identify scapegoat deviants to blame. The socially constructed deviant stereotype of Satanists and elaborate descriptions of their behavior is fabricated from stories culturally inherited from the ancient Satanic cult legend. The ways of framing the problem of Satanism are drawn from popular American explanations for the "evil" of our time. These frames provide some people with simple explanations for a variety of social problems having complex and ambiguous causes, like violent juvenile crime, teenage suicide, kidnapped children, and sexual child abuse.

These ways of framing the problem also facilitate activism against a seemingly unambiguous, concrete target: Satanism. The moral crusade against Satanism emerged as a social movement when individual activists coalesced into alliances of mutual concern. Overlapping ways of framing the problem enabled moral crusaders, with different ideologies and occupational specializations, to work together.

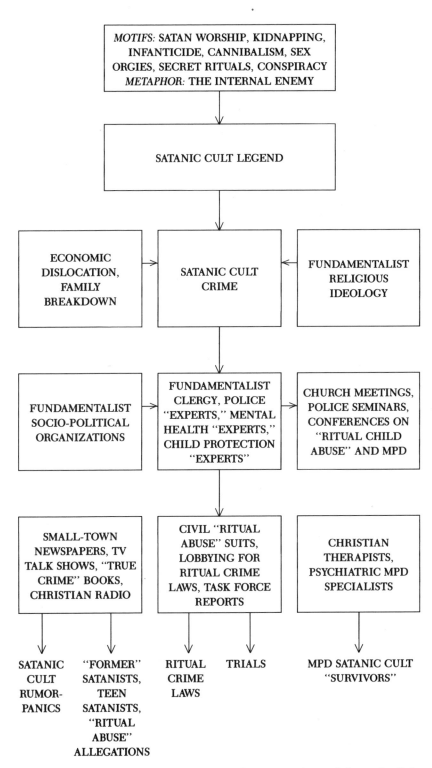

Diagram 2. Model for the Social Construction of Satanic Cult Crimes.

Chapter Twelve
The Organization of the Moral Crusade

> *Whoever fights monsters should see to it that in the process he does not become a monster.*
>
> Friedrich Nietzsche[1]

The Mobilization of Resources

A moral crusade requires more than effective rhetoric to be successful in influencing the general public. It needs effective organization. That means money, volunteer workers, paid organizers and communication channels to a wider audience. The organizational support system for the moral crusade against Satanism is distributed over a wide range of associations, many of which are fighting Satanism as a secondary concern. These organizations include associations established by religious groups, police Satan hunters, anti-cult volunteers, child protection workers, and mental health professionals. Many of the organizations have only local operations, but some of them are large-scale national membership organizations.

Many of the organizations involved in the moral crusade against Satanism were identified by a study done for the Committee for the Scientific Examination of Religion and published in the book, *Satanism in America*, by Shawn Carlson and Gerald Larue.[2] The report identified thirty-three organizations which are active in promoting the Satanism scare, as well as ninety individual activists.

Religious Organizations

Some of the organizations fighting Satanism are the vehicles of individual religious evangelists dedicated primarily to arousing public awareness of Satanism in American society.

Mike Warnke Ministries is an example. Warnke is a self-proclaimed former Satanist, who says that he committed many crimes and then repented and became a born-again Christian. His purported autobiographical testimonial, in the book *The Satan Seller*, was an early stimulus to the Satanism scare and it is now a classic of sorts, available mainly through Christian bookstores. It has recently been shown to be a fabrication, a fictional account of events which never actually took place.[3] Warnke travels the country giving revival lectures to local churches. Fighting Satanism has become a very lucrative business enterprise. In 1991, he performed at about two hundred locations, to a total audience of 500,000 people, according to a newspaper investigation of his activities. However, in the fall of 1992, the Internal Revenue Service revoked Warnke's tax-exempt status as a religious organization. It found that in 1991, Warnke Ministries: paid Warnke a salary of over $300,000; paid his wife about the same amount; paid his brother-in-law about $200,000; and contributed only $900 to charities. During their last seven years of operation, the trio earned more than $3.6 million.[4]

Another example is Jerry Johnston Ministries. Johnston offers lectures about teenage Satanism to public schools across the country, through its purportedly secular affiliate called the Jerry Johnston Association. Johnston's book about Satanism, *The Edge of Evil*, carried a foreword by Geraldo Rivera, praising its "research."[5]

Other religious organizations in the moral crusade are large national organizations which are engaged in the fight against Satanism as part of their mission to affirm traditional American "family values," and as part of their struggle against destructive "cults" which attract teenagers. These organizations are multi-million dollar operations. They sponsor radio and television shows, magazines and newsletters. A prominent example is Bob Larson Ministries. Larson is host of a Christian radio program called "Talk-Back," which is broadcast daily and received via satellite by "millions" of people, according to his own claims. He published a book about teenage Satanism, titled *Satanism: The Seduction of America's Youth*.[6] Larson writes and lectures extensively about "cults."

Another large-scale religious organization which has entered the fight against Satanism is Dr. James Dobson's Focus on the Family. Dobson is best known to the general public through his popular advocacy of parental "tough love"; this phrase refers to the policy of assuming parental authority and avoiding permissiveness toward rule-breaking by children. Dobson's radio show "Focus on the Family," heard on over 600 Christian radio stations, occasionally presents programs about the influence of Satanism on youth. Mike Warnke has been featured as an "expert" on Satanism on several of these programs. More importantly, Focus on the Family promoted the attack on the *Impressions* elementary school reading series, through its magazine, *Citizen*, as was noted in Chapter Eight.

Also, as noted in Chapter Eight, Reverend Donald Wildmon's American Family Association is helping to finance law-suits against the *Impressions* curriculum. The American Family Association is dedicated to fostering a "biblical" ethic of decency and is supported by over five hundred local chapters. Its primary concern is with obscenity in the entertainment media and in school books, and with the enhancement of traditional American "family values." The American Family Association cooperates with other conservative Christian organizations in the fight against Satanism in school books, such as the National Association of Christian Educators.

There are other organizations which serve the fundamentalist Christian subcommunity in America that contribute to the moral crusade against Satanism. Several Christian book publishers offer religiously based books about the dangers of the Satanic menace, which are widely available through Christian book stores. (Secular trade publishers seem to be much more interested in the genre of sensationalist "true crime" books about alleged Satanist murderers or child molesters.)

It should not be concluded that there is a uniformity of belief among all Christian fundamentalists in the imminent danger of a huge, secret conspiracy of Satanists. A few fundamentalist writers, most notably those working for *Cornerstone Magazine*, have provided important investigative reports, refuting false and exaggerated claims about satanic cults.[7]

As far as I can determine from my research, the Catholic subcommunity has been much less caught up in the Satanic cult scare. However, a few priests have become moral crusaders against Satanism. One example is Father Joseph Brennan of Lafayette, Louisiana, who published a book on "the secret Satanic underworld" titled, *The Kingdom of Darkness*.[8] Father Brennan gained his knowledge about Satanic cults from studying with psychiatrist Lawrence Pazder (a Catholic and the author of *Michelle Remembers*). He speaks widely to community and social groups in the South, and claims that there are 100,000 members in 8,000 Satanic cult "covens," in the United States.[9]

Law Enforcement Assistance Organizations

There are a great many police "experts" on Satanic cult crime, who travel about the country to give lectures. Sometimes they do so as private consultants, and at other times, as part of their local police community relations work.[10]

A few of the early pioneer police "experts" on Satanism have persisted and become prominent moral crusaders. Dale Griffis retired from his position as a captain in the Tiffin, Ohio, police department, after a conflict with the local government over the use of his position and department finances in pursuit of his cause, and set up a small business as a consultant for police investigations of "ritualistic crime."[11] He publishes and sells his own "cult crime" investigation manual, which is widely used by local police.

Thomas Wedge, formerly a juvenile probation officer in Logan County, Ohio, is another well-travelled consultant. His book, *The Satan Hunter*, offers a distinctly fundamentalist view of Satanism.[12] Wedge has been the main lecturer at three-day police seminars on "Satanic crime" sponsored by the University of Delaware, and offered at many locations around the country.

Robert "Jerry" Simandl, a youth officer with the Chicago police department, is another well-travelled moral crusader against Satanism. His lectures in England during September 1989, along with Pamala Klein, a Chicago "ritual abuse" counselor, at a series of seminars about "ritual" child abuse, to an audience of largely fundamentalist child protection workers, became the focus of a national scandal featured in English newspapers.[13] The Satanic cult "ritual" abuse scare which took place shortly after these seminars, resulted in many children being taken away from their parents and caused widespread outrage. Some of the children's stories were traced by investigative journalists and police detectives to child protection workers who had attended the conference, and from them back to Simandl and Klein.[14]

More important than these individual moral crusaders are organizations. Some prepare materials about Satanism for law enforcement agencies. Others sponsor police training programs about Satanic and ritualistic crime. These organizations are particularly important, because they help to manufacture more police "experts" on Satanism.

There are several small operations which specialize in supplying local law enforcement officials with materials about Satanic cult crime. Most are ideologically fundamentalist. Much of the material used at police training seminars about ritualistic crime, or distributed by police at community meetings, derive from these sources. Therefore, they convey a religious traditionalist way of framing the problem of Satanic influences in American society.

The Cult Crime Impact Network, Inc. is a private, "nonprofit" business of Boise, Idaho Police Lieutenant Larry Jones.

Jones publishes *File 18 Newsletter,* which circulates what he calls "information" about Satanic crime to police agencies which subscribe. (The newsletter is marked "Confidential: Restricted access information," a warning which presumably gives it an aura of authority.) The newsletter circulates to about two thousand subscribers.[15] The contents of the newsletter tends to focus upon "atrocity stories" about Satanism, but it also informs police about state legislation in process, police training films and materials, dates of training seminars, books, and anything else Jones finds relevant to Satanism and "cult crime." Jones's framing of the problem of Satanism is distinctly fundamentalist Christian. He identifies a very broad range of activities as "cult crime" influences, such as college courses about the history of magic, following in the tradition of anti-Communist witch hunters, who used to identify "subversive" influences everywhere.

Another outfit which produces materials for law enforcement agencies include Writeway Literary Associates of Costa Mesa, California. It sells such items as ritualistic crime investigation manuals, police training slides of ritualistic crime scenes, and calendars of supposed Satanic celebration days (when crimes can be anticipated). These items are widely used by police "experts" on Satanic cult crime at police training seminars and at community meetings; this helps to account, in part, for the consistency in these presentations coast to coast. Writeway is owned by David Balsinger, coauthor with Mike Warnke, of the book, *The Satan Seller.*[16] These purportedly "objective" police materials frame the problem of Satanism in a Christian fundamentalist ideological interpretation.[17]

Several universities sponsor regularly scheduled law enforcement training programs on Satanic cult ritualistic crime. These include the University of Delaware, through its Continuing Professional Education Program, and the University of Louisville, through its National Crime Prevention Institute. Police from around the country can attend these training programs. For the cost of several hundred dollars, they can bring back to their local communities, new "expertise" in the investigation of Satanic crime, legitimated by university training. Such university training provides these "experts" with credibility, which is useful when these policemen are called to be "expert" witnesses at trials involving allegations of Satanic cult crime. As far as I can determine, these training programs rely upon the highly questionable police materials previously noted, rather than any kind of serious behavioral science research or scholarship.

The existence of these organizing efforts does not mean that any significant number of local police are interested in spending much time and expense in the pursuit of phantom criminal Satanists, or even sympathetic to the effort to uncover supposedly secret criminal Satanists. Most professional police are skeptical about vague claims concerning crimes and prefer concrete evidence useful in prosecuting criminals in the courts. Police "experts" in ritualistic crime find considerable resistance among their colleagues. One research study of police "experts" in Satanism found that 60 percent of them complained about a lack of encouragement and support from their job superiors.[18] The same study found that these specialists in "occult crime" were more likely to speak about Satanism to non-police community and church groups than to meetings of police.[19]

Another interesting finding of this study of police Satan hunters is the correlation between religious activity and interest in Satanism. Those police who attended church most frequently, were also those who were most likely to believe that Satanic cult crime was common and should be a serious police concern.[20] This finding suggests religious ideology may be central for many police Satan hunters in motivating their concern for the pursuit of criminal Satanists. Less traditionally religious police probably give other types of crime greater priority in their expenditure of time and effort, even if they accept Satanic crime as being a real entity.

Anti-Cult Organizations

In the late 1980s, some anti-cult organizations extended their fight against the influences of "destructive cults," to embrace a concern about teenage Satanism. This was, in part, a response to the hundreds of parents who had contacted them for help in dealing with teenage Satanism, which already had become popularly defined as a "cult" activity.[21] Police and journalists also sought out their assistance in helping them to understand the juvenile delinquency and other criminal activity that they perceived as the work of Satanic "cults." The activities of these organizations play a crucial role in the dissemination of a definition of Satanism as a kind of pseudo-religious, criminal activity through their public "education" programs.[22]

The largest of these organizations is the Cult Awareness Network. The organization is a non-profit, educational association, composed of about fifty affiliated local groups across the country, with a headquarters operation in Chicago. It provides an information distribution service for the press, organizes local seminars on "destructive cults," sponsors local workshops for mental health counselors, provides volunteer speakers for conferences and community meetings on "cult crimes," sponsors a national conference for groups and individuals concerned about "cults," and mails out a monthly newsletter to about two thousand subscribers.[23]

The Cult Awareness Network is composed mainly of local volunteer parents, some youth social workers, and a few amateur cult deprogrammers, who try to draw young people out of new, unconventional religious groups. Their concern about Satanism is only secondary to their primary concern about fighting the influence of organized, unconventional religious groups. Nevertheless, they are increasingly being drawn into the moral crusade against Satanism.

The second largest anti-cult organization is the American Family Foundation. It is a non-profit educational association composed largely of mental health professionals and scholars who are concerned about the influences of "destructive cults." It is funded largely by grants from foundations. The activities of this organization involve the production of scholarly information designed for mental health professionals, such as a research journal and newsletters. The central importance of this organization is that it helped to transform the meaning of youthful conversion to new, unconventional religions, into a psychiatric problem, thus "medicalizing" the social deviance of joining a group defined as a "cult." Its activists give some professional credibility to the fight against unorthodox religions which were taking young people away from their parents.

Recently, the American Family Foundation moved, albeit cautiously, into the moral crusade against Satanism. It established study groups on Satanism and on New Age religion, composed of scholars, police Satan hunters, and anti-cult activists, designed to promote cooperative efforts. In 1990, the organization published a report about Satanism for mental health professionals, titled, *Satanism and Occult-Related Violence: What You Should Know.*[24] The Chairperson of its study group on New Age Religion, Carl Raschke, a professor of religious studies at the University of Denver, published his own book on the menace of Satanism and New Age religion, titled *Painted Black.*[25] The journal of the American Family Foundation (AFF) and its various newsletters carry articles about the dangers of Satanism. Its newsletter designed for youth workers, *Young People and Cults*, disseminates occasional information about teenage Satanism. In the March 1990 issue, for example, the newsletter carried articles praising Pat Pulling's book, *The Devil's Web*, and also Larry Kahaner's "true crime" book about Satanism, *Cults That Kill.*[26]

These educational activities of the AFF give professional credibility to the redefinition of Satanism as a psychiatric (mental health) problem, one which requires the expertise of psychiatric authorities. By the late 1980s, Satanism was increasingly seen through a lens of psychiatric thinking.[27]

Child Protection Organizations

There are a wide variety of child protection organizations which have entered the moral crusade against Satanism. Most of them have a much broader agenda of concerns about perceived threats to children beyond Satanism. Most of them assimilated claims about dangerous Satanism into their agendas, only after these claims were already widely disseminated.

Some child protection groups focus their efforts on educating the general public about dangerous Satanic influences on children from the entertainment media and children's fantasy games. The activities of these groups were described in Chapter Eight. They include: Parents Music Resource Center, the National Coalition Against Television Violence, and Bothered About Dungeons and Dragons (BADD).

Other child protection organizations focus their efforts on fighting Satanic "ritual" abuse as part of a broader agenda of concerns about child abuse. The activities of some of these groups were described in Chapter Six. They include Believe the Children, the volunteer organization composed largely of parents. It was first established by some of the parents whose children made allegations of Satanic ritual abuse against the Buckeys and other child-care workers at the McMartin Preschool in Manhattan Beach, California. It now has affiliates in Chicago, and Lincoln, Nebraska. Its advisory board is diverse and consists of several prominent therapists, clergymen, and police Satan hunters. The activities of Believe the Children are mainly directed toward educating the public about "ritual abuse" by providing information to journalists, providing speakers for community meetings and seminars about child abuse, and publishing a newsletter. Kenneth Wooden, the journalist who helped produce the "20/20" segment about Satanic cult crime, is on its advisory board. Wooden also has his own organization, the National Coalition for Children's Justice, which provides him with a forum for the fight against ritual abuse.

National and local professional associations concerned with child abuse sponsor conferences, sometimes offer special training workshops about ritual abuse for social workers and other interested professionals. These workshops are organized for the official purpose of simply sharing technical expertise. Nevertheless, they provide a vehicle for moral crusaders against Satanic "ritual" child abuse by which to manufacture more "experts." Since the work of dealing with sexual child abuse has itself taken on the character of a moral crusade, these are forums where heated scientific debate and critical analysis is neither expected nor desired.[28] There are a great many of these local conferences across the country. An example, previously noted, was a local conference on child abuse in Olean, New

York, during April 1988, at which the featured speaker was Kenneth Wooden, who spoke to child protection workers about the widespread prevalence of ritual abuse by secret cults during the time of the rumor-panic in western New York.[29]

Some of these child abuse conferences feature psychotherapists who work with MPD patients who claim to have been ritually abused by Satanic cults as children. Many of these therapists suggest that MPD "survivors" and children purported to be victims of "ritual" abuse in child-care centers are victims of the same secret Satanic conspirators.[30] Some of the training workshops on "ritual" abuse are co-sponsored by feminist groups concerned with sexual aggression. One two-day conference in Minneapolis in September 1990, for example, was sponsored by the Minnesota Awareness of Ritualistic Abuse Network and the Sexual Violence Center of Hennepin County.[31]

A number of business enterprises produce materials which have the effect of promoting the social construction of ritual abuse as a distinct form of social deviance. For example, several companies make training films about ritual abuse for therapists and law enforcement agencies. At least one company now sells sets of drawings of supposed ritual abuse scenes, which are designed for use by therapists in interviewing children suspected of having been victims of "ritual" abuse.[32] Another company publishes a children's book about "ritual" abuse, for the same purpose.[33]

Even some government agencies have entered the moral crusade against Satanism via concerns about child abuse. The Los Angeles County Commission for Women, for example, established a Ritual Abuse Task Force, which published a widely circulated report about Satanism and ritual abuse.[34] The report is as ideologically distorted as any published by fervent moral crusaders.

In sharp contrast, other child protection agencies have published reports about ritual abuse which are carefully put together and reveal an awareness of the ambiguity and lack of consensus concerning the whole issue of Satanism and ritual abuse. One example is a report published by The National Resource Center on Child Sexual Abuse titled, "Ritual Child Abuse: Understanding the Controversies."[35] A similarly well-reasoned report for therapists and the general public was published by the National Center for Missing and Exploited Children. The report, titled, *Child Sex Rings,* was written by FBI special agent Kenneth Lanning, who has been investigating stories of bizarre torture and killing of children by "cults" since 1983.[36]

Mental Health Organizations

The main organization which is disseminating claims about Satanism and "ritual abuse" to mental health professionals is the International Society for the Study of Multiple Personality and Dissociation. The organization has about eleven thousand members, including psychiatrists, clinical psychologists, social workers, and nurses, although it also has nonprofessionals as members who are interested in MPD. Some of the nonprofessionals are MPD Satanic cult "survivors."

The national and regional conferences of the Society regularly include lectures and professional training seminars for therapists about Satanic cult "ritual abuse" of MPD patients. Lecturers on the topic have included Pat Pulling. One of the missions of the Society is to educate the public about MPD, a disorder which frequently involves claims about "ritual abuse." The conferences offer training seminars on Satanic cult "ritual abuse," at which elaborate claims are presented without any scientifically verifiable evidence.[37]

As was noted in Chapter Five, papers about the ritual abuse of MPD patients from these conferences find their way into the hands of police Satan hunters and are used to give scientific credibility to various claims about Satanism. Some of the most prominent psychiatrists who specialize in the study of MPD are believers in the Satanic cult conspiracy explanation of "ritual abuse."

There are also an increasing number of psychiatric clinics and hospital programs around the country specialized in providing psychotherapy to MPD patients who claim to be victims of Satanic cult ritual abuse. The costs for a course of treatment may range up to fifteen or twenty thousand dollars. In some states, these costs are passed on to the taxpayer, through Medicaid programs. If not, the costs are paid by health insurance and ultimately result in increased costs for medical insurance.

Motives, Meanings, and Metaphors

After this examination of the organizational basis of the moral crusade against Satanism, it is useful to return once again to the question of what shared social ties link the diverse groups of people in the social movement. There is no single unifying ideology that these moral crusaders have in common as a set of beliefs and values. What, then, links them with each other in a common effort?

The beliefs that they share are those of the demonology of the Satanic cult legend, based on belief in a secret, criminal conspiracy. They hold overlapping ways of framing the problem of evil in society which reflect the metaphors of the legend, providing shared meanings for their fight against Satanism.

The various activities of the different moral crusaders are structurally integrated through participation in shared communication networks and by the cooperative integration of their different types of specialized "expertise" (supposedly acquired in the course of their roles as clergymen, police, child protection workers, mental health specialists, and anti-cult volunteers).

On a personal level, many of these "experts" in Satanism gain substantial monetary profit through their activities as consultants, guest speakers, lecturers at training seminars, and expert witnesses at trials. They also gain social prestige by being widely regarded as "experts" in dealing with a newly defined form of deviant behavior.

Considerable monetary profits are also being made out of the Satanic cult scare by organizations such as psychiatric clinics and hospital programs specialized in treating MPD "survivors."

The Career of a Moral Crusader

There have been few detailed studies of the career paths of moral crusaders fighting Satanic cult crime. However, detailed information about one prominent crusader, Pamala Klein, is available. After Klein's crucial organizing activities came to public attention during the English ritual abuse scare, journalists and court investigators gathered quite a bit of information about her background. (Much of the original source material about her background was provided to me by a private investigator, Paul Ciolino, who has investigated her credentials for attorneys in several legal cases involving allegations of "ritual abuse" in which Klein figured as an expert witness.[38]) Pamala Klein's career path illustrates many of the previous generalizations about the organization of the moral crusade against Satanism as a social movement.

Pamala Klein's formal educational training consists of an undergraduate major in psychology and a graduate school major in counselor education. She received a Master of Science degree in Education, with a specialization in counselor education in 1977, at age thirty-seven, from Southern Illinois University at Carbondale.[39] The training is designed primarily for public school counselors. It does not prepare a person to do intensive, long-term psychotherapy.

Klein's career path took her from directing a child-care center before she completed her college education, to working as a paraprofessional rape crisis counselor, to counseling child victims of sexual abuse, and ultimately to serving as an international travelling "expert" on Satanic cult "ritual abuse" and a "therapist" for child and adult victims of "ritual abuse." In the process, Pamala Klein transformed a moral enterprise into a lucrative business enterprise.

Between 1977 and 1985, Klein worked as the Coordinator for the campus Rape and Sexual Abuse Care Center at Southern

Illinois University in Edwardsville. Her responsibilities involved coordinating short-term counseling, training, and supervision of the staff at the center.[40]

Pamala Klein made her first English contacts when she resided in England, between July 1985 and January 1986. While in England, she set up a business with an English social worker, Norma Howes, as a "consultant" for cases of child sexual abuse.

Norma Howes was later an instrumental interviewing "therapist" in the first English case of alleged Satanic cult "ritual abuse," which occurred in 1988 in Kent.[41] Howes supported her claims with so-called Satanic cult ritual abuse diagnostic indicators and other American anti-Satanism pseudo-scientific propaganda materials supplied to her by Pamala Klein.[42] Journalists found that these American "diagnostic indicators" had circulated widely among British child protection social workers. Howes claimed to have identified eighteen cases of Satanic "ritual abuse" in England between 1987 and 1990.[43]

In 1987, after returning to the United States, Klein became the Director of the Children's Advocacy Center, in Hanover Park, Illinois, a suburb of Chicago. The agency was established by the Hanover Township Mental Health Board, with the sponsorship of the local government. Its purpose was to provide crisis intervention, counseling, and litigation support to victims of child sexual abuse. At the same time, Klein worked at her own counseling business, incorporated in 1984 as Klein's Consultation Service, Inc.[44] She left the Children's Advocacy Center in 1989 after being terminated by governing board.

Klein built up a wide reputation as a therapist for child victims of sexual abuse and as an expert witness in legal cases involving claims of child sexual abuse. She first began to give invited lectures about "ritual abuse" during 1988. Prior to that time, she had been invited to lecture to police and mental health conferences on the topics of sexual assault and child sexual abuse. However, by the late 1980s, Klein was lecturing in communities across the Midwest about "ritual abuse" and Satanic cult practices.[45] She also networked widely with other moral crusaders fighting Satanism. For example, she attended an annual conference of the International Society for the Study of Multiple Personality Disorder and one of Pat Pulling's conferences on ritualistic crime. She met Detective Jerry Simandl at a police conference where he offered training on Satanic cult crime and afterwards she teamed up with him for several presentations.

Klein has made a very profitable business out of the Satanic cult scare. She provides "therapy" for child victims of "ritual abuse" as well as for adult MPD "survivors" of Satanic cult torture. She gains income as an expert witness in cases of alleged "ritual child abuse" and as a consultant to several hospital programs which treat victims of "ritual abuse." In addition, she provides these same services for cases of suspected child sexual abuse not involving allegations of Satanic cult activity.

Klein's problems began when she became the focus of outrage as expressed in newspaper accounts in England, after journalists began investigating the background of the "ritual abuse" scandal there. In July 1989, a national English sensationalist television program claimed that Satanic cult ritual abuse of children was rife in that country. Journalists found that the program relied upon American "expert" Pamala Klein as a consultant for background information about Satanic cults and "ritual abuse."[46] Then, in September 1989, Klein was back in England, where she and Simandl lectured at a series of training seminars on "ritual child abuse." It was at these conferences that Klein made the infamous allegations about babies in the United States being cooked by Satanists in microwave ovens. Shortly afterwards, several major cases of alleged Satanic cult ritual abuse surfaced in child protection investigations, initiated by some of the social workers who had attended the seminars.[47] A total of fifty-two children were taken away from their parents and made wards of the court for a period of time, ultimately being returned after no evidence of Satanic cult "ritual abuse" could be found.

Pamala Klein's problems worsened back in the United States. A legal judgment disputed her qualifications in a criminal case involving allegations of ritual child sex abuse, in which

Klein functioned as "therapist" for the child. On February 13, 1991, Cook County Judge R. Morgan Hamilton ruled that "Pamala Klein is not a legitimate therapist as the term is defined by Illinois law," and dismissed her from the case.[48] Affidavits presented in the case revealed that Klein had exaggerated or falsified some of the qualifications included on her professional vitae.[49] The story made headline news in England and it was featured on a Chicago television news series.[50]

This case is worthy of brief examination because it illustrates the social dynamics of how moral crusaders facilitate children's allegations of "ritual abuse." The case began on October 16, 1990, when a five-year-old girl in Hanover Park Elementary School started to cry during a police presentation about child sexual abuse. She was taken by the police to be interviewed at the Hanover Park Children's Advocacy Center. The girl told a story of being sexually touched on her clothed genitals during the previous day, by her girlfriend's step-father, John Fittanto.[51] Fittanto was arrested on the basis of the girl's accusations. His step-daughter was taken from him and his wife by the court and placed in the custody of her natural father.

After being interviewed by Pamala Klein repeatedly over the weeks following the initial allegations, the girl elaborated her story with tales of extremely bizarre events. The girl claimed, among other things: that Fittanto committed various sexual acts with her with other men present while the acts were being videotaped; that he deliberately cut himself with a scissors and smeared blood on his face and made drawings with the blood; and that he told her that the Devil would kill her brothers if she told anyone.[52] A medical examination, however, found no evidence that the girl had had sexual intercourse. The case against Fittanto was dismissed by the trial judge, on August 23, 1991, for lack of evidence. His step-daughter was returned to him and his wife after the period of a year and a half. There is no way of determining the exact circumstances and perceptions which led to the child's initial allegations. However, the stories of "ritual abuse" have been shown to be obvious fabrications.

In a later case involving Pamala Klein, trial dispositions presented affidavits from Illinois state child protection officials stating that Klein had been involved as a consulting "therapist" in at least three other cases of alleged child sexual abuse in which children also made allegations of Satanic ritual abuse.[53] The affidavits stated further, that Klein used questionable methods of interviewing, asked leading questions, and drew conclusions not based upon facts. In none of the cases was anyone found guilty of the accusations against them. Questioning by a defense lawyer in one case revealed that all of Pamala Klein's "knowledge" of Satanic ritual abuse was derived from sensationalist popular culture books about ritual abuse and the unpublished papers of police and therapist Satan hunters, distributed at training seminars on Satanic cult ritualistic crime.[54]

These cases and many others like them cause unnecessary suffering. People accused of "ritual child abuse" must spend large sums of money in legal costs defending themselves. They may have children taken from them. They suffer from continuing community suspicion and often lose their jobs, even after they are found innocent of the charges against them. Moreover, if there has been any actual sexual molestation of children, the situation is confused and confounded by fabrications about Satanic activity.

Are there many more moral crusaders, like Pamala Klein, profiting from the Satanic cult scare? My research leads me to believe that there are many more around the country.

Chapter Thirteen
The Politics of the Moral Crusade

Social groups create deviance by making rules whose infraction constitutes deviance, and by applying those rules to particular people and labeling them as outsiders.
Howard Becker, *Outsiders*[1]

The Political Development of a Moral Crusade
A moral crusade begins with activities aimed at educating the public about its conception of a new form of deviance. These propaganda efforts are necessary to legitimize claims about a newly perceived threat. However, once a moral crusade moves from public education to action, it inevitably provokes criticism and opposition. As moral crusaders move into the political arena to call for investigations and new laws, that opposition mounts. Then a moral crusade must deal with something more than the previous disinterest and skepticism against which it initially had to struggle to legitimate its claims.

Sources of Opposition to the Moral Crusade against Satanism

The sources of opposition to an emerging moral crusade depends upon the particular claims, goals, and ideologies of a moral crusade.[2] Many opponents are simply skeptical about the claims. Some people are moved by a perception that their own religious or political values and beliefs are under threat from the moral crusade. Other people may find that the moral crusade threatens their vested interests, such as their business, career, or political power.

The moral crusade against Satanism is essentially a symbolic crusade aimed at the reaffirmation of traditional cultural values of obedience to family and religious authority. Consequently, criticism of the moral crusade is most likely to arise from groups of people who hold modernist values, or at least, people who don't feel threatened by contemporary social change.

Current Sources of Skepticism

As far as I can determine, most skeptics, if they have anything in common, are professionalized, technical specialists, in occupations in which their work values are negatively affected by the exaggerated claims about Satanism. Most of the criticism of the moral crusade against Satanism comes from people whose occupations require them to be critically analytical about claims which bear upon their occupational expertise. These people include some behavioral scientists, some professionalized law enforcement personnel, and some metropolitan and national news reporters.

The first major publication of scholarly and scientific research that offered a critical analysis of claims about Satanism was the 1991 book, *The Satanism Scare*.[3] The book presents the work of twenty-two scholars, including ten sociologists, six criminal justice specialists, three anthropologists, a historian, a folklore specialist, and an investigative journalist. There are many other behavioral scientists for whom the Satanism scare has recently become a matter of scientific curiosity and critical analysis. While there is no reason to expect uniformity in their explanations of the phenomenon, moral crusaders against Satanism are not likely to find much support for their claims from behavioral scientists. The claims contradict too much historical, sociological, anthropological, and psychological knowledge of human behavior.

Another source of opposition to claims of the moral crusaders comes from some professional police investigators, whose jobs require them to be broadly knowledgeable about criminall behavior and critically analytical about sensational claims concerning crime. One such person is Robert Hicks, a law enforcement specialist for the Department of Criminal Justice Services of the state of Virginia, who has an undergraduate degree in anthropology. His book about police involvement in the Satanic cult scare, *In Pursuit of Satan,* offers a detailed refutation of exaggerated claims about Satanic, ritualistic crime made by police Satan hunters.[4]

Another example can be found in the careful work of Kenneth Lanning, who is a member of the FBI's Behavioral Science Unit and a genuine expert in the study of crimes involving the sexual victimization of children. The Behavioral Science Unit uses behavioral science research findings in providing such services as training, lecturing, and case consultation with local law enforcement officers. (Many people are familiar with the work of the Unit in gathering and analyzing data about serial murderers.) Lanning has been trying to understand claims about ritualistic crime since 1983, when they first came to his attention. His publications are critical of vague and sensationalized claims about ritualistic crime and ritual child abuse.[5] Lanning, like most truly professionalized law enforcement agents, is primarily concerned with obtaining concrete evidence of crime that can be used in effective prosecutions of criminals, and skeptical about moralistic rhetoric which plays fast and loose with verifiable facts.

Research on police officers who are involved in investigations of alleged Satanic cult crime has shown that the longer the time local police spent investigating these allegations, generally the less likely they were to regard the claims about ritualistic crime to be a high priority matter for police concern in comparison with other crimes.[6] The researchers noted that:

"With time they may come to believe that there may be much more smoke than fire in the satanism scare. Moreover, experience may demonstrate that many apparent satanic crimes are in fact not what they seem."[7]

A survey done by the Michigan State Police asked police agencies in the state about their findings from investigations of alleged occult-related crime.[8] The survey found that the overwhelming majority of these cases of alleged occult-related crimes involved teenage males, whose "Satanism" was patched together from ideas learned from books on occult magic and heavy metal music. What this means to police Satan hunters is that they are in pursuit of juvenile delinquents, rather than conspiratorial, organized criminals, a much less glamorous moral crusade.

Another source of opposition comes from groups concerned about civil liberties. Already, the attacks upon school textbooks and library books that are alleged to promote Satanism have drawn the attention of organizations such as People for the American Way, the American Library Association, and the National Education Association. Once new state laws are passed against vaguely conceived "ritualistic crimes," it is likely that other civil liberties groups will become concerned.

Potential Sources of Opposition

Anticipating future sources of opposition to the moral crusade against Satanism is obviously a matter of informed speculation. However, the rhetoric of the moral crusaders suggests the social movement is on a collision course with certain social categories of people in American society.

One such social category includes people involved in unconventional, nature worship ("pagan") and New Age religious groups.[9] People having these religious beliefs are common secondary targets of the moral crusaders, who sometimes make no distinction between these occult enthusiasts and imaginary criminal Satanists. At the very least, they are often considered to be advocates of the same kind of dangerous magic practices as Satanists, and they are thrown into the same barrel of "occult practitioners." Organized "pagan" religionists are now keeping a close watch on the moral crusade against Satanism. A newsletter called *Cultwatch Response*, for example, publishes information about activities which defame and threaten people holding "pagan" religious beliefs by labelling them as Satanists.

It is also possible that liberal Protestants and Catholics may become concerned about the moral crusade if it continues to be used by fundamentalists as a "red herring" to indirectly attack them.

The Winds of Public Opinion

Public opinion is simply a global measure of collective attitudes in a nation or region of a nation. If accurate, the measure merges representative samples of all major segments of a population. However, global public opinion is constantly in flux, as different groups within the population influence each other's attitudes.

There have been few measures of "public opinion" about the perceived threat from Satanism. A 1989 public opinion poll in Texas found that 63 percent of Texans regarded Satanism as a "very serious" threat and another 23 percent regarded it as being "somewhat serious."[10] However, this expression of belief in the threat of Satanism may be relevant only to Texas.

My research leads me to conclude that acceptance or skepticism of any threat from Satanists varies greatly in different segments of the American population. Rural areas and areas where there are high proportions of Christian fundamentalists appear to have greater numbers of believers in the Satanism threat. Metropolitan areas and areas where there are comparatively few Christian fundamentalists appear to be areas where indifference and skepticism prevails in public opinion. I would also speculate that social class differences are important. Blue-collar workers, even in urban areas, are more likely to accept the claims about dangerous Satanists than are upper-middle class professionals, who are likely to scorn the Satanism scare as being a manifestation of superstitious ignorance.

What this means for the moral crusaders is that their claims are likely to run into a wall of harsh skepticism in metropolitan areas of the country. They are much less likely to be able to legitimize their claims through the political system in states which are primarily urban, than in states which are primarily rural and have heavy fundamentalist populations.

Conflict between Skeptics and Believers

People who are activists in a moral crusade tend to be impatient with skeptics and often intolerant toward outright critics. They often regard the expression of skepticism by critics as equivalent to giving aid and comfort to the evil they are fighting. When moral crusaders and their opponents hold very different ways of framing the problem, discourse between them is likely to be nearly impossible. Because they don't share the same frame of reference, their discourse easily degenerates into a kind of dialogue of the deaf. Miscommunication and misunderstanding can be expected as skeptics and believers attribute ulterior motives to each other.

The anti-Communist crusaders of the 1950s usually dismissed skeptics and critics as being Communist "dupes" or, worse, Communist "sympathizers." Similarly, many moral crusaders against Satanism simply dismiss critics of their efforts as being "cult apologists." This rhetorical device seeks to discredit contrary voices by painting critics as sympathizers with the evil they are fighting. In his book on the dangers of Satanism, Carl Raschke, for example, asserts: "Cult apologists are usually social scientists or general authors who hang around offbeat religious groups for such a span of time that they tend to become one with the group mind."[11] In a similar vein, Cynthia Kisser, Executive Director of the Cult Awareness Network writes:

> . . . in contrast to the mounting evidence of satanism impacting on society as a social movement a small yet persistent group of "apologists" for satanism have emerged. Their arguments for dismissing the satanism phenomena are on the whole shallow, and not well researched.[12]

Elsewhere, Kisser decries how these "cult apologists" give aid and comfort to criminals.

> The destructive cults will continue to be encouraged in acting as organized criminal groups as long as they can find unwitting

allies among respectable professionals, including those in law enforcement.[13]

Even the FBI's Kenneth Lanning has been the target of vitriolic attack from moral crusaders. In his book, Raschke wrote about Lanning that: "satanist criminals have had one of their best friends, if only for legitimate philosophical reasons, at the highest level of national law enforcement."[14]

At least one skeptic of the Satanism scare has faced official intimidation. Robert Hicks, the criminal justice analyst who wrote the highly praised book, *In Pursuit of Satan,* got caught in some bureaucratic police politics because of his sharp criticism of police "ritualistic crime" training seminars. Officials of the Virginia state police collected a confidential file of "information" about him and approached his superiors, requesting that they discipline him for challenging their competence.[15]

The Role of the Mass Media in the Satanism Scare

The belief that the Satanism scare is largely a creation of the mass media is incorrect. The mass media has functioned primarily as a vehicle through which moral crusaders and skeptics have disseminated their views, with greater ease or greater difficulty, depending on the particular media.

Most large city newspapers have so far published very little about any manifestations of the Satanism scare. The only exception concerns allegations of "ritual abuse," which are sometimes covered when they are aimed at the staffs of child-care centers, as in the McMartin case. What gets published about Satanism in large city newspapers tends to be highly skeptical toward the claims of moral crusaders.[16] While small town newspaper reporters are likely to quote local "experts" as authoritative sources, large city newspapers reach out to nationally recognized professional specialists (scholars and behavioral scientists) for authoritative quotations about phenomena labelled as manifestations of Satanism.

The vast majority of the hundreds of newspaper articles about Satanism that I have collected have been published in small town newspapers. The vast majority of these articles are about petty crimes, such as cemetery vandalism and the killing of domestic and farm animals, which reporters attribute to teenage "Satanists" by quoting local "experts." There are also an abundance of articles reporting on conferences and community meetings about "the social problem" of Satanism, most of the coverage being again directed toward the concerns of parents about teenagers. Many of these news articles offer standard "warning signs" of Satanic cult involvement among teenagers, so that parents and teachers can identify the teenage "Satanists." There are also many articles about serious crimes, such as gruesome murders and rapes, which are attributed to Satanists by reporters, once again by quoting local "experts" who note the telltale signs of Satanic cult activity. Rarely, however, is there much follow-up of the outcomes of such allegations at trials, where they are usually disconfirmed or simply ignored as being irrelevant gossip.

The influence of television has been quite different. Some national television talk shows have tended to "hype" the Satanism scare. Geraldo Rivera's special, "Devil Worship: Exposing Satan's Underground," broadcast on October 25, 1988, attracted one of the largest audiences in TV history, about fifty million people, according to the program's promoters.[17] Television critics regarded the program as an example of sensationalist "tabloid TV" and were appalled by its pretention to be a carefully crafted documentary.[18] Videotapes of that program circulate widely and are presented at community meetings and conferences about Satanism as evidence of the Satanic cult conspiracy. However, the number of talk shows featuring claims about Satanism began to decline sharply in 1991.[19]

The trade book industry, on the other hand, has been publishing a steady stream of sensationalistic books about Satanic cult crime, in the vein of popular culture "true crime" books. There were, for example, a spate of rapidly written books about the Matamoros murders, which presented them as Satanic cult murders. There are many pop culture books which purport to be about Satanic cult murders, carried out by teenage gangs or individual psychopaths. Another source of sensational stories are books about ritual child abuse. These books usually pretend to be nonfiction reports about specific cases. However, they are really another form of atrocity stories, which provide models for later rumor-allegations. Christian book publishers have also added to the list of these books.

The few skeptical books available are published by scholarly presses; this may indicate that skepticism in response to the Satanic cult scare is not seen as having as much sales potential as the "true crime" stories which promote the scare.

Science and Conflict over Claims about Satanism

Science is not an autonomous entity with its own untouched, pristine existence. Scientific investigation is never independent of the social forces which prevail in a society. Science is a human enterprise and an integral part of any society. When the phenomena subject to scientific examination are matters touched by social conflict, the community of scientists inevitably becomes an arena of conflict. It should be no surprise then that the Satanism scare has generated conflict in the community of behavioral scientists and psychotherapists, over claims concerning the "ritual" abuse of MPD patients and children.

MPD Satanic Cult "Survivor" Stories

Since the early 1980s, there has been a proliferation of cases of emotionally disturbed people, diagnosed by psychotherapists as having Multiple Personality Disorder, and increasing numbers are making allegations that they were sexually and physically tortured by Satanists. This phenomenon is a fascinating issue for scientific investigation, but it is also a matter of heated conflict.[20]

The question of whether or not Satanic cults exist which torture children is not an obscure issue for dispassionate scientific research and debate. The answer to this question has practical impact on effective therapy for the MPD patients making claims about Satanists, and on law enforcement pursuit of the perpetrators of alleged ritualistic crime. Moreover, on a broader societal level, the investigation of this question inevitably has an impact on the social dynamics of the Satanism scare.

Any bit of credibility given by significant authority figures to allegations about criminal Satanists is almost immediately employed by moral crusaders in their fight against secret, criminal Satanism.

In the small community of MPD specialists, the stakes are high. Some very prominent therapists, mostly psychiatrists, have put their professional reputations on the line by advocating that therapists accept MPD patients' allegations of Satanic cult ritual torture as being reliable reports of real events, rather than as delusions or expressions of personal fantasy.[21] If it turns out that, indeed, there exists a conspiracy of Satanists, they will be seen as courageous. In contrast, if it turns out that these therapists came to believe their patients' fantasies, they could fall into disrepute. These highly esteemed specialists in powerful positions in the mental health establishment could be caught up in one of the biggest hoaxes in the history of psychiatry.

The debate is not one between ideologues, but among people of genuinely compassionate concern. Therapists trying to help MPD patients find themselves in a particularly difficult dilemma. They worry that open scientific debate, with all its necessary skepticism toward any claims of truth lacking verifiable evidence, will undermine their ability to help the people whose suffering they see on a daily basis. One of the leading advocates of the Satanic cult explanation, psychiatrist Walter C. Young, Medical Director of the National Center for the Treatment of Dissociative Disorders, has recently expressed his view of the intense internal conflict.

> It appears that there is a distinct polarization within the field between those who look for alternative explanations to ritual abuse and those who feel that ritual abuse is still in its infancy, and like sexual abuse and child battering, will become more clear as information emerges. From the scientific point of view, having debate about ritual abuse may be healthy. On the other hand, from the clinician's perspective, immediate action is often required in order to assist a patient to gain emotional stability and recover from conditions being reported. The scholarly debate on authenticity is not of much help in the clinician's office.[22]

Young frames the problem in terms of the past "discovery" of sexual child abuse and child battering. Doing so distorts interpretation of allegations of ritual abuse in terms of that analogy, suggesting that a definite moral evil will be uncovered once sufficient evidence is accumulated. Young's statement also highlights how the Satanic cult scare has aggravated the perpetual tension between practitioners (therapists) and behavioral scientists.

These leading therapists have attempted to avoid the cauldron of public controversy by insulating their claims-making within channels of communication that exist mainly between psychotherapists. Their advocacy of elaborate Satanic cult explanations of MPD "survivor" stories (and of children's allegations of ritual abuse) is limited primarily to lectures and training workshops presented at conferences of the International Society for the Study of Multiple Personality and Dissociation, and the production of training films for therapists and law enforcement officers about "ritual" child abuse.[23] While copies of some of their conference papers circulate at police seminars on "ritualistic" crime as pieces of authoritative evidence, their work rarely finds its way into scientific research journals, where it would become subject to the cross-examination of behavioral scientists.[24]

Some less prominent psychotherapists have appeared on television talk shows which exploit the Satanism scare for sensationalized entertainment. (These shows are guided by entertainment and audience rating criteria and are not nonfiction documentaries, as many TV watchers believe.) Some therapists have already published popular culture books about their work with MPD patients who claim to be Satanic cult survivors.[25] These activities function to lend authoritative legitimacy to claims about Satanic cults.

Many local psychotherapists are now confirming the Satanic cult allegations of patients they diagnose as having MPD. As noted in Chapter Five, some therapists have made a thriving enterprise out of identifying clients who they regard as having MPD and being childhood victims of ritual abuse by Satanic cults. A recent national survey of clinical psychologists found that 1,908 clinical psychologists reported treating no cases of ritual abuse and 785 reported treating only one or two cases.[26] However, sixteen of them reported having treated over a hundred cases of ritual abuse each, indicating that a few therapists may be highly predisposed to see disturbed people as suffering from the affects of Satanic cult ritual abuse.

Potentially the most powerful source of opposition to believing psychotherapists comes from parents who have been victimized by false accusations of incest on the part of their adult children. An organization of such parents, called the False Memory Syndrome Foundation, began with several families in Philadelphia in March 1992. After only eight months, it drew together over 1,650 families from across the United States and Canada, representing about 10,500 individuals. The FMS Foundation is supported and advised by a board of nationally recognized psychologists and psychiatrists and now has chapters in several states. The amazing growth of this organization indicates the extent and seriousness of the epidemic of false accusations of incest, including accusations of Satanic ritual sex abuse. Its emergence also foretells of the intense legal and political conflict which will come.

Over the few months of its existence, the FMS Foundation has already become an active support and lobby group on behalf of victimized parents. It functions to publicize the problem of false accusations against parents and provides the mass media with scientific psychological information to counter false, pop culture assumptions about child sexual abuse and memory. The FMS Foundation also provides counseling and legal advice to accused parents. It is likely that malpractice suits against believing therapists are in the offing.

In addition, the organization plans to sponsor research on the origins of false accusations of sexual abuse against parents. It has already carried out a preliminary questionnaire survey of its members to determine the social context of these accusations. Among other things, it found that 90 percent of the accusing children are daughters, mainly in the age group of thirty to forty. About 18 percent of the accusations involved Satanic cult ritual abuse. Most of the accused parents (80 percent) are in intact marriages and never divorced, which indicates marital stability far higher than the national average. These parents also have higher than average education and income, being mainly professional people who report that they provided their children with many opportunities ranging from dancing lessons to study abroad. A majority of these parents report regularly eating together with their children, going on vacations together, and being actively involved with their children's lives, in sharp contrast to dysfunctional families. In all but a few cases, the children's supposedly repressed memories of sexual abuse were "discovered" during psychotherapy with a believing therapist, and in almost all cases the therapists provided them with pop culture incest "survivor" self-help books. Many of these therapists used highly questionable, faddish treatment techniques, such as hypnotherapy, primal scream, trance writing, and even exorcism. This suggests that many of these therapists may have been susceptible to another therapy fad—that of discovering repressed memories of sexual abuse.

Children's Allegations of Ritual Abuse

The issue of MPD "survivor" stories is inseparable from that of allegations of Satanic cult ritual abuse coming from children. The two phenomena are linked by moral crusaders, who claim that both provide eyewitness accounts that verify the existence of Satanic cult crime.

The basic research question is whether or not children's reports of extremely bizarre sexual abuse in Satanic rituals, happening mainly at child-care centers, are accurate accounts of actual incidents. Social conflict over the issue of "ritual" abuse is, if anything, more acrimonious than that over the nature of MPD "survivor" stories. The reason is that, in one way or another, children are being harmed. If children's stories of bizarre sexual abuse are accurate accounts, and if they are not given credibility, children voicing these reports are being doubly victimized by irreparable trauma and gross injustice. On the other hand, if the children's stories are not accurate accounts, the same children are being emotionally abused by overzealous child protection workers in pursuit of imaginary child molesters. Moreover, gross injustice is occurring, because some people are being falsely accused, brought to trial, and imprisoned.

Here again the stakes are high. If it turns out that some child protection workers inadvertently primed false accusations coming from the mouths of children, then they may be liable for civil suits by people having been falsely accused. (This is already happening in England.) Some prominent social workers and therapists, who have been activists crusading against Satanic cult "ritual" abuse, have their reputations on the line.[27] In addition, many child protection workers worry that, if the ritual abuse allegations are eventually discredited, the long-range effect will be also to discredit all children's testimony about their sexual victimization.

Fortunately, the issue of children's eyewitness testimony about physical and sexual abuse has not been insulated from scientific cross-examination and critical analysis. There has been an increasing number of careful research studies of this issue. The issue was considered so important by psychologists, that in 1991, the American Psychological Association published a book of research studies and scientific debate about the issue.[28] None of the studies, however, deals specifically with allegations of ritual abuse.

There are larger political implications of the whole debate. If there are, indeed, criminal Satanists who are infiltrating the nation's child-care centers, as the claims-makers assert, some action will have to be taken by law enforcement agencies and government. If children are not safe in child-care centers, most of which are privately owned today, what does that portend for any possible program of government funded child-care?

The Role of Science in the Moral Crusade

What conclusions can be drawn from the foregoing examination about the role of science in the collective definition of Satanism as a new form of deviance?

Sociologists of deviant behavior have examined the role of medicine and psychiatry in the social construction of alcoholism, drug abuse, juvenile delinquency, and homosexuality as forms of mental illness.[29] In these cases, it was practitioners, rather than researchers, who were active in attributing new psychiatric meanings to deviant behavior, previously considered simply moral and criminal offenses. These new meanings were attempts to make sense out of complex, ambiguous phenomena, with which these practitioners had to deal. Their attempts to grasp meaning framed these problems in terms of an analogy with the disease model, familiar to the medical practitioners.

Most of the people in the scientific community who are promoting elaborate claims about Satanic cults are psychotherapists rather than behavioral science researchers. This may be, in part, a result of their pressing need for immediate explanations which seem to have practical use in dealing with the ambiguous plight of their clients. In order to make sense out of ambiguity, they have framed the problem, in terms of analogies drawn from either a child advocate or from Christian fundamentalist ideologies, as being one of hidden sexual exploitation and/or the work of evil conspiracies.

Practitioners are less subject to the crucible of scientific cross-examination and dispute, a process which takes years to work itself out. These claims-making practitioners have carefully insulated their presentations about Satanism from the cross-examination of scientific researchers. At the same time, they continually organize training programs about "ritual" abuse which produce more and more believers. These new converts perceive themselves as fighting a horrendous moral evil in society. It is in this sense that they are activists in the moral crusade against Satanism.

Government and Conflict over Claims about Satanism

The most direct path that moral crusaders can take to legitimize their definitions of deviance is through the political system. The collective goal is to institutionalize a new definition of deviance, using the authority of government and law. In the United States, the collective process of the Satanism scare has involved: attempts to pass new laws; criminal trials arising from allegations of crimes such as sexual child abuse and murder, supposedly motivated by Satanic ideology; and official law enforcement task force reports about "ritualistic" crimes.

There are many past examples of how moral crusades have successfully navigated new definitions of deviance through the political system. The anti-Communist crusaders obtained a great many laws and bureaucratic regulations which allowed innocent individuals to be transformed into "subversives" because they had unpopular political beliefs. The prohibitionists were able to obtain a Constitutional amendment which transformed the production and consumption of alcohol into deviant behavior.

More recently, the moral crusade against drunk driving has been effective in getting new laws passed which permit stronger punishments for driving under the influence of alcohol. In turn, that has helped to develop stronger public condemnation of drunk driving.[30] The moral crusade against smoking has been successful in getting established new laws and company regulations against smoking in public places.[31] That has been useful in changing public opinion, so that now smoking in the presence of non-smokers is widely seen as a minor deviant act.

What is most important in all these cases is not the new laws themselves, but the symbolic legitimation of goals of moral crusaders through the authority of laws. The impact of new laws can help change public opinion about the extent of the evil that moral crusaders are fighting. (Although, as the Prohibition amendment illustrates, political struggle does not end with the passing of laws.)

New State Laws

Moral crusaders who seek new laws against "ritualistic" crimes face a major dilemma. The notion of "ritualistic" crime is so ambiguous that it is difficult to construct laws directed at criminalizing behavior which is not already criminal. In addition, attempts to criminalize particular religious beliefs or rituals run into the wall of first amendment protections of the freedom of religious expression.

Four states, Louisiana, Idaho, Texas, and Illinois, have already passed laws directed at "ritualistic" crimes, as of the end of 1991. These laws are unlikely to have any actual effects upon law enforcement. However, they do symbolically affirm the claims of moral crusaders against Satanism, who can now assert that these states "recognize" the reality of crimes committed by Satanic cults. These new laws, for the most part, simply permit harsher punishments for such crimes as: cemetery desecration, vandalism, animal mutilation, and violent crimes when they are committed by perpetrators using Satanic ritualism as a rationalization for their aggression.[32]

Political Backfire

Sometimes the attempts of moral crusaders to use the political process to provide authoritative legitimacy to their claims can backfire and result in their claims being discredited. This is what happened, for example, in the state of Virginia.

After considerable lobbying efforts by moral crusaders, the Virginia state government established a task force in its Crime Commission to study claims about "ritual" crime in Virginia. The task force carried out a rather comprehensive investigation that included surveys of reports about "ritual" crime from law enforcement agencies, school districts, and mental health practitioners in Virginia, as well as in-depth interviews with many professionals from these groups.[33] The findings of the study, made available in August 1991, largely discredited the claims of the moral crusaders about "ritual" crime.[34]

The Virginia Task Force Report came to the following conclusions about "ritual" crime in Virginia.

> Definitive documentation of ritual crime is rare. In no case was there conclusive evidence of homicide in Virginia which could be causally linked to the influence of a spiritual belief system or interest in the occult.
>
> Crimes of vandalism, trespassing, and graffiti . . . had the clearest link to occult influence. Even where these crimes were

reported, follow-up investigations revealed that an occult influence was often suspected rather than proved.

Follow-up interviews exposed no evidence of any broad conspiracy of ritual crime. Local law enforcement agencies throughout the Commonwealth and experts within the Virginia State Police insisted that their investigations failed to uncover any organized network of crime which could be attributed to the influences of a spiritual belief system.[35]

Furthermore, the Task Force Report noted that the reports and testimony they obtained from many mental health practitioners lacked verifiable evidence, because therapists, unlike police, were not required to find corroborating evidence for the claims about "ritual" crime made by their clients.

Generally, these claims involved information derived from clients, were anecdotal in nature and lacked detail concerning dates and locations of alleged offenses. Additionally, they involved incidents that were years or decades old. . . .

Disclosures by therapists and self-described victims of ritual crime included allegations of nationwide conspiracies. Alleged offenses included kidnapping, murder, and physical and emotional abuse, though witnesses were typically unable to provide specific details as to locations of events, dates on which they occurred or names of victims other than themselves.[36]

This study confirms the central role of therapists in providing legitimacy for claims about a national Satanic cult conspiracy. This role arises from the peculiar occupational requirements of psychotherapists, in contrast to those of police officers. The Task Force Report noted the conflicting occupational requirements.

Because therapists are necessarily concerned with treatment issues, their initial response to clients who report ritual abuse is to seek a determination as to what effect this has had on the client, rather than the accuracy of the client's account. Nor is it their objective to attain or compile evidence in support of a criminal investigation or prosecution. Indeed, attempts in that regard may impede effective treatment.[37]

These occupational requirements cause some compassionate therapists to become "believers" in the Satanic cult stories, which they hear voiced by their clients, who are in emotional pain. Later, some "believing" therapists go on to become moral crusaders against Satanic cult "ritual" crime. When they lecture about "ritual" crime at police and social work conferences, they assume a role quite different from that of therapist. They assume the role of authoritative expert in a moral crusade against deviant behavior.

The Courts and Conflict over Claims about Satanism

The collective behavior of the Satanism scare has intruded itself into legal processes in many ways. Many legal issues have been explored previously in this book: the criminal trials of child-care workers accused of "ritually" abusing children; the civil suits against parents accused of "ritual" abuse of their now adult children; criminal trials of rock musicians accused of encouraging suicide through Satanic music lyrics; and civil suits against school districts using books alleged to promote Satanism.

The modern-day folklore of the Satanic cult legend now circulates widely in American society. So, enterprising lawyers, for either prosecution or defense, can use it to pursue the goals of their clients.

MPD Patients' Allegations of Ritual Abuse in Court

It was only a matter of time before the allegations of MPD patients would be presented in court. Civil suits and perhaps criminal trials involving these allegations are likely to become more common in the future.

The first trial involving the allegations of MPD patients took place during March and April of 1991, in Orange County, California. Two sisters, ages forty-eight and thirty-five, brought a civil suit against their seventy-six-year-old mother, alleging that from infancy they were forced: to take part in bizarre Satanic cult ritual practices, including eating human flesh and drinking blood; to engage in prostitution in order to attract victims to be murdered; and to commit incest with both parents.[38] The older daughter claimed that she was impregnated by a cult member at the age of twelve, and then she was forced to murder her six-month-old baby by stabbing it to death. Further, the daughters accused their mother of also sexually abusing her granddaughter, now eleven years old. The girl testified in court affirming those accusations. In the suit, the sisters sought $7 million in financial compensation from the mother for their emotional suffering. (Their father died in 1986.)

The jury decided in a split 10 to 2 verdict in favor of the daughters, but awarded no financial damages. The jury charged the mother with being negligent, but did not believe that she had intentionally caused any harm to her daughters. The compromise verdict left both attorneys claiming vindication of their case.[39] The daughters claimed that their only motivation for the suit was to gain publicity for the reality of "ritual" child abuse by Satanic cults. However, their mother's defense attorney suggested that the daughters were after their mother's money, and didn't want to wait to inherit it.[40]

The central focus in the case was the influence of the daughters' psychotherapist, because they claimed to have had no memories of their childhood tortures until the memories were "brought out" by their therapist, Tim Maas, a marriage counselor.[41] Maas's professional training consisted only of a BA in business administration and a ministerial degree in pastoral counseling. He is a defrocked Evangelical Lutheran minister. His six "Christian-oriented" clinics were treating about fifty Satanic "ritual" abuse cases at the time and were receiving about two new cases each month.[42] Maas's clinics employed twenty-three "therapists," most of whom were paraprofessional interns or trainees. The defense lawyer demonstrated, by questioning Maas, that he had very little scientific knowledge about Multiple Personality Disorder and that his information about Satanic cult "ritual" abuse came mainly from pop culture books, such as *Michelle Remembers* and *Satan's Underground.*[43]

Allegations of Satanic Cult Murder in Court

One recent murder case provides an excellent example of the use of the Satanic cult legend, by a lawyer, as a defense for a client. In Palmyra, New York, on August 2, 1990, a fourteen-year-old girl and seventeen-month-old infant, whom she was babysitting, were found stabbed to death behind a local middle school. One of the classmates of the girl, fourteen-year-old Chad Campbell, was shortly thereafter arrested and charged with the murders. Initially, Campbell confessed to police investigators that he committed the murders. He also repeated his confession to two psychiatrists, who were appointed by the court to examine whether he understood the charges against him.[44]

However, Campbell later changed his story, claiming that he only raped the girl and that another teenager, a friend, had actually committed the murders. That friend was now dead, having committed suicide, so he could not be questioned about the case. According to local rumors, the friend was said to be a "high priest" in a Satanic cult. Campbell now claimed that he was fearful of implicating his friend in the murders, because his friend might use his occult powers to harm Campbell's family.[45] Campbell's defense lawyer pursued the argument that Campbell was innocent of the murders, and that his now dead Satanist friend had actually committed the murders, as a Satanic ritual sacrifice.

Before a trial could be held, Campbell's parents paid for the services of a Satan hunter, Logan Clarke, to come to Palmyra and investigate the allegations about Satanic cults in the area.[46] Clarke is a private investigator from California who has served as an "expert" witness in several trials involving alleged Satanic cult crime. He told the local press that the area of Palmyra was rife with Satanic cults, as evidenced by the abundance Satanic graffiti and local rumors about secret Satanic cult meetings. Clarke also told the press that he believed that Campbell was "brainwashed" into his participation in the crime through the influence of Satanism, thus making a case for diminished responsibility. He claimed that the day of the murder was a special day, on a so-called Satanic calendar, for making human sacrifices. These allegations precipitated a local Satanic cult rumor-panic.[47]

At the trial, Campbell's defense lawyer brought in another "expert" in Satanic cult crime, Dr. Herbert Nieberg, a psychologist working for the Department of Mental Health of Westchester County. Nieberg's testimony supported the claims about Satanic cult influences on Campbell, including the claim that the day of the murder (August 1) was a "satanist high holy day for a sacrifice." Nieberg claimed that it was the baby that the Satanists were after to sacrifice.[48] The prosecution brought in their own "expert" witness, anthropologist Dr. Phillips Stevens, from the State University of New York at Buffalo. Stevens is a respected scholar known for his studies of the Western heritage of beliefs about witchcraft and Satanism.[49] Stevens countered Nieberg's testimony, noting that there was no evidence for the existence of Satanic cults. He also noted that Nieberg's supposed day for Satanic sacrifice was actually a celebration day (Lammas Day) in the Wiccan religious calendar and that Satan hunters frequently made this mistake.[50] The prosecution's case provided an effective rebuttal of the defense's arguments about Satanic influences on the mental state of Campbell. The jury convicted Campbell of two counts of second degree murder.[51]

This case illustrates that the political struggle to define Satanism as a new form of deviant behavior has become embedded in occupational vested interests, with potential pay-offs in terms of money, prestige, and power.

Religious Conflict and Allegations of Satanism

Allegations about Satanists in the Mormon Church Hierarchy
When a scare creates widespread suspicion, allegations about involvement in an evil conspiracy are commonly used as a weapon in previously existing conflicts. These conflicts may be as personal as disputes between neighbors, or impersonal antagonisms between ideological partisans involving religious, ethnic, racial, or socio-economic groups. This was the case in all past witch hunts and it is the case in the Satanic cult witch hunt today. These conflicts are aggravated by accusations of coopera-

tion with the alleged evil internal enemy, but they also function, like a motor, to further disseminate the scare. I believe that this is the greatest danger of the Satanic cult scare.

In Utah, during November 1991, allegations surfaced in newspapers that the Mormon Church had been widely infiltrated by criminal Satanists.[52] Over the preceding weeks, one of the Salt Lake City newspapers had run a series of stories about the ritual abuse claims of MPD patients and their local therapists, offering no skeptical analysis.[53] Then, at the end of October 1991, anti-Mormon fundamentalists, Jerald and Sandra Tanner, "leaked" a confidential report about ritual abuse, written by a high level Mormon official. The Mormon official, Glenn Pace, counselor to the Presiding Bishopric of the Church of Jesus Christ of Latter-Day Saints, had investigated allegations of Satanic cult ritual abuse made by some Mormons against others in the church.

According to newspaper reports, Pace interviewed sixty people who made these allegations, including fifty-three females and seven males (eight of whom were children), from several states including Utah, Idaho, and California.[54] All of these people had been diagnosed as suffering from Multiple Personality Disorder. Almost all of them (forty-five) claimed to have witnessed or participated in human sacrifices, as well as to having been victims of sexual abuse and torture. In his confidential report, dated July 19, 1990, Pace wrote that he was convinced that there were at least eight hundred secret Satanists posing as Mormons in the Salt Lake Valley alone. Many of them were were high church officials, including bishops and patriarchs, and some were even members of the famed Mormon Tabernacle Choir.

An official public relations release from the church, in response to reporter's inquiries, stated that: "Satanic worship and ritualistic abuse are problems that have been around for centuries and are international in scope."[55] The statement denied that the problem was a major one in the Mormon Church, or particular to that church. Paradoxically, this kind of statement lends authoritative credibility to the claims of MPD patients and the therapists who believe them. It also serves to confirm people's belief in the Satanic cult legend. The statement can be seen as being very similar to those put out by organizations accused in the 1950s of being infiltrated by Communist conspirators. They affirmed that the Communist conspiracy was pervasive in American society, but denied that their particular organization was substantially infiltrated. In doing so, they perpetuated the "Red Scare."

The Struggle to Legitimize Claims about a New Form of Deviance

The process of collective behavior has a momentum of its own. The dynamic of collective behavior is not guided by people's intentions, but by the social consequences of their actions. Allegations of horrendous, organized crimes are being made. These allegations have attained popular legitimacy in many parts of the country, particularly in rural and small town areas, through the dissemination of the Satanic cult legend. However, the struggle of the claims-makers to obtain legitimacy also requires the legitimacy conveyed by authority, through science, law enforcement, government, and the courts.

The efforts of claims-makers to obtain authoritative legitimacy in these areas have met with some notable successes. These successes include receiving the endorsement of prominent psychiatrists specialized in the treatment of Multiple Personality Disorder and many other psychotherapists and child protection workers across the country. The claims-makers have also successfully agitated for the passage of a few new state laws and the preparation of a few government sponsored reports, both of which provide symbolic legitimacy to the claims.

However, there have also been some pointed failures in attempts to gain authoritative legitimacy for claims about criminal Satanic cults. Some government sponsored studies of the possible existence of ritualistic crime have backfired and provided evidence counter to the claims. Attempts to bring the claims to court, where concrete verifiable evidence is required, have usually failed to provide the claims with legitimacy. The claims have also not been able to stand the critical scrutiny of behavioral science researchers. So far, no scientifically verifiable evidence has been found through research to verify the diverse panorama of claims about secret, criminal organizations of Devil worshippers.

Given these counter-currents, it is likely that the political struggle to define Satanic cult crime as a new form of deviance will continue for at least another decade. The danger is that once a moral crusade has gained some success in legitimizing its claims about a new form of deviance, it can easily become a witch hunt.

Chapter Fourteen
The Medieval Origins of Modern Demonology

What is past is prologue.
William Shakespeare,
The Tempest[1]

Contemporary stories about Satanism and Satanic cults arise from an ancient heritage in Western societies. These stories are a product of the folklore of Devil worship accusations. The historical roots of these accusations can be traced back to the eleventh century. The motifs of the stories have been the basis of Western counter-subversion ideologies related to a host of alleged secret conspiracies. The stories have targeted groups as diverse as accused heretics, Jews, Freemasons, Catholics, and Communists.

Historical evidence indicates that a secret, organized conspiracy of Devil worshippers has never existed, except in the imagination of those people who believed in its existence. The fantasy fears of heresy and subversion represent the shadow side of the Western cultural heritage. The stories tell us nothing about supposed Devil worshippers. However, they do tell us much about the suppressed fears of people in Western cultures during times when they lose faith in the established social order.

Toward the end of the twentieth century, in Europe and the United States, the awful specter of the shadow side of Western culture has once again arisen as an explanation for disruptive change and misfortune. We see it in its many forms, in the resurgent search for scapegoats of all kinds: Jews (in Germany and Eastern Europe, once again), foreign immigrants (in France and Germany), Devil worshippers (in the United States, Canada, and Great Britain).

A Counter-Subversion Demonology

During periods of rapid, disruptive social change, many people need explanations for daily dislocations in their lives and their fears about an uncertain future. In every society, these explanations place the blame for the anxieties people feel about their fate and the fate of their group, or their society as a whole, on "evil forces." The term "demonology" has been used by some scholars to refer to these explanations of evil. Anthropologist Phillips Stevens Jr. defines a demonology as: "an ideology of evil, an elaborate body of belief about an evil force that is inexorably undermining society's most cherished values and institutions."[2] Stevens, who has done research in African societies, regards the demonology of Western, Christian cultures to be relatively distinct in structure and content, in part, because of its origin in medieval Christian beliefs about the Devil.[3] However, a demonology does not necessarily refer to beliefs about evil demons, and it may even have entirely secular, non-supernatural content today. The Satanic cult legend is only one product of the Western demonology.

The eminent British historian, Norman Cohn, has documented the cultural development and social consequences of the Western demonology in several books.[4] Its root metaphor can be found in Christian beliefs about the struggle of Satan and his earthly henchmen to undermine the Christian moral order of society. In a brilliant article titled, "The Myth of Satan and his Human Servants," Cohn concisely describes the history of this Western demonology.

> The fantasy is that there exists a category of human beings that is pledged to the service of Satan; a sect that worships Satan in secret conventicles and, on Satan's behalf, wages relentless war against Christendom and against individual Christians. At one time in the Middle Ages, this fantasy became attached to certain heretical sects, and helped to legitimate and intensify their persecution. A couple of centuries later, it gave the traditional witchcraft beliefs of Europe a twist which turned them into something new and strange. . . . And, the fantasy has also been attached to the Jews—and not only in far-off times but in the late nineteenth and early twentieth centuries, when it helped to prepare the way for the secular demonology of the Nazis. It is a long story but perfectly coherent one, and it is excellently documented.[5]

In his book, *Europe's Inner Demons,* Norman Cohn states the essence of this demonology, indicating how it forms the core metaphor of Western secular, as well as religious, counter-subversion ideologies.

> The essence of this fantasy was that there existed, somewhere in the midst of the great society, another society, small and clandestine, which not only threatened the existence of the great society but was also addicted to practices which were felt to be wholly abominable, in the literal sense of anti-human.[6]

This is the structure of the Western ideology of evil, which makes it distinct from beliefs about the nature of evil in Asian societies or in preliterate cultures.[7] It says, in essence, that the striving for moral perfection and greatness of our society is being undermined by hidden, inner enemies; and, we cannot blame ourselves for any failure to attain our ideals. The cognitive structure of this demonology encourages people to psychologically project the shadow of their fears and guilt, their inner "demons," upon convenient scapegoat groups.[8]

This demonology is particularly appealing to people who have what psychologists call an authoritarian personality. People with authoritarian personalities have a very rigid pattern of thinking, which demands complete conformity and allegiance to some ideology or religious belief system and to the conventionally accepted practices of their society. Authoritarians are extremely intolerant of anyone whom they regard as deviating from that system of thought. They tend to project their own, self-perceived sins (their "inner demons") on these scapegoat deviants.

The Medieval Origins of the Demonology

Ritual Murder Stories about the Early Christians

It is not religion but politics which accounts for the use of Western demonology in the scapegoating of imaginary secret conspirators. The seeds of the demonology lie in prehistory. However, records of its ancient European origins can be found in the political accusations of secret conspiracy that pagan Romans lodged against early Christian communities. Ironically, it was Christians who were first conceived to be a small, separate society which threatened the existence of the great society of the Roman Empire, and whose members were believed to practice abominable, inhuman rituals in secret ceremonies. Rumors and allegations of crime directed at Christians became a vehicle for their persecution and mass murder by Romans seeking scapegoats to blame for social tensions which threatened the stability of the Empire.

The inhuman practices of which Christians were accused included: the ritual murder of infants; the drinking of the infants' blood and the cannibalistic eating of their flesh at secret ceremonies; and sexual orgies and incestuous relations.[9] Early Christians were widely regarded as being a group of ruthless, power hungry conspirators. These accusations distorted the nature of early Christian rituals such as the Eucharist and the Agape feast. These accusations were essentially political rather than religious, because Christians were regarded as being subversive of the unity of Roman law.[10]

The First Allegations of Devil Worship

Accusations of the ritual murder of children did not become widespread again until the next period of great social change and religious ferment, just after the turn of the first millennium (when, according to popular belief, the world was supposed to have come to an end and Christ was supposed to have returned). At that time, religious dissent against the hierarchical Church began to gradually develop and spread.

In 1022, in Orleans, France, a group of about fourteen heretics were burned at the stake. These were the first of many hundreds of thousands of accused heretics, accused witches, and Jews to be executed in this manner over subsequent centuries.[11] The execution of the accused heretics of Orleans was also a precursor of future persecutions in several other ways. Those who were executed were, sadly, innocent victims of a power struggle between the King and local nobility. Their "heresy" wasn't substantially different than the dissenting Christian religious beliefs held by a great many religious idealists of their time. Accusations of heresy became a weapon in political disputes. More importantly, the accusations were rationalized in years after their execution, with allegations that the Orleans heretics engaged in secret rituals in which they worshipped the Devil, held sex orgies, and sacrificed infants, whose ashes they used to make a special magical ointment.[12] The Satanic cult legend that one hears repeated today was born in Orleans in the eleventh century. It was as empty of literal truth then as it is today.

The weapon of Devil worship accusations proved to be a valuable tool in political struggles, as European societies became increasingly unstable and beset by peasant rebellions against the local land owning nobility. Much of the dissent from the hierarchical medieval order took the form of increasing religious heresy.

> The message of betrayal was borne by wandering preachers, men of wild aspect, conspicuous poverty and ferocious language, who railed against the avarice and lechery of the priests and drew followers to themselves in alarming numbers.[13]

Devil Worship Stories about the Cathars

By the middle of the next century, various heresies spread widely. The most important of the religious movements against the Church hierarchy and its allies among the nobility was that of the Cathar heresy (also known as the Albigensian heresy).[14] By the 1160s, the Cathars had attracted many thousands of followers in southern France (especially in the area around Toulouse) and in northern Italy. They were even able to establish their own churches and clergy organization. In some communities, very few people continued to practice the old religion. The response of the church hierarchy to the growing heresy was the gradual organization of the Inquisition.

Eventually, in 1208, a Catholic army was sent to southern France, in a crusade ordered by Pope Innocent III to exterminate the rebellious Cathars. Over a period of about thirty years, the crusaders and the Inquisition that followed in the army's wake did so quite ruthlessly, sometimes killing the entire populations of towns: men, women, and children. At the town of Beziers, the crusaders were said to have killed twenty thousand people after they stormed the city. Considerable political benefit was reaped by the king of France, who was able to claim the region (Languedoc) for his efforts.

The Cathar heresy is not a familiar benchmark in Western history, but it was very significant to the cultural evolution of the tools of mass persecution.[15] Not only did it give impetus to the long-lasting structure of the Inquisition, but it led to a further elaboration of the demonology of persecution. Clerics and religious scholars engaged in a propaganda war against the Cathars and other heretics. The Cathars were accused of engaging in sexual orgies, sometimes involving incest, and of practicing secret rituals in worship of the Devil, involving the sacrifice of children and the eating of their flesh in cannibalistic rites.[16]

Actually, the Cathars were a rather puritanical group; they believed that the world of matter and flesh was permeated by evil. The name Cathar is derived from Greek, meaning "the purified."[17] Many of their leaders practiced life-long chastity, frequent fasting, and vegetarianism. However, surviving church polemics against the Cathars paint them as having been Devil worshippers. These documents have become part of the legacy of anti-Satanist crusaders, who point to this folkloric history of the Cathars as evidence for the centuries-old existence of Satanic cults.

Devil Worship Stories about the Knights Templars

As a consequence of the propaganda war against heresy, belief in the existence of Devil worshippers spread widely and accusations of Devil worship proved to be a useful weapon in political struggle. It didn't take long before the weapon was turned against a very reputable religious organization: the Knights Templars.

The Knights Templars were initially a special order of soldier monks, organized to guard the conquests of the crusaders in the Near East. However, the Templars became extremely wealthy after they began to function as international bankers and financiers for kings and popes, who deposited their revenues with the Templars for safeguarding. Eventually, the Knights Templars acquired estates and fortresses across Europe. Their fortress in Paris became the center of European money markets.

Unfortunately, the Templars got caught in a power struggle between the king of France, Philip IV, who desperately needed money to finance his many war-making ventures, and the Pope, to whom the Knights Templars owed nominal allegiance. Philip employed a clever strategy to appropriate the finances and lands of the Templars, and at the same time, neutralize the Pope's possible support for his religious order. In 1307, he carried out mass arrests of Templars across France. Under torture, they confessed: to having engaged in secret worship of the Devil (in the form of a black cat); to having engaged regularly in sexual orgies, sometimes involving homosexual practices; and to having sacrificed infants born out of wedlock by roasting them over fires and smearing their fat on an idol called Baphomet.[18] On the strength of these confessions, the Knights Templars were dissolved and the king acquired their property. Many of the Templars died under torture and others were executed. Their grand master, Jacques de Molay, was burned at the stake in Paris, in 1314.

Philip conducted an effective propaganda war by paying writers to justify his actions against the Templars. Even today, pseudo-histories of the Knights Templars perpetuate false claims about their Satanic cult activities.[19] These became part of the evolving Satanic cult legend. Historian Barbara Tuchman, in her book, appropriately titled A Distant Mirror, indicates the impact of this relatively obscure event upon later European culture.

> Elements of witchcraft, magic, and sorcery were taken for granted in medieval life, but Philip's use of them to prove heresy in the seven-year melodrama of the Templar's trials gave them fearful currency. Thereafter charges of black arts became a common means to bring down an enemy and a favored method of the Inquisition in its pursuit of heretics, especially those with property worth confiscating.[20]

The Origins of the Blood Libel Myth

The most familiar historical remnant of the demonology, one which arose in the eleventh century, is the "blood libel" accusation levelled against the Jews of Europe. The "blood libel" involves allegations of Jewish ritual murder of Christian children and use of their blood in secret religious rites. However, those who are familiar with the "blood libel" are usually unaware that the motif of ritual murder was only a variant of the same kind of accusation directed at other groups besides Jews, including the Cathars and Templars.

The Antecedents of European Anti-Semitism

Until the eleventh century, Christians and Jews in Western Europe lived alongside each other in relative cooperation.[21] There were scattered incidents of friction and hostility, but these incidents were exceptions. Then, after the turn of the first millennium, this cooperative relationship deteriorated rather rapidly, when Jews became targets of vilification, vicious stereotyping, and mass murder. Modern anti-Semitism has its origins in the cauldron of eleventh-century social conflicts.

What happened that so sharply changed Jewish-Christian relations in the eleventh century? Medieval historians have suggested several complementary hypotheses to explain the change. The traditional explanation has been that the moral revitalization movement of resurgent, militant Christianity leading up to the First Crusade (1095–1099) stimulated hostility toward any social group perceived as being religious deviants, including Jews as well as accused heretics. In 1063, for example, several Jewish communities in southwestern France were attacked by knights on their way to fight the Moslems in Spain.[22] Mass murder of Jews by crusaders on their way to the Holy Land became common practice after that time.

An additional explanation is that the Jews got caught up in the power struggles between different religious factions of Christians, as rival factions tried to prove the purity of their faith by the fervor of their condemnation of any rival faction perceived as being insufficiently orthodox. Anyone believed to be cooperating with non-Christians, such as Jews, could be slandered as being in league with enemies of the faith.[23] The social dynamic is similar to that which perpetuated white racism in the South, that which led white racist politicians to attack rival white politicians for being too sympathetic to Blacks, and which meant few whites would risk giving aid and comfort to the proxy scapegoat group of Blacks.

Perhaps the most penetrating analysis is suggested by social historian Gavin Langmuir, who has spent decades researching the origins of anti-Semitism in medieval European history, drawing upon both Jewish and Christian medieval writings.[24]

> I would suggest that the eleventh century marked the beginning of a period in which Christians at different social levels were assailed by doubts about their identity. Awareness of the presence and disbelief of Jews was an important reason for those doubts, but it was neither the first nor the only one. Doubt led Christians to rethink their faith and rethink it in a way that would change it radically and have baneful consequences for the Jews.[25]

We can understand this kind of cultural identity crisis by paying attention to what is happening in contemporary Western societies. I have argued previously that the Satanic cult scare is a result of a kind of incipient cultural identity crisis in American society. One aspect of that identity crisis is part of a much larger dilemma posed by vast changes in the nature of Christian religious belief, especially in beliefs about the nature of evil. This is more troubling for Americans than it is for Europeans, because so many Americans, as compared with Europeans, still believe in the existence of a willful, personalized Devil as the embodiment of evil. The faith of many traditionalist Christians that a good God exists is confirmed, in part, by a belief that an evil supernatural enemy of God also exists. In contrast, modernist Christians are moving toward a vastly different conception of good and evil, one which is more monotheistic and less dualistic.

Stories of the Jewish Ritual Murder of Children

The first accusation of the ritual murder of Christian children by Jews was recorded in the twelfth century, not long after similar accusations were made against Christian heretics. From that time onward, such accusations against Jews persisted into the twentieth century. They became so widely believed among Europeans, that stories of Jewish ritual murder were conveyed in church art and sculpture, as well as popular literature and ballads.[26] The accusations also became a justification for the murder of many thousands of Jews over the centuries, long before the same accusations were incorporated into Nazi anti-Semitic propaganda.[27]

Curiously, the first accusations arose from a local rumor which became transformed into an international legend in a matter of only few years through the efforts of effective propagandists. The first recorded story alleging the Jewish ritual murder of Christian children was made in a book written in 1150 by an English monk, Thomas of Monmouth. His book purported to be an investigation of the murder in 1144, in Norwich, England, of a twelve-year-old boy.[28] Thomas of Monmouth arrived in Norwich a few years after the boy's murder and upon learning of local rumors claiming that Jews had killed the boy, he became curious about the incident and decided to investigate it.

The first allegations that Jews killed the boy, named Thomas, were made by the boy's mother.[29] The mother had no particular evidence, other than revelations in a dream told to her by her sister. Members of the extended family made public accusations against the Jews of Norwich, but nothing much became of it. Some townspeople of Norwich believed the accusations and others did not. The accusations merely circulated in local gossip, until Thomas of Monmouth reported the results of his "investigations." Those "investigations" transformed the murdered boy into a martyr, and the murder story into a passion play about the crucifixion of innocence.[30]

Thomas of Monmouth's book, *The Life and Miracles of St. William of Norwich,* portrayed the murder as the result of an international Jewish conspiracy to sacrifice Christian children in secret religious rites.[31] His main "informant" was another monk, who was supposedly a converted Jew who had access to the secret conspiracy. According to this "informant," Jewish leaders met every year to choose a location where a Christian child would be kidnapped and crucified in a ritual murder as a symbolic insult to all Christians. Part of the concocted "evidence" against the Jews of Norwich was that the boy, Thomas, was killed during the Easter holy days, supposedly chosen specifically to offend Christians. Afterwards, according to Thomas of Monmouth, all sorts of miracles were reported to have occurred in Norwich.

The available historical research seems to indicate that the story told by Thomas of Monmouth was his original creation, fabricated from local rumors and his own imagination, possibly based upon familiar allegations against heretics.[32] There is no evidence that he copied the ideas for the story from writings about ancient ritual murder accusations against Jews and Christians. The investigations of Thomas of Monmouth are remarkably similar to the current "investigations" of some Satan hunters. We need to anticipate the distortions of perception caused by passionate ideological convictions that lead to a readiness to believe bizarre rumor allegations and anonymous "informants" (who claim to be former members of Satanic cults).

Shortly after Thomas of Monmouth's book became available, the story that Jews kidnapped and ritually murdered Christian children was quickly disseminated by word of mouth. By 1170, the rumor that Jews crucified Christian children had crossed the English Channel and was recorded in northern France.[33] Then, in 1171, in Blois, France, accusations of ritual murder led to the execution of thirty-two Jewish men and women by burning at the stake. By the turn of the century, similar accusations began to appear in Europe, beyond England and France, in Castile, Bohemia, and Germany.[34]

In England, hostility toward all Jews escalated, in part due to the rumors. In 1190, the entire Jewish community of York was massacred. About 150 men, women, and children had taken refuge from a rioting mob of townspeople in the city tower. As the tower burned, some of those inside were said to have committed suicide and those who sought to escape were slaughtered by the mob.[35] Thus, a series of mob attacks on Jews (pogroms), similar to the ones in France, lasting into the twentieth century began in England.

The myth of Jewish ritual murder persists in Europe even today, circulating in rumors whenever conditions of social stress are ripe for scapegoating. Sociological studies of the rumor-panics in France during the late 1960s in response to stories of Jewish white slavery (described in Chapter Four), found that allegations of Jewish ritual murder surfaced once again in collective behavior.[36] Accusations of this kind have even been raised in the United States during the twentieth century, indicating that some Americans are also familiar with this remnant of their European cultural heritage.[37]

The dissemination of stories of Jewish ritual murder, in medieval times and later, is instructive for our understanding of the innovation and diffusion of contemporary legends, such as those about so-called Satanic cult kidnappings, child torture, and ritual murders. The motifs of these recurrent stories do not have to be copied directly from past publications. The structure of the stories follows Western demonology. The particular target groups can easily be substituted one for another, Jews for heretics and Satanists for Catholic papist conspirators. Imaginative works, such as *Michelle Remembers*, can be innovated from a great diversity of cultural materials; and in a receptive social climate, the motifs of the tale can be quickly diffused across national borders.

We would be misguided to believe that it was mere superstition and mystical thinking which motivated the fantasies of the people of the twelfth century. They, like we today, are moved by the social dynamics of gossip, rumor, and ideological propaganda.

Stories of Jewish Blood Ritual and Devil Worship

It didn't take long before the original rumor-stories of Jewish ritual murder became embroidered with additional motifs, drawn from allegations made against the Cathar heretics. At the turn of the thirteenth century, the Inquisition against the Cathars was being organized and church propagandists were producing a lot of literature accusing the Cathars of cannibalism and Devil worship. These accusations were being used in the search for and execution of other alleged heretics across Europe.[38] It should not be surprising then, that these motifs quickly became included in accusations made against the Jews.

The first recorded case of allegations of Jewish blood ritual occurred in Fulda, in central Germany, on Christmas day of 1235.[39] The home of a miller had burned down and in it was found the bodies of his five sons. The Jews of Fulda were, in short order, accused of killing the boys. A mob then killed thirty-four local Jews to avenge the death of the boys. Afterwards, several local monks wrote justifications of the mob's violence, claiming that Jews had killed the boys, drained the boys' blood for use in Jewish religious rituals, and then burned down the miller's house to cover up their ritual murder.[40]

Later investigations of the incident commissioned by King Frederick I led to an official proclamation that all the accusations against the Jews were false. Nevertheless, the rumor-stories persisted and spread throughout Europe. By 1247, two

Franciscan monks accused Jews in the French town of Valreas of committing child murder and blood ritualism. The allegations led to the torture and execution of several Jews.[41] In the short century after Thomas of Monmouth had written his imaginative fable of Jewish ritual child murder, the "blood libel" story was fully developed.

There was a deeper, latent symbolism behind the motifs of child murder and rituals employing blood. The symbolism involves implications of Devil worship. These motifs served to reinforce beliefs that the Jews (like heretics) were in league with the Devil, that the Jews were agents of Satan on earth.[42] By the end of the thirteenth century, Jews were increasingly referred to as something worse than mere nonbelievers; they were referred to as demons and servants of Satan. Increasingly, Jews were seen as being less than human, in spirit and physical form. Popular folklore in many places even held that Jews had horns, the sign of the Devil.

The Jewish people had become transformed into a handy cultural symbol for use in times of cultural crisis. In the evolving Western demonology, the Devil was ultimately to blame for personal misfortune and social disorder. Therefore, the Jews, as the Devil's agents, could justly be punished for the pains of good and decent people. Moreover, punishing Jews had an additional symbolic function in the social control of society. Attacks upon Jews served as a warning for would-be heretics about the potential fate in store for them; and later, it served as a warning for ideological dissenters from the dominant political and social order of society.[43] Scapegoats are necessary to insure ideological conformity, when the winds of rapid change unsettle people's faith in the moral order of society. The search for Satanic cult criminals plays the same role in American society today.

The Beginning of the Great European Witch Hunt
The great European witch hunt began around 1430 and persisted over three hundred years, until about 1750. It began

as an extension of the Inquisition's search for heretics, in a rather obscure incident in the long history of persecutions. In 1428, in the Swiss canton of Valais, agents of the Inquisition were in search of Waldensian heretics who had taken refuge for generations in the remote mountain valleys.[44] Between 100 and 200 accused heretics were apprehended, tortured, and burned. In the confessions extracted, usually under torture, many of the accused were said to have admitted to have been Devil worshipping witches.

Chroniclers of the events elaborated the accusations against the heretics with stories about their purported practice of all sorts of black magic and acts of anti-Christian sacrilege. These stories, which had been circulating in oral folklore for centuries, were now added to the official allegations against heretics and formalized in church commentaries. The heretics were accused of making compacts with the Devil to obtain magical powers. This enabled them to fly at night between villages, so that they could attend conclaves of witches, called sabbats (a word derived from the Jewish celebration of Sabbath). They were also accused of killing and eating children, their own and those of other people. The women were reported to copulate with demons at night, and the infants which resulted were sacrificed at the witches' sabbats.

Historian Norman Cohn notes that in later years, some people, mainly women, came forth and voluntarily confessed to having engaged in infanticide and cannibalism. These voluntary confessions provided the inquisitors with apparent evidence to confirm the coerced confessions of Satanic witchcraft.

> It seems . . . that ecclesiastical and secular authorities alike, while pursuing Waldensians, repeatedly came across people— chiefly women—who believed things about themselves which fitted perfectly with the tales about heretical sects that had been circulating for centuries. The notion of cannibalistic infanticide provided the common factor. It was widely believed that babies or small children were devoured at the nocturnal meetings of heretics. It was likewise widely believed that certain women killed and devoured babies or small children; also at night; *and some women even believed this of themselves* (italics added). It

was the extraordinary congruence between the two sets of beliefs that led those concerned with pursuing heretics to see, in the stories which they extracted from deluded women, a confirmation of the traditional stories about heretics who practiced cannibalistic infanticide.[45]

These women's voluntary confessions closely resemble those made by women today who suffer from Multiple Personality Disorder. The women of the fourteenth century, whose delusions told them that they killed and ate their infants after being impregnated by demons, may have also suffered from the same personality disorder. In a bizarre way, history may be repeating itself. Psychologically disturbed women, who incorporate the fearful folklore of the times into their fantasies, are used by Satan hunters, who incorporate the women's testimonials into their more lucid fantasies of criminal conspiracy.

The Lack of Evidence for the Existence of Devil Worshippers

Over the following centuries, the mythology of the witch-hunters added an increasing variety of occult tales to their literature of persecution. Estimates of the numbers of people executed for demonic witchcraft are difficult to obtain, but it seems that at least sixty thousand people were victims, a disproportionate number of them elderly women.[46] The historical research suggests that none of the accusations were prompted by reactions to groups which actually practiced demonic witchcraft.

The consensus of historians who are life-long specialists in studies of social life in the Middle Ages, and who use original documents of the era, is that no Devil worshipping religious cult ever existed.[47] The stories of demonic witches, no matter how elaborately detailed, were works based upon oral folklore, confessions coerced under torture, testimonies of psychologically disordered individuals, and a vast repository of accumulated religious propaganda. This is important, because many of the Satan-hunters of today are attempting to fabricate a past history of Satan worshipping cults. They are doing it with the aid of pop culture writers about witchcraft, a few of whom claim to be spiritual descendants of medieval witches.

In his recent book, *The Witch-Hunt in Early Modern Europe,* historian Brian Levack reviews the lack of evidence for the existence of any organized cult of demonic witches.

> The evidence has never been produced in any recorded case of diabolism. Never once, for example, did the neighbors who accused witches of maleficia testify that they had witnessed the collective worship of the Devil or even the conclusion of a formal pact between a witch and the Devil. . . . Never once did authorities conduct a raid on a witches' coven, even though the same authorities showed that they were quite capable of breaking into the meetings of other subversive groups. In fact, whenever independent, impartial investigations were conducted into the alleged practice of diabolism, they produced negative results.[48]

This is not to deny that there were many peasants who practiced folk culture versions of healing magic and even sorcery. Indeed, many of these unfortunate souls got swept up in the net of the Inquisition and burned at the stake as demonic witches.[49] However, no Devil worshipping network of witches' covens ever existed in past history.

It would seem that the Satan-hunters of today, who claim that Satanic cults are so secretive that they cannot be found, are repeating a refrain heard over and over in the past. Police agents have proven quite competent at infiltrating secretive political groups, such as the Ku Klux Klan, the Communist Party, and even small groups of political terrorists. They have been able to infiltrate crime networks of drug dealers and even, with some difficulty, Mafia crime families. Police can't infiltrate secret criminal Satanist covens, however, because they simply don't exist.

The Impact of Medieval Folklore on the Modern Mind

Americans tend to hold the quaint notion that what is past is past, meaning that the present is born anew, free of any past influences. The notion is befitting to a nation of immigrants, most of whom wished to cut themselves off from painful memories of the old world.

What does this brief excursion into medieval history tell us about current claims about criminal Satanists? It seems clear to me, that we must focus our investigation on the Satan hunters, the claims-makers, rather than their claims about criminal Satanists in society. The long history of accusations against heretics, Jews, and witches, tells us nothing about heretics, Jews, and witches. However, it tells us a lot about the mind-set of the claims-makers.

The lessons of medieval history suggest that elaborate claims about secret Devil worshippers are constructed from a demonology that is now almost a thousand years in the making. Most of the motifs of that demonology originated in medieval times, including those involving: a secret conspiracy of Devil worshippers; secret ceremonial conclaves at night; sexual orgies in the presence of occult magic practices; the ritual murder of children; use of their blood in rituals; and the cannibalism of sacrificed infants.

Claims about criminal Satanic cults are woven out of the motifs of past allegations made against heretics, the Knights Templars, Jews, and accused witches. The claims-makers need not know anything at all about these past accusations and it is entirely possible that they do not. All they need is to be familiar with folklore or pop culture stories about moral subversives, be they about a supposed Masonic, Jewish, Catholic, or Communist conspiracy. Then, they can add some ideas from horror stories and the folklore of witchcraft. The essentials of our Western demonology is passed on to us through diverse elements of our cultural heritage. It is transmitted by many religious groups and by many pop culture entertainments.

Rumors of evil still have the power to create fears that some inner enemy is responsible for the grave misfortunes and social disorder of our time. Regardless of all the supposed rationality and technical progress of modern times, masses of people can still be moved to search for imaginary deviants to use as scapegoats for their inner demons. We have come so far and not far at all.

Chapter Fifteen
Conclusions: The Social Construction of Imaginary Deviance

> *The great enemy of the truth is very often not the lie— deliberate, contrived and dishonest— but the myth—persistent, persuasive, and unrealistic.*
>
> John F. Kennedy[1]

The Future of the Moral Crusade against Satanism

There are three different directions that the moral crusade against Satanism can take at this point. It may persist for a long time, or it may disintegrate, or it may become marginalized.

Paths to Permanence

The Satanic cult scare is no mere fad that will quickly expend its energy. The Satanic cult scare, and the moral crusade which is promoting it, is quite likely to last at least another decade. It will probably intensify approaching the symbolic bench mark year 2000, when abundant prophecies forecasting the end of the world at the second millennium will be heard. It will persist at least that long because of the vested interests of the many people who profit from it, in terms of gaining money, or public recognition as "experts" on Satanism, or audiences for the sale of religious ideology. It will persist at least until then, because the moral crusade is anchored in many different organizations, at least as an ancillary concern.

However, the moral crusade against Satanism must deal with major organizational problems if it is to have any chance of persisting much longer than another decade. The different moral crusaders, in widely differing occupations, will have to work together more effectively and establish some large-scale, ongoing organizations, specifically designed to fight Satanists and Satanic influences in society. Such organizations would require regular sources of financing to support their paid technical staff.

Some widely recognized leaders of the moral crusade will have to emerge, through mass media attention, to function as spokesmen for the social movement. It will also be necessary for some politicians, perhaps in primarily rural states, to find that appeals to a fear of criminal Satanists has the potential for attracting many voters. In order to do so, moral crusaders must be able to get more state laws passed against supposed ritualistic crime and win convictions of accused criminal Satanists in high profile cases that attract a lot of mass media attention.

Another possible way for the moral crusade to persist would be to merge with other moral revitalization movements. The most obvious candidate for a merger would be the Christian right socio-political movement. Some of the religiously based organizations of the Christian right have already added Satanists to their list of evil internal enemies whom they regard as being responsible for the increasing moral corruption of American society.

Given the relative success in recent years of hate-mongering politicians, like David Duke, in exploiting the politics of scapegoating, it is conceivable that the moral crusade against Satanism could move in that direction. In order to do so, however, the moral crusaders would have to modify their ways of framing the problem, and blame all non-Christians for deliberately undermining the moral values of American society. The term "non-Christians" would become a code word for New

Agers, neo-pagans, Jews, and people in unconventional new religions.

The possibility seems farfetched. However, the idea of an American Nazi being able to attract 55 percent of the white voters of a state was farfetched ten years ago. Fortunately, most of the current corps of moral crusaders have been very cautious about labelling the people of any organized religion as secret criminal Satanists, out of fear of law suits. However, the rhetoric of witch hunting is already being expressed publicly by some fundamentalists in local community lectures about Satanism. It is possible that a new generation of moral crusaders could make the shift to a new frame for the problem, scapegoating real non-Christians rather than imaginary Satanists.

The long-term persistence of the moral crusade against Satanism is likely if two social conditions develop. The first is if economic problems in American society become much more severe, manifestly obvious, and long-lasting; and this is accompanied by an obvious decline in the international power and prestige of the United States. The second is if a great many Americans become involved in unconventional, non-Christian religions, as a response to socio-economic stress. These circumstances would be likely to cause great alarm among people with very traditional religious beliefs. The conditions would precipitate a very severe national identity crisis and intensify the need for scapegoats in American society.

The one aspect of the Satanic cult scare which is likely to last longest is the witch hunt for Satanists who supposedly engage in the ritual sexual abuse of children. The reason is that the ritual abuse witch hunt has merged with the larger child protection movement and it has joined with the many ongoing organizations concerned with child abuse. It is also given credibility and legitimized by some highly reputable psychotherapists.

There should be no illusions about the matter. It is not ground-breaking scientific research which will stem the tide of the Satanic cult scare and discourage moral crusaders who are police, psychotherapists, and child protection workers.

Prominent Psychotherapist Claims Discovery of Elaborate Conspiracy

During the Fourth Annual Eastern Regional Meeting on Abuse and Multiple Personality, 25–29 June '92, Dr. D. Cory Hammond gave a workshop on treating victims of satanic ritual abuse. Hammond is a nationally respected expert on clinical hypnosis . . . ; the workshop was fully accredited as a continuing education activity by the American Medical Association . . .

During the workshop, Dr. Hammond presented the gist of information that he stumbled on concerning the origins of SRA and which he and other clinical hypnotists had independently confirmed through sessions with MPD patients. He found that they frequently mention a Dr. Green or Greenbaum as the person in charge of their torture. According to Dr. Hammond's new information, Dr. Greenbaum was a teenaged Hasidic Jew at the time of the Holocaust. To save his skin, he agreed to collaborate with Nazi doctors experimenting with mind control in the death camps. Having a profound knowledge of the Cabala and also of brainwashing tactics, he developed a nearly foolproof way of programming children to commit sexual acts and then forget about them.

After Germany fell, Dr. Greenbaum and other satanist/Nazi doctors were brought to the U.S. along with missle technicians under orders by Allen Dulles and other CIA officials. As brainwashing and mental programming was seen as a valid weapon against the Communists, he was given free rein to practice on children in U.S. military hospitals. First done among "bloodline" satanists, the programming was also extended to young children that satanists had free access to (presumably in day-care centers). Having Americanized his name and received an M. D., their leader is now known as "Dr. Green". He remains the kingpin of the secret SRA conspiracy in this country, with dozens of his henchmen keeping detailed records of

SRA victims' torture and programming in laptop computers.

These programs were frequently given Greek letters, and Hammond suggested therapists use them to prod patients to tell more about their cult abusers and their aims . . . If a cult member says, for instance, "Alpha 009", or makes a hand gesture to indicate this, Hammond said, the relevant program will automatically activate. And if exposure is ever threatened, "omega programs" in SRA victims will compel them either to "self-destruct" by committing suicide or going completely crazy, or to kill their therapists. Worse, at least 50% of MPD patients, Hammond told the group, were being "monitored" by satanic parents or overseers to make sure that they did not recover or reveal the truth. Hammond asserted (to applause from the audience) "the people who say [ritual abuse] isn't [real] are either naive, like people who didn't believe the Holocaust, or they are dirty".

This scenario reflects numerous anti-semitic government conspiracy theories. . . .

Excerpted from *FOAFtale News: The Newsletter of the International Society for Contemporary Legend Research.* Sept. 1992; Dr. Bill Ellis, Editor. Audio-tape copies of this lecture are available from: Audio Transcripts in Alexandria, VA, Telephone: 703-549-7334.

Paths to Disintegration

In order for a moral crusade to sustain the energies of its activists, it must have continuous symbolic successes. It must appear to be attracting increasing numbers of believers and gain political legitimacy. This was the situation during the last half of the 1980s.

However, the moral crusade has now run into impediments which may discourage some of its activists. It has provoked public opposition from some behavioral scientists and law enforcement officers. Even worse, it has encountered defeat in major court cases. While the moral crusaders have been successful in attracting sensationalized national mass media attention for their claims on television talk-shows, such as "Geraldo" that kind of attention has been counter-productive in influencing upper-middle class professionals. The skepticism of the national news media toward their claims remains a major obstacle to a broader dissemination of their views.

The internal differences within the moral crusade, between religious evangelists, secular psychotherapists, poorly educated volunteer activists, and self-proclaimed Satanic cult "survivors," are likely to become a source of tension and conflict in the face of discouraging opposition. When a social movement is moving from success to success in organizing and propaganda efforts, internal differences can easily be ignored. The diversity may even be regarded as being a rich source of contributions to the general effort. Activists in the social movement can initially get by with ambiguous and contradictory beliefs about the moral "evil" they are fighting.

However, in the face of substantial opposition and repeated failures, the temporary cohesiveness begins to disintegrate. The external opposition pushes moral crusaders to articulate more clearly the precise moral "evil" they are fighting. In turn, this problem drives activists with differing definitions of the "evil" into different camps and breaks down their internal unity. Different camps go off in quite different directions. The result is the disintegration of the moral crusade.

So far, this scenario has not yet begun to develop. However, it is too early in the development of the moral crusade to discount the possibility. Serious opposition to it is just beginning to coalesce.

Paths to Marginalization

If it were to become marginalized, the moral crusade would continue to be influential in certain subcultures, isolated from centers of influence in American society. I believe that the path most likely to be taken by the moral crusade against Satanism is the one toward marginalization. I am impressed by the great number of moral crusaders who are actively promoting the Satanism scare in rural areas, small towns, and small cities all around the country. These people have the greatest vested interest in keeping the Satanic cult scare going.

The moral crusade is likely to persist longest in areas where prevailing public opinion regards Satanism to be a serious problem of crime, mental health, and religious belief. Those areas remain small town and rural areas affected by lingering economic problems, and locations where there are many fundamentalists predisposed to be believers in a threat from secret Satanic criminals. I expect that the Satanism scare will continue for a long time, rumbling in the hinterlands of America.

Practical Implications of the Research Findings

This study provides the basis for conclusions about many practical concerns held by law enforcement officers, psychotherapists, social workers, and public school teachers. The specific issues are covered in the previous chapters and it serves no useful purpose to simply repeat them here. Instead, the following section presents a concise summary of the main conclusions and some practical recommendations for action.

Rumors, Allegations, and Claims about Satanic Cults

A great many people now use the phrase "Satanic cult" as if it referred to something real and concrete. However, the word is merely a vague, ubiquitous label, which doesn't identify anything in particular. The label is a garbage can category for diverse, unrelated phenomena. It may include teenagers involved in vandalism and other petty crimes, individual criminal psychopaths who threaten people by claiming to be Satanists, people suffering from painful mental illness, and even noncriminal groups of neo-pagan witches. The best reaction to people who use the label is to ask them what they mean by it.

There is absolutely no evidence whatsoever for the existence of an organized network of criminals who use Satanism as an ideology to justify criminal activities, if that is what people mean by a "Satanic cult." Quite the contrary. The conception of a dangerous, secret Satanic cult is the product of a legend, which has its origins in the Middle Ages.

Moreover, Satanic cults have never existed in reality. They have only existed in the fearful imagination of believers in their existence and in the imaginative books about occult magic of many pop culture writers. Ultimately, rumors, allegations, and elaborate claims about Satanic witchcraft and Satanic cults are a product of the cultural heritage of Western demonology. That demonology is very real. It has frequently been used as an instrument of persecution and oppression, especially during times of cultural crisis.

Claims about Satanic cults tell us much about the claims-makers and nothing whatsoever about the imaginary objects of their claims.

The Satanic cult scare is, in part, a response to people's need for simple and quick explanations for several different kinds of ambiguous social phenomena. The most publicly visible of these social phenomena, and the one which has received the greatest newspaper attention, is a rash of petty crimes by teenage delinquents, some of whom call themselves "Satanists." A second ambiguous phenomena consists of children's reports of bizarre forms of group sexual abuse at child-care centers, beginning with the allegations of children in the McMartin Preschool case. These allegations have also received a lot of sensational newspaper attention, even though the Satanic cult aspects of the allegations have often been downplayed. Finally, less publicly visible but more important are the claims of Multiple Personality Disorder patients, who tell their psychotherapists stories of childhood torture by Satanic cults. These stories are being spread across the country by believing therapists.

All three phenomena are being linked together by moral crusaders, who see themselves as fighting an organized, secret criminal conspiracy. However, the only real link consists of people's preconceptions, guided by the Satanic cult legend.

Claims about Teenage Satanism

The malicious petty crimes of pseudo-Satanist teenagers need to be taken seriously, but the phenomenon also must be de-mystified, with less emphasis upon the make-shift occult hocus-pocus accompanying the crimes. The crimes need to be rationally investigated, in the same way that crimes of cemetery vandalism and animal mutilation have been investigated in the past. Youth social workers also need to de-mystify the aggressive behavior of these teenagers and apply research on the psychology of adolescence. It is quite misleading to rely upon the distorted polemics of moral crusaders fighting Satanism. Their claims offer no basis for understanding how this latest teenage fad of pseudo-Satanism affects common teenage psychological problems and they offer no basis for understanding teenage aggression.

Allegations about Ritual Sex Abuse

The allegations of Satanic cult ritual sexual abuse of children in child-care centers need to be carefully investigated, without undue emotional over-reaction. These allegations can easily lead to false arrests and ruined community reputations, as they have in many past cases. The allegations may distort and confuse the painful realities of actual sexual abuse, perhaps experienced in a child's home. Such allegations are most likely to be an interactive product of children's fear-filled imaginings combined with the priming of unskilled interviewers. Police investigators need to be cautiously aware that allegations of Satanic ritual abuse heard from children may have been inadvertently instigated by the priming of poorly skilled and over-zealous child protection workers. Most importantly, police officers and child protection workers need to be aware that there is no evidence whatsoever for the existence of groups of so-called Satanists which sexually abuse children, but there do exist plenty of rumors about Satanic cults circulating in communities today. These rumors may influence the preconceptions of some therapists and some local police. Children may also overhear the rumors when they are the subject of adult gossip.

There is abundant research information about the sexual molestation of children by adults. Police officers and child protection workers need to be guided by that body of research, rather than by the rumors and fabrications presented at police conferences on Satanic cult crime.

The stories of Satanic cult torture told by people suffering from Multiple Personality Disorder appear to be manifestations of their deep psychological problems. The fact that many psychotherapists believe the stories, including some who are eminent psychiatrists, is another example of therapists being seduced and deceived by the fantasies of their disturbed patients. The circumstances are very similar to those in which credulous therapists believe the reincarnation stories or UFO abduction stories or the return from death stories of their patients.

The MPD "survivor" stories are manifestations of an interaction process, in which both patients and therapists are collaborative story-tellers. The contemporary legend of Satanic cults is assimilated and retold by the MPD patient and then affirmed by the authority of the therapist in search of a breakthrough discovery. Police need to keep in mind that therapists are not trained in criminal investigation and many of them are not even adequately trained in careful scientific methods of research. Moreover, many people who call themselves "therapists" or "counselors" are actually paraprofessionals, people who are not extensively trained in psychology, sociology, or anthropology.

The proliferating number of adult MPD Satanic cult "survivors," whose fantasy memories are brought out by believing therapists, has resulted in the victimization of an increasing number of emotionally troubled people and their aging parents.

Parents who are victimized by allegations that they are members of Satanic cults the members of which sexually abuse their children should seriously consider bringing civil suits against the psychotherapists who are promoting these allegations. The suits could be brought on the basis of the therapists' making false and harmful diagnoses. These Satanic cult stories are being primed by psychotherapists working with highly suggestible, psychologically disturbed clients. The process harms both the clients and their parents. When the adult children communicate these stories to acquaintances, the reputations and careers of their parents may be damaged. Taking the therapists to court is likely to be costly and humiliating. However, that may be the only way the manufacture of these allegations can be stopped. Only a small number of therapists are responsible for the vast majority of ritual abuse allegations.

Many MPD "ritual abuse" patients go through a conversion experience, with the help of "Christian psychotherapy," and become "born-again" Christians. This so-called "therapy" may be unethical if it is a form of disguised religious proselytism which preys upon the psychological problems of people, by using the pretense of therapy as a means of converting them to a particular ideology.

Responsible authorities need to investigate whether this hoax is being used by some psychiatric clinics and hospital programs, which profit from the suffering of psychologically disturbed clients and pass the cost on to taxpayers and medical insurance companies. Some hospitals may be filling hospital beds with this new source of revenue.

Responsible and properly trained psychotherapists need to be concerned that this hoax might eventually discredit the valuable scientific research currently being carried out by behavioral scientists in an effort to understand the nature and causes of Multiple Personality Disorder and other dissociative disorders. The American Psychiatric Association and the American Psychological Association need to put the investigation of this hoax on their agendas.

When accusations of ritual sex abuse are made against someone, the police, journalists, and behavioral scientists must include as part of their investigation a careful examination of the role of psychotherapists involved in the case. The investigators need to examine verifiable records of all therapy sessions before any legal charges of ritual sex abuse are brought. The possibility that the accusations were facilitated or primed by an overzealous therapist should be ruled out before legal charges are made. Legal authorities would be wise to seek a second opinion from a therapist who doesn't believe in the Satanic cult legend. Some kind of sexual abuse may (or may not) have occurred, but the actual circumstances may have become totally distorted by the allegations of Satanic cult ritualism.

Community Satanic Cult Rumor-Panics

Rumor-panics in response to stories about dangerous Satanic cults have erupted across the country in rural areas. These dramatic cases of collective behavior are also a product of the Satanic cult legend. They resemble medieval community panics in response to stories of witches or accusations of Jewish ritual murder of children. The police and responsible community leaders need be careful not to lend credibility to stories about criminal Satanic cults and thereby aggravate the panics.

This is exactly what happens when police "experts" in occult, Satanic crime or clergy "experts" in Satanism or mental health "experts" in Satanism are invited to communities to provide "explanations" for the fearful parents. Responsible community leaders, including clergymen and school officials, need to focus their response upon the dangers of rumor-mongering, rather than upon phantom Satanists.

Moral Crusaders against Satanism
Hundreds of moral crusaders are promoting unnecessary fear of imaginary deviants: secret, conspiratorial Satanists. They are propagandists for the demonology of counter-subversion, building upon a cultural legacy inherited from medieval times. These people may have the best of intentions in fighting crime and moral corruption, or they may be making a thriving business enterprise out of the Satanic cult scare. Regardless of their motives, their organizing and lecturing activities function to aggravate widespread fear in society.

The past history of the Western demonology should stand as a lesson about the often catastrophic consequences of witch hunts for imaginary moral subversives. Once the demonology is reactivated, the search for scapegoats can spread to many target groups whose existence is real, but whose character is distorted by fearful misperception.

Responsible authorities need to avoid lending legitimacy to these moral crusaders. Agencies which provide educational credit for attendance at seminars conducted by these so-called "experts" in Satanic cult crime should carefully reconsider their rationale for doing so. These seminars may be mental health seminars about teenage Satanism or "ritual abuse" or Multiple Personality Disorder Satanic cult "survivors." They may be police conferences on so-called occult or ritualistic crime.

People in this country must be free to pay their own money

to hear the freely expressed beliefs of any speaker. However, that does not mean that professional agencies must lend credibility to fear-mongering, or that taxpayers' money should to be used to support people's attendance at these conferences.

The Social Construction of Imaginary Deviance
The present interpretation of the Satanic cult scare employs theories drawn from the sociology of collective behavior and the sociology of deviant behavior. However, I have avoided burdening it with unnecessary technical jargon and unfamiliar references to sociological theories. In concluding this book, it may be useful to summarize the main lines of interpretation.

Underlying Social Dynamic Causes

Sources of Shared Social Stress
In the past, counter-subversion scares have swept over Western societies in response to shared sources of stress, such as when social conditions create sudden and widespread insecurity. The most common source of shared social stress has been a rapid decline in the economic conditions of people in a society. Other conditions, however, may also account for people's perception of a threat to their security in a society. The "Red Scare" of the 1950s, for example, arose during a period of increasing economic prosperity. However, it occurred at the beginning of the Cold War and in response to the sudden realization that the Soviets had the atom bomb which could destroy American cities.

I have argued that the current source of shared social stress is the rapid decline of occupational opportunities in the United States, especially for blue-collar workers and particularly in rural and small town areas of the country. It is in rural and small town areas that the Satanic cult scare is taken most seriously.

Several other sources of shared stress have contributed to a widespread perception that American society is beset by some kind of ambiguous threat to people's security. One is the disintegration of stable family relationships. Another is the widening gap, growing for three decades, between the ideals publicly preached by and the actual practices of powerful, wealthy, and prestigious people, people who provide the social models for others to emulate. This has led to the widespread belief that American society is in moral decline.

These conditions particularly are disturbing for young, economically stressed parents, who must worry about fragile family bonds and the difficulties of providing a moral foundation for their children. As a result, the Satanic cult scare has symbolically focussed upon perceived threats to children and teenagers.

The Search for Scapegoat Deviants to Blame

In conditions of shared social stress with complex, unclear, and ambiguous causes, people need a quick, easy explanation for their plight. The easiest solution is to blame scapegoats. In Western societies, the scapegoating process has traditionally been guided by the blueprint provided in a demonology, which attributes the causes of evil to a small, conspiratorial group seeking to undermine the moral order of society. The contemporary Satanic cult legend is a product of that Western demonology.

The Western demonology doesn't cause scapegoating in itself. Instead, the ideas provide an instrument (or weapon) for people to use when they seek scapegoats. The Western demonology is always in circulation, but large audiences are usually not receptive to it unless people are motivated to accept the ideas by a climate of widespread social stress. In the past, the demonology has been used in different times and places to scapegoat such groups as heretics, Jews, witches, Catholics, and Freemasons.

Satanic Cult Rumors and Rumor-Panics

One manifestation of the Satanic cult scare has been community-wide and regional rumor-panics in response to stories about dangerous, secret Satanists. At least sixty-two of them have occurred in rural and small town areas of the United States since 1984.

These rumor-panics are not eruptions of irrational "mass hysteria." Instead, they arise from underlying sources of shared social stress, which become translated into the symbolism of the rumor stories about dangerous Satanists. Much like nightmares, these collaboratively created, fear-filled stories express in symbolic form, the shared anxieties of communities of people. The stories first evolve out of purely local gossip about some ambiguous incidents which are perceived to be threatening. The Satanic cult legend then becomes incorporated into the ongoing rumors, as an explanation for the ambiguous incidents. The underlying anxieties then become aggravated by these fear-provoking rumors about criminal Satanists who are supposedly lurking hidden in communities. The rumors provide a seemingly concrete, specific object for the anxieties.

The social process of consensual validation of reality makes the stories believable to people who hear them repeated over and over from many different sources. Ultimately, people may react to the rumors with panic, manifested by exaggerated protective behavior, aggression, and information-seeking. They are reacting rationally to a threat that they believe to be true. When people collectively believe that a threat is real, it is very real for them at the time.

In attempts to understand persistent rumors and rumor-panics, it is crucial to pay attention to the beliefs that people hold and to interpret their symbolic meanings, rather than to disregard them as if these beliefs were irrelevant misconceptions of reality.

The Cognitive Basis

The Symbolic Message of a Contemporary Legend
A contemporary legend is a cultural script which provides guidelines for understanding ambiguous social conditions that

provoke widespread anxiety. The Satanic cult legend is a counter-subversion, scapegoating metaphor about the origins of evil forces which are threatening the moral order of society. It has its roots in Medieval Europe. The legend serves the social function of providing a useful, although imaginary, target for the displacement of collective frustration and anxiety about an uncertain future.

The symbolism embedded in the contemporary Satanic cult legend communicates a collaboratively created message, with several levels of culturally shared meanings. It expresses a loss of confidence (or "faith") in society to provide the security and prosperity that people had previously come to expect. It also expresses shared feelings that the traditional values of the past are being threatened by destructive, "heretical" forces whose nature is ambiguous and unclear.

In its American cultural context, the Satanic cult legend focusses upon perceived threats to children for several reasons. First, children symbolically represent the future of society. Secondly, the perceived threats to children reflect social conditions in American society, including the disintegration of stable family bonds, economic stress on young families with children, and a host of other social problems which do endanger the well-being and security of children.

At a deeper level of unconscious personality dynamics, the rumors, claims and allegations express a projection of parental guilt feelings and inner conflicts over stressful demands upon parenting in contemporary American society.

Ideology and Framing the Problem

The Satanic cult meanings that moral crusaders attribute to ambiguous social phenomena do not derive directly from any one ideology. Instead, ambiguous incidents and events are attributed Satanic cult meanings through very specific frames for interpreting experience. The most common frames for interpreting ambiguous social phenomena attributed to criminal Satanists derive from the Christian religious ideology, the social conservative ideology, and the child advocate ideology. Claims about Satanic cult crime serve to support the differing ideologies. When the claims are taken seriously by a wide public audience, the claims provide exemplars that moral crusaders use to affirm the validity of their broader ideology.

Zealous Christian traditionalists and child advocates are likely to be particularly receptive to believing claims about Satanic cult crimes against children.

The Organizational Basis

The Moral Crusaders against Satanism

The activists who are promoting and disseminating the Satanic cult legend follow in the long tradition of American moral crusaders. It is they who have reactivated an ancient legend and reshaped its content for contemporary audiences. They are the shapers and molders of a contemporary legend.

Moral crusaders against Satanism come from a wide variety of occupations. Some are evangelists and clergymen who are "experts" in identifying the signs of Satanism. Some are police specialists in ritualistic crime. Some are psychotherapists specialized in treating MPD patients who claim to have been victims of ritual abuse. Some are child protection workers specialized in helping child victims of ritual sexual abuse. Some are youth workers who are "experts" in understanding teenage Satanism. Some are volunteers in anti-cult organizations.

They are drawn together in a loose communication network, aided by training seminars, conferences, and newsletters. Many of them are fundamentalist Christians. Some of them are social conservatives and child advocates. Although they may frame the problem quite differently from each other, their differences are bridged by belief in the Satanic cult legend. Even if they differ in ways of framing the problem, their specialized forms of occupational "expertise" confirms each others' belief in the Satanic cult legend.

The Organization of the Moral Crusade against Satanism

A wide variety of specialized associations provide an organizational foundation for the moral crusade against Satanism. These associations include: volunteer anti-cult organizations; volunteer organizations of parents concerned about sexual child abuse; mental health organizations of therapists concerned with Multiple Personality Disorder or child abuse; and some religious lobby groups concerned with the climate of morality in American society. These associations do not focus their agendas exclusively upon fighting Satanism. Instead, they provide an organizational forum and propaganda vehicle for moral crusaders fighting Satanism as an adjunct to their more specialized concerns.

The Satanic cult scare has already generated a host of business enterprises. These enterprises also provide an organizational basis for the moral crusade. Some of them produce materials such as: training films and audiotapes, interviewing materials, police investigation manuals, and information newsletters. Some of these enterprises provide services such as therapy clinics and hospital programs specialized in treating MPD "survivors" of ritual abuse, or teenage Satanists, or identifying child victims of "ritual abuse." In addition, a few religious evangelists have made lucrative careers out of travelling the country to lecture about the growing dangers of Satanism.

The Political Legitimation of Claims about Satanism

In order to legitimize its claims about a newly identified form of deviance, a moral crusade must do so through the legal and political system of a society and through reference to scientific authority. The attempts of moral crusaders to obtain new state laws and legal precedents in court decisions which affirm their claims have not been particularly successful. At this point, Satanic cult crime is not yet legally and politically defined as a distinct form of deviance.

The most important authorities who are lending legitimacy to the Satanic cult scare are psychotherapists who believe the Satanic cult "survivor" stories of MPD patients. Their affirmation of stories of Satanic ritual sex abuse and the torture of children lends credibility to the Satanic cult legend, by giving it the aura of having been confirmed by science. The social role of these psychotherapists is similar to the role of medieval monks in articulating, disseminating, and legitimizing the ancient Satanic cult legend. They are the main conduit through which the contemporary Satanic cult legend is being transmitted across national borders to Great Britain, Holland, and Australia.

The moral crusaders against Satanism face several sources of opposition in their attempts to obtain legal and political sanctions for their claims. Their opponents in court cases and in political lobbying for new laws include some professionalized law enforcement officials and some behavioral scientists, whose occupational expertise causes them to be highly skeptical of the claims about Satanism. The moral crusaders are also burdened by the skepticism of journalists working for major metropolitan newspapers and national news organizations. In contrast, local sources of authority, including clergymen, school officials, and local police officers in rural areas and small towns, have lent credibility to the moral crusaders' claims about Satanic cult crime.

The Dissemination of Satanic Cult Stories

Hundreds of articles have appeared in small town newspapers, which portray Satanic cult crime as a taken-for-granted reality and rarely offer any skeptical analysis. The reason is that these newspaper reports rely upon local "experts," clergymen, police "experts" on ritualistic crime, and therapists, many of whom are themselves moral crusaders against Satanism. In addition, out-of-town "experts" on Satanism who are moral crusaders, are commonly brought into an area to offer their advice in response to some heinous crime, a case of teenage suicide, or rampant rumors about Satanic cults. Their presentations are then covered in the local press, giving credibility to the Satanic cult legend.

It is inaccurate to say that the mass media has promoted the Satanic cult scare. Different elements of the mass media have handled the claims about Satanic cult crime in different ways. What may be said with some accuracy about the mass media is that different media have reflected and served different audiences, some receptive to belief in the Satanic cult legend and others unreceptive.

Other means by which Satanic cult stories are being disseminated include: seminars and workshops about Satanic cult crime; the newsletters and publications of organizations fighting Satanic cult crime; television talk shows; popular culture "true crime" books; Christian books about Satanism; Christian radio program; and local rumors.

The effect of the dissemination process is to create vicious circles in which Satanic cult stories are encountered by so-called "experts" on Satanism, such as the local police, child protection workers, psychotherapists, and clergymen, and the stories are then given credibility by these "experts" who promote the stories once more.

Rumors of Evil

This study has provided abundant evidence that the Satanic cult scare is not the product of ignorance and superstition, nor emotional hysteria, nor the fantasies of a medieval mentality. The rumors, claims, and allegations about dangerous, criminal Satanists arise from people's attempts to grasp meaning out of the mist of ambiguous experience and uncertainty. People today, just like people in the Middle Ages, often fall back upon belief in ancient legends to deal with the phantoms of their fears. It is through ancient legends that rumors of evil from the past shape people's preconceptions of the present.

Hopefully, this study of the germinal stages of a witch hunt for contemporary witches will deepen our understanding of the social conditions which lead to witch hunts and mass persecutions, when societies construct imaginary scapegoat deviants as a way of dealing with rapid change and social stress.

Appendix I
Bibliography of Resource Books, Articles, and Periodicals

Overviews of the Satanic Cult Scare

Hicks, Robert. *In Pursuit of Satan*. Buffalo, NY: Prometheus Books, 1991. [Focusses upon "cult cops" and misguided law enforcement.]

Richardson, James; Best, Joel; and Bromley, David, eds. *The Satanism Scare*. New York: Aldine de Gruyter, 1991. [Eighteen chapters written by different social science specialists.]

Understanding Allegations of "Ritual" Child Abuse

1. How to investigate claims about "ritual abuse".

Lanning, Kenneth V. *Investigator's Guide to Allegations of "Ritual" Child Abuse*. National Center for the Analysis of Violent Crime (NCAVC FBI Academy, Quantico, VA 22135), January 1992.

2. The social construction of "ritual abuse" as imaginary deviance.

Nathan, Debbie. *Women and Other Aliens*. El Paso, TX: Cinco Puntas Press, 1991. [Reprints Nathan's articles: "The Ritual Sex Abuse Hoax." and "The Making of a Modern Witch Trial."]

Nathan, Debbie. "Satanism and Child Molestation: Constructing the Ritual Abuse Scare." In: James Richardson, Joel Best, and David Bromley, eds. *The Satanism Scare*. Aldine de Gruyter, 1991, pp. 75–94.

3. The origin of false accusations of sexual child abuse due to improper interviewing of children; and, how to distinguish valid

accusations from invalid ones.

Coleman, Lee, and Clancy, Patrick E. "False Allegations of Child Sexual Abuse." *Criminal Justice* (Fall 1990): 14–20, 43–47.

Doris, John, ed. *The Suggestibility of Children's Recollections.* Washington, D.C.: American Psychological Association, 1991.

Ekman, Paul. *Why Kids Lie.* New York: Penguin Books, 1989.

Gardner, Richard A. *True and False Accusations of Child Sex Abuse: A Guide for Legal and Mental Health Professionals.* Cresskill, NJ: Creative Therapeutics, 1992.

Loftus, Elizabeth F. *Eyewitness Testimony.* Harvard University Press, 1979.

Loftus, Elizabeth F. *Witness for the Defense.* New York: St. Martin's Press, 1991.

Perry, Nancy W., and Wrightsman, Lawrence S. *The Child Witness.* Newbury Park, CA: Sage Publications, 1991.

Underwager, Ralph, and Wakefield, Hollida. *Accusations of Child Sexual Abuse.* Springfield, IL: Charles C. Thomas, 1988.

Underwager, Ralph, and Wakefield, Hollida. *The Real World of Child Interrogations.* Springfield, IL: Charles C. Thomas, 1989.

Wakefield, Hollida, and Underwager, Ralph. "Sexual Abuse Allegations in Divorce and Custody Disputes." *Behavioral Sciences and the Law.* Vol. 9. 1991, pp. 451–68.

4. The national over-reaction to the reality of sexual child abuse and the false accusations which result from propaganda and fear.

Best, Joel. *Threatened Children.* Chicago: University of Chicago Press, 1990.

Gardner, Richard A. *Sex Abuse Hysteria.* Cresskill, NJ: Creative Therapeutics, 1991.

Wexler, Richard. *Wounded Innocents.* Prometheus Books, 1990.

Understanding Multiple Personality Disorder and Satanic Cult Survivor Stories

1. Research on the origins of MPD patients' claims about "ritual abuse."

Mulhern, Sherrill. "Satanism and Psychotherapy: A Rumor in Search of an Inquisition." In *The Satanism Scare,* edited by James

Richardson, Joel Best, and David Bromley. New York: Aldine de Gruyter, 1991, pp. 145–74.

2. Understanding Multiple Personality Disorder and fantasies about Satanic cult torture.

Aldridge-Morris, Ray. *Multiple Personality: An Exercise in Deception.* London, United Kingdom: Lawrence Erlbaum Associates, 1989. [Especially Chapter 8: "Multiple Personality as a Cultural Phenomena."]

Ganaway, George K. "Historical Versus Narrative Truth: Clarifying the Role of Exogenous Trauma in the Etiology of MPD and Its Variants." *Dissociation* 2, no. 4 (Dec. 1989): 205–20.

Jenkins, Philip, and Maier-Katkin, Daniel. "Occult Survivors: The Origins of a Myth." In *The Satanism Scare*, edited by James Richardson, Joel Best, and David Bromley. New York: Aldine de Gruyter, 1991, pp. 127–44.

Spanos, Nicholas P.; Weekes, John R.; and Bertrand, Lorne D. "Multiple Personality: A Social Psychological Perspective." *Journal of Abnormal Psychology* 94, no. 3 (Aug. 1985): 362–76.

Spiegel, Herbert. "The Grade 5 Syndrome: The Highly Hypnotizable Person." *Journal of Clinical and Experimental Hypnosis* 22, no. 4 (1974): 303–19.

3. MPD fantasies about Satanic cults and similarities to fantasies about demonic possession and abductions by UFO aliens.

Bartholomew, Robert E.; Basterfield, Keith; and Howard, George S. "UFO Abductees and Contactees: Psychopathology or Fantasy Proneness?" *Professional Psychology: Research and Practice* 22, no. 3 (1991): 215–22.

Goodman, Felicitas D. *How about Demons? Possession and Exorcism in the Modern World.* Bloomington, Indiana: Indiana University Press, 1988.

Spanos, Nicholas P., and Gottlieb, Jack. "Demonic Possession, Mesmerism, and Hysteria: A Social Psychological Perspective on Their Interrelationships." *Journal of Abnormal Psychology* 88, no. 5 (Oct. 1979): 529–46.

Wilson, Ian. *All in the Mind.* Garden City, NY: Doubleday & Co., 1982.

Understanding Claims about "Satanic," "Occult," or "Ritualistic" Crime

Hicks, Robert. *In Pursuit of Satan.* Buffalo, NY: Prometheus Books, 1991.

Hicks, Robert D. "The Police Model of Satanism Crime." In *The Satanism Scare,* edited by James Richardson, Joel Best, and David Bromley. New York: Aldine de Gruyter, 1991, pp. 175–89.

Crouch, Ben, and Damphousse, Kelly. "Law Enforcement and the Satanic Crime Connection: A Survey of 'Cult Cops.'" In *The Satanism Scare,* edited by James Richardson, Joel Best, and David Bromley. New York: Aldine de Gruyter, 1991, pp. 191–217.

Lanning, Kenneth V. "Satanic, Occult, Ritualistic Crime: A Law Enforcement Perspective." *The Police Chief* (Oct. 1989): 62–83.

Jenkins, Philip, and Maier-Katkin, Daniel. "Satanism: Myth and Reality in a Contemporary Moral Panic." *Crime, Law and Social Change* 17 (1992): 53–75.

Michigan State Police Occult Survey. Michigan State Police, Investigative Resources Unit. June, 1990. (714 South Harrison Road, East Lansing, Michigan, 48823)

An Introduction to the Sociology of Deviant Behavior

Goode, Erich. *Deviant Behavior.* 3rd ed. Englewood Cliffs, NJ: Prentice-Hall, 1990.

Thio, Alex. *Deviant Behavior.* 3rd ed. New York: Harper & Row, 1988.

Identifying Moral Crusaders against Satanism

Carlson, Shawn, and Larue, Gerald; with O'Sullivan, G.; Masche, A.; and Frew, D. *Satanism in America.* Buffalo, NY: Committee for the Scientific Examination of Religion, 1989. Published by Gaia Press, El Cerrrito, CA, 1989.

Understanding the Current Cultural/Moral Crisis in American Society

Hunter, James Davison. *Culture Wars: The Struggle to Define America.* New York: Basic Books, 1991.

Understanding the History and Heritage of the Satanic Cult Legend

1. Analysis of the contents and effects of the Western demonology of evil.

Cohn, Norman. "The Myth of Satan and his Human Servants". In *Witchcraft Confessions and Accusations*, edited by Mary Douglas. New York: Travistock, 1970, pp. 3–16.

Oplinger, Jon. *The Politics of Demonology.* Cranbury, NJ: Associated University Presses, 1990.

Russell, Jeffrey Burton. "The Historical Satan." In *The Satanism Scare*, edited by James Richardson, Joel Best, and David Bromley. New York: Aldine de Gruyter, 1991, pp. 41–48.

Stevens, Phillips, Jr. "The Demonology of Satanism: An Anthropological View." In *The Satanism Scare*, edited by James Richardson, Joel Best, and David Bromley. New York: Aldine de Gruyter, 1991, pp. 21–40.

2. The Medieval origins of the Satanic cult legend.

Cohn, Norman. *Europe's Inner Demons.* New York: Basic Books, 1975.

Levack, Brian P. *The Witch-Hunt in Early Modern Europe.* New York: Longman, 1987.

Moore, R.I. *The Formation of a Persecuting Society.* Cambridge, MA: Basil Blackwell, 1987.

3. The blood libel and ritual murder accusations against the Jews.

Dundes, Alan, ed. *The Blood Libel Legend: A Casebook in Anti-Semitic Folklore.* Madison, WI: University of Wisconsin Press, 1991.

Hsia, R. Po-Chia. *The Myth of Ritual Murder: Jews and Magic in Reformation Germany.* New Haven, CN: Yale University Press, 1988.

Tractenberg, Joshua. *The Devil and the Jews.* New Haven, CN: Yale University Press, 1943. (Republished by The Jewish Publication Society, New York, 1983.)

Understanding Rumors and Rumor Control

1. The scientific study of rumors and rumor control.

Kapferer, Jean-Noel. *Rumors: Uses, Interpretations, and Images*. New Brunswick, NJ: Transaction Publishers, 1990.

Koenig, Frederick. *Rumor in the Marketplace: The Social Psychology of Commercial Hearsay*. Dover, MA: Auburn House, 1985.

Rosnow, Ralph L., and Fine, Gary Alan. *Rumor and Gossip*. New York: Elsivier, 1976.

Rosnow, Ralph L. "Inside Rumor: A Personal Journey." *American Psychologist* 46, no. 5 (May 1991): 484–96.

Rosnow, Ralph L. "The Psychology of Rumor Reconsidered." *Psychological Bulletin* 87, no. 3 (1980): 578–91.

Shibutani, Tamotsu. *Improvised News: A Sociological Study of Rumors*. Indianapolis: Bobbs-Merrill, 1966.

2. Critique of the concept of "mass hysteria."

Bartholomew, Robert E. "Ethnocentricity and the Social Construction of Mass Hysteria." *Culture, Medicine and Psychiatry* 14, no. 4 (Dec. 1990): 455–95.

Understanding Contemporary Legends

1. A popular and original study of urban legends.

Brunvand, Jan Harold. *The Vanishing Hitchhiker: American Urban Legends and Their Meanings*. New York: W.W. Norton, 1981.

2. An introduction to the scholarly study of contemporary legends.

Ellis, Bill. "Introduction." *Western Folklore*. Special Issue: "Contemporary Legends in Emergence." 49, no. 1 (1990): 1–10.

Goode, Erich. "Contemporary Legends and Collective Delusions." Chapter 8 in *Collective Behavior*. New York: Harcourt Brace Jovanovich, 1992.

Information about Attempts to Censor Books

Attacks on the Freedom to Learn. Published annually by People for the American Way, 2000 M Street, N.W., Suite 400, Washington, D.C., 20036.

Newsletter on Intellectual Freedom. Published bi-monthly by the American Library Association, 50 Huron Street, Chicago, IL 60611.

Resources in Periodical Publications

Scholarly Publications

FOAFtale News: The Newsletter of the International Society for Contemporary Legend Research. (FOAFtale is an abbreviation for "friend-of-a-friend tale.") This publication regularly reports stories of the Satanic cult legend from around the world, sent in by members of the Society, as well as other rumors and contemporary legends, both funny and fearful. The newsletter provides a means of keeping up to date with strange events in popular culture, which are commonly not widely reported in the national mass media. Sample copies can be obtained for $2.50 from the editor: Dr. Bill Ellis, Department of English and American Studies, Pennsylvania State University, Hazleton Campus, Hazleton, PA 18201. Published quarterly.

Contemporary Legend. This is the scholarly journal of the International Society for Contemporary Legend Research. It provides current research and theory in the study of contemporary legends. Published annually. Both *Contemporary Legend* and *FOAFtale News* come with the $18 membership in ISCLR. Contact the editor: Dr. Paul Smith, Department of Folklore, Memorial University, St. John's, Newfoundland, CANADA A1C 5S7.

Issues in Child Abuse Accusations. This journal provides specialized articles about accusations of sexual child abuse mainly from psychologists, psychiatrists, and lawyers. It sometimes also offers articles about ritual abuse allegations. The emphasis of the journal is upon detecting false accusations and "mistakes of the rush to solve the problem of child abuse." The Summer 1991 issue focussed on ritual abuse allegations. Published by The Institute for

Psychological Therapies, 13200 Cannon City Blvd., Northfield, MN 55057. Quarterly.

Non-Scholarly Publications

Cornerstone.   This is an evangelical Protestant religious magazine, which has published some excellent investigative reports about the harmful effects of the Satanic cult scare. The articles focus upon false accusations of Satanic cult ritual abuse which may discredit sincere Christian belief. Copies are available from: Cornerstone Magazine, 939 W. Wilson, Chicago, IL 60640.

CultWatch Response.   This bi-monthly newsletter is put together by a members of the WICCA religion. It is designed to monitor efforts to defame and harass people who follow neo-pagan religions. It is a useful resource for evaluations of police "occult crime" training materials and for monitoring the public activities of anti-cult organizations. Sample copies are available for $2 from: CultWatch Response, Inc., P.O. Box 1842, Colorado Springs, CO 80901-1842.

Appendix II
Resource Persons Who May Be Contacted for Assistance

Allegations of Ritual Sex Abuse of Children

Paul Ciolino
20 North Clark Street, Suite 3500
Chicago, IL 60602-5002

Private investigator. Experienced in working on cases of false accusations of sexual child abuse.

Dr. Lee Coleman, M.D.
1889 Yosemite Road
Berkeley, CA 94704

Psychiatrist. Has written articles about false allegations of child sexual abuse. Has testified at hundreds of trials involving child sexual abuse allegations.

Dr. Richard A. Gardner, M.D.
155 County Road
P.O. Box R
Cresskill, NJ 07626-0317

Psychiatrist. Has written books about evaluating allegations of child sex abuse. Has testified at many trials involving allegations of child sex abuse.

Debbie Nathan
511 Randolph Street
El Paso, TX 79902

Journalist. Investigated several trials of women falsely accused of sexual abuse of children in day-care centers.

Dr. Martha Rogers, Ph.D.
17662 Irvine Blvd., Suite 12
Tustin, CA 92680

Clinical Psychologist. Does forensic psychology in criminal cases. Has testified in trials involving allegations of ritual abuse.

Dr. Ralph Underwager, Ph.D.
Institute for Psychological Therapies

Clinical Psychologist. Has written books about interviewing children in cases of alleged sex-

13200 Cannon City Blvd.
Northfield, MN 55057

ual child abuse to distinguish valid from false accusations. Has testified at hundreds of trials involving child sexual abuse, including "ritual abuse."

Multiple Personality Disorder Patients' Claims about Satanic Cults

Dr. George Ganaway, M.D.
Program Director
Ridgeway Center for
Dissociative Disorders
Ridgeway Institute
3995 South Cobb Drive
Smyrna, GA 30080

Psychiatrist, specialized in therapy for MPD. Has written articles skeptical of MPD claims about Satanic cults. Has consulted in legal cases.

Dr. Elizabeth Loftus
Department of Psychology
University of Washington
Seattle, WA 98195

Nationally recognized expert on the psychology of memory and on eyewitness testimony in legal cases.

Dr. Sherrill Mulhern
Laboratoire des Rumeurs
92 rue Perronet
92200 Neuilly, France

Anthropologist, specialized in study of culture and psychopathology. Did research on MPD patients' claims about Satanic cults and the therapists who believe them.

Dr. Richard Noll, Ph.D.
2005 Walnut Street
Philadelphia, PA 19103

Clinical Psychologist. Has written articles skeptical of MPD patients' claims about Satanic cults. Has private psychotherapy practice.

False Memory Syndrome
Foundation
3508 Market Street, Suite 128
Philadelphia, PA 19104
(Telephone: 800-568-8882 or
215-387-1865)

Organization of parents who have been falsely accused by their adult children of sexual child abuse. Acts as a support and information resource group for parents.

Criminal Justice and Claims about Satanic Cult Ritualistic Crime

Robert Hicks
Department of Criminal Justice Services
Commonwealth of Virginia
805 East Broad Street
Richmond, VA 23219

Law Enforcement Specialist. His book, *In Pursuit of Satan*, details how local police "experts" in ritual crime are promoting the Satanic cult scare. Experienced in correct police investigation procedures.

Dr. Philip Jenkins
Administration of Justice Department
Pennsylvania State University
901 Oswald Tower
University Park, PA 16802

Professor of Criminal Justice. Has written articles critical of police investigations of crimes attributed to Satanists. Specialist in the history of law enforcement.

Kenneth V. Lanning
Supervisory Special Agent
F.B.I. Behavioral Science Unit
F.B.I. Academy
Quantico, VA 22135
(Telephone: 703-640-1191)

FBI Special Agent. Provides advice to criminal justice professionals investigating crimes against children, including sex abuse and kidnapping. Has investigated claims about Satanic and ritual crime.

Detective David Minzey
Michigan State Police
Investigative Resources Unit
714 South Harrison Road
East Lansing, MI 48823

Police Detective. Helped to prepare the Michigan State Police study of "occult" crime. Experienced in the investigation of violent crimes attributed to supposed Satanists.

Dr. James T. Richardson
Department of Sociology
College of Arts and Sciences
University of Nevada–Reno
Reno, NV 89557-0067

Sociologist, specialized in the study of religion and law. Has done research on religious conversion, "deprogramming," and allegations of religious brainwashing in court cases. Trained as a lawyer (J.D.).

Research on Groups and Individuals Promoting the Satanism Scare

Dr. Joel Best, Chairman
Department of Sociology
Southern Illinois University at
Carbondale
Carbondale, Illinois 62901

Sociologist. Has done research on crimes against children, including kidnapped and missing children, and groups promoting unnecessary fear.

Dr. David G. Bromley
Department of Sociology
College of Humanities and
Sciences
Virginia Commonwealth
University
312 Shafer Street
Richmond, VA 23284-2040

Sociologist, specialized in the study of religion. Has written extensively about anti-cult volunteer organizations, including those promoting claims about criminal Satanic cults.

Shawn Carlson
P.O. Box 466
El Cerrito, CA 94530-0466

Co-author of *Satanism in America* report on anti-Satanist crusaders. Has information on many individuals and groups promoting claims about secret, criminal Satanists.

Vicki Copeland
CultWatch Response Inc.
P.O. Box 1842
Colorado Springs, CO 80901

Keeps a computer data bank on groups and speakers promoting the Satanic cult scare, focussed upon false allegations against neo-pagan religious groups.

Dr. J. Gordon Melton, Director
Institute for the Study
of American Religion
P.O. Box 90709
Santa Barbara, CA 93190

Minister and noted scholar on religious diversity in America. Expert on new religious groups (including religious Satanists) and anti-cult organizations.

Gerry O'Sullivan
4617 Pine Street, Apt. H518
Philadelphia, PA 19143-1855

Co-author of *Satanism in America*, report. M.A. degree in religion. Legally certified as expert to testify about occult religious groups. Has collected information on religious and rightist groups which are promoting the Satanism scare.

Dr. Anson Shupe
Department of Sociology and Anthropology
Indiana University–Purdue University
2101 Coliseum Blvd., East
Fort Wayne, IN 46805-1499

Sociologist. Specialist in the sociology of religion. Has done research on the Satanic cult scare and groups promoting it in Indiana and the Midwest.

Dr. Jeffrey S. Victor
Department of Sociology
Jamestown Community College
Jamestown, NY 14701

Sociologist. Author of this book and a textbook in the psychology of human sexuality. Can help in understanding the distortions in accusations and allegations about Satanic cult crime.

Help in Dealing with Censorship Attacks on Schools, Libraries, and Teachers

Office of Intellectual Freedom
American Library Association
50 East Huron Street
Chicago, IL 60611
(Telephone: 312-280-4223)

Provides information about groups promoting censorship of library books, including those making claims of occult or Satanic influences in books.

Mark Sedway
Director, School Censorship Program
People for the American Way
2000 M Street, N.W., Suite 400
Washington, D.C., 20036
(Telephone: 202-467-4999)

Provides information about groups attempting to censor school materials, including those making claims of occult and Satanic influences. Can be contacted about legal assistance for teachers and school districts.

The Cultural Heritage of the Satanic Cult
Contemporary Legend

Dr. Bill Ellis
Department of English and American Studies
Pennsylvania State University
Hazleton Campus
Hazleton, PA 18201

Editor of the newsletter of the International Society for Contemporary Legend Research. Did research on adolescent, legend trips and local legends in the Midwest about magic, the

Devil, demons, and witches. Expert on American folklore.

Dr. Gary Alan Fine, Chairman
Department of Sociology
Baldwin Hall
University of Georgia
Athens, GA 30602

Sociologist. Has written about children's fantasy games, the subculture of preadolescents, and contemporary legends. Co-author of a scholarly book about rumors.

Dr. Phillips Stevens, Jr.
Department of Anthropology
Ellicott Complex
SUNY University Center at
Buffalo
Buffalo, NY 14261

Anthropologist, specialized in the study of witchcraft, magic, and occult beliefs, including Santeria and Voodoo. Has written about the heritage of beliefs about Satanism and has testified in court.

The Satanic Cult Scare In Other Countries

Dr. Robert Bartholomew
R.F.D. # 2, Box 2886
Whitehall, NY 12887

Sociologist. Collects information about the Satanic cult scare in Australia. Specialist in the study of collective behavior.

Dr. Benjamin Rossen
Meerssenerweg 5p
6222 AE Maastricht
The Netherlands

Sociologist. Did research on a Satanic "ritual abuse" scare in Holland. Experienced as an expert witness in sex abuse trials.

Dr. Bill Thompson
Department of Sociology
University of Reading
Whiteknights, Reading
United Kingdom, RG6 2AA

Criminologist. Does research on the Satanic ritual abuse scare in England and Scotland. Member of the Society for Contemporary Legend Research.

Rosie Waterhouse
The Independent on Sunday
40 City Road
London, EC1Y 2DB
United Kingdom

Journalist. Has written extensively about the ritual abuse scare in England and Scotland.

Appendix III
Guidelines for Dealing with Satanic Cult Rumors in a Community

The following suggestions for dealing with rumors have been adapted from the book *Rumors: Uses, Interpretations and Images* by Jean-Noel Kapferer.

A. Denials, refutations, or silence about the validity of the rumors won't work.

1. Rumors are constantly being repeated over and over. In contrast, simple denials of the rumor stories are not interesting and newsworthy enough to be repeated.
2. Denials of the rumor stories are commonly either ignored or distorted by rumor-mongers, so that they become seen as confirmation of the rumors.
3. Even refutations of the rumor stories by authority figures often backfire and become seen as evidence of the rumor's essential validity.

B. The best anti-rumor strategy is to promote a counter-explanation.

1. The rumors should constantly be referred to as a hoax, false reports, or even as pranks.
2. The counter-explanation needs to be designed to divert the growing energy of the rumor process, rather than to attempt to block it. It must be simple and believable, so that it can gradually gain credibility.
3. The counter-explanation must focus upon: a) the underlying anxieties triggered by the rumor stories; and 2) the symbolism embedded in the rumor stories.
4. The underlying anxieties triggered by Satanic cult rumors are

parents' fears about the safety of their children. Therefore, a counter-explanation must focus upon those fears (without denying them).

5. The symbolism embedded in Satanic cult rumors refers to a malicious conspiracy, which is secretive, hidden, and not easily identified and which is to blame for vicious, criminal acts. The symbolism appeals to the need to blame some entity, or group, for threats to our well-being which are ambiguous and cannot easily be comprehended.

6. Therefore, a useful counter-explanation is that "certain" (unidentified) rumor-mongers are stirring-up trouble and endangering the safety of our children. Children may be endangered by "unstable" people who might use the hoax, by self-appointed vigilantes, and by a climate of fear designed to frighten children.

7. The target of the anti-rumor strategy needs to be the communication process of transmitting "exciting" Satanic cult stories, rather than any specific people or groups. The aim is to stigmatize rumor-mongering about Satanic cults, so that it becomes seen as being disreputable and dangerous. The objective is to promote an anti-rumor, a substitute for the Satanic cult rumor, which people find interesting to transmit. (This is a variation of the World War II anti-rumor strategy, embodied in the slogan: "Loose lips sink ships.")

8. Note that it is neither useful or necessary to identify any specific rumor-mongers, because they will be everywhere and don't constitute a group. However, asserting that "certain" rumor-mongers are creating a hoax counters the symbolism of a malicious, conspiratorial group of people, by substituting malicious rumor-mongers for malicious Satanists.

9. Obviously, this anti-rumor strategy cannot be employed by individuals alone. It needs to be adopted by community authorities or groups, working in concerted action.

C. An anti-rumor campaign must use multiple modes of publicity.

1. Different individuals are selectively exposed to different media and most people only give selective attention to the ideas they encounter in any single medium.

2. Therefore, it is best to use a variety of communication media, including radio, newspapers, fliers, posters, and public meetings.
3. An anti-rumor campaign must aim publicity at specific audiences, rather than at a mass audience. The most important audiences in a community where Satanic cult rumors emerge, include local government officials, the police, church groups, social workers, school administrators, teachers, school students, and parents of school children. Each of them needs to be approached in different ways, through different media.

D. Avoid focussing attention on "Satanism" as the issue.

1. Don't allow "Satanism" to be made the issue in conversation and public discourse. Don't argue with rumor believers. Don't debate the issue of "Satanism." Don't attempt to refute the Satanic cult rumor stories. Doing so only lends credibility to rumor-mongers. People's selective attention and preconceptions will distort any such effort.
2. Don't invite public speakers who are "experts" on Satanism or occult crime, even to refute the rumors. Don't publish so-called "indicators of Satanic cult involvement." Doing so only focusses attention upon the Satanic cult rumors.

E. Other suggestions.

1. Establish a rumor control center which can be reached by telephone. People can call a specific location for information to dispel rumor misinformation.
2. A reward can be offered for information leading to the detection of the supposed groups originally starting the rumor stories. No such group will ever be found, but the reward serves to discredit rumor-mongering.

What Parents Can Do: Dealing with Gossip and Rumors

1. Be careful of the labels people put on pre-packaged ideas. Realize that a few malicious youth in every generation have done things like kill cats and dogs, overturn cemetery tombstones, mess up people's property with graffiti, or vandalize churches. A few vicious kids have also tortured and killed other kids. These are crimes which deserve to be punished. However, labelling such viciousness as "Satanic cult activity" adds nothing new to our understanding of it.

2. Beware of well meaning gossip-mongers. Some people are always trying to give you "gifts" of alarming bits of information that they have heard through their special grapevine. Just realize from whom it comes.

3. Remember that when "everyone" gets carried away by fear, "everyone" can be wrong. Trust your own good judgment and reasoning ability. Avoid getting caught up in the crowd mentality, because that is what can most easily poison your own good judgment. If "everyone," for example, says that those kids with the strange clothing and hair must be "Satanists," your own good judgment tells you that every generation of youth has some rebels who like to wear shocking new styles.

4. Remember "where there is smoke," there is often a lot of hot air. You might be inclined to think that when most of the people you meet just happen to repeat a similar story, there must be some truth to it. Don't be misled. A fiction told in a thousand ways by a thousand people is still a fiction. Repeating the myth that a Satanic cult is kidnapping and killing children, does not make it so.

5. Remember that shared fear makes the "big lie" credible. When a shared fear affects a whole community, just as during a natural catastrophe or urban riot, many people become emotionally ready to listen to the most alarmist claims and accusations. Realize that, unfortunately, the verifiable facts don't matter to many people until their emotions have cooled off.

6. Contact people whose job it is to know about what is happening in your community. Call your local police chief, school principal, youth bureau director, city news editor, and animal protection society. Ask for any reliable information they may have about rumors circulating in your area that involve claims of animal killings or kidnappings by so-called Satanic cults. Always seek a second opinion. Local authorities can also get caught up in a community-wide scare.

Appendix IV
Descriptions of Satanic Cult Rumor-Panics in the United States and Canada, 1982–1992

This material provides a historical record of the contemporary legend about Satanic cults, as it is expressed through rumor-panics. (Total = 62)

These descriptions offer information from the sources about possible antecedent triggering events, content of the rumor stories, behavioral indicators of fear, possible rumor propagandists, and the reactions of local authorities. This list includes only those rumor-panics for which the author has reliable sources of information and is not necessarily inclusive of all such events. It does not include reports about locations where Satanic cult rumors were merely in wide circulation.

Prelude

In the 1970s, these rumor-panics were preceded by widely reported rumors about cattle mutilations attributed to Satanic cults, which circulated across the rural West and Midwest. There were also rumors about teenage Devil worshipping cults, which circulated in some urban areas of the West and East coasts.

Date and Location	Source of Information and Relevant Incidents
(1) June 16, 17, 1982. June 14, 17. Area around City of Victoria, British Columbia, Canada	*Vancouver Sun* (British Columbia, Canada). *The Province.* Rumors appear to have begun after publication of the book, *Michelle Remembers*, two years earlier, which purports to be a story about secret Satanic cult crime and torture in the Victoria area. In the spring of 1982, a group of fundamentalist churches sponsor a series of seminars and religious rallies to warn people about Satanic cults in the area. Ru-

mors predict that a newborn baby will be kidnapped by the cult for sacrifice on June 14. A child abuse hotline in Vancouver is called with reports of the rumor, which is taken seriously by authorities in Victoria. Security guards are posted in the maternity ward of the hospital to protect against an attempted kidnapping of a newborn baby. Rumors proliferate about Satanic cult animal sacrifices and drug use. The Province ministry alerts social workers to be on the lookout for babies in danger.

Oct. 13, 1983

Vancouver Sun.
Rumors recur about the planned kidnapping of a newborn baby. Guards are again posted at the hospital.

(2)
Sept. 22, 1984.
Edinburg,
Christian County,
(south of
Springfield)
Illinois

Associated Press news release.
Rumors of animal sacrifices. Town meeting with local sheriff. High school teens are accused of being in a "Devil worshipping cult."

(3)
Oct. 31, 1984.
Greene,
Craighead,
Poinsett counties,
(northeastern)
Arkansas

Mid-American Folklore 13, no.2, 1985. (Research article by Martha Long.)
Reports of widespread fear among children, parents, and teachers in response to rumors about a "Devil worshipping cult," focussed on Halloween night. Rumors of ritual cattle mutilations and of the planned kidnapping and ritual sacrifice of a blond, blue-eyed virgin child. Rumors persist for months after.

(4)
Apr. 14, 1985.
Union County,
(northwest of
Columbus) Ohio

Columbus Dispatch.
Local deputy sheriff claims that a series of pet animal mutilations are the work of Satanists. He claims that he has identified "five cells of

Satanists" in the area and that there are 1,500 secret Satanists in Ohio. He claims that many are homosexuals.

(5) May 14, 1985. Village of Delhi (southwest of London) Ontario, Canada	*Toronto Star.* Intense rumors about a Satanic cult supposedly meeting in an abandoned barn cause widespread fear among parents. Rumors of animal mutilations. Some parents hold children home from school. Police identify a group of six teenagers who met at barn to perform magic rituals. Police caution parents not to over-react. The teenagers are sent for counseling.
[May 16, 1985.	"20/20" TV segment, "The Devil Worshippers"]
(6) June 11, 21, 23, 1985. Akron, Ohio	*Akron Beacon Journal.* Intense rumors of Satanic cult animal mutilations and ritual sacrifice of children begin when a local Baptist minister organizes a community meeting to hear "former Satanic cult members" of Akron Cult Watch. The meeting attracts several hundred people. They are shown a videotape of the "20/20" show about "devil worshippers." Parents' concerns focus on a neighborhood park "taken over" by teenagers at night for drinking and drug use, where "Satanic symbols" are found. A group of residents organize patrols for the neighborhood at night.
(7) June 1985. Holland, (18 miles from Toledo) Ohio	*Cleveland Plain Dealer,* June 21, 22, July 7, Aug. 4. *Akron Beacon Journal,* June 21, 22. *Columbus Dispatch,* June 21, 22. National mass media focus attention on local

claims of Satanic cult murders. A local sheriff orders an excavation of a garbage-strewn wooded area, acting on claims of confidential "informants," that 50 to 80 victims of Satanic cult murders, mostly children, have been buried there since 1969. The dig attracts about 100 reporters, including television crews, from across the country and about 50 law enforcement officers from several states. Dale Griffis is hired as a consultant "authority" on Satanic cult crime and his wild claims are widely quoted by reporters. Although no evidence of any murders is found, Griffis claims that some items are "occult ritual relics."

Later (July 7), it is reported that the sheriff's main "informant" was a local Baptist minister who owned the land excavated. It was also later reported that a dilapidated shack on the land was once inhabited by a homeless, psychiatric patient, who would try to scare away curious teenagers with a variety of hocus-pocus items.

In a related incident, the police "raid" a nearby home that sheriff claims is a "cult house," where police confiscate a Bible and rock music records. The "cult house" story makes the cover of the Toledo newspaper. Later, the police admit mistake.

---

(8)
Aug. 31, 1986.
Denair, Stanislaus
County, (near
Modesto)
California

Modesto Bee.
Grave robbery, cemetery vandalism, graffiti symbols, mutilated animals, and burglaries of homes with the burglars leaving symbols provokes panic. Entire town said anxious to arrest supposed Devil worshippers.

San Jose Mercury News (follow up), Sept. 5, 1986. Vigilante patrols in rural areas. Rampant gossip. Denair High School spray-painted with symbols. Students are searching for suspects in Satanic cult. Reward is offered for information. Reporters come from San Francisco, with TV crew to cover story.

(9)	
Sept. 27–31, 1986. Schoharie County, (Catskill Mountains area) New York	*Schenectady Gazette.* Rampant rumors of Satanic cult activity. Rumors of animal sacrifices, ritual meetings, and planned human sacrifice on Halloween night. Graffiti found at high school. A community meeting about the rumors attracts 700 people and provides forum for lecture by police "expert" on dangers of teenage Satanism. Three youths arrested for graffiti vandalism. They say it was done as prank.
(10)	
Oct. 30, 1986. Counties of Beckham, Greer, Kiowa, Jackson, (southwestern) Oklahoma	*The Daily Oklahoman.* Rumors of planned Satanic cult kidnapping and sacrifice of a virgin on Halloween night causes panic. Police are swamped by telephone calls.
(11)	
Mar. 13, 1987. Mar. 14, 1987. South Carolina (from coast to mountains)	*Myrtle Beach Sun-News.* *Columbia State/Spartanburg Herald-Journal.* Intense rumors for several weeks about Devil worshippers over much of the state including: planned kidnappings of "blond, blue-eyed virgins" for ritual sacrifice on Friday the 13th. Flood of calls to police. Police radio is monitored by locals, who distort messages and then spread rumors. Concerns expressed about teenagers wearing black clothes.
(12)	
June 30, 1987. Benton County, (near Lafayette) Indiana	*Lafayette Journal and Courier.* Intense rumors about animal mutilations and possible kidnappings of children, in response

to graffiti symbols and cemetery vandalism. Gun sales increase.

(13)
Aug. 1987 and after.
City of Rockford, and Winnebego County, Illinois

Rockford Register Star (and an informant). Persistent rumors of Satanic cult activity (Aug. 26, 1987). A teenager and adult were found murdered. Police find books on "Satan worship" in room of son of murdered man (Sept. 6, 1987). The son confesses to killing his father after a family dispute. Mother of the murdered teenager claims that Satanism motivated the killing. Police deny claim (Apr. 2, May 3, Nov. 11, Dec. 7, Dec. 10, 1988). Newspaper reports of graffiti, arson, vandalism, assaults, and burglaries, all attributed to Satanism (Apr. 19, 1989). Workshop about dangers of Satanism presented for parents and teenagers, by police and clergy "experts" (Sept. 26, 1989). Woman at a prayer meeting goes into trance and says that Satanists plan to kidnap and kill her 5-year-old daughter. The woman is in psychiatric treatment. Court orders hearing for custody of daughter, but church members support her claims (Oct. 1988). Report from an informant in Rockford. Rumors circulate widely through city of a secret Satanic cult of adults who are sexually abusing children. Rumors name prominent professionals and clergy as leaders of the "cult." (These names are told to my informant by the Chief of Police, who takes the rumors seriously.)

(14)
Oct. 24, 1987.
St. Joseph County, (outside South Bend) Indiana

The Indianapolis Star.
Rumors of animal killings, ritual meetings, and planned human sacrifices on Halloween night cause widespread panic.

[Nov. 19, 1987.	"Geraldo" show on "Satanic Cults and Children"]

(15) Nov. 21, 1987. Towns of Island Falls and Smyrna Mills, (northeastern) Maine	*Bangor Daily News.* Intense rumors of a teen Devil worshipping cult and of animal killings. Graffiti symbols found. Punk teens, who dress differently, accused of being members of a Satanic cult. One youth rumored to be leader. A minister claims daughter was brainwashed by the cult.

(16) Mar. 20, 1988. Ft. Collins area, Larimer County, Colorado	*Fort Collins Coloradan.* Intense rumors about a teenage Satanic cult. Only "evidence" found are graffiti symbols. Some parents and teachers urge action against teens rumored to be a Satanic cult. Community conflict erupts over accusations of Devil worship and threats of violence from and against rumored cult members.

(17) Mar. 26, 1988. Kansas City, and surrounding area in Missouri and Kansas	*Kansas City Times* (Missouri). Rumors of children ritually murdered by Satanists. Newspaper reports claims of child sexual abuse made by self-proclaimed former Satanists and links them with claims of police Satan hunters about a national network of Satanic cults. It cites claims of Satan hunter "experts": Dale Griffis, Larry Jones, Sandi Gallant, Maury Terry, Craig Hill, Larry Dunn, and Jacquie Balodis (a self-proclaimed former Satanist). They make claims about thousands of child kidnappings and ritual sacrifices carried out by network of Satanic cults. The "Lost Child Network" of 50 police and therapists in Kansas City area is established to investigate Satanic cult activity.

Some therapists report having teenage patients who are Satanists.

---

(18)
Apr. 1, 2, 1988.
Town of McComb,
Pike County,
Mississippi

Jackson Clarion-Ledger.
New York Times (Apr. 3, 1988).
Rumors began to spread March 20–25, after Baptist revival against Satanism, followed by TV report on Satanic cults. Rumors of animal killings, secret ritual meetings, group sex, and planned kidnapping and sacrifice of a child. Sheriff says he has a list of 22 members of a Satanic cult in the county. During panic, 30% of children kept home from school. Gun sales increase.

---

(19)
Apr. 12, 1988.
Wilkes-Barre and
Scranton area,
Luzerne County,
Pennsylvania

Citizen's Voice (Wilkes-Barre, Pennsylvania).
Rumors began in January, after news reports of the Tommy Sullivan case, in nearby New Jersey, and of cemetery vandalism. Rumors of animal killings and planned kidnapping of a child by a Satanic cult. Reports of "near hysteria" among parents. Report notes some people buying guns for protection. Schools preparing to educate children and parents about dangers of Satanic cults. Newspaper publishes list of "indicators" of teenage Satanism.

---

(20)
Apr. 19, 1988.
Town of Lancaster
Grant County,
(southwestern)
Wisconsin

Capital Times (Madison, Wisconsin).
Rumors start when some dead cats are found. Rumors accuse group of five teenagers of being a Satanic cult, killing cats, and planning to sacrifice babies. These teens merely play *Dungeons and Dragons* games and draw tattoos on their arms. Parents and children are frightened. Police and schools are swamped

by telephone calls. (Police determine that cats were killed by owner.)

(21)	
May 13, 1988.	*Tuscaloosa News.*
Tuscaloosa	Rumors that a Devil worshipping cult plans to
County, Alabama	kidnap a girl on Friday the 13th cause widespread fear. Police and schools are swamped by telephone calls. Many parents keep children home from school. Police sent to guard all schools in county.
(22)	
May 13, 1988.	See chapters 2 and 3 for details of this rumor-
Southwestern	panic.
New York State,	
northwestern	
Pennsylvania,	
northwestern	
Ohio	
(23)	
July, 1988.	*Steubenville Herald-Star.*
Counties of	(From letter from reporter.)
Jefferson and	Rumor-panic occurs after a two-day seminar
Columbiana,	by Larry Nelson from Mike Warnke
(near town of	Ministeries, in town of Richmond, Ohio. He
Steubenville),	was invited to speak at a church and was paid
Ohio	$1500. Many parents kept their children home, due to fear that they might be kidnapped and sacrificed by the "cult." At a press conference, County Sheriff announces that a dozen teenagers are involved in Satanism and two are getting therapy.
(24)	
Sept. 25, 26,	*Lexington Herald-Leader.*
1988. Sept. 12,	Rumors of planned kidnapping and sacrifice
20, 1988.	of a "blond, blue-eyed virgin," animal muti-

Covers 25 counties; centered in Breathitt County, eastern Kentucky

lations, planned mass murders cause panic. Rumors began two months before, in response to grave robbery and arrest of two teens and four adults for vandalism. During panic, 350 students leave school building and many others are kept home by parents, in response to rumor that cult would come to Caldwell County High School to kill students. Gun stores sold out. Rumors spread rapidly from eastern counties to western counties.

---

(25)
Sept. 30, Oct. 7, 1988. Sept. 30, 1988.
Kanawha, Raleigh, Putnam Counties, (near Charleston) West Virginia

Charleston Gazette.
Charleston Daily Mail.
Rumor of planned kidnapping and sacrifice of a "blond, blue-eyed virgin" and animal mutilations cause rumor-panic. Many children kept home from elementary schools in area. Four hundred people attend a meeting about the problem in Coal City. Vigilante groups form and patrol looking for Satanists. Police flooded with telephone calls (as is Humane Society) from people making claims and asking for information. Evidence only of cemetery vandalism.

---

(26)
Oct. 21, 1988.
town of Chinook, Blaine County, (north central) Montana

Great Falls Tribune.
Rumors of planned kidnapping and sacrifice of "blond, blue-eyed virgins" and animal mutilations cause panic. Four youths arrested for alleged threats and assaults "related to Satanic practices." Reports of widespread fear among parents and children, in days before Halloween night. Parents advisory group forms to patrol area looking for Satanic cult. Local Sheriff "expert" in finding Satanists. Librarian reports to school officials, a youth asking to read "Satanic Bible."

[Oct. 6, 1988.	"Geraldo" show—"Teenage Satanism"]
[Oct. 24, 1988.	"Geraldo" show—"Satanic Breeders: Babies for Sacrifice"]
[Oct. 25, 1988.	"Geraldo" TV special on "Devil Worship"]

(27)

Oct. 28, 1988.
Counties around
Richmond (VA)
Chesterfield,
Dinwiddie,
Henrico,
Hanover,
Goochland,
Powhatan,
Virginia

The Richmond News Leader.
Rumors began in Sept. after a conference on Satanism offered by police, counselors, and "cult survivors." Rumors intensify after parents at a day-care center were given a memo to be on the alert for a Satanic cult, which was supposedly planning to kidnap and sacrifice a child. Rumors of animal killings and the planned kidnapping of "blond, blue-eyed" children by a Satanic cult. Newspaper reports that "parents have become overly alarmed." Satanic graffiti found on abandoned house rumored to be cult ritual site. Rumor-panic in rural and suburban areas near city. *Richmond News Leader,* April 6 and 7, 1989 (follow up). Newspaper report attributes origin of rumors to three local Satan hunters who were widely quoted in the media of Richmond area, including two local police and Patricia Pulling (head of B.A.D.D.), making claims about Satanic cult crime. Local "cult survivors" (Multiple Personality Disorder patients) make claims. Claims are also made by children that they know of Satanic cult ritual activities.

(28)

Oct. 25, 30,
1988. Oct. 25.
Oct. 25.
Counties of
Whitley, DeKalb,
Steuben,
(northeastern)
Indiana

Fort Wayne Journal Gazette.
Post & Mail (Columbia City, Indiana).
Auburn Evening Star (Indiana).
Rumors began after sex-murder of a "blond, blue-eyed" 8-year-old girl in April, in DeKalb County. Rumors intensified after the suicide of a teenager in Whitley County. Rumors of animal killings, human sacrifice,

secret ritual meetings, a criminal Satanic cult network, and police cover-up of kidnappings cause panic. Public meeting about rumors attracts 700 people. "Task force" organized to investigate Satanism in the area. A local police chief lectures about Satanic cult kidnappings and sacrifice of children. He claims that a local murder was "related to Satanic activity," but covered up by police. Rumors that a Satanic cult plans to kidnap and sacrifice a "blond, blue-eyed" teenage girl on Halloween night. Rumors of lists of potential victims. Many parents keep their children home from school. Rumor that some local stores are holding secret Satanic rituals in basements at night results in financial losses.

---

(29)
Oct. 31, 1988
Counties of
Washburn, Rusk,
Taylor, Lincoln,
Marathon, (north
central)
Wisconsin

Capitol Times (Madison, Wisconsin).
Rumors began the previous month, in Washburn County, after a 17-year-old murdered both parents. Spray-painted graffiti are found at a high school. Rumors of slaughtered cattle and of the planned kidnapping of "blond, blue-eyed" children on Halloween night. Schools and churches hold meetings to dispel wild rumors among frightened parents. Police say that they are worried about threats by citizens "to take things into their own hands." Local humane societies have stopped giving black cats, due to fear that they might be used in ritual sacrifices.

---

(30)
Nov. 16, 1988.
Juneau, Alaska

Juneau Empire.
Rumors began to circulate in 1987, after a wife accused her husband of ritually sexually abusing her children and also of murdering

another child in Satanic rituals. Police find no evidence of Satanism or murder, but husband was convicted of child sexual abuse. Rumors intensify after an October workshop on Satanic cult child sex abuse, sponsored by a local fundamentalist minister, in response to the wife's claims. Local school board send staff to the workshop for training, because of concerns of parents and teachers. Local therapists report having treated former "Satanic cult" members. Intense rumors of animal mutilations, Satanic cult ritual meetings, and child sexual abuse by Satanic cult cause panic. Police find no evidence to support the rumors of Satanic cult crimes.

(31)
Dec. 4, 1988.
Kansas City area,
counties of
Wyandotte,
Leavenworth,
Shawnee, Kansas

Kansas City Star (Missouri).
Intense rumors of Satanic cult ritual meetings, animal mutilations, and planned kidnappings of blond, blue-eyed children. Rumors began after Geraldo Rivera's special TV show on Satanism on Oct. 25, in which a Kansas City crime case was featured as an example of Satanic ritual torture. Some Kansas City police claim on TV show, that the crimes were activities of a Satanic cult. Newspaper notes that other local police are skeptical about these claims. A citizen's task force on Satanism has been operating since April. At a local school, 300 people attend a meeting on the problem where they are told that "Satanic ritualism is a growing problem" by the Kansas City police detective from the TV show (Lee Orr). A concerned parents group draws up a list of books that they believe promotes Satanism, which they want removed the school library.

(32)
Dec. 19, 1988.
Pinal County,
towns of Eloy and
Casa Grande
(north of Tucson)
Arizona

Tucson Citizen.
Rumors start after a murder, in which a
teenage suspect was reported to have a tattoo
of the Devil on his chest. Rumors of Satanic
cult ritual sacrifices of animals and children
and teenage suicides caused by Satanism.
Police find no evidence of such crimes.

(33)
Jan. 15, 1989.
Fort Bend
County, towns of
Richmond and
Rosenberg (west
of Houston) Texas

Dallas Morning News.
Rumors may have started after a community
conference on Satanism was attended by 350
people, on Nov. 14. Intense rumors about
Satanic cult activity emerge after a series of
murders by a teenage gang, who attempt to
kill their parents. One teenager killed his
mother. Prosecutor claims that gang is led by
a 16-year-old girl, who used Satanism to
influence the others.

(34)
Feb. 21, 23,
1989.
Village and
county of
Hillsdale, (south)
Michigan

Detroit Free Press.
Rumors probably spread from nearby Indiana
counties experiencing the same rumors,
noted above, on Oct. 25, 1988. Two gutted
goats are found with horns removed. Rumors
of Satanic cult rituals cause panic. At a town
meeting, 800 people show up to hear local
police lecture on "how to recognize signs of
Devil worship." Police use videotape of
"Geraldo" TV show as information and present "psychological profile of devil worshippers" to audience.
Detroit News, March 22, 1989, (follow up
report).
Rumors persist in area of Hillsdale. Police
receive daily claims of Satanic cult crimes,
including many kidnappings and murders.
Report gives details about various supposed

"Satanic cult crimes" in the Detroit area. (The 1985 Ohio search for secret Satanists is covered extensively in the article, as affirmation of Satanic crime.)

---

(35)
Mar. 20, 1989.
Towns of Peoria
and Glendale,
(near Phoenix)
Arizona

Arizona Republic.
Intense rumors and fears of Satanic cults after incidents of cemetery vandalism. Four youths are arrested for the crime. Police present seminar on Satanism to a meeting of parents and teachers.

---

(36)
Mar. 23, 1989.
Mar. 26, 1989.
Village of Corith,
(south of Glens
Falls) New York

Post-Star (Glens Falls, New York).
Sunday Times Union (Albany, New York).
A wave of Satanic cult rumors begins after suicide of local teenager. Rumors of animal killings and human sacrifice. Graffiti symbols found. A town meeting attracts about 600 people, who hear Father LeBar caution parents to be calm. High school Superintendent says that four teenagers are in a "cult." Local Sheriff cautions against witch hunt.

---

(37)
Apr., 1989.
Area around Rock
Springs,
(southwestern)
Wyoming

Local Informant and *Rock Springs Rocket-Miner* (Apr. 18, 1990, follow up).
Widespread, intense rumors cause panic. Rumors of animal killings, ritual meetings, strange lights at night, and planned kidnapping of a blond, blue-eyed virgin girl by Satanic cult. Graffiti symbols found. Many parents keep their children home from school. Local group of teenagers becomes target of accusations and harassment. Fundamentalist police "expert" invited to lecture. He claims that there is evidence of Satanic cult in the area, in lecture to community meeting and on local radio. List of "Satanic

indicators" circulated. Panic persists through
month of April.

(38)
Apr. 17, 1989.
May 14, 1989.
Rural counties
around
Pittsburgh,
Washington,
Fayette, Greene,
Westmoreland,
Indiana; Butler,
Armstrong,
Pennsylvania

Valley News Dispatch.
The Pittsburgh Press.
A long lasting rumor-panic over a very large
area. Rumors may have started after the local
murder of two teenage girls by a teenage boy,
when defense attorney claimed that the killer
was under the influence of Satanism. Police
then announce finding a Satanic cult ritual
meeting site (which is later identified as a
picnic area). Other incidents include some
animal mutilations by teenagers, cemetery
vandalism, and spray-painted graffiti symbols
on churches across area. There are a great
variety of rumor stories, including the
planned kidnapping and ritual sacrifice of
blond, blue-eyed children, animal sacrifices,
and secret meetings of Satanic cults. Many
local town meetings are held about the rumors. Hundreds of telephone calls come to
local police and school officials with claims
about Satanic cult activities. Hundreds of
children were kept home from school. School
meetings are held to calm fearful parents and
their children.

(39)
May 5, 28, 1989.
May 21, Apr. 21.
May 3, 4, 12.
(state wide) New
Hampshire

Boston Globe (Massachusetts).
Boston Globe.
Union Leader (Manchester, New Hampshire).
Widespread rumors and fear start after a
state-wide 3-day police conference on "Satanic cult crime," earlier in April, which
attracted 170 police and received much media coverage. A featured speaker was police
Satan hunter, Dale Griffis, billed as "nation-
wide consultant to police departments," who

is quoted as saying that "some Satanic cults are criminal cartels." Newspapers quote other claims from the conference, that there are over two million members of Satanic cults in the U.S. and that a great many serial murders and teenage suicides are caused by Satanism. After the conference, local police consult with San Francisco policewoman Sandi Gallant about local incidents. Gallant then informs them that they have found "signs" of Satanic cult activity. Then, across the state, police mistakenly perceive many situations as "signs" of Satanic cult crime. A skinned beaver and raccoon are found in a state park, resulting in rumors and media stories of Satanic cult ritual animal mutilations. Later, it is determined that it was the work of fur trappers. Police find some dead animals hanging from a shed in the woods and report it as being animal sacrifices by "cult" members. Later, it is determined that the dead animals were road kills cleaned up by state road crews. A teenage girl reports her ex-boyfriend as the Satanic animal killer and is believed by police and the announcement made to local media. Police arrest a group of youths who are meeting in the woods dressed in Medieval garb and using strange paraphernalia, including an animal skull, candles, daggers, and swords. The incident is widely reported in the local media, as a police arrest of "cult" members. Later, it is determined that they are college students working on an film project for a college art course.

(40)
May 28, 1989.
Across rural areas
of Iowa

Des Moines Register.
A "prairie fire" of rumors across the rural areas of Iowa, causing widespread fear among parents for months. Rumors may have begun

in response to media attention given to suicides of teenagers alleged to be involved in "Satanism." Rumors of secret ritual meetings, animal sacrifices, drinking of blood, planned kidnappings, and human sacrifices. Community meetings across the state are packed with concerned parents. Police in small towns are swamped by telephone calls with rumors and try to check stories, finding nothing. Survey of Iowa principals ranks "cult involvement" as one of the major concerns of educators in state. Mental health and social service professionals hold 2-day seminar on "ritual abuse" of children.

(41)
May 30, 1989.
Town of Lake
City, Anderson
County,
Tennessee

Oak Ridger (Oak Ridge, Tennessee).
"Rampant rumors" limited to small town, about cult of Devil worshippers who kill animals. Graffiti symbols found. Three teenagers arrested for the graffiti vandalism. Dead dog was a road kill.

(42)
July 21, 1989.
Town of
Hereford, Deaf
Smith County
(near Amarillo)
Texas

Amarillo Daily News and *Hereford Brand*.
Intense rumors of Satanic cult murders begin after fundamentalist minister reports claims of two women who told him that 40 to 50 people have been ritually mass murdered and buried in the area. Police find no evidence of missing persons or murder.

(43)
Aug. 6, 1989.
Sept. 3, 1989.
Beaver County,
(north of
Pittsburgh)
Pennsylvania

Beaver County Times.
Pittsburgh Press.
Intense rumors in western Pennsylvania persist. Widespread fear reported in rural areas. Claims constantly reported to police, such as Satanic altars in the woods, animal mutila-

tions, and planned sacrifices of blond, blue-eyed children.

(44)
Aug. 13, 1989.
Big Pine Key,
Florida

Miami Herald.
Intense rumors and fear in response to the murders of two women and a 4-year-old girl. The first murder occurred in July. The bodies were mutilated by killer or by vultures. Graffiti symbols found on road near one victim. Rumors allege that the murders are the work of a drug dealing Satanic cult.

(45)
Sept. 10, 1989.
Counties of
Greene, Sevier,
Cocke, Hamlen,
Hawkins,
Washington,
(eastern)
Tennessee

Knoxville News Sentinel.
Persistent rumors previous two years over a broad region. Rumors of Satanic cult animal mutilations and sacrifice of human fetuses. Police find only graffiti symbols in several caves. Therapists report that they treat many teenagers for drug abuse, who are also involved in Satanism. Personnel at shelters for runaway teenagers also report that Satanism commonly accompanies drug abuse.

(46)
Sept. 17, 1989.
Joplin, Jasper
County, Missouri

Kansas City Star (Missouri).
Persistent rumors over previous two years since the murder at nearby Carl Junction, in which three teenagers beat to death another teenager with a baseball bat, labelled by media a "Satanic cult sacrifice." Local churches campaign against Satanism among teenagers. A major concern is an abandoned shopping center, decorated with "Satanic" graffiti. Another concern is that a self-proclaimed Satanist now has a telephone listing for his "religion," which has a recorded telephone message recruiting new members.

(47)

Oct. 24, 1989.	*Dickinson Press* (North Dakota).
Oct. 28, 1989.	*Fargo Forum* (North Dakota).
Oct. 28, 1989.	*Bismarck Tribune* (North Dakota).
Towns of Jamestown, Dickinson, Belfield, New England; across southern North Dakota	A great variety of Satanic cult rumors sweep across southern section of rural North Dakota, focussed on Halloween. Rumors may have been triggered by media attention given to the kidnapping of child from nearby Minnesota (Jacob Wetterling). Rumors of animal sacrifices, planned kidnapping, and sacrifice of blond children or women. Police swamped by telephone calls with rumors to investigate. Police caution parents to accompany their children while trick-or-treating on Halloween night. Graffiti symbols found on abandoned houses and photos printed in small town newspapers. Minister "cult expert" is quoted advising parents to take the rumors seriously, "because Halloween is known as a Satanic holy day."

(48)

Oct. 28, 1989.	*Raleigh News and Observer.*
Eastern area of North Carolina	Rumors spread "like wildfire" across eastern section of North Carolina, about planned Satanic cult kidnapping of blond, blue-eyed children for ritual sacrifice on Halloween. Police swamped by telephone calls from worried parents.

(49)

Oct. 31, 1989.	*Albuquerque Tribune.*
Rural villages east of Albuquerque, New Mexico	Intense rumors circulate through elementary schools and day-care centers that a Satanic cult plans to kidnap and sacrifice a "blond, blue-eyed" child on Halloween.

(50)

Nov. 1, 2, 1989. *Columbus Ledger-Enquirer.*
Nov. 2, 1989. *Waycross Journal-Herald.*
Town of Butler, Newspapers report "mass hysteria" in re-
Taylor County, sponse to rumor that Satanic cult planned to
Georgia kidnap children from schools for human sacrifice. About 300 parents invade county elementary, middle, and high school buildings to
remove their children. On previous day, 25%
of parents kept children home from school, in
response to rumors that blond, blue-eyed
children would be kidnapped by cult on
Halloween.

(51)

Nov. 1989. *Evening Telegram* (St. John's, Newfoundland)
Village of Intense rumors of Satanic cult activity are
Bonavista (north sparked by graveyard vandalism and disinter-
of St. John's) ment. Crosses on tombs were knocked off and
Newfoundland, set upside down. An 18-year-old youth ar-
Canada rested. Widespread fear reported.

(52)

Dec. 7, 1989. *Journal-Tribune* (Biddeford-Saco, Maine).
Town of Fear of Satanic cult crime, in response to
Biddeford York arson at high school and several local
County, churches, at which "Satanic" graffiti symbols
(southern) Maine are found. Conference held on problems of
"Satanism."

(53)

Feb. 2, 1990. *Easton Star-Democrat.*
Caroline County, A "crisis situation" in response to rumors
on eastern shore triggered by the suicides of three teenage
of Maryland boys over previous months. Rumors that teenage Satanic cults are promoting the suicides
worry parents. Hundreds of parents attend
two community meetings. "Cult expert," Michael Rokos, is invited to investigate. He finds

graffiti symbols on abandoned house and is quoted as saying that there is a surprising amount of occult activity taking place in the county.

(54)
Mar. 12, 13, 14, 17, 1990. Mar. 10, 11, 13. Feb. 19, Mar. 26. City of Lethbridge and southern Alberta, (north of Montana border) Canada

The Calgary Sun (Alberta, Canada).
The Herald (Calgary, Alberta).
Alberta Report (Edmonton, Alberta).
A series of three teenage suicides causes intense rumors and fear among parents about suicide pacts, supposedly motivated by Satanic cult influences. Evidence is found that the teenagers were involved in black magic practices. Rumors allege adult leaders, cult brainwashing, secret ritual meetings, and drug use in rituals. School board chairman claims that as many as 100 youths are involved in Satanism in the area of Lethbridge. Some parents threaten to form a vigilante group and attack suspected adult cult leaders and burn their homes. A group of parents demonstrate outside police station. Police and other authorities caution calm. Fundamentalist churches in nearby Calgary organize a public seminar on the dangers of Satanism. Eight teenagers are put in psychiatric or foster care. Police find no organized cult.

(55)
Mar. 28, 1990. Across northern sections of South Dakota

Aberdeen American-News.
Rumors across north central South Dakota, including towns of Aberdeen, Webster, and McLaughlin. Rumors of human sacrifices, secret ritual sites in abandoned buildings, animal mutilations, and of teenagers involved in Satanism. Community meetings held in many locations. Law enforcement officers, clergy, school officials, and counselors speak publicly

about the dangers. Graffiti symbols seen as evidence of Satanic cult activity.

(56)
Aug. 7, 1990.
Town of Sierra
Vista, Cochise
County,
(southeastern)
Arizona

Sierra Vista Herald/Bisbee Review.
Persistent rumors of human sacrifices by Satanic cults in the area. Town meeting draws 300 people to hear local police "expert" on Satanic cult crime. He tells them that there are seven Satanic cults in the town and that he has evidence that they practice human sacrifice in ceremonies out in desert canyons.

(57)
Sept. 28, 1990.
Palmyra, New
York (near
Rochester)

Democrat and Chronicle (Rochester, New York).
Rumors started after local murder of a teenage girl and infant (Chad Campbell case), previous month. Community meeting about Satanism attracts about 1,200 people, who hear local police "expert" tell about cult symbols and activities of Satanists. A family therapist also talks about "ritual abuse." However, they caution that there is "no epidemic" of Satanism among area youth.

(58)
Oct. 20, 1990.
Monroe County,
(outside
Bloomington)
Indiana

The Herald-Times (Bloomington, Indiana).
"Rampant" rumors about Satanic cult plans to kidnap and sacrifice as many as 100 blond, blue-eyed children. Police inundated by telephone calls. Graffiti symbols found.

(59)
Oct. 23, 1990.
Jefferson County,
West Virginia

Martinsburg Journal.
Intense rumors of Satanic cult animal sacrifices and the kidnapping and sacrifice of blond, blue-eyed children in Harpers Ferry area. Many parents call schools about rumors. School has safety assemblies.

(60)
Nov. 14, 15,
1990.
Village of
Kremmling,
(northwest of
Denver) Colorado

Rocky Mountain News (Denver).
Reports of hysteria in town on Halloween,
due to rumors of Satanic cult activity, after
police find graffiti symbols, altar, candles,
lanterns, and Satanic bibles at abandoned
shack. Police arrest six teenagers for trespassing. Rumors that Satanic cult planned sacrifices of neighbor's pets, desecration of
churches, and sacrifice of children. About a
third of town attends meeting to hear local
police "expert" on Satanic cult crime.

(61)
Nov./Dec. 1991.
Counties of
Minidota and
Cassia, (southern)
Idaho

Twin Falls Times-News, Nov. 8, 9; Dec. 15.
Rumors started in Nov. 1989, after finding of
the mutilated and burned corpse of a baby in
a landfill, that baby was Satanic cult ritual
sacrifice. Frequent articles in local newspapers about "Baby X" investigation attract
much attention to rumor allegations. Rumors
proliferate about black robed figures having
rituals in woods and dogs sacrificed. Local
psychiatrist is quoted in newspaper as believing that secret Satanists practice in the area
and sacrifice babies. Area clergy organize
candlelight vigil in Rupert on Nov. 8, protesting "ritual abuse," which attracts about 500
people from several states. The vigil is covered by television news from Idaho and even
Salt Lake City.

(62)
Mar. 6, 7, 10, 14,
1992. Mar. 10,
11, 1992.
Carbon County,
Pennsylvania

The Morning Call (Allentown, Pennsylvania).
The Times News (Carbon County).
Intense rumors start among school children in
town of Lehighton, that a teenage Devil worshipping cult plans to kidnap and sacrifice a
blond, blue-eyed virgin on Friday the Thirteenth. Rumors claim that more than 100

students are involved in the cult. Police question suspected cult members and stake out houses. Police inundated by telephone calls from worried parents. Graffiti symbols found at abandoned houses. A local police chief circulates letter through area churches stating that "Satan is alive and well in Carbon County," inviting parents to attend a community meeting that he will address about the danger "signs to watch for." Rumor-panic is covered by distant television news.

Appendix V
Some Satanic Ritual Abuse Cases, 1983-1987

Source: Benjamin Rossen. "Zedenangst: Het verhaal van Oude Pekela." (Moral Panic: The story of Oude Pekela.). Amsterdam and Lisse, The Netherlands: Swets and Zeitlinger, 1989. English language version, translated by the author. [Original Source: *Memphis Commercial Appeal*, January 1988.]

August 1983. Manhattan Beach, California. A woman told the police that her son had been abused by his teacher at the McMartin Preschool. As a result of the investigation, seven people were indicted in what authorities called "the largest child molestation ring in the country." Ray Buckey and his mother, Peggy McMartin Buckey faced trial on more than 100 counts of child abuse. More than 349 children were interrogated repeatedly by therapists at the Children's Institute. Children told incredible stories about airplane flights, submarine rides, teachers dressed as witches and flying naked, nude photography, Satanic rituals in churches and graveyards, animal sacrifices and blood-drinking. Massive police investigations were unable to find concrete evidence. Charges were dropped five defendants, including the school's owner, Virginia McMartin, after an 18-month preliminary hearing. In January 1990, Peggy and Ray Buckey were found innocent of most of the charges against them and later that year, the remaining charges were dropped by the prosecution.

August 1983. Concord, California. A vehicle mechanic was accused by his stepdaughter of being part of a Satanic cult that forced her to kill an infant and eat feces as well as engage in ritualistic sex abuse during the previous three years. No concrete evidence could be found. The man was arrested and tried. A locked jury, 6 to 6, defeated the case. No new trial is scheduled.

September 1983. Jordan, Minnesota. James Rud, a garbage collector, was arrested and charged with the indecent assault of three children. The resulting investigation lead to the arrest of 24 adults. Stories told by James Rud and five children formed the basis for the charges. As the children were repeatedly interviewed, their stories grew increasingly bizarre and included reports about the murder and mutilation of other children. Rud pleaded guilty to unremarkable indecent assault charges. Months of police investigation failed to produce concrete evidence of any other offenses. Parents, Robert and Louis Bentz, were acquitted a year later. Scott County prosecutor, Kathleen Morris, dismissed charges against the remaining 21 defendants. A state attorney investigation, chaired by Hubert Humphrey III, concluded that the Morris investigation had been flawed and contained extensive fabrication of stories of sex, torture, and murder.

October 1983. Bouse, Arizona. Children in foster care in Omaha, Nebraska told of children being kidnapped from shopping malls, drugged, abused and sacrificed by their natural parents and other adults in rituals dating to 1980 and 1981 in southwestern Arizona. Authorities, guided by photos on which the children had drawn X's excavated the area for remains. Huge areas of desert were searched and satellite photographs were used. No concrete evidence was found to substantiate the accounts. No children were reported missing from the area.

April 1984. Pico River, California. Deputies arrested two men and two women on kidnapping and conspiracy charges based on the accusations of two children who made continuing detailed claims of Satanic rituals and child sacrifice. A judge dismissed the charges against the four suspects a year later saying that the two boys who made the charges had lied.

April 1984. Chicago, Illinois. Deloartic Parks was charged with the sexual assault of preschoolers at Rogers Park Day Care Center, where he was a janitor. Children soon began to accuse teachers of abusing them in Satanic rituals. No teachers were arrested. Parks was acquitted. The Illinois Department of Children and Family Services concluded most of the 246 allegations against other staff members were unfounded. In February 1986, prosecutors dropped the remaining charges.

May 1984. Reno, Nevada. The owner of a Montessori day school babysitting service and two co-workers were indicted on 69 charges of sexual assault, lewdness, and mental harm to 26 children. Several children talked of chanting, singing, and 'naked movie star' games. Charges were dismissed against one defendant after a judge ruled that the children had been subject to leading questioning. The charges against all defendants in the case were eventually dropped.

June 1984. Memphis, Tennessee. Georgian Hills Early Childhood center teacher's aid Frances Ballard was charged with the sexual assault of 19 children. The next May, a Baptist minister, the Reverend Paul Shell, and two day-care workers were charged with similar offenses involving 26 children. The children told about airplane flights, satanic rituals, pornography, the slaying of animals, and threats. They were said to have been locked in cages, burned with candles and baptized in the name of the Devil. Mrs. Ballard was convicted on one count of sexual battery and acquitted on 15 others. In 1991, an appeals court overturned Ballard's conviction and the charges were dropped. The charges against the other defendants were dropped in 1987.

June 1984. Sacramento, California. Gary A. Dill and four other men were accused of sexually assaulting Dill's children, who told about orgies, cannibalism, and the making of 'snuff' movies. Charges were dropped when the Municipal Court Judge, Ronald Robie, said that there was no credible evidence against the men, and that the children had been contaminated by 'inhumane' interrogation techniques of their 'severely mentally ill' grandmother. Two girls testified that they made up stories on their grandmother's orders. The two girls were in the McAuley Neuropsychiatric Institute being treated for 'post trau-matic stress syndrome' months after the supposed reason for the treatment had been found to be false. Judge Ronald Robie com-mented: "Sadly health professionals and law enforcement officials were unable to recognize or do anything about the senseless harm being done to these children."

June 1984. Bakersfield, California. The first of several defendants in the so called 'Gonzales-Thomas-Nokes child sex abuse ring' were arrested and charged with child sexual abuse. Children talked about Satanic ceremonies, including the slaying of 29 infants. By the end of the investigation there were 88 suspects, including a prosecutor, a social worker, a deputy sheriff, and a mortician. Authorities removed 21 children from the homes of their parents, including some parents who had not been charged with any offenses. The children were placed in protective custody where many began to show signs of serious behavioral disturbance. No evidence of ritual crime was found. The allegedly slain children were found to be alive and well. Leroy George Stowe was convicted and received a 30-year sentence which was overturned on appeal. Two defendants pleaded guilty to lesser charges in exchange for the dismissal of more than 300 counts against four other defendants. There have been suggestions that the American plea bargaining system in these cases results in innocent people making untrue guilty pleas.

July 1984. West Point, New York. An investigation of the Army's day-care program began after a girl returned home from it bleeding in her vaginal area. During the investigation, which continued throughout the next year, more than 950 people were interviewed, including hundreds of children. The allegations grew to include several children, animal sacrifices, pornography, and rituals involving people wearing bloody Dracula type masks. Dr. Walter Grote, a general practitioner who had played a central role in promoting the myths of Satanic ritual child molestation, accused West Point officials of covering up. Eight families have filed damages claims amounting to $110 million. An investigation concluded that there were indications of abuse of one child but insufficient evidence to prosecute.

Summer 1984. Los Angeles County, California. Michael Ruby (17), a teacher's assistant at the Manhattan Ranch Preschool, was arrested on 11 counts of child molestation. Pretrial testimony centered on children's reports of underground passages and haunted houses. The school grounds were dug up to find the passages. No evidence could be found. After a 4-month trial Ruby was released when the jury deadlocked. Jurors said that contradictory children's testimony was the main reason for the impasse.

October 1984. Los Angeles County, California. Allegations of Satanic ritual abuse, similar to those in the McMartin case, involved 63 other day-care centers and included references to hooded figures in dark robes dancing and chanting in circles. A sheriff's task force and state social services department investigated cases and closed down some preschools. At a cost of more than $1 million more than 100 adults and several hundred children were interviewed. Homes and businesses were searched and 56 suspects were identified. No criminal charges were made when no evidence could be found. Investigations centered on facilities in several communities, including Torrence, Whittier, Placentia, Covina, and Lomita. Late last year insurers of one school reached a $1 million out-of-court settlement with the families who alleged their children had been abused. In large areas around Los Angeles, preschool and day-care services are no longer available for preschool children.

October 1984. Atherton, California. A 17-year-old high school honor student accused her stepfather and 10 other adults of sexual abuse. The girl said she witnessed blood drinking, animal mutilations, and human sacrifices. No evidence to support the allegations could be found. Dead cats were found in the girl's school locker and under the porch at her home. According to investigators the girl had marks that could indicate physical abuse.

Fall 1984. Richmond, Virginia. Two children who may have had incestuous relations with other family members, began telling of rituals they allegedly took part in nearly a year earlier. They said they had been forced to witness the slaying of a child, a friend of theirs whose decomposed body had been discovered in the woods the year before. Children told of adults wearing red robes and said they had to eat parts of the girl's body. The police found burn rings, similar to those left by candles, on the floor of the apartment where the acts were said to have occurred. The police said: "the children would freeze up . . . we couldn't decide whether the children were telling the truth or fantasizing." No charges have been filed and the death from the previous year remains unsolved.

January 1985. Fort Bragg, California. Authorities conducted a nearly year long investigation of the Jubilation Day Care Center, where two teachers, sisters from Illinois, were accused of molesting more than a dozen children, some as young as two. Children said that women cut them with long jeweled knives and sucked their blood, sacrificed an infant and animals, and photographed them. Authorities brought no criminal charges although the child-care license was revoked. No concrete evidence of any of the allegations could be found. Assistant District Attorney Hugh Cavanagh said: "All we really have is the testimony of very young kids, who probably couldn't qualify as competent witnesses."

January 1985. Cornelius, Oregon. The investigation involved nine children, some as young as three. Three adults at a day-care center were accused. An investigator said: "Little by little, children have talked of robes, candles and murder." No evidence could be found and no arrests were made.

June 1985. El Paso, Texas. Police and social workers began an investigation after parents questioned their four-year old daughter about a word she had used. Several employees of East Valley YMCA Day Care Center were investigated. Teachers Gayle Dove and Michelle Noble were indicated. Eight children talked about monsters, being kissed and fondled, and having pennies put into their 'pee-pees', drinking drugs, and being forced to eat body parts, and watching murders of adults and children. They also said that knives were used in rituals. The police investigations failed to discover the whereabouts of any monsters, cauldrons, or skeletons. No evidence of any kind was found. Michelle Noble was convicted in March 1986. An appeals court overturned the conviction. In a new trial in 1988, she was found innocent. Gayle Dove was convicted separately in March 1987. An appeals court overturned the conviction, and in 1990, the charges were dropped.

September 1985. Carson City, Nevada. An investigation was spawned by the comment of a five-year-old male while watching television. Martha Helen Felix, who ran a baby-sitting service, and her nephew, Felix Ontiveres, who lived in the home, faced trial on 25 counts of felony child abuse involving 14 children. Children told of the murders of adults, animal killings, drinking blood, and other rituals. The police discovered a photograph of mummified children. Ontiveres gave evidence that the picture was taken at a museum in his native Mexico. No evidence of murders or animal killings was ever found.

April 1986. Sequim, Washington. A woman noticed vaginal redness in her granddaughter. A preschool owner and her son were charged with three counts of indecent liberties involving five children, who said they had been assaulted by adults who wore hooded robes and wielded sticks, and that they had been taken to graveyards and witnessed animal sacrifices and cutting up babies. Charges were dropped a year later when no evidence to substantiate the allegations could be found.

December 1987. Roseburg, Oregon. Trial began in the case of Ed Gallup and his son Chip, accused of sexually abusing children at their religious schools. Allegations, which stemmed from a parent's discovery of two boys playing sexually at home, included Satanic rituals and the shooting of people who were said to have been brought back to life. No concrete evidence of any abuse has been found.

Jesus is Lord God Almighty.
Jesus said "I am the Way, the Truth and the Life".
Satan is real.
Jesus said, "I saw Satan fall from heaven like lightening".
This means he (satan) was cast out of heaven. He is called The Prince of this World System. He is the Father of Lies and Seeks to destroy, to deceive and to kill!
Satan wants people to believe he doesn't exist and has blinded men to the Truth of Jesus.
Satan will, in the future, become ruler of this earth and will demand that YOU WORSHIP him.

Notes

Chapter One: Rumors, Claims, and Allegations about Satanic Cult Crimes

1. Antoine de Saint-Exupéry, *Wind, Sand and Stars*, trans. Lewis Galantiere (1939).
2. Phil Sahm, "Are Satanists Practicing Locally?", *Times-News* (Twin Falls, Idaho), Nov. 8, 1991, pp. A5–A6; Phil Sahm, "Anti-Abuse Vigil Draws 500," *Times-News* (Twin Falls, Idaho), Nov. 9, 1991.
3. Tamarkin, Clivia. "Police on Halloween Alert for Satanic Cults." *Chicago Sun-Times*, Oct. 28, 1990.
4. Sally Hill and Jean Goodwin, "Satanism: Similarities Between Patient Accounts and Pre-Inquisition Historical Sources," *Dissociation* 2, no. 1 (March 1989): 39–43.
5. I used a wide range of research methods to collect information for this book. The methods include interview studies, participant observation studies, the use of local documents and the publications of organizations, the use of newspaper reports and a content analysis of newspaper articles, the use of court records, audio-tapes of speeches, videotapes, and transcripts of television shows.

Chapter Two: The Evolution of the Satanic Cult Legend

1. Alexander Pope, *Temple of Fame*, Line, 468.
2. Neil J. Smelser, *Theory of Collective Behavior* (New York: Free Press, 1962); David Miller, *Introduction to Collective Behavior* (Belmont, CA: Wadsworth, 1985).
3. Brend Van Driel and James Richardson, "Print Media Coverage of New Religious Movements: A Longitudinal Study," *Journal of Communication* 38, no. 3 (Summer 1988): 37–61.
4. J. Gordon Melton, *Encyclopedic Handbook of Cults in America* (New York: Garland Pub., 1986).
5. *New York Times*, " 'Satan Cult' Death, Drugs, Jolt Peaceful Vineland N.J.," July 6, 1971, p. 29.
6. Kenneth V. Lanning, "Satanic, Occult, Ritualistic Crime: A Law Enforcement Perspective," *The Police Chief* (Oct. 1989): 62–83.
7. Daniel Kagan, and Ian Summers, *Mute Evidence* (New York: Bantam Books, 1983).

8. *Ibid.*
9. The symbolic connection between the ritual sacrifice of animals and of children was not clear to me at first. Satan hunters commonly claim that the ritual sacrifice of animals inevitably leads to human sacrifice. In traditional European-American folklore, the association of animal with human sacrifice has often been used as an accusation against non-Christian religions. It is an integral part of the blood ritual myth.
10. "Satanism's Wings Cast Shadows in Corners of North Texas," *Fort Worth Star-Telegram*, April 16, 1989.
11. James Stewart, "Cattle Mutilations: An Episode of Collective Delusion," *The Zetetic* (Spring-Summer 1977): 55–66; James Stewart, "Collective Delusion: A Comparison of Believers and Skeptics," paper presented to the Midwest Sociological Society, April, 1980.
12. Frederick Koenig, *Rumor in the Marketplace: The Social Psychology of Commercial Hearsay*, (Dover, MA: Auburn House, 1985).
13. *Ibid.*
14. "Satanism Trademark Rumors Again Denied," *Richmond News Leader*, April 28, 1990; "P & G Sick of Rumors and Flyers," *Chronicle* (Augusta, GA) April 24, 1990, pp. 7C, 10C; "Old Rumor is Giving P & G Devil of a Time," *Herald-Leader* (Lexington, K.Y.), April 7, 1990, pp. A11, A13; "Satanism Rumor Resurfaces", *News & Courier* (Charleston, SC), May 4, 1990, pp. 1B, 3B; "Procter & Gamble Files Suit to Stop Satanism Symbol Rumor," *Capital-Journal*, Aug. 1, 1990. For details about more recent developments in the P & G rumors, see: "Procter & Gamble's Devil of a Problem," *Washington Post*, July 15, 1991, pp. B1, B3.
15. Koenig, 1985.
16. Michelle Smith and Lawrence Pazder, *Michelle Remembers* (New York: Congdon and Latte, 1980). Paperback edition by: Pocket Books Division of Simon & Schuster, New York, 1981.
17. Tom Charlier and Shirley Downing, "Facts, Fantasies Caught in Tangled Web," Jan. 17, 1988; "Allegations of Odd Rites Compelled Closer Look," Jan. 17, 1988; "Allegations Rife, Evidence Slight," Jan. 18, 1988; "Links to Abuse of Children Hard to Prove," Jan. 18, 1988, *Memphis Commercial Appeal.*
18. Debbie Nathan, "Satanism and Child Molestation: Constructing the Ritual Abuse Scare," *The Satanism Scare*, ed. J. Richardson, J. Best, and D. Bromley (New York: Aldine de Gruyter, 1991), pp. 75–94.
19. Shawn Carlson and Gerald Larue, with G. O'Sullivan, A. Masche, and D. Frew, *Satanism in America* (Buffalo, N.Y.: Committee for the Scientific Examination of Religion, 1989). Published by Gaia Press, El Cerrito, CA, 1989.
20. "McMartin Case: Swept Away by Panic About Molestation," *New York Times*, Jan. 24, 1990, p. A1; "Longest Trial Over, Child Abuse Suspect Now Faces a Retrial" *New York Times*, Feb. 1, 1990, p. A1.

21. Nathan, 1991.
22. "Longest Trial Over, Child Abuse Suspect Now Faces a Retrial" *New York Times*, Feb. 1, 1990; "7 Years Later, McMartin Case Ends in a Mistrial," *New York Times*, July 28, 1990.
23. Michael Snedeker, "The Rise and Fall of the Devil in Kern County, California," *California Prisoner*, April 1988, Part I; and Part II, June 1988.
24. "In California, a Question of Abuse," *Washington Post*, May 31, 1989, p. D1.
25. James T. Richardson, "Satanism in the Courts: From Murder Heavy Metal," *The Satanism Scare*, ed. J. Richardson, J. Best and D. Bromley (New York: Aldine de Gruyter, 1991), pp. 205–20.
26. Charlier and Downing, Jan. 17–18, 1988.
27. *Ibid.*
28. Debbie Nathan, "The Making of a Modern Witch Trial," *The Village Voice*, Sept. 29, 1987; Debbie Nathan, "Victimizer or Victim? Was Kelly Michaels Unjustly Convicted," *The Village Voice*, Aug. 2, 1988; Dorothy Rabinowitz, "From the Mouths of Babes to a Jail Cell," *Harper's Magazine*, May, 1990; Snedeker, 1988; *Washington Post*, May 31, 1989.
29. Charlier and Downing, Jan. 17–18, 1988.
30. Charlier and Downing, *Commercial Appeal* (Memphis, TN). "Allegations Rife, Evidence Slight," Jan. 18, 1988.
31. Robert Hicks, "Satanic Cults: A Skeptical View of the Law Enforcement Approach, in Shawn Carlson and Gerald Larue, 1989, Appendix, pp. 1–25; Robert Hicks, "Police Pursuit of Satanic Crime," *Skeptical Inquirer* 14, no. 3 (Spring 1990): 276–86.
32. Kenneth Wooden also produced the "Geraldo" television special on Satanism, which was broadcast on Oct. 25, 1988, to one of the largest audiences in American history. Wooden gave a speech in April 1988, at a conference on child abuse in Olean, New York, attended by social work professionals who were worried about rumors of local Satanic cults. Wooden was quoted in the local newspaper as claiming: "Twenty-five percent of all unsolved murders are ritualistic in nature. The victims are women and children. In twenty-five percent of incest cases, we've found the occult or ritual abuse. Ritual abuse is new and rampant and moving around the country right now. I've seen so many children's bodies on slabs, whose deaths could be associated with the occult". ("Children's Advocate Addresses Seminar," *Olean Times-Herald*, April 24, 1988.).
33. "The Devil Worshippers," a segment of the "20/20" show (ABC. News), May 16, 1985. Transcript from Journal Graphics, New York.
34. *Ibid.*
35. William Arens, *The Man-Eating Myth* (New York: Oxford University, 1979).
36. "Lucas County Clues Vague," *Akron Beacon Journal* (Ohio), June 21,

1985; "Hunt for Graves Comes up Empty," June 22, 1985; "Hunt Near Toledo Fails to Find 80 Sacrifices," *Cleveland Plain Dealer*, June 21, 1985; "No Bodies Found Yet in Cult Probe," *Columbus Dispatch* (Ohio), June 21, 1985; "Satanic Murders: a Great Story That Wasn't There," *Columbus Dispatch* (Ohio), June 23, 1985.

37. *Ibid.*
38. One newspaper did investigate the "Toledo dig" a bit further. It found that the main "informant" of Sheriff Telb was a local Baptist minister, who happened to own the wooded lot alleged to be the Satanic cult burial site. On that wooded lot was an abandoned, run-down shack, which at one time was inhabited by a homeless old man. He was a mental patient at a local hospital according to a local policeman who drove him to the hospital. He used to chase away children playing in the area by threatening them and scaring them with a variety of makeshift magic artifacts. "Bedeviled Searchers Call It Off," *Cleveland Plain Dealer*, June 22, 1985. "The Devil You Say," *Cleveland Plain Dealer*, July 7, 1985, pp. 200–208.
39. "As Satan Worship Heats Up, Area Police Uncover Some Grisly Clues," *Detroit News*, March 22, 1989.
40. Carlson and Larue, 1989; "Potent Mix of Ritual and Charisma," *Los Angeles Times*, May 16, 1989.
41. "Cult of the Red Haired Devil," *Time Magazine*, April 24, 1989, p. 30.
42. "Pizza Evangelism—Premeditated, Purposeful, and Profitable", report of Sept. 1989, pp. 2–3; and "Rescuing Our Children from the Edge of Evil," report of Dec. 1989, p. 3; National Education Association, Division of Human and Civil Rights, *Preserving Public Education*.
43. Jerry Johnston, *The Edge of Evil* (Dallas: Word Pub., 1989).
44. Ray Allen Billington, *The Protestant Crusade, 1800–1860: A Study of the Origins of American Nativism* (New York: Macmillan, 1938).
45. George Johnson, *Architects of Fear: Conspiracy Theories and Paranoia in American Politics* (Los Angeles: Jeremy P. Tarcher, 1983); David H. Bennett, *The Party of Fear: From Nativist Movements to the New Right in American History* (Chapel Hill, NC: University of North Carolina, 1988).

Chapter Three: The Social Dynamics of a Rumor-Panic

1. Gustave Le Bon, *The Crowd: A Study of the Popular Mind*, 1st ed. (1886, London: Ernest Benn Ltd., 1952), p. 110.
2. A more detailed version of this chapter was previously published in: Jeffrey S. Victor, "A Rumor-Panic about a Dangerous Satanic Cult in Western New York," *New York Folklore* 25, nos. 1–2 (1989): 23–49.

3.   "Geraldo," "Satanic Cults and Children," Nov. 19, 1987 (New York: Journal Graphics, Inc.).

4.   "Boy Scout Kills His Mom, Then Himself," *Jamestown Post-Journal*, Jan. 12, 1988, p. 15.

5.   Jack T. Chick, *The Poor Little Witch* (Chino, Calif.: Chick Publications, 1987).

6.   "Police, Schools Say Cult Rumors Unfounded," *Jamestown Post-Journal*, May 12, 1988.

7.   Jean-Noel Kapferer, *Rumors: Uses, Interpretations, and Images* (New Brunswick, N.J.: Transaction Publishers, 1990).

8.   *Ibid.*

9.   Ralph L. Rosnow, "Inside Rumor: A Personal Journey," *American Psychologist* 46, no. 5 (May 1991): 484–496; See also: Ralph L. Rosnow and Gary Alan Fine, *Rumor and Gossip* (New York: Elsivier, 1976).

10. Hadley Cantril, *The Invasion from Mars: A Study in the Psychology of Panic* (Princeton, N.J.: Princeton University Press, 1940; Republished by Harper, 1966).

11. Robert E. Bartholomew, "Ethnocentricity and the Social Construction of Mass Hysteria," *Culture, Medicine and Psychiatry* 14, no. 4 (Dec. 1990): 455–95.

12. Rosnow, 1991.

13. Neil J. Smelser, *Theory of Collective Behavior* (New York: Free Press, 1962).

14. For a similar analysis of a Satanic cult rumor-panic, see: Bill Ellis, "The Devil Worshippers at the Prom: Rumor-Panic as Therapeutic Magic," *Western Folklore*, 49, no. 1 (Jan. 1990): 27–49.

15. Kapferer, 1990.

16. *Ibid.*

17. In his study of the "War of the Worlds" panic, Cantril (1940) found that the rumor of the Martian invasion was more likely to be believed by people with lower education and more likely to be regarded skeptically by people with higher education. Cantril found that a much greater percentage of people with a high school education tried to verify the authenticity of the supposed radio "news broadcast" about the Martian invasion, compared with people having less than a completed high school education.

18. James Stewart, "Collective Delusion: A Comparison of Believers and Skeptics," paper presented to the Midwest Sociological Society, 1980.

19. His name is Reverend Everett E. Seastrum. He used a questionnaire as well as open-ended questions. All of these ministers preferred to label themselves as "born-again Christian" ministers rather than "fundamentalists." Nine of them described their political attitudes as being either "very conservative" or "conservative."

20. Unfortunately, I was not able to collect specific information about what

was happening in mainline Protestant churches for a useful comparison. However, none of the interviews revealed any activities of this sort going on in the mainline churches.

21. Smelser, 1962.
22. William P. O'Hare, *The Rise of Rural Poverty in America* (Washington, D.C.: Population Reference Bureau, 1988) p. 1 and p. 8. Also see: Kathryn H. Porter, *Poverty in Rural America: A National Overview* (Washington, D.C.: Center on Budget and Policy Priorities, 1989); Lawrence Mishel and Jacqueline Simon, *The State of Working America* (Washington, D.C.: Economic Policy Institute, 1988). For data on the effects of underemployment upon marital relations, see: Anisa M. Zvonkovic, "Underemployment: Individual and Marital Adjustment to Income Loss," *Lifestyles: Family and Economic Issues* 9, no. 2 (Summer 1988): 161–78.
23. "Overall Economic Development Plan," mimeographed report, Southern Tier West, Regional Planning Board (Salamanca, New York, 1988).
24. John Leunsman, "A Review of Recent Population and Economic Data From State and Federal Agencies for Chautauqua County," Chautauqua County Department of Planning and Development, mimeographed report, 1987.
25. "Annual Report," Chautauqua County Department of Social Services, 1988.
26. "School and Community," Jamestown Senior High School, mimeographed report, 1986.
27. Kapferer, 1990, p. 145.
28. Kapferer, 1990.
29. *Ibid.*
30. Victor, 1989.
31. Clyde Z. Nunn, "The Rising Credibility of the Devil in America," *Listening*, 9, 1974, pp. 84–99.; George Gallup, Jr. *Adventures in Immortality* (New York: McGraw-Hill, 1982).
32. Seymour M. Lipset and William Schneider, *The Confidence Gap* (New York: Free Press, 1983); Louis Harris, *Inside America* (New York: Random House, 1987).

Chapter Four: Rumor-Panics across the Country

1. This chapter is an updated and revised version of my previous publication: Jeffrey S. Victor, "The Dynamics of Rumor-Panics about Satanic Cults," in *The Satanism Scare*, ed. J. Richardson, J. Best, and D. Bromley (New York: Aldine de Gruyter, 1991), pp. 221–36.

2. Kai T. Erikson, *Wayward Puritans: A Study in the Sociology of Deviance* (New York: John Wiley and Sons, 1966), p. 153.
3. Ralph L. Rosnow, "The Psychology of Rumor Reconsidered," *Psychological Bulletin* 87, no. 3 (1980): 578–91; Jean-Noel Kapferer, *Rumors: Uses, Interpretations and Images* (New Brunswick, New Jersey: Transaction Publishers, 1990).
4. Tamotsu Shibutani, *Improvised News: A Sociological Study of Rumors* (Indianapolis: Bobbs-Merrill, 1966).
5. Ralph L. Rosnow and Allan J. Kimmel, "Lives of a Rumor," *Psychology Today* (June 1979): 88–92; Rosnow, 1980.
6. Neil Smelser, *Theory of Collective Behavior* (New York: Free Press, 1962).
7. "Reports of Satanism Prove Unfounded, Far-Reaching Rumors Trigger Fear, Anxiety," *Erie Times-News* (PA), May 12, 1988.
8. William P. O'Hare, *The Rise of Poverty in Rural America* (Washington, D.C.: Population Reference Bureau. July, 1988); Kathryn H. Porter, *Poverty in Rural America: A National Overview* (Washington, D.C.: Center on Budget and Policy Priorities, 1989).
9. *Ibid.*
10. Doris Helge, "National Study Regarding Rural, Suburban and Urban At-Risk Students," (Bellingham, Wash.: National Rural Development Institute, Western Washington University, 1990, mimeographed research report).
11. "Geraldo," "Satanic Cults and Children," Nov. 19, 1987. Transcript from Journal Graphics, New York.
12. "Boy Scout Kills Mom, Then Himself," *Jamestown Post-Journal*, Jan. 15, 1988.
13. Everett M. Rogers and D. Lawrence Kincaid, *Communication Networks*, (New York: Free Press, 1981).
14. "No Bodies Found Yet in Cult Probe," *Columbus Dispatch* (Ohio), June 21, 1985.
15. "Rumor of Satanic Cult Ritual Spooks McComb, Children Kept Home," *Jackson Clarion-Ledger*, April 1, 1988; "Police Source Says Most Satanists in Cult to be in its Orgies," April 2, 1988.
16. "Cult Scare Seen as Overrated," *Boston Globe*, May 28, 1989.
17. "Rumors of Satanic Cult Murders Sweep Hereford," *Amarillo Daily News*, July 21, 1989; "Minister Airs Claims of Cult Activity," *Hereford Brand*, July 21, 1989.
18. Jan Harold Brunvand, *The Vanishing Hitchhiker: American Urban Legends and Their Meanings* (New York: W. W. Norton, 1981), p. 3.
19. Bill Ellis, "Introduction," *Western Folklore*, Special Issue: "Contemporary Legends in Emergence," 49, no. 1 (1990): 1–10.
20. Linda Milligan, "The 'Truth' about The Bigfoot Legend," *Western*

Folklore, Special Issue: "Contemporary Legends in Emergence," 49, no. 1 (1990): 83–98.

21. Joel Best, *Threatened Children: Rhetoric and Concern about Child-Victims* (Chicago: University of Chicago, 1990).

22. Patrick B. Mullen, "Modern Legend and Rumor Theory," *Journal of the American Folklore Institute* 9 (1972): 95–109.

23. Linda Degh and Andrew Vazsonyi, "Does the Word Dog Bite? Ostensive Action: A Means of Legend Telling," *Journal of Folklore Research* 20 (1983): 5–34; Bill Ellis, "Death by Folklore: Ostension, Contemporary Legend, and Murder," *Western Folklore* 48 (1989), p. 201–20; Bill Ellis, "Legend-Trips and Satanism: Adolescents' Ostensive Traditions as 'Cult' Activity," *The Satanism Scare*, ed. James Richardson, Joel Best, and David Bromley (New York: Aldine de Gruyter, 1991), pp. 279–96; Bill Ellis, "Satanic Ritual Abuse and Legend Ostension," *Journal of Psychology and Theology* 20, no. 3 (Fall 1992): 274–77.

24. Edgar Morin, *Rumour in Orleans* (New York: Random House, 1971).

25. Kapferer, 1990.

26. Morin, 1971.

27. *Ibid.*

28. Phillips Stevens, Jr., "The Demonology of Satanism: An Anthropological View," *The Satanism Scare*, ed. J. Richardson, J. Best, and D. Bromley (New York: Aldine de Gruyter, 1991), pp. 21–40.

29. R. Po-Chia Hsia, *The Myth of Ritual Murder: Jews and Magic in Reformation Germany* (New Haven, Conn.: Yale University, 1988). Florence H. Ridley, "A Tale Told Too Often," *Western Folklore* 26 (1987): 153–56.

30. Bill Ellis, "De Legendis Urbis: Modern Legends in Ancient Rome," *Journal of American Folklore* 96, no. 380 (1985): 200–208.

31. Norman Cohn, *Europe's Inner Demons: An Enquiry Inspired by the Great Witch-Hunt* (New York: New American Library, 1975); R. I. Moore, *The Formation of a Persecuting Society: Power and Deviance in Western Europe, 950–1250* (New York: Basil Blackwell, 1987); Joshua Tractenberg, *The Devil and the Jews* (New Haven, Conn.: Yale University, 1961, 1983; Reprint of 1943 publication).

32. Stevens, 1991.

33. Brian P. Levack, *The Witch-Hunt in Early Modern Europe* (New York: Longman, 1987); Thomas J. Schoeneman, "The Witch Hunt as a Culture Change Phenomenon," *Ethos* 3, no. 4 (Winter 1975): 529–54.

34. Erikson, 1966.

Chapter Five: Satanic Cult "Survivor" Stories

1. William Shakespeare, *A Midsummer-Night's Dream*, Act V, Scene 1.
2. Maria Monk, *The Awful Disclosures of Maria Monk* (Manchester, United Kingdom: Pemberton, Ltd., 1836; reprinted).
3. Ray Allen Billington, "Maria Monk and Her Influence," *Catholic Historical Review*, vol. 23 (Oct. 1936): 238–96; Ray Allen Billington, *The Protestant Crusade, 1800–1860* (New York: Macmillan, 1938); Carleton Beals, *Brass-Knuckle Crusade* (New York: Hastings House, 1960); David H. Bennett, *The Party of Fear* (Chapel Hill, N.C.: University of North Carolina Press, 1988).
4. Michelle Smith and Lawrence Pazder, *Michelle Remembers* (New York: Congdon and Lattes, 1980; republished by Pocket Books Division of Simon & Schuster, New York, 1980).
5. Paul Grescoe, "Things That Go Bump in Victoria," *Maclean's* (Canada) (Oct. 27, 1980): 30–31.
6. Smith and Pazder, 1980, pp. 188, 194.
7. Kristin McMurran, "A Canadian Woman's Bizarre Childhood Memories of Satan Shocks Shrinks and Priests," *People Weekly*, vol. 14 (Jan. 1, 1980): 28–30.
8. Arthur Lyons, *Satan Wants You* (New York: Warner Books, 1988).
9. Other books by Satanic cult survivors include: Lauren Stratford, *Satan's Underground* (Eugene, Oregon: Harvest House, 1988); Judith Spencer, *Suffer the Child* (New York: Pocket Books, 1989). See also: Joyce Price, "I Started Screaming as Followers of Satan Sacrificed a 17-year-old," *Washington Times* (D.C.), Sept. 14, 1989.
10. "Satanic Breeders: Babies for Sacrifice," the "Geraldo" show, *Journal Graphics*, Oct. 24, 1988; "Satan's Black Market: Sex Slaves, Porno and Drugs," the "Geraldo" show, *Journal Graphics*, March 1, 1989; "Investigating Multiple Personalities: Did the Devil Make Them Do It?" the "Geraldo" show, *Journal Graphics*, Sept. 10, 1991.
11. "Baby Breeders," the "Sally Jesse Raphael" show, *Journal Graphics*, Feb. 28, 1989; "Devil Babies," the "Sally Jesse Raphael" show, *Journal Graphics*, July 24, 1991.
12. "Satanism," "The Oprah Winfrey Show," *Journal Graphics*, Sept. 30, 1986; "Satanic Worship," "The Oprah Winfrey Show," *Journal Graphics*, Feb. 17, 1988; "Headlines That Shocked the Nation: Mexican Satanic Cult Murders," "The Oprah Winfrey Show," *Journal Graphics*, May 1, 1989.
13. "Baby Breeders," the "Sally Jesse Raphael" show, *Journal Graphics*, Feb. 28, 1989.
14. "Baby Breeders," the "Sally Jesse Raphael" show, *Journal Graphics*, Feb. 28, 1989. Cheryl Horton also appeared as the guest, "Cheryl" on: "Satanic Breeders: Babies for Sacrifice," the "Geraldo" show, *Journal Graphics*, Oct. 24, 1988.

15. Sherrill Mulhern, "Satanism and Psychotherapy: A Rumor in Search of an Inquisition," *The Satanism Scare*, ed. J. Richardson, J. Best, and D. Bromley (New York: Aldine de Gruyter, 1991), pp. 145–74.
16. Norman MacKenzie, ed., *Secret Societies* (New York: Macmillan, 1967).
17. Philip Jenkins and Daniel Maier-Katkin, "Occult Survivors: The Origins of a Myth," *The Satanism Scare*, ed. J. Richardson, J. Best, and D. Bromley (New York: Aldine de Gruyter, 1991), pp. 127–44.
18. Ian Wilson, *All in the Mind* (Garden City, NY: Doubleday, 1982).
19. Wilson, 1982.
20. Personal communication from Martin M. Segall, Dec. 23, 1989.
21. Nicholas P. Spanos and Jack Gottlieb, "Demonic Possession, Mesmerism, and Hysteria: A Social Psychological Perspective on Their Interrelationships," *Journal of Abnormal Psychology* 88, no. 5 (Oct. 1979): 529–46; Felicitas D. Goodman, *How about Demons? Possession and Exorcism in the Modern World* (Bloomington, Indiana: Indiana University Press, 1988).
22. For an understanding of the personality syndrome of people who are highly hypnotizable, see: Herbert Spiegel, "The Grade 5 Syndrome: The Highly Hypnotizable Person," *Journal of Clinical and Experimental Hypnosis* 22, no. 4 (1974): 303–19. For an application to UFO abduction stories, see: Robert E. Bartholomew, Keith Basterfield, and George S. Howard, "UFO Abductees and Contactees: Psychopathology or Fantasy Proneness?" *Professional Psychology: Research and Practice* 22, no. 3 (1991): 215–22.
23. Wilson, 1982.
24. Goodman, 1988; Spanos and Gottlieb, 1979; Wilson, 1982.
25. For an understanding of the functional similarities between witchcraft and psychiatric beliefs, see: E. Fuller Torrey, *Witchdoctors and Psychiatrists* (New York: Jason Aronson, 1986); and Phillips Stevens, Jr., "Some Implications of Urban Witchcraft Beliefs," *New York Folklore* 8, (Winter 1982): 29–45.
26. Mulhern, 1991.
27. Richard P. Kluft, ed., *Childhood Antecedents of Multiple Personality* (Washington, D.C.: American Psychiatric Press, 1985).
28. Sherrill Mulhern, "Ritual Abuse: Defining a Syndrome versus Defending a Belief" (abstract of a paper presented the International Congress on Child Abuse and Neglect. Hamburg, Federal Republic of Germany, Sept., 1990, unpublished paper).
29. Irving L. Janis, *Victims of Groupthink* (Boston: Houghton Mifflin, 1972).
30. Thomas A. Fahy, "The Diagnosis of Multiple Personality Disorder: A Critical Review," *British Journal of Psychiatry* 153 (1988): 597–606.
31. Nicholas P. Spanos, John R. Weekes, and Lorne D. Bertrand, "Multiple Personality: A Social Psychological Perspective," *Journal of Abnormal Psychology* 94, no. 3 (Aug. 1985): 362–76; Fahy, 1988.

32. Mulhern, 1991.
33. D. Sexton, "Gaining Insights into the Complexity of Ritualistic Abuse" (paper presented at the Eigth National Conference on Child Abuse and Neglect, 1989, audio-tape #28) (quoted in Mulhern, 1991.)
34. George K. Ganaway, "Historical Versus Narrative Truth: Clarifying the Role of Exogenous Trauma in the Etiology of MPD and Its Variants," *Dissociation* 2, no. 4 (Dec. 1989): 205–20.
35. Fahy, 1988.
36. Mulhern, 1991.
37. The particular paper was one by Kaye and Klein, whose ideas are presented in the next section. Maribeth Kaye and Lawrence Klein, "Clinical Indicators of Satanic Cult Victimization" (unpublished paper presented at the Fourth International Conference on Multiple Personality/Dissociation, Chicago, Oct. 1987).
38. Mulhern, 1991.
39. "Programs That Treat Occult Believers," *Medical World News,* Oct. 9, 1989, p. 28.
40. Bennett G. Braun and Roberta G. Sachs, "Recognition of Possible Cult Involvement in MPD Patients" (paper presented at the Fifth International Conference on Multiple Personality/Dissociation States, 1988, audio-tape #IVd-436). (Quoted in Mulhern, 1991.)
41. "Culture, Cults and Psychotherapy: Exploring Satanic and Other Cult Behavior" (Harding Hospital, Worthington, Ohio, March 26, 1990), audio-tapes no. 3 and no. 4.
42. *Ibid.*
43. Gretchen Passantino, Bob Passantino, and Jon Trott, "Satan's Sideshow," *Cornerstone* 18, issue 90 (1990): 24–28.
44. Lauren Stratford, *Satan's Underground* (Eugene, Oregon: Harvest House, 1988).
45. Lauren Stratford appeared as a featured guest on: "Satanic Worship," "The Oprah Winfrey Show," *Journal Graphics,* Feb. 17, 1988; and "Headlines That Shocked the Nation: Mexican Satanic Cult Murders," "The Oprah Winfrey Show," *Journal Graphics,* May 1, 1989.
46. Passantino, et al, 1990.
47. "Statement Regarding *Satan's Underground,*" letter from the publisher, Harvest House, Jan. 26, 1990.
48. Mulhern, 1991.

Chapter Six: Satanism and Alleged Threats to Children

1. Charles W. Upham, *Salem Witchcraft,* vol. 2 (Williamstown, MA.: Corner House Publishers, 1867; reprinted 1971), pp. 387–88.

2. *Occult Crime: A Law Enforcement Primer* (Office of Criminal Justice Planning, State of California, Sacramento, California, Winter 1989–1990) p. 39.

3. *Ibid.*, p. 39.

4. *Ibid.*, p. 39.

5. *Ibid.*, p. 39.

6. "Characteristics of Schools in which Satanic Ritual Abuse Occurs," (Believe the Children, mimeographed paper, no date).

7. "Ritual Abuse: Definitions, Glossary, the Use of Mind Control," (The Ritual Abuse Task Force, Los Angeles County Commission for Women, printed Pamphlet, September 15, 1989), p. 2.

8. Office of Criminal Justice Planning, State of California, Winter, 1989–1990, p. 33.

9. Susan J. Kelley, "Parental Stress Response to Sexual Abuse and Ritualistic Abuse of Children in Day-Care Centers," *Nursing Research* 39, no. 1 (Jan./Feb. 1990): 25.

10. Kenneth V. Lanning, "Satanic, Occult, Ritualistic Crime: A Law Enforcement Perspective," *The Police Chief* (Oct., 1989 (a)), pp. 69–70.

11. Jeffrey S. Victor, *Human Sexuality: A Social Psychological Perspective* (Englewood Cliffs, NJ: Prentice-Hall, 1980), p. 312.

12. Debbie Nathan, "The Ritual Sex Abuse Hoax," *The Village Voice*, June 12, 1990, 38. Reprinted in Debbie Nathan, *Women and Other Aliens* (El Paso, Texas: Cinco Puntas Press, 1991), pp. 148–67. See also: Debbie Nathan, "Satanism and Child Molestation: Constructing the Ritual Abuse Scare, *The Satanism Scare*, ed. J. Richardson, J. Best, and D. Bromley, (New York: Aldine de Gruyter, 1991), pp. 75–94.

13. The following is a list of sources about cases involving false allegations of ritual child sex abuse: Debbie Nathan, *Ibid.*; Debbie Nathan, "Victimizer or Victim? Was Kelly Michaels Unjustly Convicted," *The Village Voice*, Aug. 2, 1988, 31–39; Debbie Nathan, "The Making of a Modern Witch Trial," *The Village Voice*, Sept. 29, 1987, 19–32; Dorothy Rabinowitz, "From the Mouths of Babes to a Jail Cell," *Harpers Magazine*, May 1990, 52–63; Michael Snedeker, "The Rise and Fall of the Devil in Kern County, California," *California Prisoner*, April 1988, 4–6; "In California, a Question of Abuse" *Washington Post*, May 31, 1989; Mary Ann Williams, "Witch Hunt," *Chicago Lawyer* 11, no. 10, (Oct. 1988): 1, 7–9, 24–27; Lawrence Buser, "Court Voids Child Abuse Conviction of Ballard," *Commercial Appeal* (Memphis, TN), Feb. 21, 1991; Keith Bernhart, *Guilty Until Proven Innocent* (Hannibal, MO: Hannibal Books, 1990); Michael Bamberger, "Sons Tell a D.A. that They Lied," *Philadelphia Inquirer*, Oct. 21, 1989.

14. Richard Wexler, *Wounded Innocents* (Prometheus Books, 1990).

15. Personal letter from Sharon R. Goretsky, Research Associate, Center on Children and the Law, American Bar Association.

16. David Mills, "The Limits of Innocence," *Washington Post*, May 5, 1991, pp. B1 & B8. See also: Joe Dew, "Seven in Day Care Case to be Tried Together," *News and Observer* (Raleigh, N.C.), Feb. 22, 1990; Joe Drape, "Child Sex Abuse Trial to Open," *The Journal* (Atlanta), July 22, 1991; Jon Glass, "N.C. Molestation Trial is Progressing Slowly," *Virginia-Pilot* (Norfolk), Aug. 8, 1991; "Carolinan is Convicted of 99 Child-Abuse Charges," *New York Times*, April 23, 1992, p. A16.

17. Joe Southern, "Abuse Case Defense Seeks More Information," *Daily Advance* (Elizabeth City, NC), Feb. 27, 1990, p. 1.

18. The name of the "therapist" is Judy Abbot. She lectured in a seminar titled, "Satanism and Ritualistic Abuse," held on Feb. 1 and 2, 1990, in Greensboro, North Carolina. See: *Crime Prevention Bulletin*, A publication of North Carolina Department of Crime and Public Safety (Winter, 1990), p. 7. According to the "Frontline" documentary, Abbot treated about 85% of the children in the Edenton case.

19. David Finkelhor, Linda M. Williams, and Nanci Burns, *Nursery Crimes: Sexual Abuse in Day Care* (Newbury Park, CA: Sage Pub., 1988).

20. Kathleen C. Faller, "Women Who Sexually Abuse Children," *Violence and Victims* 2, no. 4 (Winter 1987: 263–76).

21. Leslie Margolin and John L. Craft, "Child Sexual Abuse by Caretakers," *Family Relations* 38, no. 4 (Oct. 1989): 450–55.

22. Susan J. Kelley, 1990; Susan J. Kelley, "Ritualistic Abuse of Children: Dynamics and Impact," *Cultic Studies Journal* 5, no. 2 (1988): 228–36; Susan J. Kelley, "Stress Responses of Children to Sexual Abuse and Ritualistic Abuse in Day Care Centers," *Journal of Interpersonal Violence* 4, no. 4 (Dec. 1989): 502–13. Barbara Snow and Sorenson, "Ritualistic Child Abuse in a Neighborhood Setting," *Journal of Interpersonal Violence* 5, no. 4 (Dec. 1990): 474–87; Pamela S. Hudson, "Ritual Child Abuse: A Survey of Symptoms and Allegations," *Journal of Child and Youth Care* (Canada), Special Issue, 1990, 27–53; Louise M. Edwards, "Differentiating Between Ritual Assault and Sexual Abuse," *Journal of Child and Youth Care* (Canada), Special Issue, 1990, 67–90.

23. Lee Coleman and Patrick E. Clancy, "False Allegations of Child Sexual Abuse," *Criminal Justice* (Fall 1990): 14–20, 43–47.

24. *Ibid.*, p. 18.

25. *Ibid.*

26. *Ibid.*

27. Paul M. Herr, "Consequences of Priming: Judgement and Behavior," *Journal of Personality and Social Psychology* 51, no. 6 (1986): 1106–115; K. James, "Priming and Social Categorizational Factors: Impact on Awareness of Emergency Situations," *Personality and Social Psychology Bulletin* 12 (1986): 462–67.

28. Alfred R. Lindesmith, Anselm L. Strauss, and Norman K. Denzin, *Social Psychology*, 7th ed. (Englewood Cliffs, NJ: Prentice-Hall, 1991).

29. Elizabeth F. Loftus, *Eyewitness Testimony* (Cambridge, MA: Harvard University Press, 1979); Elizabeth F. Loftus, "The Eyewitness on Trial," *Trial*, Oct. 1980, 31–36; Steven Penrod, Elizabeth Loftus, and Winkler John, "The Reliability of Eyewitness Testimony: A Psychological Perspective," *The Psychology of the Courtroom*, ed. Norbert Kerr and Robert Bray (New York: Academic Press, 1982), pp. 119–68.

30. Kenneth V. Lanning, *Child Sex Rings: A Behavioral Analysis* (National Center for Missing and Exploited Children, Dec. 1989.)

31. Michael Bamberger, "Sons Tell a D.A. That They Lied," *Philadelphia Inquirer*, Oct. 21, 1989.

32. Ian MacKinnon, "Sister in 'Ritual Sex' Trial Lied Over Names," *The Independent* (London, U.K.), Nov. 19, 1991; Martin Linton, "Satan Case Collapses after Girl's Evidence," *The Guardian* (London), Nov. 20, 1991.

33. David Shaw, "Where Was Skepticism in Media?" *Los Angeles Times*, Jan. 19, 1990; David Shaw, "Reporter's Early Exclusiveness Triggered a Media Frenzy," *Los Angeles Times*, Jan. 20, 1990; David Shaw, "Times McMartin Coverage Was Biased, Critics Charge," *Los Angeles Times*, Jan. 22, 1990.

34. Shaw, Jan. 19, 1990, p. A20.

35. Jean-Noel Kapferer, *Rumors: Uses, Interpretations and Images* (New Brunswick, NJ: Transaction Publishers, 1990).

36. Sarah E. Foster, "The Satanic Preschool: A Contemporary Legend," *California Folklore Society Newsletter*, Summer 1990, p. 9.

37. Rosie Waterhouse, "Satanic Cults: How the Hysteria Swept Britain," *The Independent*, Sept. 16, 1990; Rosie Waterhouse, "The Making of a Satanic Myth," *The Independent*, Sept. 23, 1990, p. 8; Rosie Waterhouse, "NSPCC Questions Led to Satan Case," *The Independent*, Sept. 30, 1990, p. 8; Rosie Waterhouse, "Satanic Inquisitors from the Town Hall," *The Independent*, Oct. 7, 1990, p. 6.

38. Rosie Waterhouse, Sept. 16, 23, 30 and Oct. 7, 1990.

39. Adam Sage, "Parents May Sue after Ritual Abuse Cases Are Dropped," *The Independent*, March 10, 1991, *p. 10.*

40. Rosie Waterhouse, Sept. 16, 23, 30 and Oct. 7, 1990.

41. Rosie Waterhouse, Oct. 7, 1990.

42. Joel Best, *Threatened Children: Rhetoric and Concern about Child-Victims* (Chicago: University of Chicago Press, 1990).

43. *Ibid.*, p. 152.

44. Bob Larson, *Satanism: The Seduction of America's Youth* (Nashville: Thomas Nelson, 1989), p. 125.

45. Jerry Johnston, *The Edge of Evil: The Rise of Satanism in North America* (Dallas: Word Publishing, 1989), p. 4.

46. Robert Hicks, *In Pursuit of Satan: The Police and the Occult* (Buffalo, NY: Prometheus Press, 1991).

47. Ben M. Crouch and Kelly Damphousse, "Law Enforcement and the Satanism Crime Connection: A National Survey of 'Cult Cops'," *The Satanism Scare*, ed. James Richardson, Joel Best, and David Bromley (New York: Aldine de Gruyter, 1991) p. 00.
48. Jim Bryant, "Occult Crimes," *Police Marksman*, May/June 1987, 30–33.
49. "Children's Advocate Addresses Seminar," *Olean Times Herald*, 1988, p. 3.
50. Kenneth Wooden, "Light Must Be Shed on Devil Worship," letter to the editor, *New York Times*, Nov. 23, 1988, p. A22. Wooden is the founder of an organization called the National Coalition for Children's Justice, for which he lectures about child victim issues around the country.
51. Best, 1990.
52. See, for example, "Stolen Children," *Newsweek*, March 19, 1984, 78–86.
53. Joel Best, "Missing Children, Misleading Statistics," *The Public Interest* 92 (1988): 84–92; Leroy G. Schultz, "The Ethics of Inflated Numbers: The Case of the Missing Children," *Journal of Ethical Studies* (April 1988): 3–5.
54. "Stolen Children," *Newsweek*, March 19, 1984, 78–86.
55. David Finkelhor, Gerald T. Hotaling, and Andrea Sedlak, *Missing, Abducted, Runaway, and Throwaway Children in America* (Executive Summary. U.S. Department of Justice, Office of Juvenile Justice and Delinquency Programs. Rockville, Maryland, May, 1990).
56. Gerald T. Hotaling and David Finkelhor, "Estimating The Number of Stranger-Abduction Homicides of Children: A Review of Available Evidence," *Journal of Criminal Justice* 18 (1990): 385–99.
57. "Seminar Puts Group Face-to-Face With Satanism," *Wichita Eagle* (Kansas), Nov. 4, 1990.
58. "Suspect Claims Courts Stole Girl," *The Daily Pilot* (Costa Mesa, CA), Oct. 24, 1988, p. A1.
59. Veronique Campion-Vincent, "The Baby-Parts Story: A Latin American Legend," *Western Folklore*, Special Issue: Contemporary Legends in Emergence, Bill Ellis, ed., 49, no. 1 (Jan. 1990): 9–26.
60. Charles W. Upham, *Salem Witchcraft*, vol. 2 (Williamstown, MA: Corner House Publishers, 1867; reprinted 1971), p. 422.

Chapter Seven: Satanism and Teenage Crime

1. W. H. Auden, "September 1, 1939, *W. H. Auden, Selected Poems*, ed. Edward Mendelson, (New York: Random House, 1976).
2. Pat Pulling, *The Devil's Web* (Lafayette, LA: Huntington House, 1989), pp. 41–42.

3. Ronald M. Holmes, "Youth in the Occult: A Model of Satanic Involvement," *The Journal* (Official Publication of the National Fraternal Order of Policey, vol. 18, no. 3 [Summer 1989]: 20–23; reprinted in *CJA File*, pp. 13–20, quote from p. 16–17).

4. Paula K. Lundberg-Love, "Update on Cults Part I: Satanic Cults," *Family Violence Bulletin* (Summer 1989): 9–10, published by University of Texas at Tyler.

5. Lundberg-Love, 1989, p. 9.

6. Bill Ellis, "Adolescent Legend-Tripping," *Psychology Today*, August 1983, 68–69; Bill Ellis, "Legend-Trips and Satanism: Adolescents' Ostensive Traditions as 'Cult' Activity," *The Satanism Scare*, ed. J. Richardson, J. Best, and D. Bromley (New York: Aldine de Gruyter, 1991) pp. 279–96.

7. Jan Harold Brunvand, *The Study of American Folklore: An Introduction*, 3rd edition (New York: W. W. Norton, 1986).

8. Ellis, 1983; Ellis, 1991.

9. Ellis, 1983, p. 68.

10. Ellis, 1991.

11. Ellis, 1983.

12. Ellis, 1991.

13. Ellis, 1983.

14. Ellis, 1991.

15. *Ibid.*

16. *Ibid.*

17. Michigan Department of State Police, "Michigan State Police Occult Survey," (Investigative Service Bureau, Michigan Department of State Police, June, 1990).

18. *Ibid.*, p. 9.

19. Kelly Richard Damphousse, *Did the Devil Make Them Do It? An Examination of the Etiology of Satanism among Juvenile Delinquents.* (Unpublished Masters Thesis, Department of Sociology, Texas A & M University, May 1991.)

20. Damphousse, 1991, p. 30.

21. Damphousse, 1991.

22. Dominique Bourget, Andre Gagnon, and John Bradford, M. W., "Satanism in a Psychiatric Adolescent Population," *Canadian Journal of Psychiatry* 33, no. 3 (April 1988): 197–202.

23. Amy M. Speltz, "Treating Adolescent Satanism in Art Therapy," *The Arts In Psychotherapy* 17 (Summer 1990): 147–55.

24. Jack Katz, *The Seductions of Crime*, (New York: Basic Books, 1988).

25. William J. Chambliss, "The Saints and the Roughnecks," *Society* 11, no. 1 (Nov./Dec. 1973); reprinted in *Deviance: The Interactionist Perspective*, 4th ed., ed. Earl Rubington and Martin S. Weinberg (New York: Macmillan, 1981), pp. 236–47, (p. 246).

26. Thomas J. Scheff, Suzanne M. Retzinger, and Michael T. Ryan, "Crime, Violence and Self-Esteem: Review and Proposals," *The Social Importance of Self-Esteem*, ed. Andrew M. Mecca, Neil Smelser, and John Vasconcellos, (Berkeley, CA: University of California, 1989), pp. 165–99.

27. Morris Rosenberg, Carmi Schooler, and Carrie Schoenbach, "Self-Esteem and Adolescent Problems: Modeling Reciprocal Effects," *American Sociological Review* 54, no. 6 (1989): 1004–1018.

28. C. Daniel Batson and W. Larry Ventis, *The Religious Experience: A Social-Psychological Perspective* (New York: Oxford University Press, 1982). (See chapter 7, "Mental Health or Sickness?")

29. Michael Beck, "Acquisition and Loss of an Evil Self-Image," *Evil: Self and Culture*, ed. Marie C. Nelson and Michael Eigen (New York: Human Sciences Press, 1984), pp. 170–80, (p. 172).

30. Beck, 1984, p. 177.

31. Speltz, 1990, p. 150.

32. Robert D. Hicks, *In Pursuit of Satan: The Police and the Occult* (Buffalo, N.Y.: Prometheus Press, 1991).

33. Anton S. LaVey, *The Satanic Bible* (New York: Avon, 1969).

34. Gwynn Nettler, *Killing One Another* (Cincinnati, Ohio: Anderson, 1982).

35. Aminah Clark, Harris Clemes, and Reynold Bean, *How to Raise Teenagers' Self-Esteem* (Los Angeles: Price, Stern and Sloan, 1978).

36. Jeff Brookings and Alan McEvoy, "Satanism and Schools," *School Intervention Report* 3, no. 5 (April–May 1990), Learning Publications Inc.: Holmes Beach, Florida, pp. 9–10.

37. California State Department of Education, *Toward A State of Esteem*, The Final Report of the California Task Force to Promote Self-Esteem and Personal and Social Responsibility, January, 1990; Andrew M. Mecca, Neil J. Smelser, and John Vasconcellos, eds., *The Social Importance of Self-Esteem* (Berkeley, CA: University of California, 1989).

Chapter Eight: Searching for Satanism in Schools, Books, Music, and Games

1. Arthur Miller, *The Crucible*, 1953. Reprinted in Arthur Miller, *Arthur Miller's Collected Plays* (NY: Viking Press, 1957), pp. 228–29.

2. Quoted in: "Worst Year for School Censorship," *Newsletter on Intellectual Freedom*. Chicago: American Library Association, Nov. 1991, p. 189.

3. People for the American Way, *Attacks on the Freedom to Learn: The 1990–1991 Report* (Washington, D.C.: People for the American Way, Aug. 1991).

4. "Schools Taking Devilish View of Once-Benign Peace Symbol," *Houston Chronicle*, June 18, 1989, pp. C1., C4; "The 'Horrors' of Halloween," *NEA Today*, Oct. 1990, p. 6.

5. "More Impressions Attacks Continue Nation-wide," *NEA Report, Human and Civil Rights*, May 1991, p. 3–4.

6. *Ibid.*

7. *Ibid.*

8. "Are Kids Ready for Literature?" *Los Angeles Times*, Dec. 13, 1989, pp. A1, A38–A40; "Trouble's Brewing Over Witch in School Reader," *Buffalo News*, March 10, 1991, pp. A1, A14.

9. Jeff Meade, "A War of Words," *Teacher Magazine*, Nov./Dec. 1990, pp. 37–45.

10. Deborah Mendenhall, "Nightmarish Textbooks Await Your Kids," *Focus on the Family—Citizen* 4, no. 9 (Sept. 17, 1990): 1–7; Deborah Mendenhall, "Chasing Impressions Out of the Schools," *Focus on the Family—Citizen* (Jan. 21, 1991): 5; Deborah Mendenhall, "The Secret Campaign Against Parents," *Focus on the Family—Citizen* (Feb. 18, 1991): 1–5.

11. Mendenhall, Sept. 17, 1991, 5–6.

12. *NEA Report, Human and Civil Rights*, May 1991, 3–4.

13. "Groups Unite to Ban Textbooks," *Freedom Writer* 8, no. 2 (March/April 1991): 1–2, (Great Barrington, MA.: Institute for First Amendment Studies, Inc.).

14. "Christian Group's Lawsuit Says Reading Series Promotes Witchcraft," *Education Daily*, Dec. 31, 1990, p. 5.; NEA Report, May 1991.

15. "Controversy Brewing Over New Books at SWCS," *Jamestown Post-Journal*, Jan. 26, 1991; "SWCS To Continue Using Controversial Book Series," *Jamestown Post-Journal*, Feb. 12, 1991; "Impressions Meeting Termed Successful," *Jamestown Post-Journal*, April 12, 1991.

16. "Trouble's Brewing Over Witch in School Reader," *Buffalo News*, March 10, 1991, pp. A1, A14.

17. Marcia A. Ryan, "Our Children Are Not Safe in School," Guest Editorial, *Jamestown Post-Journal*, Feb. 7, 1991.

18. Janette Martin, "*Shame on Protesters At SWCS*," Guest Editorial, *Jamestown Post-Journal*, Feb. 16, 1991.

19. "Trouble's Brewing Over Witch in School Reader," *Buffalo News*, March 10, 1991, pp. A1, A14.

20. Marcia A. Ryan, "Our Children Are Not Safe in School," Guest Editorial, *Jamestown Post-Journal*, Feb. 7, 1991.

21. "Trouble's Brewing Over Witch in School Reader," *Buffalo News*, March 10, 1991, pp. A1, A14.

22. "Controversy Brewing Over New Books at SWCS," *Jamestown Post-Journal,* Jan. 26, 1991.
23. People for the American Way, *Attacks on the Freedom to Learn: The 1990–1991 Report,* Washington, D.C.: People for the American Way, Aug. 1991.
24. "Florida Library Censorship Survey," *Newsletter on Intellectual Freedom,* Nov. 1990, p. 228, Chicago: American Library Association.
25. "Librarians Fight to Keep Book Checkouts Secret," *Jamestown Post-Journal,* Dec. 6, 1988.
26. "Zodiac Cops Quiz Broker About Library Books," *New York Post,* July 17, 1990, p. 15.
27. Robert Hicks, *In Pursuit of Satan: The Police and the Occult* (Buffalo, NY: Prometheus Press, 1991).
28. Will Shaw, "Characterizing Rock Music Culture," *On Record: Rock, Pop, and the Written Word,* ed. Simon Firth and Andrew Goodwin (New York: Pantheon, 1990), pp. 97–110; Jennifer Foote, "Making It In Metal Mecca," *Newsweek,* Aug. 7, 1989, 56–58.
29. Joe Stuessy, *Rock & Roll: Its History and Stylistic Development* (Englewood, NJ: Prentice-Hall, 1990), p. 306.
30. Joe Stuessy, 1990, p. 378.
31. J. D. Considine, "Metal Mania," *Rolling Stone,* Nov. 15, 1990, 102.
32. Jennifer Foote, "Making It In Metal Mecca," *Newsweek,* Aug. 7, 1989, 56–58.
33. Joe Stuessy, 1990; Jennifer Foote, Aug. 7, 1989.
34. Michael Langone, and Linda Blood, *Satanism and Occult-Related Violence: What You Should Know* (Weston, MA.: American Family Foundation, 1990); Carl A. Raschke, *Painted Black* (San Francisco: Harper & Row, 1990).
35. Paul King, "Heavy Metal Music and Drug Abuse in Adolescents," *Postgraduate Medicine* 83, no. 5 (April 1988): 295–304.
36. Paul King, 1988, p. 298.
37. Paul King, 1988, p. 301.
38. Paul King, 1988, p. 301.
39. Will Shaw, 1990.
40. Jeffrey H. Goldstein, *Aggression and Crimes of Violence,* 2nd ed. (New York: Oxford University Press, 1986).
41. James M. Schaefer, "Slow Country Music and Drinking" (paper presented to the American Anthropological Association, Nov. 17, 1988).
42. "The Devil's Music," *New York Post,* March 5, 1990, p. 3.; Rob Tannenbaum, "Church Assails Heavy Metal," *Rolling Stone,* April 19, 1990.
43. "Boy Kills Mother and Himself," *New York Times,* Jan. 11, 1988, p. B2; "Occult Killings Stun Area," *North Jersey Herald & News,* Jan. 12, p.

A1; "Satanic Warning Signs Unveiled," *North Jersey Herald & News,* Jan. 22, 1988, p. A1.

44. Ester Davidowitz, "Die Mother, Father, Brother," *Redbook,* 1989, 132–34, 168–71; Claire Safran, "The Devil Made Me Do It," *Woman's Day,* Nov. 22, 1988, 146–47, 152–53.

45. Personal letter from Detective Paul Hart.

46. Michael Beck, "Acquisition and Loss of an Evil Self-Image," *Evil: Self and Society,* ed. Marie Nelson and Michael Eigen (New York: Human Sciences Press, 1984), pp. 170–80.

47. Mary Billard, "Heavy Metal Goes on Trial," *Rolling Stone,* July 12–26, 1990.

48. "Judas Priest Plays Reno to Thank Fans for Support During Trial," *Reno Gazette-Journal,* Nov. 4, 1990.

49. "Family Blames Music for Love One's Death," *Gainesville Times* (Georgia), Oct. 28, 1990, pp. A1, A6.

50. Jean-Noel Kapferer, *Rumors: Uses, Interpretations and Images* (New Brunswick, NJ: Transaction Publishers, 1990).

51. John R. Vokey and J. Don Read, "Subliminal Messages: Between the Devil and The Media," *American Psychologist* 40, no. 11 (1985): 1231–239.

52. Stephen B. Thorne and Himelstein, "The Role of Suggestion in the Perception of Satanic Messages in Rock-and-Roll Recordings," *Journal of Psychology* 116, no. 2 (1984): 245–48.

53. Lorraine E. Prinsky, and Jill L. Rosenbaum, "'Leer-ics' or Lyrics: Teenage Impressions of Rock 'n Roll," *Youth and Society* 18, no. 4 (1987): 384–97.

54. George H. Lewis, "Patterns of Meaning and Choice: Taste Cultures in Popular Music," *Popular Music and Communication,* ed. James Lull, (Beverly Hills, CA: Sage Publications, 1987), pp. 189–211; James Lull, "Listeners' Communicative Uses of Popular Music," *Popular Music and Communication,* ed. James Lull (Newbury park, CA: Sage Publications, 1987), pp. 140–74; Keith Roe, "The School and Music in Adolescent Socialization," *Popular Music and Communication,* ed. James Lull (Newbury park, CA: Sage Publications, 1987), pp. 212–30.

55. Jeffrey Goldstein, 1986.

56. Jeffrey Goldstein, 1986.

57. David O. Sears, and Jonathan L. Freedman, "Selective Exposure to Information: A Critical Review," *The Process and Effects of Mass Communication,* ed. Wilbur Schramm and Donald F. Roberts (Urbana, IL: University of Illinois Press, 1967), pp. 209–34.

58. Michael A. Stackpole, "The Truth About Role Playing Games," *Satanism in America,* ed. Shawn Carlson and Gerald Larue; with G. O'Sullivan, A. Masche, and D. Frew, (Buffalo, N.Y.: Committee for the Scientific Examination of Religion, published by Gaia Press, 1989).

59. Joyce Brothers, "Dungeons and Dragons Role-Playing Game and Game Play," (Lake Geneva, WI: TSR Hobbies, Inc., 1983).
60. Pat Pulling, *The Devil's Web* (Lafayette, LA: Huntington House, 1989).
61. "Game Cited in Youth's Suicide," *Washington Post*, Aug. 13, 1983, pp. A1, A8; "Judge Rejects Suit Tying Suicide to Fantasy Game," *Washington Post*, Oct. 27, 1983.
62. "Satanic Cults Said to Entice Teens with Sex, Drugs," *Richmond Times-Dispatch* (VA), March 5, 1988, p. B4; "In Harm's Way," *Virginian-Pilot* (Norfolk, VA), Feb. 12, 1989.
63. Pat Pulling, Patrick Dempsey, and Rosemarie Loyacono, "Dungeons and Dragons," (pamphlet published by B.A.D.D., no date).
64. Daniel Martin, and Gary Alan Fine, "Satanic Cults, Satanic Play: Is Dungeons & Dragons a Breeding Ground for The Devil?" *The Satanism Scare*, ed. James Richardson, Joel Best, and David Bromley, (New York: Aldine de Gruyter, 1991), pp. 107–27.
65. Bob Larson, *Satanism: The Seduction of America's Youth* (Nashville, TN: Thomas Nelson, 1989), p. 52.
66. *Ibid*, p. 53.
67. Pat Pulling, 1989, p. 81.
68. Pat Pulling, 1989, p. 82.
69. Robert Hicks, 1991.
70. "Friends Say Teen Held in Deaths Played Fantasy Games," *Richmond News Leader* (VA), March 18, 1991, p. 15.
71. Luis H. Zayas and Bradford H. Lewis, "Fantasy Role-Playing for Mutual Aid in Children's Groups: A Case Illustration," *Social Work in Groups* 9, no. 1 (Spring 1986): 53–66.
72. Armando Simon, "Emotional Stability Pertaining to the Game of Dungeons and Dragons," *Psychology in the Schools* 24 (Oct. 1987): 329–32.
73. Daniel Martin and Gary Alan Fine, 1991.
74. Daniel Martin and Gary Alan Fine, 1991.
75. "Police Question Teens in Anti-Cult 'Vigilante' Case," *Harrisburg Patriot* (PA), March 23, 1990; "Gun Totting Teen Vigilantes Arrested," A.P. news release, March 23, 1990.
76. "Witch Rumors, Alleged Murder Plot Linked," *Tuscaloosa News* (AL), Aug. 9, 1990.
77. "Police Almost Shoot Student in What Prof Says Was Satanic Spoof," A.P. news release, Nov. 1, 1988.
78. "Teacher—Rumors," A.P. news release, Oct. 3, 1988.
79. "Teenagers Sue, Claim to Be Victims of Witch-Hunt," *Ann Arbor News* (Michigan), Nov. 1, 1989.
80. "Rumors of Satanism Closes Montazuma Creek School," *Cortez Montazuma Valley Journal*, Nov. 11, 1988, pp. A1, A18.

Chapter Nine: The Moral Crisis in American Society

1. Robert Heilbroner, "Lifting the Silent Depression," *New York Review of Books* 38, no. 17 (1992) p. 6.
2. Teresa C. Martin and Larry L. Bumpass, "Recent Trends in Marital Disruption," *Demography* 26, no. 1 (Feb. 1989), pp. 37–51.
3. Lawrence A. Kurdek, "Divorce History and Self-reported Psychological Distress in Husbands and Wives," *Journal of Marriage and the Family* 52 (Aug. 1990): 701–8; Lawrence A. Kurdek, "The Relations between Reported Well-Being and Divorce History, Availability of a Proximate Adult, and Gender," *Journal of Marriage and the Family* 53 (Feb. 1991): 71–78.
4. Deborah A. Dawson, "Family Structure and Children's Health and Well-Being: Data from the 1988 National Health Interview Survey on Child Health," *Journal of Marriage and the Family* 53 (Aug. 1991): 573–84; David H. Demo and Alan C. Acock, "The Impact of Divorce on Children," *Journal of Marriage and the Family* 50 (Aug. 1988): 619–48.
5. Marilyn Coleman and Lawrence H. Ganong, "Remarriage and Stepfamily Research in the 1980s: Increased Interest in an Old Family Form," *Journal of Marriage and the Family* 52 (Nov. 1990): 925–40.
6. David H. Demo and Alan C. Acock, "The Impact of Divorce on Children," *Journal of Marriage and the Family* 50 (Aug. 1988): 619–48; Paul R. Amato and Bruce Keith, "Parental Divorce and Adult Well-being: A Meta-analysis" 53 (Feb. 1991): 43–58.
7. Deborah A. Dawson, "Family Structure and Children's Health and Well-Being: Data from the 1988 National Health Interview Survey on Child Health," *Journal of Marriage and the Family* 53 (Aug. 1991): 573–84.
8. Sara McLanahan and Julia Adams, "The Effects of Children on Adults' Psychological Well-Being: 1957–1976," *Social Forces* 68, no. 1 (Sept. 1989): 124–46.
9. Andrew J. Cherlin, *The Changing American Family and Public Policy* (Washington, D.C.: The Urban Institute Press, 1988).
10. *Ibid.*
11. "Results from the National Adolescent Student Health Survey". *Morbidity and Mortality Report* 38, no. 9 (March 10, 1989).
12. Roper Organization, *The American Dream: A National Survey by the Wall Street Journal* (Princeton, NJ: Dow Jones Company, Feb. 1987), pp. 50–51.
13. "Research and Forecasts," *The Ethan Allen Report: The Status and Future of the American Family* (Danbury, CT: Ethan Allen, 1986).
14. Alexander W. Austin, et. al. *The American Freshman: National Norms for Fall 1986* (Los Angeles: University of California at Los Angeles Higher Education Research Institute, Dec. 1986).
15. Louis Harris, *Inside America* (New York: Vantage Press, 1987), p. 113.

16. James Trussell, "Teenage Pregnancy in the United States," *Family Planning Perspectives* 20 (Nov./Dec. 1988): 262–72.
17. Syed A. Husain, "Current Perspective on the Role of Psychological Factors in Adolescent Suicide," *Psychiatric Annals* 20 (March 1990).
18. Harris, 1987.
19. Stephen Rose and David Fasenfast, *Family Incomes in the 1980s: New Pressures on Wives, Husbands, and Young Adults* (Washington, D.C.: Economic Policy Institute, Nov. 1988); Lawrence Mishel and Jacquiline Simon, *The State of Working America* (Washington, D.C.: Economic Policy Institute, 1988); William P. O'Hare, *The Rise of Poverty in Rural America* (Washington, D.C.: Population Reference Bureau, Inc., July 1988; Kathryn H. Porter, *Poverty in Rural America* (Washington, D.C.: Center on Budget and Policy Priorities, 1989); Kevin Phillips, *The Politics of Rich and Poor* (New York: Harper-Collins, 1990).
20. Patricia Voydanoff, "Economic Distress and Family Relations: A Review of the Eighties," *Journal of Marriage and the Family* 52 (Nov. 1990): 1099–115.
21. Mishel, and Simon, 1988.
22. Voydanoff, 1990.
23. Voydanoff, 1990.
24. George Gallup, Jr. and Sara Jones, *100 Questions and Answers: Religion in America* (Princeton, NJ: The Princeton Religion Research Center, 1989), p. 108.
25. "A U.S. News Poll: Echoes of Watergate," *U.S. News & World Report*, Feb. 23, 1987, 56–57.
26. Ingrid Groller, "Is Society Morally Bankrupt?" *Parents*, June 1989, p. 35.
27. David J. Lewis and Andrew Weigert, "Trust as a Social Reality," *Social Forces* 63 (June 1985): 967–85.
28. Michele N. Collison, "Apparent Rise in Students' Cheating Has College Officials Worried," *Chronicle of Higher Education,* Jan. 17, 1990, pp. A. 33, A. 34; Michele N. Collison, "Survey at Rutgers Suggests That Cheating May Be on the Rise at Large Universities," *Chronicle of Higher Education,* Oct. 24, 1990, pp. A31–A32.
29. Rushworth M. Kidder, "Children's Moral Compass Wavers," *Christian Science Monitor*, May 16, 1990, p. 12; Louis Harris & Associates, *Girl Scouts Survey on the Beliefs and Moral Values of America's Children*, Executive Summary, Fall, 1989.
30. *Ibid.*
31. Ron Lesthaeghe and Johan Surkyn, "Cultural Dynamics and Economic Theories of Fertility Change," *Population and Development Review* 14 (March 1988): 1–45; Duane F. Alwin, "Changes in Qualities Valued in Children in the United States, 1964 to 1984," *Social Science Research*

18 (1989): 195–236; Ronald Inglehart, *Cultural Shift in Advanced Industrial Society* (Princeton, NJ: Princeton University Press, 1990).

32. James Davison Hunter, *Culture Wars: The Struggle to Define America* (New York: Basic Books, 1991).

33. Gallup, 1989, pp. 108–9.

34. Harris, 1987, pp. 31–38.

35. *Ibid.*

36. *Ibid.*, p. 38.

37. Robert N. Bellah, *The Broken Covenant* (New York: Seabury Press, 1975).

Chapter Ten: The Search for Scapegoat Deviants

1. Robert Lynd (cited in Rudolf Flesch) *The Book of Unusual Quotations* [New York: Harper Bros., 1957], p. 80.

2. Nachman Ben-Yehuda, *The Politics and Morality of Deviance* (Albany, NY: State University of New York Press, 1990).

3. Erich Goode, *Deviant Behavior*, 3rd ed. (Englewood Cliffs, NJ: Prentice-Hall, 1990).

4. Nachman Ben-Yehuda, "The European Witch Craze of the 14th to 16th Centuries: A Sociologist's Perspective," *American Journal of Sociology* 86, no. 1 (1981): 1–31; Elliott P. Currie, "Crimes Without Criminals: Witchcraft and Its Control in Renaissance Europe," *Law and Society Review* 3, no. 1 (August 1986): 7–32.

5. Albert J. Bergesen, "Political Witch Hunts: The Sacred and the Subversive in Cross-National Perspective," *American Sociological Review* 42, (April 1977): 220–33; Jerry D. Rose, *Outbreaks: The Sociology of Collective Behavior* (New York: The Free Press, 1982).

6. Brett Silverstein, "Enemy Images," *American Psychologist* 44 (June 1989): 903–13; Jerome D. Frank, "The Face of the Enemy," *Psychology Today*, Nov. 1968, 24–29.

7. Howard F. Stein, "The Indispensable Enemy and American-Soviet Relations," *Ethos* 17 (Dec. 1989): 480–503.

8. Joseph T. Hepworth and Stephen G. West, "Lynchings and the Economy: A Time-Series Reanalysis of Hovland and Sears," *Journal of Personality and Social Psychology* 55, no. 2 (1988): 239–47.

9. Michael Reich, "The Economics of Racism," *Problems in Political Economy: An Urban Perspective*, ed. David M. Gordon (Lexington, MA: D. D. Heath, 1971): pp. 107–13.

10. Lynn S. Kahn, "The Dynamics of Scapegoating: The Expulsion of Evil," *Psychotherapy: Theory, Research and Practice* 17 (Spring 1980): 79–84;

Jeffrey Eagle and Peter M. Newton, "Scapegoating in Small Groups: An Organizational Approach," *Human Relations* 34, no. 4 (1981): 283–301; Fred Wright, et. al. "Perspectives on Scapegoating in Primary Groups," *Group* 12 (Spring 1988): 33–44; Gary Gemmill, "The Dynamics of Scapegoating in Small Groups," *Small Group Behavior* 20 (Nov. 1989): 406–18.

11. Ezra F. Vogel and Normal W. Bell, "The Emotionally Disturbed Child as the Family Scapegoat," *The Family*, rev. ed. (New York: Free Press, 1960, 1968), pp. 412–25.

12. Lewis Coser, *The Function of Social Conflict* (New York: Free Press, 1956), p. 107.

13. "Panel: Hate crimes grow worse in Vt.," *Burlington Free Press*, Jan. 11, 1990; "Trouble Trend: Experts See Rise in Racism in U.S.," *Virginian-Pilot* (Norfolk), April 29, 1990; " 'Hate Crime' Reports up 70% in Monmouth," *Asbury Park Press* (NJ), May 1, 1990; "Prejudice Based Crimes on Rise in Texas, U.S.," *American-Statesman* (Austin, TX), May 5, 1990.

14. "Race on Campus: Failing the Test," *Newsweek*, May 6, 1991, 26–27.

15. Gregory M. Herek, "Hate Crimes against Lesbians and Gay Men," *American Psychologist* 44 (June 1989): 948–55; David M. Wertheimer, "Victims of Violence: A Rising Tide of Anti-Gay Sentiment," *USA Today*, Jan. 1988, pp. 52–61; "Battling the Bias," *Newsweek*, Nov. 25, 1991, p. 25.

16. "Anti-Semitic acts increase during '90," *Houston Post* (Texas), Feb. 11, 1991; "Jewish Groups Disagree on Significance," *Detroit Free Press*, Feb. 7, 1991; "Jersey Posts a Drop in Anti-Semitic Vandalism Amid a national Upsurge," *Star-Ledger* (Newark, N.J.), Feb. 7, 1991; "Report Shows 12% Rise in Anti-Semitic Incidents," *New York Times*, Jan. 27, 1988, p. A13.

17. *Ibid.*

18. Anson, Shupe, "Constructing Evil as a Social Process: The Unification Church and the Media," *Uncivil Religion: Interreligious Hostility in America*, ed. Robert Bellah and Frederick E. Greenspahn (New York: Crossroad Press, 1987), pp. 203–18.

19. Phillips Stevens, Jr., "The Demonology of Satanism: An Anthropological View," *The Satanism Scare*, ed. James Richardson, Joel Best, and David Bromley (New York: Aldine de Gruyter, 1991), pp. 21–40.

20. Jeffrey Burton Russell, "The Historical Satan," *The Satanism Scare*, ed. James Richardson, Joel Best, and David Bromley (New York: Aldine de Gruyter, 1991), pp. 41–48.

21. Clyde Z. Nunn, "The Rising Credibility of the Devil in America," *Listening* 9 (1974): 84–99; Clyde Z. Nunn, Harry J. Crockett, and J. Allen Williams, *Tolerance for Nonconformity* (San Francisco: Jossey-Bass, 1978).

22. George Gallup, Jr. and Frank Newport, "Belief in Paranormal Phenomena among Adult Americans," *Skeptical Inquirer*, Winter 1991, 137–46.

23. George Gallup, Jr., *Adventure in Immorality* (New York: McGraw-Hill, 1982), p. 98.

24. George Gallup, Jr., and Jim Castelli, *The American Catholic People* (Garden City, NY: Doubleday, 1987), pp. 15–16.

25. Kahn, 1980.

26. William A. Miller, *Make Friends with Your Shadow* (Minneapolis: Augsburg, 1981).

27. *Mother Jones*, Special Issue: "America's Dirty Little Secret: We Hate Kids," May/June, 1991.

Chapter Eleven: The Rhetoric of the Moral Crusade against Satanism

1. Eric Hoffer, *The True Believer* (New York: Harper and Row, 1951), p. 89.

2. Howard S. Becker, *Outsiders: Studies in the Sociology of Deviance* (New York: Free Press, 1963).

3. J. Gusfield, "Moral Passage: The Symbolic Process in Public Designations of Deviance," *Social Problems* (Fall 1967): 175–88.

4. D. Bennett, *The Party of Fear: From Nativist Movements to the New Right in American History*, (Chapel Hill, NC: University of North Carolina Press, 1988).

5. Becker, 1963.

6. Doug McAdam, John D. McCarthy, and Mayer N. Zald, "Social Movements," *Handbook of Sociology*, ed. Neil J. Smelser (Newbury Park, CA.: Sage Publications, 1988), pp. 695–737.

7. Albert James Bergesen, "Political Witch Hunts: The Sacred and the Subversive in Cross-National Perspectives," *American Sociological Review* 42 (April 1977): 220–33.

8. Peter Conrad and Joseph W. Schneider, *Deviance and Medicalization* (St. Louis, MO.: C. V. Mosby Co., 1980).

9. For a similar analysis of the Satanism scare in Canada, see: Randy Lippert, "The Social Construction of Satanism as a Social Problem in Canada," *Canadian Journal of Sociology* 15, no. 4 (1990), pp. 417–37.

10. R. Po-Chia Hsia, *The Myth of Ritual Murder* (New Haven: Yale University Press, 1988).

11. David Caute, *The Great Fear* (New York: Simon and Schuster, 1978), pp. 122–33.

12. According to most MPD patients' testimonials, Satanic cults were torturing them when they were children in the 1950s. Yet during the

1950s, the secret conspiracy found in social paranoia consisted of Communists and nothing whatsoever was heard about Satanists.

13. Robert D. Hicks, "The Police Model of Satanism Crime," *The Satanism Scare*, ed. James Richardson, Joel Best, and David Bromley, (New York: Aldine de Gruyter, 1991), pp. 175–89.

14. Peter L. Steinberg, *The Great "Red Menace"* (Westport, CT: Greenwood, 1984), p. 183.

15. "Satanic Cults and Children," "Geraldo," Nov. 19, 1987 (transcript from: Journal Graphics, Inc., New York).

16. Phillips Stevens, Jr., "The Demonology of Satanism: An Anthropological View," *The Satanism Scare*, ed. J. Richardson, J. Best, and D. Bromley (New York: Aldine de Gruyter, 1991), pp. 21–40.

17. David A. Snow, et. al. "Frame Alignment Processes, Micromobilization, and Movement Participation," *American Sociological Review* 51 (August 1986), pp. 464–81.

18. Daniel Goleman, "Therapists See Religion as Aid, Not Illusion," *New York Times* Sept. 19, 1991, pp. C1, C8.

19. M. Scott Peck, *People of the Lie: The Hope for Healing Human Evil* (New York: Simon and Schuster, 1983).

20. Glenna Whitley, "The Seduction of Gloria Grady," *D Magazine* (Dallas), Oct. 1991, pp. 45–49, 66–71.

21. Carl A. Raschke, *Painted Black* (San Francisco: Harper and Row, 1990).

22. Debbie Nathan, "The Ritual Abuse Hoax," *Village Voice*, June 12, 1990, pp. 36–44. Reprinted in Debbie Nathan, *Women and Other Aliens* (El Paso, Texas: Cinco Puntas Press, 1991), pp. 148–76; Debbie Nathan, "Satanism and Child Molestation: Constructing the Ritual Abuse Scare," *The Satanism Scare*, ed. J. Richardson, J. Best, and D. Bromley (New York: Aldine de Gruyter, 1991), pp. 75–94.

23. E. Sue Blume, *Secret Survivors: Uncovering Incest and its Aftereffects in Women* (New York: John Wiley and Sons, 1990), p. 60.

24. McAdam, et. al., 1988.

Chapter Twelve: The Organization of the Moral Crusade

1. Friedrich Nietzsche, *Beyond Good and Evil*, trans. by Walter Kaufmann (New York: Vintage, 1986), p. 146.

2. Shawn Carlson and Gerald Larue, *Satanism in America* (El Cerrito, CA: Gaia Press, 1989).

3. Mike Warnke, with Dave Balsinger and Les Jones, *The Satan Seller*

(South Plainfield, NJ: Bridge Publishing, 1972); Jon Trott and Mike Hertenstein, "Selling Satan: The Tragic History of Mike Warnke," *Cornerstone* 21, issue 98 (1992): 7–9, 30.

4. Jay Grelen and Kit Wagar, "IRS May Have the Last Laugh on Comedian," *Buffalo News*, New York, Aug. 8, 1992.

5. Jerry Johnston, *The Edge of Evil* (Dallas: Word Publishing, 1989).

6. Bob Larson, *Satanism: The Seduction of America's Youth* (Nashville: Thomas Nelson, 1989).

7. Gretchen Passantino, Bob Passantino, and Jon Trott, "Satan's Sideshow: The True Lauren Stratford Story," *Cornerstone* 18, issue 90 (1990): 24–28.

8. Joseph Brennan, *The Kingdom of Darkness* (Lafayette, LA.: Arcadian House Publishing, 1990).

9. "La. Priest Presses Fight against Satanic Cults," *Times-Picayune* (New Orleans, LA), Jan. 20, 1990; "Burden that Robs Them of Joy," *Times* (Shreveport, LA) Oct. 21, 1989.

10. Ben Crouch and Kelly Damphousse, "Law Enforcement and the Satanic Crime Connection: A Survey of 'Cult Cops'," *The Satanism Scare*, ed. James Richardson, Joel Best, and David Bromley, (New York: Aldine de Gruyter, 1991), pp. 191–217; Robert Hicks, *In Pursuit of Satan* (Buffalo, NY: Prometheus Books, 1991).

11. "Tiffin's 1-Man Satan Squad Draws Fire," *Cleveland Plain Dealer*, Aug. 4, 1985.

12. Thomas W. Wedge, *The Satan Hunter* (Canton, Ohio: Daring Books, 1987).

13. Rosie Waterhouse, "Satanic Cults: How the Hysteria Swept Britain," *The Independent on Sunday*, Sept. 10, 1990; Rosie Waterhouse, "The Making of a Satanic Myth," *The Independent on Sunday*, Sept. 23, 1990; Rosie Waterhouse, "Satanic Inquisitors from the City Hall," *The Independent on Sunday*, Oct. 7, 1990; "Where the Devil is the Evidence?" *The Mail on Sunday*, Sept. 16, 1990; "We Reveal 3 Experts Behind the Gory Tales," *Daily Star*, Sept. 20, 1990.

14. *Ibid.*

15. Crouch and Damphousse, 1991.

16. Warnke and Balsinger, 1972.

17. David Alexander, "Giving the Devil More Than His Due," *The Humanist*, March/April 1990.

18. Crouch and Damphousse, 1991.

19. *Ibid.*

20. *Ibid.*

21. Cynthia S. Kisser and Bette Naysmith, "Toward a Better Understanding of Satanism as a Social Movement," *Free Inquiry*, Spring 1992.

22. Some other anti-cult groups which are particularly active in the moral crusade against Satanism are Watchmen Alert to Cultic Harassment

(WATCH) of El Paso, Texas, and the Council on Mind Abuse of Toronto, Canada.

23. Cult Awareness Network, New York and New Jersey, pamphlet.
24. Michael D. Langone and Linda O. Blood, *Satanism and Occult-Related Violence: What You Should Know* (Weston, MA: American Family Foundation, 1990).
25. Carl Raschke, *Painted Black* (San Francisco: Harper and Row, 1990).
26. *Young People and Cults*, March 1990, American Family Foundation.
27. Anson Shupe and David Bromley, "The Modern American Anti-Cult Movement: A Twenty Year Retrospective" (paper presented at the annual meeting of the Association for the Sociology of Religion, August, 1991).
28. Richard Wexler, *Wounded Innocents* (Buffalo, NY: Prometheus Books, 1990).
29. "Children's Advocate Addresses Seminar," *Olean Times-Herald*, April, 29, 1988.
30. Sherrill Mulhern, "Satanism and Psychotherapy: A Rumor in Search of an Inquisition" *The Satanism Scare*, ed. James T. Richardson, Joel Best, and David Bromley, (New York: Aldine de Gruyter, 1991), pp. 145–72.
31. Ralph Underwager and Hollida Wakefield, "Cur Allii, Prae Aliis? (Why Some, and Not Other?) *Issues in Child Abuse Accusations* 3, no. 3 (1991): 178–93.
32. "Projective Story Telling Cards," (Northwest Psychological Publishers, 1990).
33. Doris Sanford, *Don't Make Me Go Back, Mommy* (Portland, OR: Multnomah Press, 1990); also see book review: Gretchen Passintino, "Stolen Innocence," *Cornerstone* 19, issue 94, (1991): 14.
34. Report of the Ritual Abuse Task Force of the Los Angeles County Commission for Women, September 15, 1989.
35. David W. Lloyd, "Ritual Child Abuse: Understanding the Controversies" (Wheaton, MD: The National Center on Child Sexual Abuse, Aug. 10, 1990).
36. Kenneth V. Lanning, "Child Sex Rings: A Behavioral Analysis" (Arlington, VA: National Center for Missing and Exploited Children, December, 1989).
37. Mulhern, 1991.
38. Paul Ciolino & Associates, 20 North Clark Street, Suite 3500, Chicago, Illinois 60602.
39. Unofficial college transcript of Pamala Gay (Morris) Klein, Southern Illinois University, Carbondale, Illinois, Oct. 7, 1977.
40. Position description, Coordinator, Rape and Sexual Abuse Care Center, Southern Illinois University at Edwardsville, July 13, 1977.
41. Mike Dash, "Satan and the Social Worker," *Fortean Times*, vol. 57, 1991, pp. 46–61.

42. Rosie Waterhouse, "Judge Dismisses Status of Satanic Abuse 'Therapist'," *The Independent on Sunday*, March 24, 1991.
43. Dash, 1991.
44. Articles of Incorporation, Office of the Secretary of State, Illinois, July 1, 1984.
45. Background vitae of Pamala G. Klein, no date.
46. Nicki Pope, "The Root of All This Evil," *Today* (U.K.), April 6, 1991; Waterhouse, March 24, 1991.
47. Dash, 1991.
48. Ruling on Supplemental Motion No. 12, Judge R. Morgan Hamilton, Circuit Court of Cook County, Feb. 13, 1991. (Case of the People vs. John Fittanto.)
49. Affidavits submitted for: Ruling on Supplemental Motion No. 12, Judge R. Morgan Hamilton, Circuit Court of Cook County, Feb. 13, 1991. (Case of the People vs. John Fittanto.)
50. Transcripts from Paul Hogan of WMAQ-TV News, Chicago; May 2, 1991, May 3, 1991, May 10, 1991, Aug. 23, 1991.
51. Law suit of John Fittanto and Teresa Fittanto vs. Pamala Klein; No. 91C6934, no date. United States District Court for the Northern District of Illinois.
52. *Ibid.*
53. Affidavits submitted in the case of Harry J. Johnson and Kristine Short; Emergency Motion for Temporary Restraining Order and Preliminary Injunction. May 6, 1991. No. 90 D 13399. Circuit Court of Cook County, Illinois, Domestic Relations Division.
54. Discovery Disposition in the interest of Marie Lodge and Sarah Fittanto. Circuit Court of Cook County, Illinois; City Department, Juvenile Division. Feb. 7, 1991. No. 89J20642.

Chapter Thirteen: The Politics of the Moral Crusade

1. Howard Becker, *Outsiders: Studies in the Sociology of Deviance* (New York: Free Press, 1963), p. 9.
2. Doug McAdam, John D. McCarthy, and Mayer N. Zald, "Social Movements," *Handbook of Sociology*, ed. N. Smelser (Newbury Park, CA: Sage, 1988), pp. 695–737.
3. James Richardson, Joel Best, and David Bromley, eds., *The Satanism Scare* (New York: Aldine de Gruyter, 1991), pp. 3–17.
4. Robert Hicks, *In Pursuit of Satan* (Buffalo, NY: Prometheus Books, 1991).
5. Kenneth V. Lanning, "Satanic, Occult, Ritualistic Crime: A Law Enforcement Perspective," *The Police Chief*, Oct. 1989, pp. 62–83;

Kenneth V. Lanning, *Child Sex Rings: A Behavioral Analysis* (Arlington, VA: National Center for Missing and Exploited Children, Dec. 1989).

6. Ben Crouch and Kelly Damphousse, "Law Enforcement and the Satanic Crime Connection: A Survey of 'Cult Cops'," *The Satanism Scare*, ed. J. Richardson, J. Best, and D. Bromley (New York: Aldine de Gruyter, 1991), pp. 191–204.

7. *Ibid.*, p. 202.

8. "Michigan State Police Occult Survey" (East Lansing: Investigative Services Bureau, Michigan State Police, June, 1990).

9. Margot Adler, *Drawing Down the Moon* (Boston: Beacon Press, 1986).

10. Richardson, Best, and Bromley, 1991, p. 3.

11. Carl A. Raschke, *Painted Black* (San Francisco: Harper & Row, 1990), p. 132.

12. Cynthia S. Kisser and Bette Naysmith, "Toward a Better Understanding of Satanism as a Social Movement," *Free Inquiry*, Spring 1992.

13. Cynthia Kisser, "Destructive Cults: A New Organized Crime," *Law Enforcement News*, March 15, 1991, 8–9.

14. Raschke, 1990, p. 75.

15. Andrew Petkofsky, "Author on Occult Sees Intimidation," *Richmond News Leader*, Dec. 13, 1991, p. 24.

16. A few newspaper reports about the Satanic cult scare with a skeptical slant include the following. Rex Springston, "Experts Say Tales Are Bunk," *Richmond News Leader* (VA), April 6, 1989; Rex Springston, "Local Believers Short on Evidence," *Richmond New Leader*, April 7, 1989; Dave Condren, "Rumors Feed Satanism Fears, Experts Say," *Buffalo News*, Oct. 8, 1989; Anson Shupe, "Pitchmen of the Satanism Scare," *Wall Street Journal*, March 9, 1990; John Johnson and Steve Padilla, "Satanism: Skeptics Abound," *Los Angeles Times*, April 23, 1991.

17. Debbie Nathan, "Exposing Geraldo's Special". *Village Voice*, Nov. 8, 1988, 57–58.

18. "Trash TV," *Newsweek*, Nov. 14, 1988, p. 72–78; "Devil Worship: Exposing Satan's Underground," *Variety* Nov. 9, 1988, p. 43.

19. As far as I could determine, "Geraldo" had twelve programs related to Satanism from 1987 to 1991; "Sally Jesse Raphael" had four from 1989 to 1991; "The Oprah Winfrey Show" had three from 1986 to 1989; and "Donahue" only one in 1989. The peak year for these programs was 1988.

20. Sherrill Mulhern, "Satanism and Psychotherapy: A Rumor in Search of an Inquisition," *The Satanism Scare*, ed. J. Richardson, J. Best and D. Bromley (New York: Aldine de Gruyter, 1991), pp. 145–74.

21. Some of the most prominent psychiatric advocates of the Satanic cult explanation include: Bennett G. Braun (M.D.), Medical Director of the

Dissociative Disorders Program at Rush Presbyterian—St. Lukes Medical Center at Rush North Shore Medical Center in Chicago; Roberta G. Sacks (Ph.D.), Director of Training, Dissociative Disorders Inpatient Unit of Rush Presbyterian—St. Lukes Medical Center at Rush North Shore Medical Center in Chicago; Walter C. Young (M.D.), Director of the National Center for the Treatment of Dissociative Disorders in Denver; Jean Goodwin (M.D., M.P.H.), Professor of Psychiatry at the Medical College of Wisconsin in Milwaukee; and Roland C. Summit (M.D.), Professor of Psychiatry at Harbor-U.C.L.A. Medical Center.

22. Walter C. Young, "What's New in Dissociation," *Violence Update* 1, no. 10 (1991): 3.

23. Some of ritual abuse training videos for therapists and law enforcement officers include the following: "Sessions and Sand Trays," featuring Roberta Sachs (Ph.D.); "Treatment of the Ritually Abused Child," featuring Pamela Hudson (LCSW); "Identification of the Ritually Abused Child", featuring Catherine Gould (Ph.D.); "Ritual Child Abuse: A Professional Overview," featuring Bennett Braun (M.D.), Jean Goodwin (M.D.), Catherine Gould (Ph.D.), Roberta Sachs (Ph.D.), Roland Summit (M.D.), Walter Young (M.D.) and others. The videotapes are available from several companies, including Cavalcade Productions of Ukiah, CA and R. & E. Publishers of Saratoga, CA.

24. One exception can be found in the article: Walter C. Young, Roberta G. Sachs, Bennett G. Braun, and Ruth T. Watkins, "Patients Reporting Ritual Abuse in Childhood: A Clinical Syndrome. Report of 37 Cases," *Child Abuse and Neglect*, vol. 15, 1991, pp. 181–89.

Unfortunately, this study, like all others by therapists, is based upon clinical case studies of the allegations of MPD patients and lacks any external verification. None of the patients' allegations of crime were referred to police for criminal investigations. As the therapists themselves note: "They [the patients] could have incorporated certain incidents from articles or books as 'pseudo-memories,' and retrieved them with the same conviction as real memories (p. 185)."

These therapists have been considerably less cautious in their conference papers and training videos. (See Mulhern, 1991).

25. Robert S. Mayer, *Satan's Children: Case Studies in Multiple Personality* (New York: G. P. Putnam, 1991); James G. Friesen, *Uncovering the Mystery of MPD* (San Bernardino, CA: Here's Life Publishers, 1991).

26. Bette L. Bottoms, Philip R. Shaver, and Gail G. Goodman, "Profile of Ritualistic and Religion-Related Abuse Allegations Reported to Clinical Psychologists in the United States," (paper presented to the annual meeting of the American Psychological Association, Aug. 19, 1991). (Available from: B. Bottoms, Dept. of Psychology, State University of New York, Buffalo, NY.)

27. Some social workers who are prominent moral crusaders against Satanic cult "ritual" abuse include: Kee MacFarlane, Pamela Hudson, Kathy Snowden, and Maribeth Kaye. Pamala Klein may be included here, as an untrained, uncertified "ritual" abuse counselor.

28. John Doris, *The Suggestibility of Children's Recollections: Implications for Eyewitness Testimony* (Washington, D.C., 1991).

29. P. Conrad and J. Schneider, *Deviance and Medicalization* (St. Louis: C.V. Mosby, 1980).

30. Joseph Gusfield, *The Culture of Public Problems: Drinking and Driving and the Symbolic Order* (Chicago: University of Chicago Press, 1981).

31. Ronald J. Troyer and Gerald E. Markle, *Cigarettes: The Battle Over Smoking* (New Brunswick, NJ: Rutgers University Press, 1983).

32. "Governor Gets Satanic Crimes Bill," *Chicago Sun-Times*, June 26, 1989; "Bill Would Make Things Hot for Devil-May-Care Satanists," *Times-Picayune*, April 28, 1989.

33. *Final Report of the Task Force Studying Ritual Crime* (Richmond, VA.: Crime Commission Task Force Studying Ritual Criminal Activity).

34. "State Task Force Finds No Major Cult Activity," *Richmond New Leader*, Aug. 15, 1991.

35. *Final Report of the Task Force Studying Ritual Crime*, pp. 17–18.

36. *Ibid.*, p. 18.

37. *Ibid.*, p. 19.

38. "Woman Tells Satanic Horror Story to Jury," *Los Angeles Times*, March 22, 1991, pp. A37, A45; "Girl Tells Court in Satanic Trial of Blood Ritual," March 22, 1991, pp. B1, B6; "Jurors Hear Lurid Testimony in Abuse Case," *Orange County Register*, March 23, 1991, pp. A1, A14; "Satanic Abuse: Truth or Modern Legend," *Orange County Register*, March 25, 1991, pp. A1, A14; "Witness Denies Defense Allegation in Cult Case," *Los Angeles Times*, April 2, 1991. Also see the transcript for the television program: "Larry King Live," May 13, 1991 (Journal Graphics, New York, transcript # 300). This author was interviewed about the case on the program, along with the two sisters.

39. "Jury Splits Its Verdict in Cult Trial," *Los Angeles Times*, April 13, 1991, pp. A1, A12; "Satanic Child Abuse Suit May Lend Credibility to Future Cases," *Los Angeles Times*, April 23, 1991, pp. A1, A22.

40. David Alexander, "Still Giving the Devil More than His Due," *The Humanist*, Sept/Oct. 1991, 22–33, 42.

41. "Satanic Abuse: Truth or Modern Legend," *Orange County Register*, March 25, 1991, pp. A1, A14; "Roe Case Delved into Ritual Abuse, Repressed Memories and Disorders," *Orange County Register*, April 14, 1991, pp. A1, A26; "Witness Denies Defense Allegation in Cult Case," *Los Angeles Times*, April 2, 1991.

42. "Roe Case Delved into Ritual Abuse, Repressed Memories and Disorders," *Orange County Register*, April 14, 1991, pp. A1, A26.

43. David Alexander, "Still Giving the Devil More than His Due," *The Humanist*, Sept/Oct. 1991, 22–33, 42.

44. "Satanism in the Campbell Case?" *Rochester Times-Union*, Oct. 16, 1990.

45. *Ibid.*

46. *Ibid.*

47. Bennett Loudon and Jack Jones, "Rumors Run Rampant in Wake of Palmyra Killings," *The Democrat and Chronicle* (Rochester, NY), Aug. 5, 1991, pp. 1A, 4A; Jack Jones and Bennett Loudon, "Youths Wonder if Suicide, Slayings Were Linked," *The Democrat and Chronicle* (Rochester, NY), April 4, 1991, p. 6A.

48. Personal communication from Phillips Stevens.

49. Phillips Stevens, Jr., "The Demonology of Satanism: An Anthropological View," *The Satanism Scare*, ed. J. Richardson, J. Best, and D. Bromley (New York: Aldine de Gruyter, 1991), pp. 21–40.

50. "Anthropologist: No Proof of Satanism," *Finger Lakes Times*, Sept. 26, 1991; "Testimony Ends in Cambell Case: Jurors to Begin Deliberations Today," *Rochester Democrat and Chronicle*, Sept. 27, 1991.

51. "Chad Campbell: Guilty as Charged," *Times* (Wayne County, NY), Oct. 1, 1991, pp. 1,. 6, 13.

52. Dawn House, "LDS Church Reviewing Abuse Claims," *Salt Lake City Tribune*, Oct. 25, 1991; "Mormons Probing Reports of Satanism, Human Sacrifices," *St. Paul Pioneer Press* (Minnesota), Nov. 2, 1991.

53. Patty Henetz, "Are Accounts of Ritual Child Abuse for Real—or a Mass Delusion?" *Deseret News* (Salt Lake City), Sept. 8, 1991; Patty Henetz, "Is Disorder Caused by Ritual Abuse?" *Deseret News* (Salt Lake City), Sept. 9, 1991; Patty Henetz, "S.L. Child Who Used to be 'Daddy's Girl' Now Troubled by Images of Ritual Abuse," *Deseret News* (Salt Lake City), Sept. 11, 1991.

54. Dawn House, "LDS Church Reviewing Abuse Claims," *Salt Lake City Tribune*, Oct. 25, 1991; "Mormons Probing Reports of Satanism, Human Sacrifices," *St. Paul Pioneer Press*, Nov. 2, 1991.

55. Dawn House, "LDS Church Reviewing Abuse Claims," *Salt Lake City Tribune*, Oct. 25, 1991.

Chapter Fourteen: The Medieval Origins of Modern Demonology

1. William Shakespeare, *The Tempest*, Act I, Scene 1, line 261.

2. Phillips, Stevens, Jr., "The Demonology of Satanism: An Anthropological View," *The Satanism Scare*, ed. J. Richardson, J. Best, and D. Bromley (New York: Aldine de Gruyter, 1991), p. 21.

3. Phillips, Stevens, Jr., "Satanism: Where are the Folklorists?" *New York Folklore* 15, no. 1–2 (1989): 1–22; "The Dangerous Folklore of Satanism," *Free Inquiry* 15, no. 3 (1990): 28–34; Stevens, 1991.
4. Norman Cohn, "The Myth of Satan and his Human Servants," *Witchcraft Confessions and Accusations,* ed. Mary Douglas (New York: Travistock, 1970) pp. 3–16; Norman Cohn, *Europe's Inner Demons* (New York: Basic Books, 1975).
5. Cohn, 1970, p. 3.
6. Cohn, 1975, p. xi.
7. David Parkin, ed., *The Anthropology of Evil* (New York: Basil Blackwell, 1985). (See especially: D. Parkin, "Introduction," pp. 1–25; and D. Taylor "Theological Thoughts about Evil," pp. 26–41; Vytautas Kavolis, "Civilizational Models of Evil," *Evil: Self and Society,* ed. M. Nelson and M. Eigen (New York: Human Sciences Press, 1984), pp. 17–35.
8. William A. Miller, *Make Friends with Your Shadow* (Minneapolis: Augsburg Publishing House, 1981).
9. Bill Ellis, "De Legendis Urbis: Modern Legends in Ancient Rome," *Journal of American Folklore* 96, no. 380 (1983): 200–208; Cohn, 1975.
10. Cohn, 1975.
11. R. I. Moore, *The Formation of a Persecuting Society* (Cambridge, MA: Basil Blackwell, 1987); Cohn, 1975.
12. Cohn, 1970; 1975; Moore, 1987.
13. Moore, 1987, p. 19.
14. Joseph R. Strayer, *The Albigensian Crusades* (New York: Dial Press, 1971).
15. Moore, 1987.
16. Cohn, 1975.
17. Strayer, 1971.
18. Cohn, 1975.
19. Peter Partner, *The Murdered Magicians: The Templars and Their Myth* (Oxford, U.K.: Oxford University Press, 1981).
20. Barbara W. Tuchman, *A Distant Mirror: The Calamitous 14th Century* (New York: Knopf, 1978), p. 43.
21. David Berger, "Mission to the Jews and Jewish-Christian Contacts in the Polemical Literature of the High Middle Ages," *American Historical Review* 91, no. 3 (1986), pp. 576–91; Gavin Langmuir, "Comment," *American Historical Review* 91, no. 3 (1986): 614–24; Moore, 1987.
22. Moore, 1987.
23. Berger, 1986.
24. Gavin I. Langmuir, *Toward a Definition of Antisemitism.* Berkeley, Ca.: University of California Press, 1990.
25. Langmuir, 1986, p. 619.
26. Alan Dundes, "The Ritual Murder or Blood Libel Legend: A Study of

Anti-Semitic Victimization through Projective Inversion," *Temenos: Studies in Comparative Religion* 25 (1989): 7–32; Florence H. Ridley, "A Tale Told Too Often," *Western Folklore* 26 (1967): 153–56.

27. R. Po-Chia Hsia, *The Myth of Ritual Murder: Jews and Magic in Reformation Germany* (New Haven, CN: Yale University Press, 1988).

28. Gavin I. Langmuir, "Thomas of Monmouth: Detector of Ritual Murder," *Speculum* 59, no. 4 (1984): 820–46. (Republished in Langmuir, 1990.)

29. *Ibid.*

30. M. D. Anderson, *A Saint at Stake* (London, U.K.: Faber and Faber, 1984); Langmuir, 1984.

31. Langmuir, 1984.

32. *Ibid.*

33. *Ibid.*

34. Erhrman, "The Origins of the Ritual Murder Accusation and Blood Libel," *Tradition* 15, no. 4 (1976): 83–90; Hsia, 1988.

35. R. B. Dobson, *The Jews of Medieval York and the Massacre of March 1190* (York, U.K.: University of York, 1974). (Borthwick Paper No. 45.)

36. Edgar Morin, *Rumour in Orleans* (New York: Random House, 1971); Freddy Raphael, "Le Juif et le Diable dans la civilisation de Occident," *Social Compass* 4 (1972): 549–66.

37. Abraham Duker, "Twentieth-Century Blood Libels in the United States," *Rabbi Joseph H. Lookstein Memorial Volume*, ed. L. Landman (Hoboken, NJ: KTAV Publishing House, 1980), pp. 85–97; Saul S. Friedman, *The Incident at Massena: The Blood Libel in America* (New York: Stein and Day, 1978). As recently as 1989, blood libel accusations circulated in anti-Semitic propaganda in the U.S. in response to the kidnapping and disappearance of a child. See: Barry Cytron, "St. Cloud Flier Revives an Ancient Attack on Jews," *Star Tribune* (Minneapolis), Dec. 3, 1989.

38. Gavin Langmuir, 1990, Chapter 11, "Ritual Cannibalism," pp. 263–81.

39. *Ibid.*

40. *Ibid.*

41. *Ibid.*

42. Joshua Tractenberg, *The Devil and the Jews* (New Haven, CN: Yale University Press, 1943). (Republished by The Jewish Publication Society, New York, 1983.) Raphael, 1972.

43. Moore, 1987.

44. Cohn, 1975.

45. *Ibid.*, p. 228.

46. Brian P. Levack, *The Witch-Hunt in Early Modern Europe* (New York: Longman, 1987).

47. Cohn, 1975; Levack, 1987; Moore, 1987.

48. Levack, 1987, pp. 12–13.

49. Cohn, 1975; Levack, 1987.

Chapter Fifteen: Conclusions: The Social Construction of Imaginary Deviance

1. John F. Kennedy, Commencement address, Yale University, June 11, 1962.

Index